Using Assessment to Reshape Mathematics Teaching

A Casebook for
Teachers and Teacher Educators,
Curriculum and Staff Development Specialists

STUDIES IN MATHEMATICAL THINKING AND LEARNING

Alan H. Schoenfeld, Series Editor

Carpenter/Fennema/Romberg (Eds.) • Rational Numbers: An Integration of Research

Cobb/Bauersfeld (Eds.) • The Emergence of Mathematical Meaning: Interaction in Classroom Cultures

English (Ed.) • Mathematical Reasoning: Analogies, Metaphors, and Images

Fennema/Nelson (Eds.) • Mathematics Teachers in Transition

Fennema/Romberg (Eds.) • Mathematics Classrooms That Promote Understanding

Lajoie (Ed.) • Reflections on Statistics: Learning, Teaching, and Assessment in Grades K–12

Lehrer/Chazan (Eds.) • Designing Learning Environments for Developing Understanding of Geometry and Space

Ma • Knowing and Teaching Elementary Mathematics: Teachers' Understanding of Fundamental Mathematics in China and the United States

Martin • Mathematics Success and Failure Among African American Youth: The Roles of Sociohistorical Context, Community Forces, School Influence, and Individual Agency

Reed • Word Problems: Research and Curriculum Reform

Romberg/Fennema/Carpenter (Eds.) • Integrating Research on the Graphical Representations of Functions

Schoenfeld (Eds.) • Mathematical Thinking and Problem Solving

Sternberg/Ben-Zeev (Eds.) • The Nature of Mathematical Thinking

Wilcox/Lanier (Eds.) • Using Assessment to Reshape Mathematics Teaching: A Casebook for Teachers and Teacher Educators, Curriculum and Staff Development Specialists

Using Assessment to Reshape Mathematics Teaching

A Casebook for Teachers and Teacher Educators, Curriculum and Staff Development Specialists

Edited by

Sandra K. Wilcox
and
Perry E. Lanier

Michigan State University

2000

LAWRENCE ERLBAUM ASSOCIATES, PUBLISHERS
Mahwah, New Jersey London

Lawrence Erlbaum Associates, Inc., Publishers
10 Industrial Avenue
Mahwah, NJ 07430

Cover design by Kathryn Houghtaling Lacey

Library of Congress Cataloging-in-Publication Data

Using assessment to reshape mathematics teaching : a casebook for teachers and teacher educators, curriculum and staff development specialists / edited by Sandra K. Wilcox and Perry E. Lanier.

p. cm.

Includes bibliographical references and index.

ISBN 0-8058-2962-8 (pbk : alk. paper)

1. Mathematics—Study and teaching—United States—Case studies. 2. Mathematical ability—Testing. I. Wilcox, Sandra K. II. Lanier, Perry E.

QA13.U78 2000

371.3 —dc21 98-24193
CIP

Books published by Lawrence Erlbaum Associates are printed on acid-free paper, and their bindings are chosen for strength and durability.

Printed in the United States of America
10 9 8 7 6 5 4 3 2 1

List of Contributors

Teacher Collaborators

Sandra Bethell
Patti Bick
Greg Burmester
Danise Cantlon
Brenda Duckett-Jones
Greg Mickelson
Karen Rohrs
Marie Sahloff
Karma Vince
Cindy Simon
Patti Sommers
Linda Stoyk
Linda Tisdale
Mike Vince
Patricia Wagner
Greg Williams
Ron Zielinski

Graduate Student Collaborators

Melissa Dennis
Jenny Jorgensen
Sonia Marsalis
Maria Salih
Kara Suzuka
Jeff Wanko

Consultants

Glenda Lappan
John Masterson
Daniel Chazan
Bill Rosenthal

Contents

Acknowledgments

We first thank the collaborating teachers with whom we worked on this project and from whose classrooms these cases (and many others) came. They teach in urban, suburban, and rural districts in Michigan, Ohio, and Maine. They teach in heterogeneously grouped regular education classrooms, "honors" course classrooms, and classrooms for the learning disabled. Their students reflect the diversity of race–culture–ethnicity and social class that characterizes our nation's schools. Prior to this project, each of the teachers participated with MSU faculty in curriculum development, classroom research, professional development, and/or teacher preparation. In some cases, the collaboration goes back 10 years.

Each, in her or his own way, was trying to shape a practice in which *all* students could develop mathematical power. They took the risk and the opportunity to share episodes from their classrooms, knowing that the materials they brought would be subject to close scrutiny but trusting that it would be done in the interest of furthering the learning of us all. They helped us learn more than we could have imagined about how professional development through assessment can contribute to teacher learning and teacher change.

We thank our colleagues James Gallagher and Joyce Parker, who led the work with science teachers in this project. Although the two subject-matter teams ultimately went in somewhat different directions, the four of us worked closely to shape a pattern of activity aimed at developing resources to help teachers learn to use assessment in the service of instruction.

We owe a great debt to our many colleagues (faculty and graduate students) at Michigan State who sat with us to analyze case data, used early drafts of the cases in their own teaching and provided us with critical feedback, and invited us to use cases with teachers with whom they were working. A special thanks to Glenda Lappan, Dan Chazan, Pamela Schram, Bill Rosenthal, Bill Fitzgerald, Betty Phillips, John Masterson, Mary Bouck, Helene Furani, Judi Zawojewski, and the faculty and graduate students who participate in the Math Ed Seminar.

Our work was enhanced by the development work of the Balanced Assessment Project, of which the senior editor was a Director. We used many of the performance assessment tasks developed by BA to support teachers' efforts as they sought a richer understanding of what their students knew and could do. We are grateful to Alan Schoenfeld and Hugh Burkhardt for their comments on and support of our case development work.

We owe a special thanks to Diana Lambdin, Carne Barnett, and Mary Lynn Raith who reviewed this manuscript—we were impressed with the detail of the feedback. They will see the ways in which their commentaries contributed to the shape the cases took in the end.

Naomi Silverman, acquisitions editor at LEA, deserves a medal for perseverance. She persisted in securing a contract when common sense might have argued for giving the whole thing up. Thanks, Naomi, for your enthusiasm for this project and for sticking with us to see it happen.

Several other individuals made valuable contributions. Kaijun Hon produced the video that accompanies the casebook. She faced considerable challenges in assembling a product of reasonable quality from raw material shot by nonprofessional videographers. At the same time, she captured the reality of daily life in these classrooms. Kyle Ward, Pamela Dismuke, and Mary Hartwig did some of the tedious work of cleaning up student work and making photocopies. Jean Beland, the project secretary, kept things running smoothly, helping us meet deadlines and making sure our teacher participants were well cared for at our retreats.

We are grateful to the National Science Foundation for supporting this work through grant number MDR 9252881.

Preface

This casebook grows out of a 4-year collaborative project that brought together a group of mathematics teachers, mathematics educators, and mathematicians to learn more about how assessment can be used by teachers to improve their teaching and their students' learning. Our project is one of a number of research and development efforts undertaken this decade to increase our understanding of the role that assessment can and should play in reforming mathematics education. The work across projects has been wide-ranging—from the design of performance and authentic assessment tasks and the development of various kinds of rubrics that assess multiple dimensions of mathematical performance, to the implementation of alternative assessment systems (e.g., portfolios, the addition of constructed-response items to district- and state-mandated tests) for monitoring student achievement and program effectiveness, to the study of psychometric issues that arise in the context of these new assessments. Some of this work has focused primarily on high-stakes, on-demand assessment; some has centered on classroom-based or curriculum-embedded assessment.

The point of departure in our project was the use of assessment as ongoing activity in the classroom to help teachers reshape their instructional practice. The work was shaped by several key questions: How can teachers learn to assess multiple aspects of students' mathematical understanding? How can teachers gather information about what students are coming to understand as they teach? How can teachers use analysis of this information to help them make instructional decisions? At the heart of this casebook is using assessment to make sense of what students understand and how they understand it, deciding what counts as evidence of that understanding, and using that analysis to consider what the teacher's next instructional moves might be.

There is a growing interest in the use of cases as a pedagogical tool in teacher professional development. The value of cases resides in their power to stimulate analysis and reflection; to provoke various, and sometimes conflicting, interpretations of a classroom event; to bring to the fore deeply held beliefs of beginning and experienced teachers so they can be reconsidered; to engage in pedagogical problem solving in the context of episodes from complex classroom settings. The cases in this book take a particular form that Merseth (1992) called decision-making cases. As a genre, they have certain features:

- They are built around actual teaching and learning episodes from mathematics classrooms
- They present the raw data of classroom events in a straightforward way, with the intent of describing the event as it happened
- They are richly complex and can be viewed through a variety of analytic lenses
- They are typically open-ended, presenting situations for which there can be multiple interpretations and for which there may be more than one possible course of action

- They have been crafted to engage groups of professionals in analysis, reflection, problem-solving, and decision-making
- They allow for several levels of investigation, from interrogating the raw data of a specific case to considering a more general line of inquiry about the value of engaging in deep analysis of classroom events in the company of other professionals

A special feature of this casebook is that four of the seven cases are accompanied by video recordings of the classroom event. This further documentation provides additional insights into how students reason about and make sense of mathematical ideas in ways that students' written work or teacher's summaries alone cannot capture.

Each case is composed of two sections. The first is the case narrative. This section is written to the teacher educator, the teacher leader, and the workshop facilitator who uses the case as part of the curriculum in a professional development setting (e.g., an undergraduate or graduate teacher education course; a series of in-service teacher workshops; a teacher-led, school-based study group). The narrative sets the context for the case including what preceded the event and the learning/assessment task that shaped the event. It provides a suggested set of activities for investigating the case and sets of questions for analyzing the case materials and shaping subsequent discussion. In some, there are ideas for further activities related to, but going beyond the specifics of the case. These suggestions grow out of our use of the cases in extended, multisession professional development workshops. They invite teachers to take a step that is closer to home, moving from analysis of data from another's classroom to analysis of data collected from their own classroom.

A unique feature of each case is the summary of the deliberations that took place within our project team meetings around the data teachers brought documenting events in their classrooms. We include this component to show the variety of analytic lenses we used across the cases. With all cases, we tried to make sense of what students understood and what they were struggling with, what counted as evidence of the claims we made, and how we could use this collective analysis to help the teacher think about choices for his or her next instructional moves.

The second section contains a set of blackline masters of case materials and discussion questions suitable for making photocopies and overhead transparencies. This section contains all or some of the following: a learning–assessment task; samples of student work on the task; transcripts of audio and video recordings of whole class and small group discussions that accompany the case narrative; questions to frame analysis and discussion; samples of problems from the curriculum-in-use.

The casebook is organized into three chapters. The three cases in chapter 1, Listening to Students, center around classroom events where students and teachers are engaged in conversations about mathematical ideas. The cases raise issues about what it means to listen to students and to take seriously the ways in which they are trying to make sense of important ideas. The cases illustrate some of the dilemmas teachers face in trying to decide when to give students information and when to hold back and let students struggle with a complex idea. The cases exemplify the efforts of teachers trying to orchestrate conversations when they encounter unexpected ways in which students are reasoning about an idea.

The two cases in chapter 2, Assessing the Potential of Tasks, focus on using worthwhile tasks for assessment. By worthwhile tasks, we mean tasks that provide opportunities for students to show what they know and what they can do, that encourage them to demonstrate how they are making connections—among mathematical ideas and to real-world situations—and that call on them to communicate how they are reasoning about important ideas. Worthwhile assessment tasks are also good learning tasks, for students and teachers. In working on them, students can increase their own levels of understanding about ideas. Worthwhile tasks also provide a rich data source for teachers' analysis to help them make sense of what students are coming to understand and to use their analysis to make choices about next instructional moves.

The two cases in chapter 3, Capturing Students' Engagement with a Task, focus on analysis of teaching and learning through examination of data collected in multiple ways. The cases highlight the limitations of relying solely on students' written work to make claims about what they understand and how they understand it. Both cases provide data collected from audio or video recordings of small groups as they worked on a task. This additional documentation provides insights into how students reason about and solve a problem that is not apparent in their written work.

Those who will find these materials useful include mathematics teachers, curriculum and assessment specialists, staff-development facilitators, and mathematics educators. The casebook is deliberately designed to foster conversations among groups of professional colleagues. A central premise that has guided the construction of these cases is that the kind of deep analysis we are promoting is enhanced when groups of individuals can consider together the issues embedded in using assessment in the service of instruction. As our project evolved, we came to see the power of engaging in a collective process where a community of professional colleagues struggle to make sense of what students are coming to understand, what they are struggling with, what counts as evidence, and how to use that analysis to decide on next instructional moves.

At the same time, there is much that an individual can learn from reading these cases—what it means to listen to students, what makes a good instructional–assessment task, how a teacher can collect information about students' understanding in multiple ways, what other forms of documentation reveal that students' written work alone cannot, what counts as evidence of claims about student understanding, how to use assessment to consider possible courses of further action. Taken together, these cases are designed to support professionals who are working in a variety of contexts to use assessment more effectively to support teacher learning and teacher change and to enhance the opportunities for all students to develop mathematical power.

REFERENCE

Merseth, K. (1992). Cases for decision making in teacher education. In J. Shulman (Ed.), *Case methods in teacher education* (pp. 50–63). New York: Teachers College Press.

Introduction

Classroom-based assessment is a powerful, yet underused tool in improving teaching and learning in mathematics classrooms. In traditional practice, assessment is used by teachers primarily to assign grades at the end of a unit of instruction and to identify which students are successful and which are not. Teachers rely heavily on students' written work on completing imitative exercises and solving routine, stylized problems as evidence of learning. Students are tested, their efforts are measured, and they are evaluated.

There is another conception of classroom-based assessment, promoted by the *Standards* documents of the National Council of Teachers of Mathematics (NCTM, 1989, 1991, 1995). Central to this view is the importance of teachers using assessment as an ongoing activity to gain insights about students' understandings, and to judge the usefulness of teaching practices and learning activities. In this conception, assessment is not a separate activity disconnected from other aspects of classroom practice. On the contrary, assessment is seen as the critical link among curriculum, teaching, and learning.

This casebook is grounded in this broader conception of classroom-based assessment. The cases are intended to help teachers learn to assess for understanding and to use that assessment of student learning to reshape their own instructional practices—what we call *assessment in the service of instruction*.

Assessment is probably the most neglected area in the professional studies of mathematics teachers. Stiggins (1989) reported that when it is attended to, it is almost always focused on pencil-and-paper tests that teachers use for summative evaluation. There is precious little attention to using multiple forms of assessment, including observing and talking with students, to develop more complex pictures of student learning within classrooms. Because instruction and assessment are generally separated, teachers do not learn how to use assessment as a teaching tool.

The very terms we use to talk about ascertaining students' knowledge reveal stances about what it means to know mathematics, what counts as evidence of knowing, and to what ends the processes of assessment are aimed. Lesh and Lamon (1992) draw distinctions between two set of terms: testing, measuring, and evaluating; and examining, documenting, and assessing. They described *testing* as "creating an ordeal (or a barrier, or a filter) to inform decisions about acceptance or rejection, passing or failing," *measuring* as "specifying both 'how much' and 'of what,'" and *evaluating* as "assigning a value to it." In contrast, they described *examining* as "inspecting it closely," *documenting* as "gathering tangible evidence to demonstrate what occurred" and *assessing* as "describing its current state—probably with reference to some conceptual, or procedural or developmental landmarks" (p. 7).

The dominant practice of testing, measuring, and evaluating stands in sharp contrast to the visions of assessment reflected in the current national reform efforts in mathematics education. In the *Assessment Standards for School Mathematics* (NCTM, 1995), the National Council of Teachers of Mathematics considered multiple ways to characterize assessment including purposes of assessment, phases of assessment, and

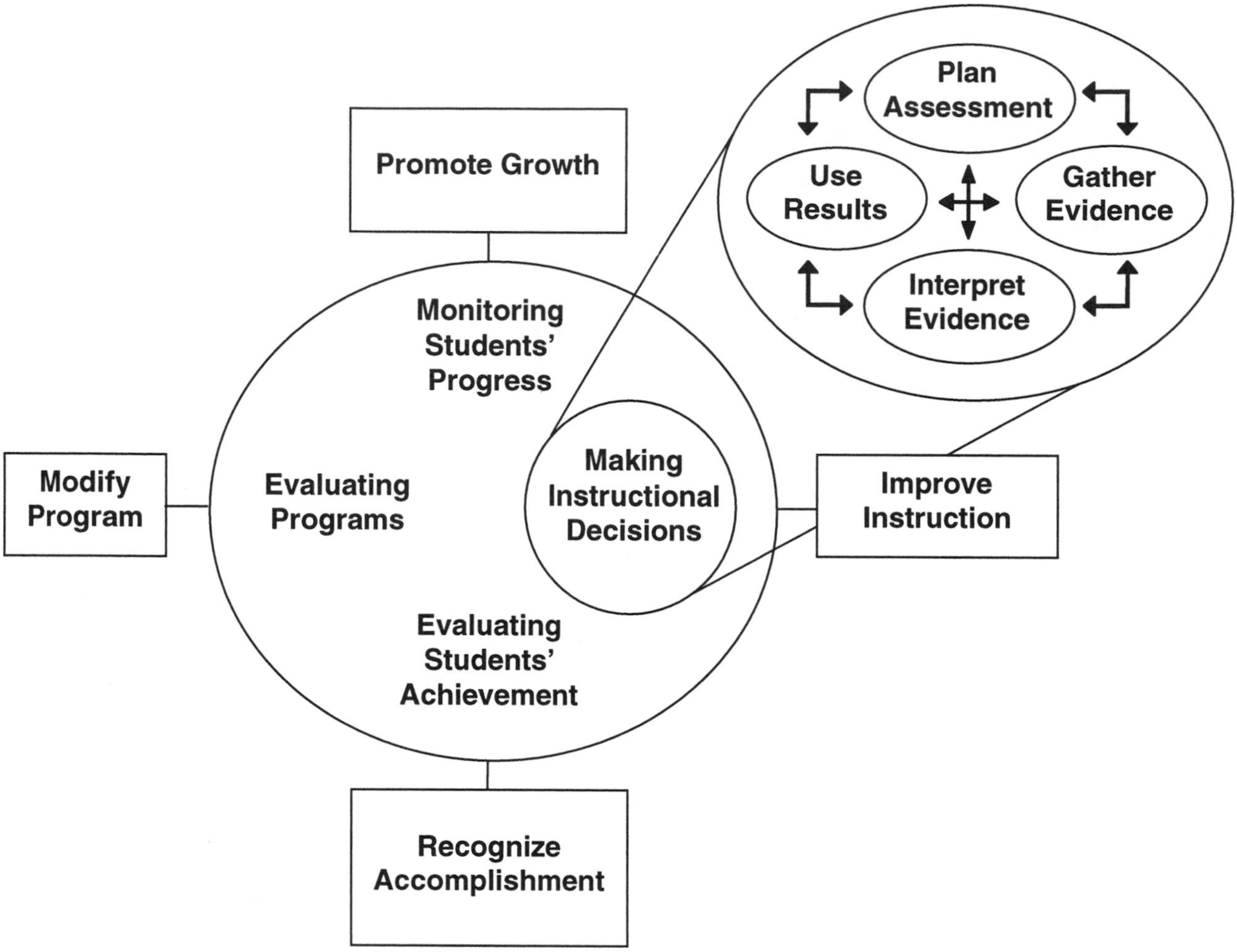

FIG. I.1. Multiple Dimensions of Mathematics Assessment (NCTM,1995)

the results of assessment. The graphic Fig. I.1 from that document illustrates the relationship among these various dimensions of assessment.

Although all assessments involve planning, gathering evidence, interpreting the evidence, and using the results, engaging in this process for the purposes of promoting student growth and improving instruction has not been prominent in practice.

The reform agenda in mathematics education aims to provide all students with opportunities to develop robust understandings about number and quantity; geometry, shape, and space; algebra, patterns, and functions; and probability and statistics. The reform also aims to develop students' abilities to engage in mathematical problem solving and reasoning, to make connections—among mathematical ideas, between mathematics and other school subjects, between mathematics and situations in the real world—and to communicate their mathematical understandings to themselves and others. A commitment to helping all students learn powerful mathematics brings with it the challenge to develop a broader perspective on the purposes, modes, and substance of assessment in the classroom.

A more expansive conception and use of assessment can contribute to teachers coming to believe that all students can succeed in mathematics—in contrast to the still-prevailing notion that some are destined to fail. Wiggins (1993) contended that conventional wisdom about student ability in mathematics emanates largely from the use of standardized tests.

> Is it any wonder, then, that a fatalism pervades education? The tests we use result in a self-fulfilling prophecy about student ability. ... Few educators really end up believing (no matter what a school mission statement says) that "all children can learn" to high standards, given that test results rarely show dramatic change. (And they *won't* change, because of their design and our current patterns of use.) To develop an educational system based on the premise that "all children *will* learn," we need assessment systems that treat each student with greater respect, assume greater promise about gains, (and seek to measure them), and offer more worthy tasks and helpful feedback than are provided in our current culture of one-shot, "secure" testing. (pp. 5–6)

When used in a broader and more constructive manner, assessment can help teachers gain better insights into students' understandings, including their partial conceptions and poorly integrated ideas. By using assessment as an ongoing activity in the mathematics classroom, teachers can gauge students' progress toward desired learning goals in ways that can guide teaching and foster successful learning for all.

The *Standards* documents of the National Council of Teachers of Mathematics emphasize the importance of using assessment as ongoing activity—for gaining insights about what students know and how they know it; for judging the usefulness of the learning activities they provide for their students; and for evaluating the effectiveness of their own teaching practices.

> [Assessment serves] to help teachers better understand what students know and make meaningful instructional decisions. The focus is on what happens in the classroom as students and teachers interact. (NCTM, 1989, p. 189)

> Assessment of students and analysis of instruction are fundamentally interconnected. Mathematics teachers should monitor students' learning on an ongoing basis in order to assess and adjust their teaching. (NCTM, 1991, p. 63)

> Assessment is the link between teaching and learning. As such, it is a dynamic, ongoing, and critical process that shapes classroom environments and students' opportunities to learn. Through assessment, teachers monitor the success of their practice and make instructional decisions. (NCTM, 1993, p. 59)

This casebook has been developed to assist teachers, teacher educators, and curriculum and staff-development specialists in their efforts to eliminate the separation of assessment, curriculum, teaching, and learning in mathematics classrooms.

THE CASES

A number of the cases in this casebook arose from classroom events that we came to call *moments*. These were episodes where the teacher or participant-observer was taken aback because a student in the class had a remarkable insight or because a student made a comment that seemed totally off the mark. These included instances of students' diverse and unexpected ways of working on problems; oftentimes solutions appeared, at first glance, not to make sense at all. There were occasions where students' searches for patterns in a problem produced conjectures that had the potential to lead to serious misunderstandings. In some instances, students seemed to hold on to informal, intuitive, or real-world meanings and resisted drawing on relevant mathematics to develop more robust mathematical meanings and understandings. These puzzling episodes became a site for collective analysis and sense making within our project as we considered the implications for shaping ongoing instructional decisions. At the heart of each case is making sense of what students understand about a particular idea or set of ideas in mathematics and how they understand it, and using analyses of the case materials to consider what a teacher's next instructional moves might be. Every case can be minimally interrogated with a core set of questions:

- What do I see going on here?
- What do students seem to understand and what am I taking as evidence?
- What are students struggling with and what am I using as evidence?
- What does this analysis of students' understanding suggest about where a teacher might go next in instruction? What would I do next?

Where to go next can mean thinking about what to do the next day. It can mean noting some important ideas to come back to in subsequent units. Or it can mean making changes in instruction when teaching the ideas the next year.

A few cases provide a narrative that can be transformed into multiple cases, depending on the analytic framework used to examine the case. For example, one of our project teachers works with students who are labeled "learning disabled." Case 7 in chapter 3 is from her classroom and describes work on a task in which students showed reasonable conceptual understanding of the measurement ideas they had been studying, but considerable confusion about applying computational procedures. One direction for analysis would be to consider what students understood about the mathematics embedded in the task at a conceptual and a procedural level, what they struggled with, and what might account for that. This could be followed with a discussion about possible future action the teacher might take to help students deepen their procedural knowledge. Another line of inquiry could be to consider the particular task, what mathematics students would need to bring to its solution, what it had the potential to reveal about multiple dimensions of students' understanding, and their ability to use their knowledge flexibly. The task could be contrasted with more conventional measurement assessment tasks. But a quite different set of issues could emerge having to do with the kinds of learning opportunities that should be available to students with special needs. Far too often, well-intentioned adults hold minimal expectations for students with learning disabilities. This case could provide an occasion to consider what it means to develop the mathematical power of *all* students. The case provides an excellent opportunity to consider the links across teachers and teaching, learners and learning, curriculum and assessment.

Case 4 in chapter 2 uses a specific assessment strategy—concept maps—and invites a consideration of the strengths and weaknesses of the strategy. It is unique in that it focuses on student self-assessment, an often neglected area of assessment.

THE COMPONENTS OF A CASE

Cases are composed of the following components.

- *Overview*: describes briefly the kinds of explorations to which the case lends itself, the mathematical content of the case, the case materials, and a minimum amount of time that is needed to engage in deep analysis of the materials.
- *Introduction*: includes relevant information about what preceded the immediate events of the case and the learning–assessment task that shapes the event.
- *Using the case materials*: describes the different levels with which a group might work with the materials. All the cases lend themselves to investigation at three levels minimally. At one level, participants can analyze the raw data of the case to make sense of what students understand and what counts as evidence of understanding. At another level, participants can consider what they might do next if they were the teacher in this classroom. At yet another level, participants can stand back and ask how engaging in this kind of deep analysis of classroom events, in the company of other professionals, might contribute to their own professional growth and changes in their teaching practices.
- *Activities*: describes in detail a suggested set of activities for investigating the case. This section is written with the workshop facilitator, the teacher leader, and the teacher educator as audience. We have tried to not be overly prescriptive about how to use the cases. We expect a facilitator to carefully work through the narrative of the case in advance of using it with a group. Drawing on our own experiences in field-testing the cases, we have tried to provide the kinds of information and suggestions that we hope will support a facilitator's efforts in working with a group of educators. In those cases where there is a substantial amount of data, we offer a way of organizing materials and participants and of structuring the investigation around a series of activities so that there are opportunities for deep, thoughtful analysis. In instances where we have found that "setting the stage" is critical (especially when a key piece of data is a video recording of a teacher's classroom), we provide specific suggestions about how to introduce the case.

For each activity, we reference the case materials that need to be reproduced in advance of a session for distribution to the participants. In most cases, one copy per participant is needed. All case materials are organized in a separate section following the case narrative, in the order in which they are used in the activities. Four of the cases include video clips that are collected together on the 70-minute video that accompanies this casebook.

- *Beyond the Case*: includes suggestions for extending participants' professional development with activities related to but going beyond the specifics of the case. This section, which accompanies some of the cases, grows out of our use of them in multisession workshops where participants met regularly over a period of several months. Such a structure allowed us to give "assignments" that they carried out in their own classrooms (or in the case of specialists or administrators, in the classrooms of colleagues). The data collected in such assignments—samples of their own students' written work on a task, insights from observing students engage with a task, video recordings of a teaching episode—then became the curriculum of a part of the subsequent session.
- *Deliberations Within the Project*: provides some insight into the project team's engagement with the raw data of the case. The cases were shaped by the process of deep analysis at two sites. The first occurred with the individual teacher in whose classroom the event took place. Teachers often brought classroom vignettes to our project meetings because they were truly puzzled about what was going on. The second place of analysis was within the collectivity of our group. Together, we joined the teacher in looking carefully at what she/he presented. We posed questions about what we saw, or what we were told, or what students had written. We asked about earlier events that might shed some light on the situation. We offered conjectures about what students understood, what they seemed to be having trouble with, and what we were using as evidence to support our conjectures. We speculated about possible explanations for what we observed. And we considered how the teacher might use this analysis to make decisions about where to go next.

  We have included this component to show the variety of analytic lenses we used across the cases. In every instance, we faced a complex situation and a rich data set of which we tried to make sense. With all cases, we tried to make sense of what students understood and what they were struggling with to help the teacher think about choices for next instructional moves. However, this always led us to other considerations. Sometimes our investigation moved to consider the strengths and weaknesses of a particular task. At other times, our focus shifted to what students were saying and our interpretations of their sense-making. In some instances, we considered the challenges that nearly all teachers face in trying to teach a particular set of ideas. On more than one occasion, issues surfaced about the feasibility of documenting students' learning in multiple ways. What a facilitator will find in this section is a glimpse of one group of professionals trying to come to grips with a classroom situation for which there are many possible roads of inquiry. In some cases, we admit to still being puzzled about some aspects and sufficiently curious about it that we continue to revisit the case because with each additional interrogation we develop new insights. A facilitator might choose to share some of this with participants after they themselves have carefully investigated the case.
- *Materials for making photocopies and transparencies*: includes materials for using the case in a professional learning context, including blackline masters suitable for photocopying and for making overhead transparencies. A case may contain all or some of the following:

  - a learning/assessment task that shapes the event;
  - samples of students' work on a task;
  - recorded observations of students' engagement with a task. These observations may be documented with video recordings along with a transcript of the recording; a transcript only of conversations among students in small groups or as a whole class; a teacher's summary of the event;
  - questions to engage participants in analysis of the case materials;
  - samples of problems from the curriculum-in-use.

AUDIENCES FOR THE CASES

Those who will find these materials useful include mathematics teachers, curriculum and assessment specialists, staff development facilitators and teacher educators. Although individuals will find a case contains many ideas for linking assessment with curriculum and instruction, the most powerful use of these materials resides in a deliberate design intended to foster conversations among groups of professional colleagues. A central premise that has guided the construction of these materials is that the kind of deep analysis we are promoting is enhanced when groups of individuals can consider together the issues embedded in using assessment in the service of instruction. Key to connecting assessment with curriculum, teaching, and learning is engaging in a collective process where a community of professional colleagues struggle to make sense of what students are coming to understand, what counts as evidence of student understanding, and how to use that information to decide where to go next in instruction.

Continuing Professional Development Workshops

Curriculum, assessment, and staff development specialists will find the cases useful as catalysts for conversations in teacher inservice workshops. The materials are designed to engage workshop participants in inquiry about and deep analysis of specific classroom events—analyzing student actions and student work, making sense of what students are doing and saying, considering various claims about student understanding and what counts as evidence for each of the claims, deciding what a teacher might do next based on the analysis of the information presented by the case materials. Cases allow for inquiry into learning–assessment tasks—what a task has the potential to reveal about multiple dimensions of assessment (problem solving and reasoning, communication, connections, concepts and procedures, dispositions), and what different response modes (e.g., oral, written explanation, picture/graph, posing a new question) might reveal about student understanding. Sense-making is at the heart of these materials and we have assembled a collection of artifacts that allow participants to dig deep into a specific piece of data as well as into a range of data from different sources.

School-Based Mathematics Collectives

Small groups of mathematics teachers within a school will find the conceptual model that guided our project helpful as they seek to use assessment to enhance their teaching and their students' learning. Because assessment is a crucial link connecting curriculum, teaching and learning, we began our work in the project by considering: "What are the big ideas in a mathematical domain and what is important for students at a particular level to know about those ideas?" Teachers might construct a concept map (White & Gunstone, 1993) as a representation that extracts and connects the key ideas within a mathematical domain. In Case 4, we include two concept maps that we created in the project for the domain of statistics. Our experience is that in the process of constructing the map with others, educators engage in lively and rich conversations about what they think are key aspects of a "big idea" and the linkages among those aspects.

Teachers will find the tasks that are often the starting point of a case to be examples of the kinds of learning/assessment tasks that can provide rich data about student understanding. Some of the cases present samples of student work on the tasks. Teachers might want to try some of the tasks in their own classrooms and continue a conversation using their own students' work as the point of departure.

Teachers tend to rely heavily on written work to make judgments about students' understanding. These artifacts are permanent, visible records that teachers can examine at length. What teachers learn in other ways—by listening, observing, talking with students, posing questions—is idiosyncratic and seldom documented in a way that it can be returned to for further reflection and analysis. Some of the cases are designed to have groups of teachers consider ways of collecting and documenting information as students work on learning–assessment tasks. Some of the cases are accompanied by video recordings of classroom vignettes or transcripts of conversations as they occurred in small or whole-class discussions.

One way in which groups of teachers might choose to use these materials is to read a case before coming together. Two questions could frame reading and reflecting on a case: "What are the implications of this case for my own teaching? and "What could I individually and we collectively learn from reading and discussing this case?"

Teacher Preparation and Graduate Education Courses

These cases can support teacher educators in teacher preparation programs as they work with their teacher candidates to develop the knowledge, skills, and dispositions to help them link curriculum, teaching, learning, and assessment. Those cases that include video recordings of classroom vignettes are especially powerful for teacher candidates. They provide glimpses into real classrooms where experienced mathematics teachers encounter puzzling situations. They provide the teacher educator with tools to challenge beginning teachers' expectations that they will find right answers to their questions about how to handle the complexity of daily life in classrooms. We have found that initially, teacher candidates can be quite judgmental about what they see going on in a vignette. The case materials allow the teacher educator to move candidates from a critique toward a consideration of what they see going on, what interpretations they make of the situation, what interpretations seem more plausible and why, and how different interpretations of events may lead to different courses of action. Although this can be quite unsettling to novice teachers, they come to appreciate that learning teaching is filled with uncertainty, even for the most accomplished teacher.

We have used the cases as models of teachers engaged in inquiry about aspects of their own practice. One of us has interns in the fifth year of our initial certification program develop their own inquiry project about an aspect of practice about which they are curious. This is a first formal experience they have in the role of teacher-as-researcher. The cases help them think about multiple ways of documenting events in their own classrooms. The cases give them insights into the ways in which their own situations are open to more than one interpretation. And the cases push them to consider how different interpretations of their situations might lead them to make different instructional decisions.

We recently offered a summer graduate level teacher education course on alternative assessment in mathematics and used several cases as part of the curriculum. The teachers in the course taught in elementary, middle and high school, and adult education. One participant was the mathematics consultant in her district and another was a teacher educator in an Asian university. Their years of experience in the classroom ranged from less than 5 years to more than 20. The cases proved to be a powerful environment to bring together a diverse group of professionals to consider what is entailed in (a) providing opportunities in mathematics for *all* students to demonstrate what they know, (b) figuring out what they are coming to understand and what counts as evidence of that understanding, (c) developing ways to document and report on students' accomplishments, and (d) deciding how to use that information to make ongoing instructional decisions.

The cases also helped create dissonance with some of their more traditional views about teaching, learning, and assessment in mathematics. One of the participants had quite strong beliefs about how students should solve the *Fractions of a Square* task in Case 6. After working on the case in class, he took the problem home and had his two children work on it. He was surprised that their approach was not what he had expected even though they got the "right answer." He asked them to explain to him how they thought about the problem and again was surprised to hear two quite different ways of reasoning that the youngsters employed. This was a potent experience that caused him to begin to reconsider what it might mean to know and do mathematics.

Perhaps the most important outcome of the use of these cases is that teacher candidates and experienced teachers alike seem to develop a new appreciation for the role of evidence in making claims about student learning. Global claims about student understanding—"I think Katie has a good understanding about equations"—shift to more specific claims—"Katie knows about distinguishing features of systems of linear equations as shown in the matrix on her concept map where she describes how they vary by their graph, the slopes of the lines in a system, and the number of solutions." The cases also tend to raise issues about how much and what kind of evidence is needed to make defensible claims about student learning.

Your Professional Community

Sense making, analysis, reflection, and decision making are at the heart of these cases. They are intended to engage mathematics professionals in yet another site—your own professional learning community. The lenses that you bring to bear will be conditioned by a number of factors: the circumstances of your local context; the focus of a meeting in which a case is featured; the aims of a workshop facilitator; the goals of a teacher educator; the aspects of practice that a group of teachers are working to reshape in their classrooms. The materials can serve as models for you to construct cases from your own experiences. Most importantly, the cases allow close examination and interrogation of episodes that are common in mathematics classrooms where teachers are working to introduce *Standards*-based curricula, teaching, and assessment.

We have much to learn about using assessment as an ongoing activity to inform instructional decision making. We believe these materials will help professionals in a variety of contexts develop their own expertise in using assessment to reshape instructional practices.

REFERENCES

Lesh, R., & Lamon, S. (1992). Trends, goals, and priorities in mathematics education. In R. Lesh & S. Lamon (Eds.), *Assessment of authentic performance in school mathematics* (pp. 3–15). Washington, DC: American Association for the Advancement of Science.

National Council of Teachers of Mathematics. (1989). *Curriculum and evaluation standards for school mathematics*. Reston, VA: Author.

National Council of Teachers of Mathematics. (1991). *Professional standards for teaching mathematics*. Reston, VA: Author.

National Council of Teachers of Mathematics. (1993). *Assessment standards for school mathematics: Working draft*. Reston, VA: Author.

National Council of Teachers of Mathematics. (1995). *Assessment standards for school mathematics*. Reston, VA: Author.

Stiggins, R. (1989). Teacher training in assessment: Overcoming the negelct. In S. Wise (Ed.), *Teacher training in assessment*. Hillsdale, NJ: Lawrence Erlbaum Associates.

White, R., & Gunstone, R. (1993). Concept mapping. In *Probing understanding* (pp. 15–43). London, UK: The Falmer Press.

Wiggins, G. (1993). *Assessing student performance: Exploring the purpose and limits of testing.* San Francisco, CA: Jossey-Bass.

1

Listening To Students

The cases in this chapter focus on conversations in mathematics classrooms about mathematical ideas. Each narrative is accompanied by a video recording and transcript of the whole-class discussions that are the raw data of the cases. The teachers from whose classrooms these cases come are all engaged in a kind of teaching in which they pose questions or problem situations for their students to investigate. After students have had sufficient time to investigate the problem, the teacher facilitates a discussion in which students present their results for their classmates' consideration. In the three cases that follow, the question or problem posed led to a variety of ways in which different students made sense of the situation and tried to justify their views to others in the class. As you read these cases, consider the following questions. They have been framed to help you stand back from the particulars of a specific case and reflect on what you might learn from reading the case and how it might influence your own classroom practice.

- What does it mean to listen to students, to try and understand how they are making sense of a situation or an idea?
- What might account for the different ways in which students interpret or make sense of a situation or an idea?
- How can I respect students' ways of making sense, particularly when their ideas have the potential to lead to incorrect conclusions or misconceptions?
- How do I help my students construct deep understandings of mathematical concepts and procedures when they have different ways of making sense and when these ways may be in conflict with more mathematically acceptable views?
- What challenges have I faced or will I face if I open my classroom to this kind of mathematical investigation, discussion, and reflection?
- What do I need to know—about the mathematical content, about constructivist teaching and learning, about a particular classroom of students—to engage in the kinds of practices embodied in these cases? How, where, and with whom might I lear n what I need to know?

CASE 1—"They Favor Each Other": Making Sense of Similarity—is crafted around a short video segment in which a class of middle-school students are talking about what they think makes figures similar. The case highlights important issues that often emerge when teachers move from a traditional curriculum to a problem-centered, inquiry-focused curriculum. The case raises a key question: How can a teacher listen to and honor students' knowledge built from previous experiences and, at the same time, challenge their currently held views in ways that lead to the construction of more powerful and mathematically acceptable views?

CASE 2—Nurturing a Disposition for Inquiry—comes from a first-year algebra class for students in grades 10–12 who have not been very successful in previous mathematics classes. It is built around video segments of a whole class conversation about whether the point (0,0) on the coordinate grid is in four quadrants or in no quadrants. The vignettes portray multiple instances of where the teacher is using assessment in the moment-to-moment of the discussion to pose questions, to help clarify issues, and to resist telling students "who is right." A special feature of this case is the commentary of the teacher where she shares how she thinks about her role in relation to this particular set of students and the decisions she makes to foster their inquiry. The case raises issues about the nature and role of definitions in the mathematics classroom, and what teachers and students do when the curriculum does not set a definition that clarifies whether answers are right or wrong.

CASE 3—Learning Children's Understandings of Algebra comes from an elementary classroom where children in a 3rd–4th-grade classroom are exploring ideas about patterns and generalizing about patterns with algebraic sentences. The teacher created the unit following a persistent request from some of her students to "learn algebra." The case is unique in two ways; first, it contains data collected over several lessons to show the various ways in which students encountered a search for patterns. Second, it provides a glimpse into the classroom of a teacher engaged in adventuresome teaching, exploring new mathematical territory to learn more about the content and what her young students could do in this area.

Case 1: "They Favor Each Other": Making Sense of Similarity

From the classroom of Mike Vince in collaboration with the Project Team

OVERVIEW

This case provides opportunities to:

- *Examine the curriculum in use*: looking at a sample of the learning activities that students had engaged—how the unit approached teaching the concept of *similarity*, what teacher and students might find challenging or unfamiliar about the approach, what the investigations might contribute to students' understanding of similarity;
- *Analyze a video segment of a whole-class conversation*: making sense of what students are saying about what they think makes figures similar—what they seem to focus on, what they seem to be bringing to the conversation, and what might account for this;
- *Consider instructional options based on analysis of video*: using analysis of a class discussion for the purpose of considering next moves in instruction—what a teacher might do next to help students build a deeper understanding of mathematical similarity;
- *Explore the complexity in helping students construct robust and personally meaningful mathematical definitions*: considering the role of reflection to help students attend to the salient characteristics embedded in investigations that are intended to build an understanding of mathematical similarity; considering how to acknowledge and build on the meanings that grow out of students' lived experiences;
- *Consider a more general line of inquiry about documenting and analyzing classroom events*: using videotapes to document classroom events—what they can contribute to making sense of student learning; how analysis and conversation among a group of professionals might contribute to reshaping teaching and enhancing learning in the classroom.

Mathematical Content: Similarity of geometric figures.

Case Materials: Video recording and transcript of a 10 minute segment of a whole class discussion. Sample problems from the curriculum-in-use.

Additional Materials Needed: Centimeter grid paper; rubber bands (3 for each participant).

Suggested Time: Minimum of 2.5 hours to investigate the case.

INTRODUCTION

This case is built around a 10-minute video segment of a whole-class conversation where students are talking about what they think makes figures similar. The students had been working for more than a week on investigations intended to help them build a mathematical concept of similarity. They had done some stretching investigations with a rubber band, noting what changed and what stayed the same in the figures. They had used an overhead projector to make enlargements of figures, investigating how moving the projector in different orientations to the screen changed the image. The students had been introduced to the idea of scale factor and had applied it to several problems. They had used coordinate rules to draw enlarged and distorted figures. Following these several investigations, the teacher asked them what they thought would always be true about two figures that are similar to each other, and video recorded the conversation.

The video invites participants to make sense of what students are saying about similar figures. On what do they seem to be focusing? What might account for their persistence in using common meanings rather than more precise mathematical ones that the teacher had expected would grow out of the several investigations?

This case has an interesting and unexpected twist. An examination of sample problems from the curriculum in use provides insights into what might account for some of the ideas students had about similar figures. It gives participants an opportunity to consider how curriculum materials themselves might inadvertently contribute to students' misconceptions about mathematical ideas. Also, it raises issues about whether doing a set of investigations, answering questions, and solving problems is sufficient for students to come to grips with the mathematics embedded in the investigations. The case highlights the importance of the teacher leading a reflection on mathematical activity so that students can build a coherent conception of a "big idea" from discrete but connected activities.

USING THE CASE MATERIALS

Introducing the Case

Because of the complexity of this case and the sensitive nature of visiting others' classrooms via brief video recordings, we have given considerable thought to the use of the materials that constitute this case. The teacher, Mike Vince, was using a new curriculum unit that introduced students to the idea of mathematical similarity in a way quite different from previous ways he had taught the concept.[1] In past years, Mr. Vince had given students the definition of similarity and then assigned problems that had students apply the definition to determine whether figures were similar, and to calculate measures of similar figures using a scale factor. In this new unit, students were engaged in several "hands-on" investigations to explore what happens when figures are enlarged or reduced. The aim of the unit was to help students build a personally meaningful, mathematically robust conception of similarity.

About midway through the unit, Mr. Vince asked his students the following question: "At this point, what do you think will always be true about two figures that are similar to each other?" He was completely taken aback by their responses. It seemed to him that students were unable or unwilling to draw on any of the mathematical ideas he thought they had been developing over the several investigations.

In this case, participants try to make sense of how the students are reasoning about similarity and what might account for their ways of making sense. Participants examine sample problems from the several investigations students worked on in the unit, to anticipate how students might respond to Mr. Vince's question about similar figures. They view a clip of a video recording that Mr. Vince made during the whole-class discussion about their responses. They re-examine the curriculum materials in light of the whole-class discussion, to consider what might account for the students' responses, and to pose choices that Mr. Vince might consider about where to go next in instruction.

Introducing the video to an audience is perhaps the most critical aspect of using these materials. We have found that a kind of "stage setting" is effective in focusing the participants' attention on making sense of what they are seeing and hearing in the video rather than taking a judgmental stance on the actions of the teacher or the students. We include a script to provide guidance about what we have found useful in introducing the video.

You might introduce the case investigation with something like the following.

> It is common for teachers, like yourselves, to have the experience of guiding students through a series of problem situations intended to develop their knowledge and understandings about a particular mathematical idea. After several days you may pause and take stock of where students are in their understanding. A typical way of doing this assessment is to ask students to tell you what they know about the particular idea. For example, if students have been working on a geometry unit that involves tesselations, you might ask what they can say at this point

[1]The curriculum unit that Mike was using was a draft of *Similarity: Stretching and Shrinking*, a unit developed by the Connected Mathematics Project, which Mike was field-testing. The Connected Mathematics Project is supported, in part, by the National Science Foundation to develop a mathematics curriculum for grades 6–8. The project directors are Glenda Lappan, James Fey, William Fitzgerald, Susan Friel, and Elizabeth Phillips. The units are available through Dale Seymour Cuisenaire Publications.

about figures that tesselate. Taking stock at several points in a unit can reveal to you and to the students themselves how they are building their knowledge of the ideas within the unit.

In the case that we are going to consider, the teacher, Mike Vince, is taking stock in this manner. His 7th-grade students had been working for about a week on some problems intended to develop their understandings of similarity. About mid-way through the unit he had posed the following question: At this time, what do you think will always be true about two figures that are similar to each other? We will be looking at a video clip of a whole class conversation about this question but first it might be helpful in making sense of this conversation to first look at the investigations in the curriculum unit that Mr. Vince was using in his class.

Activity 1: Examining the Curriculum-in-Use

The following materials will need to be distributed.

- *Similarity: A Sample of Activities From Investigations 1–3.* Provide one set of these curriculum materials for each participant.
- *Mugwumps 1, 2, and 3 and Cuzz and Wuzz* . A sample of student work from Investigation 3. Provide one set of these drawings for each participant.
- *Questions for Discussion: The Curriculum in Use*. These questions can help frame participants' examination and discussion of the curriculum materials: How does this unit approach teaching the concept of similarity? How might the investigations help students build a mathematical definition and understanding of similarity? What might students and their teacher find challenging or unfamiliar about this approach? What demands does it make of teacher and students? What might a teacher expect that students would be able to say about what makes figures similar following these three investigations?

The case investigation begins by having participants examine some of the activities of the first three investigations in the Similarity unit. Give participants an opportunity to work on the activities. We have found that some teachers themselves are unfamiliar with these sorts of activities and their own experience at working on the problems helps them appreciate the mathematics embedded in them. Have participants work in small groups, using the discussion questions to help them examine the nature of the activities and the particular stance these materials take on developing an understanding of the concept of similarity. It will be useful to record (on large paper or transparency) their reactions to the activities and their responses to the discussion questions so they are available later.

Activity 2: Viewing and Discussing the Video—What Do Students Seem To Understand and What is the Evidence?

We suggest an introduction something like the following extract. It works well to create empathy for a professional whom the participants are about to observe. They can anticipate the frustration of the teacher who is trying to orchestrate the conversation. This kind of introduction also seems to preclude any inappropriate evaluation of the teacher's actions. There is not a teacher who has not experienced this kind of situation in her or his classroom before.

> In Investigation 3, students created several figures by plotting points using the rules: Mugwump 1 (x, y); Mugwump 2 $(2x, 2y)$; Mugwump 3 $(3x, 3y)$; Cuzz $(3x, y)$; Wuzz $(x, 3y)$. After students had completed the drawings, they were to respond in writing to the following question: Which of the figures do you think are similar and why? Mr. Vince had read students' written responses and was surprised by the number of students who thought all 5 figures were similar. The next day he decided to pursue this with them in a whole-class discussion, which he documented with a video recording.
>
> We will now watch about 10 minutes of this whole-class discussion. Every teacher has been in a situation like the one we are going to see. Close your eyes and imagine this scenario in your own classroom. You and your students have been working hard at developing their knowledge about some new ideas. You think the work has gone well. Students have completed the problems and have answered the questions, in most cases correctly. You are feeling fairly confident about where they are and so you pose a question, like the one Mr. Vince posed, to get an overall assessment of what students are able to communicate about what they have learned. What happens takes you to-

tally by surprise. The students respond to your question in ways that you had not anticipated. You cannot figure out where they are coming from. You continue to pose your question, sometimes rephrasing it, but to no avail. There you are, on your feet, trying to make sense of what students are saying, trying to figure out what to do and what to say next.

This is the situation that Mr. Vince found himself. As we watch this segment of a whole class discussion, we want to consider what it is that makes figures seem similar to students.

The following materials will need to be distributed, one copy to each participant.

- *Transcript of Video Recording*. There are some places where the discussion is difficult to follow and you will find the transcript helpful in following along with the video and for referral back to during the discussion about the case materials;
- *Questions for Discussion: The Video*. The following questions can help frame the viewing of the video and the subsequent small group conversations. What understandings about similarity of figures do you think exist among the students in the class? What sense do you make of the students' arguments, and Jessica's in particular, about what makes figures similar? In light of your examination of the investigations in the unit, what surprised you about students' responses? Why do you think the youngsters are not drawing on or making connections to the relevant mathematical ideas that these investigations were intended to develop? What do you think Mr. Vince might do next—either in this conversation, in the next class session, or in preparing to teach this unit again?

Suggest that small groups of participants arrange themselves so they can view and talk about the video together. Usually groups of four to five work best. Again, draw their attention to the questions as a helpful way to frame their viewing of the video.

After viewing the video, have groups take up the discussion questions. As you move around listening to conversations, push participants to be specific about claims they make about what students seem to understand and what evidence supports their claims. The notion of having evidence for claims about student understanding is central to the discussion at this point. Given that the video segment is fairly short, participants may want to view it a second time. They often notice new things in a second viewing.

There can be a tendency for teachers to focus on what students do not understand. Try to get them to talk first about what they think students do understand about similarity and what might account for this. After they have had sufficient time to consider the video, you might offer the following anecdote.

This class discussion continued for a bit longer. By the end of class, most students appeared to be convinced by Jessica's argument that all five figures were similar because "they favored each other" and because "they all had the same shape, just in a different form."

Activity 3: What Might Mr. Vince Do Next in Instruction?

You will need to distribute the following materials, one copy to each participant.

- *Additional Questions for Discussion: Next Instructional Moves* What might Mr. Vince do when teaching this unit again to draw out the relevant mathematics that students would need to construct a deep understanding of similarity? What are the implications for a teacher's practice when using materials that are based on a constructivist view of learning? How does a teacher help students construct a rich, deep understanding of similarity that does not begin with giving students a definition and then having them apply it to stylized, routine exercises? With what would teachers want students to leave each investigation and how can she or he help students gain that knowledge? What role does reflection on mathematical activity play in using these kinds of curriculum materials effectively? How does a teacher take into account the experiences and meanings that students bring with them to the mathematics classroom that may interfere with the teachers main idea? How can a teacher acknowledge and build on the meanings that grow out of students' lived experiences?

In the next section, Deliberations Within the Project, a discussion of our own inquiry is provided as we tried to make sense of the whole-class discussion, closely examined the nature of the curriculum materials, and considered how Mike Vince might think about next instructional moves.

Activity 4: Stepping Back

This case provides an opportunity for participants to step back and consider the potential for continued professional learning when groups of educators engage in dialogue about particular classroom events. It also highlights the utility of capturing events in ways that allow one to revisit those events. Without the video recording, our group would have been severely limited in helping Mr. Vince make sense of what had occurred in his classroom. The very use of video recordings in mathematics classrooms is likely to raise a number of issues, not the least of which is a feasibility concern. What may be most useful here is to have participants consider when a teacher might want to document classroom events with video or audio recordings, for what purposes, with what kinds of support, and whether the benefits might override some of the feasibility concerns.

BEYOND THE CASE

The video recording that Mike Vince brought to our project retreat engaged us in extended conversations over the three days we met and beyond. This case exemplifies key aspects of our project—the willingness of teachers to take risks by bringing to the group instances from their own classroom of students struggling with new ideas, to reveal their frustrations at not being able to make sense of students' answers, and to disclose their own uncertainty about what they might have done differently or where to go next. We think this is professional collaboration at its best.

If the group working through this case has developed a level of trust that allows sharing of lessons from their own classrooms, inquire if one or two participants would volunteer to have a whole-class discussion videotaped for the group's consideration at the next session. It must be made clear that the purpose is not to judge a teacher's actions but to use the recording as a site to investigate what students seem to understand, what they are struggling with, and what counts as evidence of these claims. There may be teachers in the group who are teaching a topic that is difficult for her or his students to come to grips with. The topic may lend itself nicely to the kind of mid-unit assessment that engaged Mr. Vince and his students. We have found that many teachers welcome the opportunity to talk with colleagues about the challenges in helping students develop a robust, deep understanding of difficult topics. The power of the video recording is that it is concrete, does not rely on a teacher's selective and partial summary of the event, and allows participants to revisit the event as new questions and insights emerge while viewing and talking about the specific event.

DELIBERATIONS WITHIN THE PROJECT

Making Sense of What Students Understand

What Does it Mean to "Listen to Students"? During the whole class discussion, Mike Vince was working hard at listening to what students were saying about what makes figures similar. He was puzzled by their persistence at hanging on to their common, nonmathematical meanings of similar, and their inability or resistance to draw on the relevant mathematics that he thought had been developed in the several previous lessons. We speculated that there is a tendency for teachers to listen in response to their instruction, not anticipating how the views that students developed from prior experiences could be so powerful or so deeply held that it shapes their answers to a teacher's questions.

For example, almost buried in this conversation was Jessica's reference to the names of the figures. It appeared as if she initially thought the names given to objects were salient. Mugwumps 1, 2, and 3 were similar because they had the same name, Cuzz and Wuzz were similar because they had names that sounded alike, but the two sets were not similar to each other because the names were different. But then Jessica seemed to change her mind about that in favor of another reason to classify figures as similar—if they "favor each other." Later in the exchange (not included in the transcript), there was reference again to names of objects; if the names were alike, the figures were similar.

Interrogating the Curriculum. Another teacher in our project, whose students were studying the same unit said he had experienced some similar problems in his class. His students, too, seemed to place particular relevance on the names of objects. We reviewed the first several investigations in the unit. In the investigation with the overhead projector of sailboats, students initially moved the projector perpendicular to the screen to make enlargements of the image. These figures were called sailboats. Then they angled the projector so the image of the sailboat was distorted, producing either a very long or very tall boat. The long boat was called a battleship, the tall boat was called a clipper. The teacher said that when his students were asked which boats were similar, they said the sailboats, but not the battleship or the clipper. When he asked why the sailboats were similar, several students responded, "The name's the same." We began to see that from the students' point of view, whether figures were similar might have something to do with the names of the figures.

Looking back at the curriculum unit, we realized the possibility that the materials themselves may have inadvertently contributed to students' misconceptions. Students giving the same name to similar figures happened in two different investigations—the sailboat activity and the Mugwump activity. In both instances, the similar figures had the same name (sailboats; Mugwumps), whereas those that were not similar were assigned different names (clipper and battleship; Cuzz and Wuzz).

We found instances where the use of the word *similar* encouraged students to think of similarity in a common, everyday use of the idea. We wondered whether the intention of linking new learning to previous experiences—a frequently used method to help students associate new ideas with things they already know—could have contributed to students' persistence with nonmathematical meanings for similar. For example, one question following Investigation 2 asks: Aunts are notorious as experts on similarities between a parent and a child. According to Aunt Brenda, "Jill looks the same as her mother." What does she mean? We wondered whether this question at this particular point in the unit might actually retard students moving from common to mathematical meanings.

The close examination of the investigations in the unit led us to consider whether we needed to approach all curriculum materials with a more critical eye. The experience forewarned us to be on the lookout for ways in which approaches in a text might unintentionally lead to confusion rather than clarity. An interesting footnote to our inquiry was our ability to help reshape this curriculum unit as it was under development. We provided very important feedback to the curriculum writers who revised the unit in light of Vince's experience with and our collective analysis of the curriculum materials.[2]

Getting it Right or Making Sense. In our conversations, we experienced Mike Vince's frustration at trying to figure out what he could have done differently, or what he could follow up with, so that the youngsters would move toward a mathematical definition of similarity. We had noticed in our group a range of responses to surprising student actions across several of the case materials we were developing. In some instances, we focused on where students were wrong in their thinking or understanding and how we

[2]The curriculum writers took care to name objects so as not inadvertently to lead students to conclude that the name given to figures was a salient attribute of similar figures. In addition, and far more significantly, the writers have developed a Reflections activity that follows each investigation, with the intent of helping teachers help their students extract the relevant mathematics from the investigation and put new learnings together with previous learnings continually to build their understandings of a new and important mathematical idea.

could get students to "get it right." In other instances, we tried to make sense of student actions or responses from the students' perspectives. We were particularly curious about what kinds of things in our own teaching—prior experiences, ideas not sufficiently explored or developed, shortcomings in carrying out instruction—contributed to a puzzling action or response.

In the particular instance of Mike's efforts, he had the intention of providing the opportunity for students to construct the mathematical definition of similarity. Like many other teachers who are taking the reform of mathematics teaching seriously, he tried to avoid "telling" students what they needed to know—in this case, telling them the definition of similarity. But this raises some interesting questions. What needs to be on the table, in the conversation, to enable students to construct robust definitions of similar figures (or other definitions of mathematical terms)? Mike had tremendous faith in the few tasks on scale factor to reveal to students the critical aspects that make figures similar and to supersede the common sense meanings they brought from everyday use of the term. What accounted for their persistence in using everyday meanings to talk about similarity? Why didn't they draw on the mathematical ideas that were embedded in the several activities on stretching and scale factor? Why did they not mention anything about the angles in the drawings? What could be done differently next time?

Doing or Reflecting on Doing. Students often view the goal in the mathematics classroom as completing the assignment, getting the work done. We considered that there may also be a tendency on the part of teachers to focus more on doing and less on thinking about or reflecting on the doing. Mike Vince had engaged his students in several investigations intended to explore aspects of similarity. They had made enlargements with rubber-band stretchers and asked what things were changed and what things were not. They used overhead projections of objects to make enlargements and distortions, and considered how edge and angle measures of projected figures compared with the original figure. They were introduced to scale factor. They drew figures on grid paper using rules to generate pairs of numbers. They had done the exercises and answered the questions. However, it seemed from the video of the conversation that students had not linked the mathematics embedded in these investigations with what it might mean to say that figures were mathematically similar.

This particular episode pushed us all to think about what teachers need to do to make the mathematics in a problem explicit. The relevant mathematics in a task are not automatically revealed to youngsters through their doing of the task. Teachers need to consider what she or he needs to do to extract the mathematics, to link the work of the task to the direction in which the investigations are headed. In this case, Mr. Vince and his students were working toward a mathematical definition of similarity. What the students seemed to miss was what each task was contributing to constr ucting a mathematical definition.

Deliberation Prompts Looking Back. The conversations we had about this case helped us to see that using assessment in the service of instruction may involve looking back, to see whether and in what ways prior experiences may account for the place students are in their understandings or in their ability to bring relevant mathematics to bear on problem situations and questions. Our reflection led us to ask more questions: What might Mr. Vince have done to draw out the relevant mathematics that students needed to construct a working definition of similarity? How does a teacher take into account the experiences and meanings that students bring with them to the mathematics classroom that may interfere with the point?

Thinking About Next Steps

One course of action available to Mr. Vince was to acknowledge the common meanings that students attached to the term *similar* and where those meanings came from. For example, talking about kin "favoring each other" is common among African-American communities. The youngsters in Mr. Vince's class were bringing meanings from their everyday lives to make sense of an idea in their mathematics classroom. We considered how he could honor and build on the meanings that grew out of his students' lived experiences.

We thought Mr. Vince needed to alert students early on that mathematicians use the term *similar* in a special way and that this unit is intended to help them learn about the mathematical meaning of similarity and the properties of similar figures. One possible course of action Mr. Vince could take was to revisit the previous investigations, pointing out which figures mathematicians would call similar. Then the students could consider specific attributes of the figures, which changed and which did not change when a figure was enlarged or shrunk.

This case highlighted for us important issues that arise when teachers move from a traditional curriculum (where students are given definitions that they memorize and then apply to stylized exercises) to a problem-centered, inquiry-focused curriculum – where students investigate situations intended to help them construct mathematically robust and personally meaningful definitions. The issues are embedded in the link between curriculum and teaching. A problem-centered curriculum implies different modes of teaching. This can create a tension for teachers between wanting their students to "get it right" and wanting ideas to "make sense." Teachers may resist "telling" students what they want them to know but feel quite uncertain about how to help students construct their own understandings from mathematical investigations.

A number of issues that emerge as teachers change multiple aspects of their practice are embedded in this case, to which we have returned many times over the past 3 years.

MATERIALS FOR MAKING PHOTOCOPIES AND TRANSPARENCIES

- *Similarity: A Sample of Activities from Investigations 1–3*. Prepare one copy for each participant.
- *Mugwumps 1, 2, 3, and Cuzz and Wuzz*. Prepare one copy for each participant.
- *Questions for Discussion*. Prepare one copy for each participant and prepare an overhead transparency.
- *Transcript of Video Recording*. Prepare one copy for each participant.
- *Some Additional Questions for Discussion*. Prepare one copy for each participant and prepare an overhead transparency.

SIMILARITY: A SAMPLE OF ACTIVITIES FROM INVESTIGATIONS 1–3

Investigation 1: The Stretcher

In this investigation, students experiment with an activity in which they use two rubber bands knotted together to draw enlargements of pictures. To make an enlargement of the apple pictured below, a student holds down one end of the rubber band with a finger, puts a pencil in the end of the other rubber band, stretches the rubber band and guides the knot around the apple, while the pencil traces out the new figure.

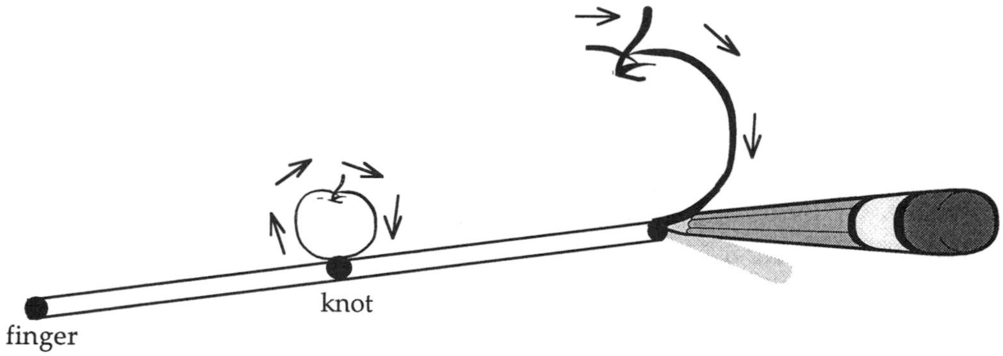

One activity has students use the stretcher to make an enlargement of rectangle ABCD below. Then students are asked questions such as:

- How do the lengths of corresponding sides compare?
- How many rectangles ABCD can fit inside the enlarged rectangle?
- What things were changed in the rectangle by the enlargement process?
- What things were not changed in the rectangle by the enlargement process?

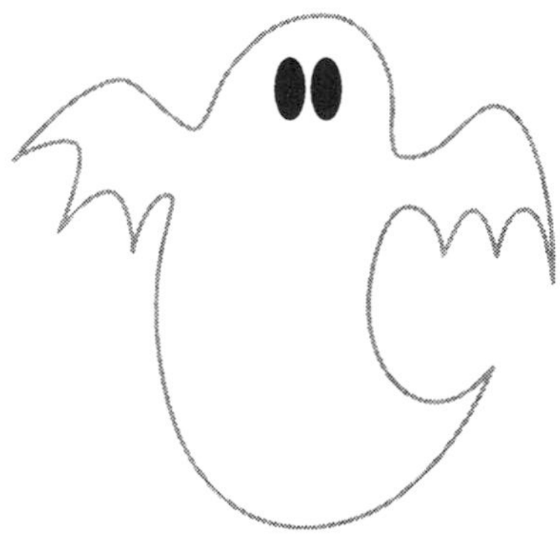

In this investigation, students make enlargements of a variety of shapes with the stretcher. One extension question invites students to investigate what happens if they make a super-stretcher by knotting three rubber bands and guiding the knot closest to the anchor point around the original figure. Another extension question asks students what will happen if they move the projection point to a different location.

Investigation 2: Projecting Models of Sailboats

In this investigation, students investigate the images they can get by projecting an object from an overhead projector. They complete a chart to help them look for patterns in predicting the size of the projection.

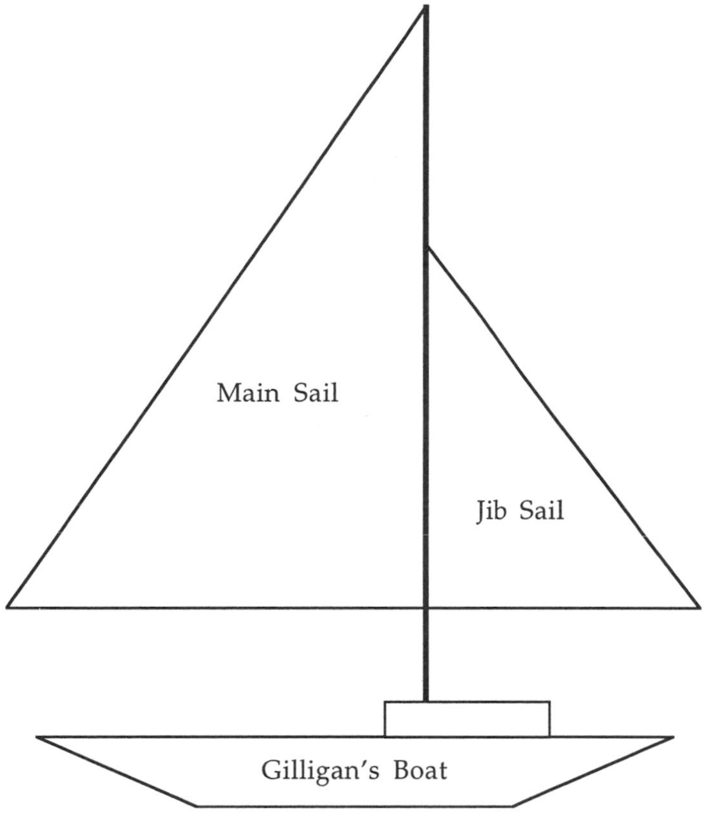

	Length of the Boat	Main Sail Height	Main Sail Base	Distance of Projector to Screen
Original Picture				
Projection 3 times				
Projection 6 times				
Projection 9 times				

Then students are asked questions such as:

- How do the angle measures of the projected pictures compare with the angle measures of the original picture?
- What properties of the original picture did not change?
- Experiment with the overhead projector to make a picture of a "battleship" about 6 times as long but only 3 times as high as the original. Record the measurements of your battleship. Describe how the projector was arranged to get the battleship.
- Make a picture of a "clipper" about 3 times as long and 6 times as high as the original. Record the measurements of your clipper. Describe how the projector was arranged to get the clipper.

At the completion of these activities, students are introduced to scale factor.

> The **scale** is the **factor** that is *multiplied* by the measures of lengths of a figure to get the corresponding measures of lengths on an enlargement. We call this number the **scale factor** because it tells us how to scale a figure to get a new figure.
>
> For example, if the measures of the edges of a figure are tripled to get the length of the edges of a new figure the same shape, but a larger size, then the scale factor from the small figure to the larger figure is 3.

Then students examine drawings of similar figures and determine the scale from the smaller to the larger and from the larger to the smaller.

Investigation 3: Mugwump's Cousins

In this investigation, students are given a table of sets of points—with their coordinates and rules—to produce members of the Mugwump family. They are given the following directions:

1. Label the point in the lower left corner of the grid paper as 0,0.
2. From the column marked Mugwump 1, plot the points on the grid paper. Connect the points, as you go, with line segments.
3. Following the same steps, list all the pairs of numbers for each figure and make drawings of the other Mugwumps and Cuzz and Wuzz.

Points		Mugwump 1 (x,y)	Mugwump 2 (2x,2y)	Mugwump 3 (3x,3y)	Cuzz (3x,y)	Wuzz (x,3y)
Set 1	A	2,0	4,0			
	B	2,4				
	C	0,4				
	D	0,5				
	E	2,5				
	F	0,8				
	G	0,12				
	H	1,15				
	I	2,12				
	J	5,12				
	K	6,15				
	L	7,12				
	M	7,8				
	N	5,5				
	O	7,5				
	P	7,4				
	Q	5,4				
	R	5,0				
	S	4,0				
	T	4,3				
	U	3,3				
Connect V to A	V	3,0				
Set 2						
Start over	W	1,8				
	X	2,7				
	Y	5,7				
	Z	6,8				
Set 3						
Start over	AA	3,8				
	BB	4,8				
	CC	4,10				

Connect DD to AS	DD	3,10				
Set 4						
	EE	2,11 dot				
	FF	5,11 dot				

Then students are asked to examine their drawings.

- As Mugwump grew into 2 and 3, what things remained the same and what changed?
- How do the angles in Mugwump 1 compare to the corresponding angles in Mugwump 2 and Mugwump 3?
- How do the angles in Mugwump 1 compare to the corresponding angles in Cuzz and Wuzz?

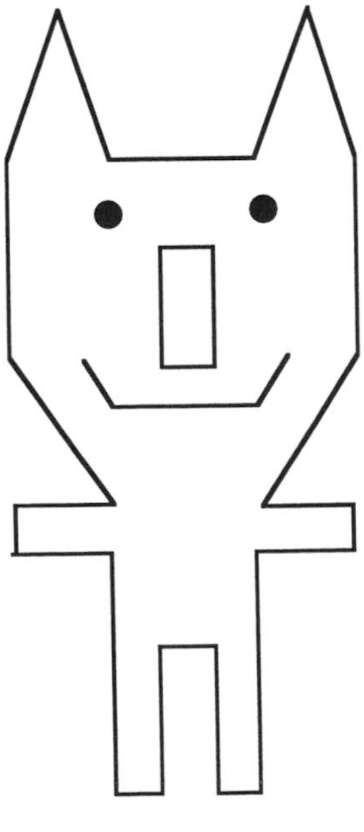

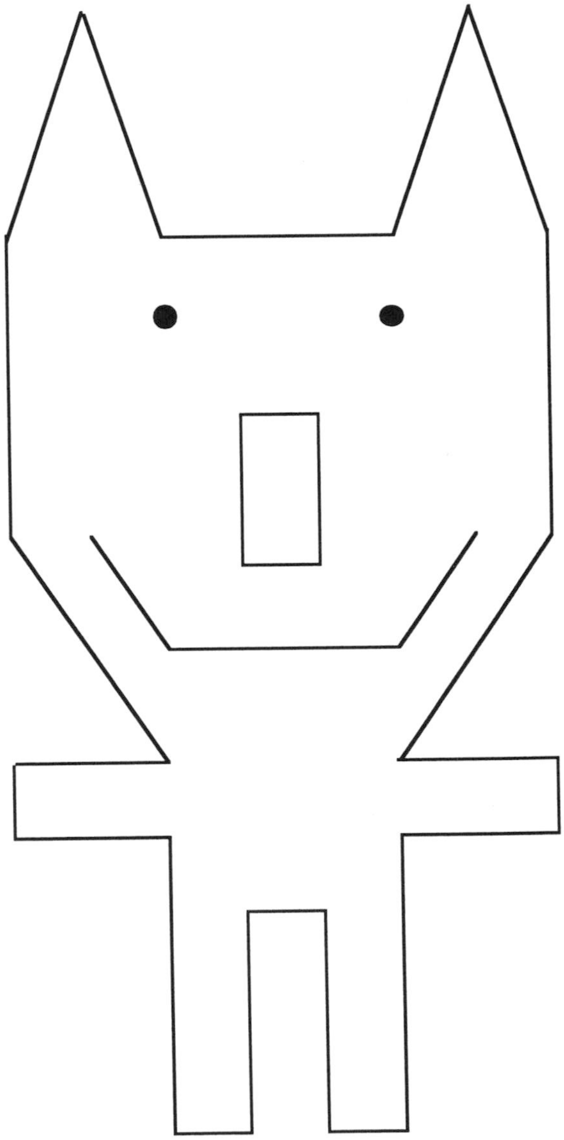

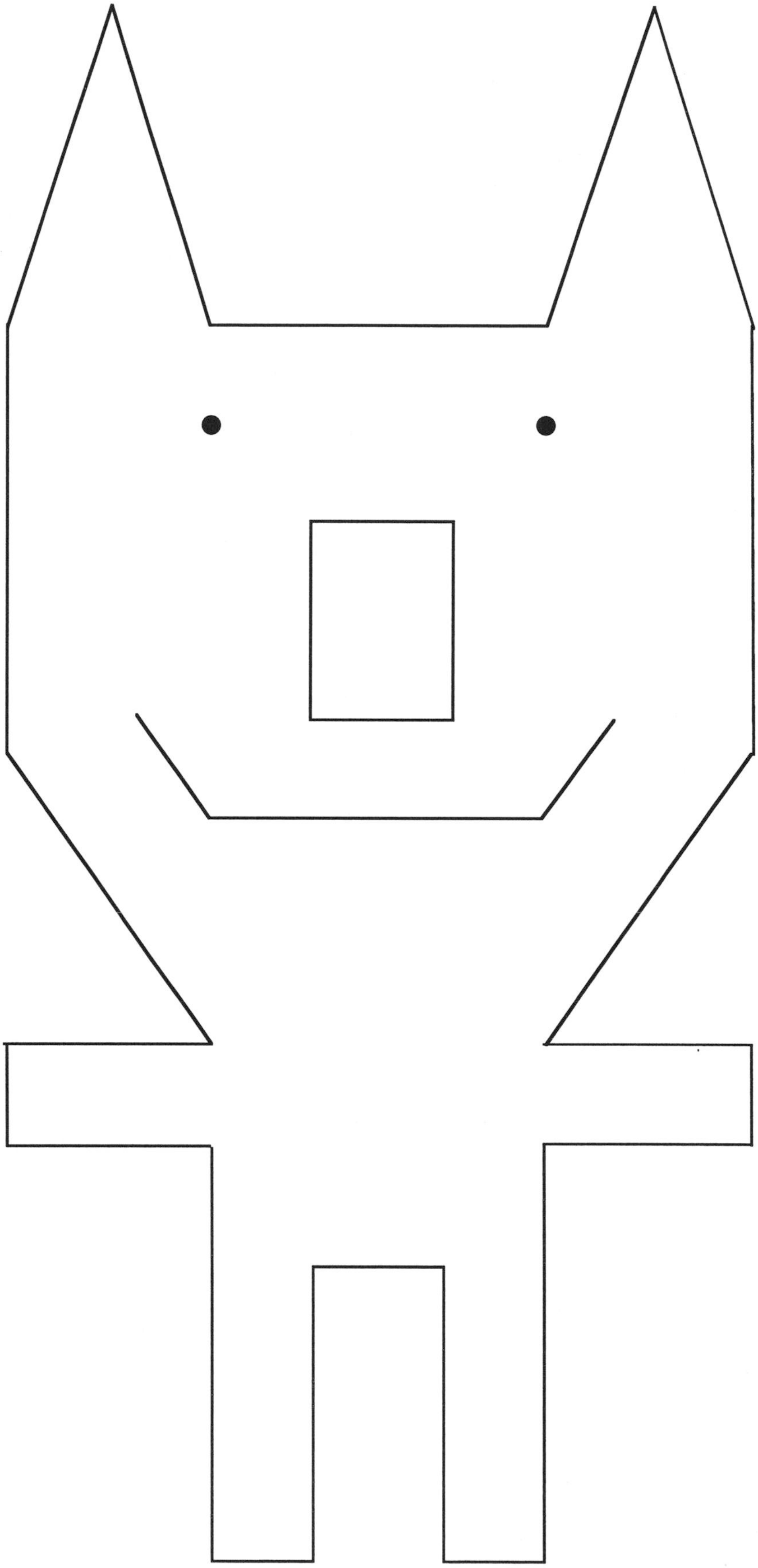

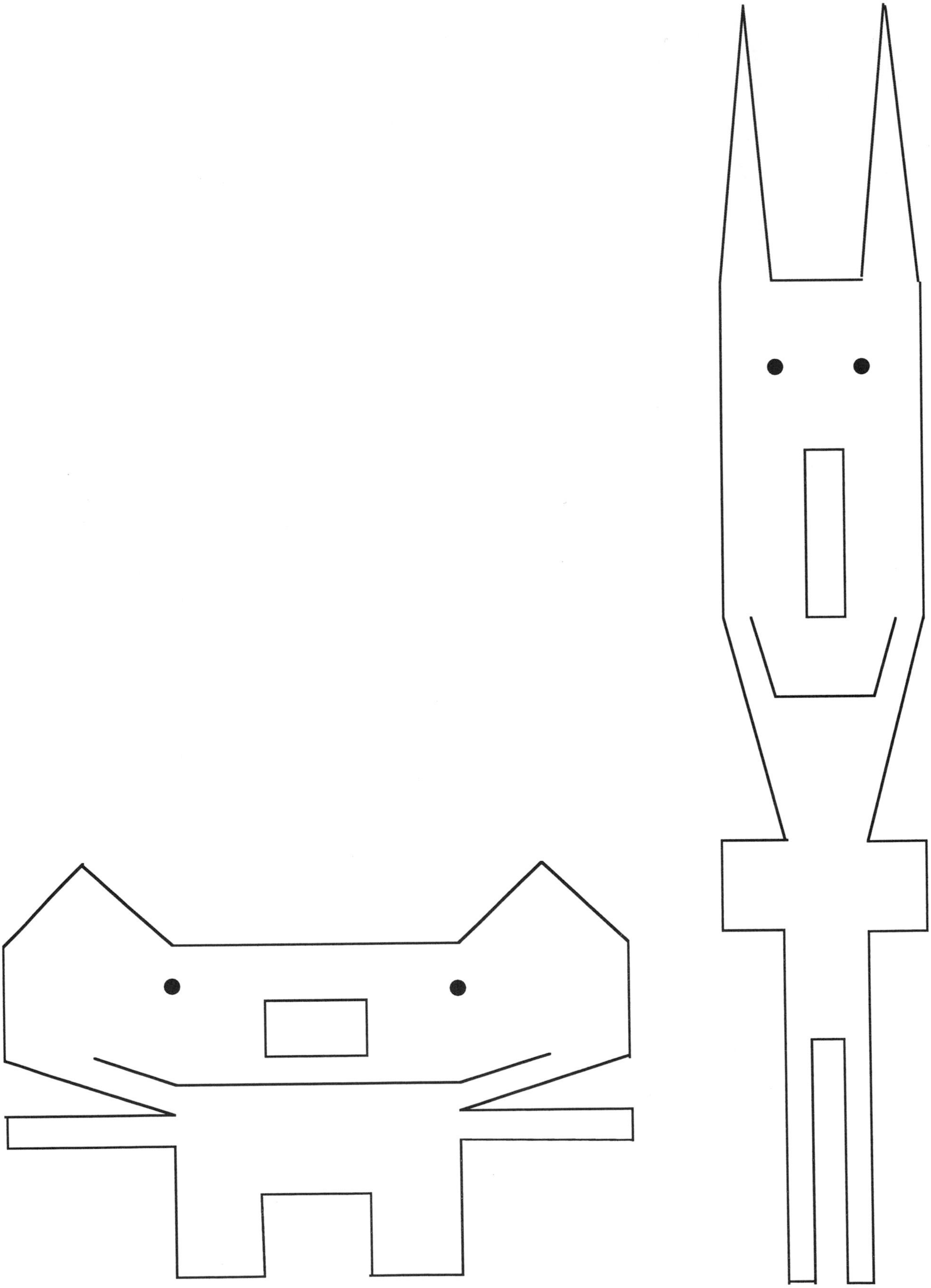

QUESTIONS FOR DISCUSSION: THE CURRICULUM-IN-USE

- How does this unit approach the teaching of the concept of similarity?
- How might the investigations help students build a mathematical definition and understanding of similarity?
- What might students and their teacher find challenging or unfamiliar about this approach?
- What demands does it make of teacher and students?
- What might a teacher expect that students would be able to say about what makes figures similar following these three investigations?

TRANSCRIPT OF VIDEO RECORDING

Mr. Vince: I want you to think about what we've done thus far. What activities and experiments and investigations have we done thus far toward the idea of learning what similarity means? What have we done?

Student: What was that rubber band thing?

Mr. Vince: Okay, one of the things we did was the stretcher rubber band where we produced a figure that was larger than the one that we were tracing. Okay. The large figure. What else did we do?

Student: The mugwump thing.

Mr. Vince: We did the coordinate graph where we put down the different figures based upon the different coordinates that they gave us. What else? What else?

Student: We did a couple of pages.

Mr. Vince: Was there another investigation right there that we did?

Student: We did the boats, did the boats.

Mr. Vince: We did the boats, the overhead projector about moving the overhead projector closer or farther away or at an angle and so forth. Now thinking about all those things we've done and talked about. Here's what I want you to think about now. What do you think will always be true about two figures that are similar to each other? Now, I'll tell you ahead of time that most of you, I have only glanced at some of the responses that you guys gave me yesterday, about which figures were similar. Now some people, of the five figures yesterday that you said were similar, how many said that they were all similar? All five were similar, one, two, three, Cuzz and Wuzz? ... How many said that just one, two, three were similar? [4 hands raised]. Anybody say anything different? All right, the discussion that I had with my 7th hour class yesterday, and I want to see how you guys respond to this because it may help us answer again this first question. It should make more sense here what do you think will always be true about two figures that are similar. How would you feel if somebody answered the question this way as compared to the way you would answer it. They told me yesterday, some people yesterday that all five figures are similar.

Student: They are.

Mr. Vince: They are Jessica?

Jessica: (Shakes her head yes).

Mr. Vince: You, did you say that all five, when you wrote yesterday, did you say all five were similar?

Jessica: (Shakes her head no).

Mr. Vince: What did you say were similar?

Jessica: One, two, three.

Mr. Vince: Why didn't you include Cuzz and Wuzz in there?

Jessica: Because, I didn't think at the time, you know [inaudible] 'cause one, two, three look the same, Cuzz and Wuzz got a different name. So ...

Mr. Vince: Because they have different names that makes them not similar?

Students: No, no ...

Jessica: Not that they have a different name. It just didn't dawn on me that they [inaudible].

Mr. Vince: Now, I really don't want to be, I know that this strikes some people as funny and comical but I really want people to be serious about this because, see I want to understand what it is that you people are knowing about this or are not knowing about this or what you are confused about or what you don't understand about. So if I ask the question all over again, Jessica, how would you tell me, if I said, Which of the drawings Mugwump one, Mugwump two, Mugwump three, Cuzz and Wuzz, if I asked you which ones of those were similar to each other? What would be your answer today?

Student: The same.

Mr. Vince: No, let her answer.

Jessica: All of them.

Mr. Vince: They're all similar. Can you tell me why you think that way?

Jessica: Because, they all favor each other.

Mr. Vince: They all what please?

Jessica: Favor each other.

Mr. Vince: What do you mean favor each other. What do you mean by favor?

Jessica: They have the same body, same nose, same shape.

Mr. Vince: Do they have the same body, same nose?

Jessica: Don't have the same body but they have the same shape of body, just in different forms.

Mr. Vince: Now wait a minute. They have the same shape of body but in different forms?

Jessica: Yeah, a smaller, a bigger, a larger, a longer, a taller, they all the same, all same arms, all got the same boxed off ... same square ears.

Mr. Vince: How many disagree with what Jessica is saying?

Student: I don't understand. [Student responding, inaudible].

Mr. Vince: Does anybody else understand what Jessica is trying to get at here? 'Cause I think, 'cause I think that this is, this is the same thing that came up yesterday in the seventh hour and I'm trying to understand the view of those people, 'cause they were, they were not trying to be funny about this. They were serious about the fact that they firmly believed that all of them in a way, because of what they felt or what they thought of as similar, that they all five of those drawings fit, met that category. And I think I'm hearing that from Jessica, but I don't want to put words in her mouth, so I want people who think they understand what she is saying to help out on this, because I really need to understand why some of you think that way and why some of you don't think that way. Now obviously there's a number of people that heard what she said that don't agree with that. Is that correct?

Student: If I knew what she said.

Jessica: What I'm saying is they got the same blocked off arms and blocked off face, same square nose, same eyes, same mouth, same ears but they just in different form. Longer, fatter, taller, shorter. Just different forms.

Mr. Vince: Now does everybody understand what she's talking about?

Students: Yes.

Mr. Vince: Do you agree that those, that those common things that she is talking about are good enough to make figures similar? Now at this point, remember the questions says, "At this point." Meaning as far as we've gone thus far, with the understanding of the idea about similarity. What is it that we say is true about two similar figures? Let's go back to the people who said one, two, three were similar. Why did you guys figure that ... Who said that one, two, three were similar? [hands up]. All right, I mean that's all. Not, Cuzz and Wuzz. Can you tell me why you thought those three were similar?

Student: Because they have the same shape.

Mr. Vince: They have the same basic shape. What does that, how does that, how does that differ from what Jessica said? Which is they have the same basic form, but they're different sizes. Is that what you said? Now when you say size, are you just talking about, one being bigger?

Jessica: It's like with Cuzz, you just stretched Cuzz out, Cuzz is still Wuzz. And so Cuzz (inaudible, continues to explain).

Mr. Vince: That's what we need to talk about. That's what I'm trying to get you guys to open up a little more. Now does everybody understand what Jessica was saying?

Students: Yes, yes.

Mr. Vince: Now, how, how do those figures that are stretched out either widthwise or lengthwise. How do those figures differ from one, two and three?

Student: 'Cause of the size. They're different in the ...

Mr. Vince: Well, now, wait a minute, wait a minute. Ah, Mugwump two and Mugwump three were bigger than Mugwump one.

Student: Yeah.

Mr. Vince: So, their size is different too, but they don't look like Cuzz and Wuzz.

Student: 'Cause they all look the same.

Mr. Vince: Well that's what I'm trying to figure out here. So in terms of what we're saying here, I want, help me figure this out, help me find out why, why these are. So, so how are we going to decide this? How are we going to decide about what things are going to be called similar and what things are not going to be?

QUESTIONS FOR DISCUSSION: THE VIDEO

- What understandings about similarity of figures do you think exist among the students in the class?
- What sense do you make of the students arguments, and Jessica's in particular, about what makes figures similar?
- In light of your examination of the investigations in the unit, what surprised you about students' responses?
- Why do you think the youngsters are not drawing on or making connections to the relevant mathematical ideas that these investigations were intended to develop?
- What do you think Mr. Vince might do next—either in this conversation, in the next class session, or in preparing to teach this unit again?

ADDITIONAL QUESTIONS FOR DISCUSSION: NEXT INSTRUCTIONAL MOVES

- What might Mr. Vince do when teaching this unit again to draw out the relevant mathematics that students would need to construct a deep understanding of similarity?
- What are the implications for a teacher's practice when using materials that are based on a constructivist view of learning?
- How does a teacher help students construct a rich, deep understanding of similarity that does not begin with giving students a definition and then having them apply it to stylized, routine exercises?
- What would a teacher want students to leave each investigation with and how can she/he help students gain that knowledge?
- What role does reflection on mathematical activity play in using these kinds of curriculum materials effectively?
- How does a teacher take into account the experiences and meanings that students bring with them to the mathematics classroom that may interfere with where the teacher wants to take them? How can a teacher acknowledge and build on the meanings that grow out of students' lived experiences?

Case 2: Nurturing a Disposition for Inquiry

From the classroom of Sandra Bethell in collaboration with Daniel Chazan, Melissa Dennis, Bill Rosenthal, Perry Lanier, and Sandra Wilcox

OVERVIEW

This case provides opportunities to:

- *Consider a teacher's decision to set aside her agenda and pursue a student's question*: Why does she pursue a disagreement among students about whether the point (0,0) is in four quadrants or one, and what purposes might be served by taking up this disagreement?
- *Debate the question of whether there are always right answers in mathematics*: Is there a "right" answer to the question of whether (0,0) is in four quadrants or none, on what does the answer depend, is it the answer or the question that is important, and what purposes might be served by highlighting (or avoiding) this and other examples where there may not be strong pressure to choose between contradictory views?;
- *Consider how a teacher portrays to students the nature of definitions in mathematics*: How do definitions arise, when does it become important to set a definition, and can students make definitions for use by their class or should they always look to texts and teachers to tell them what definitions have been accepted by mathematicians?;
- *Consider how and why a teacher elicits students' intuitions about standard mathematical topics*: What intuitions do students have about the geometry of the Cartesian plane, what are they using to reason about the plane, how does the teacher follow up with questions that focus on these intuitions, what purposes might she have in eliciting these intuitions, and how might such a discussion shape future discussions in this class?;
- *Explore ways of working with students who have been largely unsuccessful in mathematics*: How does a teacher try to engage students who like to be contrary, and who may differ in their willingness to work with mathematical definitions and topics that are new to them?

Mathematical Content: Reasoning about definitions in mathematics and mathematical consistency with regard to the origin and axes in the Cartesian plane.

Case Materials: Edited video recording and transcript of the whole-class discussion, and of the teacher's after-class reflections.

Suggested Time: Minimum of 2 hours to examine a portion of the case materials, and at least 3 hours to engage in a full analysis.

INTRODUCTION

This case is built around a discussion in an Algebra I class that centers on the question of whether the point (0,0) is in four quadrants or no quadrants. This question is not one that the teacher had intended to pose. Rather, it surfaced as students were discussing their work on problems in which they were to decide, among other things, whether a line always, sometimes, or never passes through exactly two quadrants. When one student identified a line that passed through quadrants one and three and through the origin, it set off a controversy about how to describe the location of (0,0) on the plane. Although the question was not one the teacher had set out to raise, she decided to pursue it with the class. The case provides an opportunity to consider, in the context of a particular lesson, the intentions and actions of a teacher whose central aim is to foster the mathematical inquiry of her students.

About the Teacher and Students in This Algebra Class

Sandra Bethell's classroom looks different from more-conventional Algebra I classes. Here students are engaged with her in developing an understanding of algebraic concepts and having conversations about how they are making sense of these ideas. Bethell's stance toward teaching reflects important aspects of her experiences, her beliefs, and her values. Her students are working class youth in grades 10–12 who have generally had unpleasant and unsuccessful experiences in previous mathematics classes. In her teaching, Bethell manifests a concern for her students, an appreciation for their intellectual prowess, and a commitment to help them develop their power to express what they are coming to understand.

Bethell identifies strongly with her students; she grew up in circumstances similar to theirs. As a young teacher, she hoped that through her example her students would come to value and appreciate mathematics as she had. But her early experiences were disappointing. It seemed that mathematics created too large a chasm between her and the students she hoped would identify with her. After a temporary detour to pursue a doctoral degree in education, Bethell turned to her undergraduate minor, to the teaching of Spanish. Here she felt she had opportunities for rich engagement with students and their intellectual life while she helped them gain the ability to express themselves in a different language. This stood in stark contrast to her earlier mathematics teaching in which she felt she had not helped students gain the ability to express their own ideas.

Several years ago, the opportunity to reshape her mathematics teaching drew Bethell back into the mathematics classroom. Recently, she completed a master's program in mathematics for teacher-leaders in the state. She has done intensive work with colleagues on understanding the high-school mathematics curriculum. From her teaching of a language, Bethell now brings a new appreciation for helping students articulate their mathematical ideas as they become immersed in a mathematical culture. Her advanced training in mathematics helps her appreciate the advanced mathematical thinking often found in the intuitions her students express about topics in the curriculum. Furthermore, she remains committed to demonstrating to her students that they are good thinkers who can understand complex mathematical ideas.

About the Curriculum in This Algebra Class

Bethell has taught this Algebra I course for several years. The course was developed in collaboration with Daniel Chazan, a mathematics educator at Michigan State University with whom Bethell taught for 2 years, and several of her colleagues. In this course, *variables* and *functions* are the objects of study, with a primary emphasis on linear functions and some investigation of quadratic functions. Students encounter polynomial expressions as representations of "number recipes" that can be expressed *symbolically* (e.g., $5x + 2$), as input and output *tables*, and as *graphs* in the two dimensional Cartesian plane.[3] There is no conventional textbook for the course, although the teachers have a set of problems from which they choose. These problems are located on a file server that the teachers access. Some were written by Chazan, others by Bethell and some of her colleagues, and a few by the students themselves.

This event took place during the study of the unit titled, "Families of Functions". In this unit, students classify functions into different categories of their own construction. The unit begins with Bethell giving students particular rules and having them create corresponding tables and graphs. Students investigate a wide range of rules (e.g., $y = x$; $y = x^2$; $y = 3x$; $y = 2x + 5$; $y = 2x^2$; $y = x^2 + 4$; $y = \sin x$; $y = \cos x$; $y = \ln x$). The use of a graphing calculator as a regular tool in this classroom makes this exploration possible with minimal help from Bethell. Once students have constructed their tables and graphs, they compare the rules with the corresponding graphs and devise ways to classify the functions by their graphs. This provides Bethell an opportunity to learn what sorts of categories students make on their own, and to what aspects of the graphs of

[3]The mathematical point of view that Bethell and Chazan have taken grows out of the work of Judah Schwartz and Michal Yerushalmy. For an elaboration of this particular stance on algebra see Schwartz and Yerushalmy (1992).

functions they pay particular attention. Bethell then introduces classifications that are typically used in mathematics, and standard mathematical terminology (e.g., *increasing*, *decreasing*, *quadrants*, *origin*) about graphical representations of functions.

In earlier units, students had investigated how symbolic rules compare with their tabular outputs; what inputs result in a zero output; what information can be discerned from particular features of a graph; how to decide between graphs, tables, or rules within a given context. They also had investigated *quantities* and relationships between quantities, and how tables, graphs, and symbolic expressions represent relationships between quantities.

In the particular lesson of this case, students were completing a worksheet that asks them to decide whether a line always, sometimes, or never passes through exactly two quadrants. As students made arguments about their ideas, they were to provide examples and counterexamples. During the whole class discussion, there was a surprise event. As students tried to make lines go through two quadrants, some of them came up with a line that passed through the origin. This led to students questioning whether the point (0,0) is in four quadrants or in no quadrant. The question then led to a lengthy discussion in which various students argued for one or the other of the positions.

This classroom event highlights an important aspect of student understanding: How to help students discuss their intuitions as they explore mathematical topics that are new to them. It also highlights a kind of teaching practice in which Bethell acts as a facilitator, providing tools and tasks that can support students' sense-making, and orchestrating conversations that make their reasoning public and available for others to consider, challenge, reshape, and confirm. Interestingly, it is an example of a learning situation in which Bethell values the question but does not think it is important to come to a consensus on the answer. From her perspective, the value of the question lies, in part, in what it can reveal to her about students' conceptions so she knows what they think and can plan appropriate instr uction.

The Case Materials

The materials for this case consist of an edited video recording of a whole class discussion, divided into five short segments, and a transcript of the recording. The case also includes a video recording of Bethell's after-class reflections on the discussion. In her reflections, the teacher provides insights into her stance on teaching, what she thinks it means to know mathematics, and how she conceives her role with this particular class.

USING THE CASE MATERIALS

Levels of Working With the Materials

Describing Teacher Actions. One lens for analyzing the tapes is to follow closely the actions of the teacher. At one level, participants may simply want to describe what they see, noting what actions Bethell takes at various points during the discussion. In fact, this is not a simple thing to do. Participants are likely to notice quite different things and to recall teacher actions with varying levels of detail.

Analyzing and Interpreting Teacher Actions. At another level, participants should be encouraged to engage questions about why Bethell takes the actions she does. The intent here is not to make judgments about the wisdom of those actions, but to try and make sense of them within the context of (a) the class, (b) the goals Bethell has for her students generally and in this lesson in particular, (c) her views of what it means to know mathematics and how one comes to know, (d) her views of learning and the role of learners, and (e) her views of teaching and the role of the teacher. Here the task moves participants from description of actions to analysis and interpretations of those actions.

Describing Student Actions. Another lens for viewing the tapes is to follow closely the participation of the students. At one level, each participant may want to focus on a specific student and describe the ways in which the student engages in the discussion. What does the student say? When and how does the student respond to a contribution by another student? As with close attention to the teacher, participants are likely to take note of different aspects of students' participation in this whole-class discussion.

Analyzing and Interpreting Student Actions. At yet a different level, participants may try to understand a particular student's participation. When does the student make a contribution? Does it seem to be shaped by what others have said, including the teacher, and if so, in what ways? What do students' contributions suggest about her or his understanding of the mathematical idea under consideration? Here, the task for participants is to move from rich description of student actions to analysis and interpretation of those actions, and what they might reveal about students' understandings of an important and complex idea.

Participants are likely to notice and comment on the apparent lack of participation of some of the students. It would be useful to probe what it means to participate in this class, and how a teacher can know whether students are engaging with the ideas under consideration.

Looking for Evidence of Ongoing Assessment. These case materials can be used to consider whether and in what ways Bethell is engaged in assessment of what her students understand. Participants can be asked to consider the following: When is she assessing? What is she assessing? Who is she assessing? How is she assessing? For each question, participants should be challenged to provide evidence to support any claims they make in response to the questions. Finally, participants can consider what actions they think Bethell takes during the discussion based on her ongoing assessment while the students are engaged in conversation.

Tackling Issues of Definitions, Right Answers, and Students' Intuitions. As mathematics is commonly portrayed, mathematicians have the right to make their own definitions. These case materials raise issues about the role of definitions, how they might arise in mathematics classrooms, and what teachers and students do when the curriculum does not set a definition that clarifies whether answers are right or wrong.

Activity 1: Viewing and Analyzing the Video Segments of the Class

We edited the video recording into five segments and then organized the transcript and questions so that each of the five segments is coupled with its own particular set of questions.

How you decide to use this case will depend, in part, on the time you have available. We have developed sets of discussion questions for each video segment assuming a 3-hour session. You may find it useful to group participants to view and discuss the video recording. One group could analyze the event from the teacher's perspective, trying to imagine itself as this teacher—making sense of what students are saying, facilitating the conversation, and using assessment to orchestrate the discussion. The other group could analyze the event from the students' perspective—making sense of the big questions, responding to others' comments, reconciling various points of view.

However, if you have less time, you may want to make some adaptations. For example, you could decide to focus primarily on the class discussion from the teacher's point of view. What actions does she take? To what does she seem to be paying attention? How does she facilitate the discussion? To what extent does she acknowledge students' contributions? Where does she seem to want to take them mathematically? How does she seem to be using assessment? Or you might decide to view the video primarily through the eyes of particular students. Ken, Matie, Jake, and Kyle may be especially interesting to follow. What ideas do they have about the question? What analogies or representations do they find useful? How do they respond to the contributions of others? The transcript will help participants identif y particular students in the class.

We have scaffolded the questions so that participants move from description to analysis and interpretation. You may find it helpful to have participants frame their viewing of the first two segments of the video with the question, What do you see going on here? This encourages them to describe in detail what they are seeing and holds off for a moment a typical desire to move quickly to interpreting or evaluating the event.

This sets the stage for more in-depth analysis of later segments by drawing out initial impressions of the classroom environment, the roles of teacher and students, and the nature of mathematical activity and discourse.

What follows is a brief commentary on each of the video segments and questions that are intended to support you as you guide participants in a discussion of each segment. In addition, we provide Bethell's reflections on some of the questions for each segment.

You will need to distribute the following, one set to each participant.

- *Transcript: Segment One* and *Questions for Discussion: Segment One*
- *Transcript: Segment Two* and *Questions for Discussion: Segment Two*
- *Transcript: Segment Three* and *Questions for Discussion: Segment Three*
- *Transcript: Segment Four* and *Questions for Discussion: Segment Four*
- *Transcript: Segment Five* and *Questions for Discussion: Segment Five*
- *Transcript: After Class Conversation With Bethell* and *Questions for Discussion: After Class Reflections*

Segment One

The first segment introduces the question that led to an extended discussion about the origin and its location in relation to the four quadrants. Bethell began the class intending to engage students in a discussion about linear functions, their graphs, and the slopes of the graphs. They had begun class with a discussion of whether increasing lines (lines with a positive slope) always, sometimes, or never pass through exactly two quadrants. Kyle had provided an example of a line that passed through three quadrants. Bethell then asked for an example of a line that passes through just two quadrants. Ken suggested a line in the first and third quadrants that passed through the origin. We join the class discussion at this point.

The following Questions for Discussion are intended to help participants get into the class discussion, to locate particular students, and to describe in some detail what they are seeing.

What do you see going on here?

How does the point (0,0) get introduced into the conversation?

What initial ideas do Ken, Matie, and Jake seem to have about how many quadrants a line goes through if it goes through (0,0)?

How are the ideas of individual students treated by Bethell and by the other students?

Why might this be an important question for Bethell to pursue with her students?

What might be a direction Bethell could take at this point and why?

Bethell's Reflections.

The problem they were working on—trying to decide whether a line always, sometimes, or never passes through exactly two quadrants—is very important at this point in the class because our whole goal, before we get into linear functions, is to help them understand what we call the Cartesian connection. If we have two variables that are in a dependence relation, those relationships can be represented in a number of ways. One is with a rule, one is in words—the actual situation, one is a table, and one is a graph. Understanding the connection between a rule, a table, a graph, and what that might mean in terms of a situation is fundamental to our whole program. So an exploration of what the graph is and what's going on in the graph—what the domain is, what the range is, how to consider the points on the graph, and how to relate that to the table—that's just fundamental to the study of functions.

We're also getting conversant about the quadrants. As we talk about the quadrants I refer to them as quadrant one, quadrant two, quadrant three and quadrant four. In using these words, I'm introducing some mathematical conventions and some terminology, to give them tools to talk about their ideas. They are using lines and axes in-

terchangeably. I think the discussion is critical because how we define things is real important to how we later interpret things. That's not so important as following up on a question they have or a disagreement they have—any kind of dissonance. I'm helping them use more precise vocabulary as they try to do that.
What happened today surprised me. Usually when students try to find a line in only two quadrants, they either try to find a line with their calculator that goes straight up and down or a line with a slope of zero. But in this instance, Ken suggested a line with a positive slope that passes through the origin. I wasn't expecting this. But given this particular line, it seemed important to try and learn more about what they were thinking about the point (0,0). Pursuing the question is also important at this point because it can give me some insights about conceptions and intuitions they have about the Cartesian plane.

Segment Two

In this segment, Bethell pursues two ideas with students: Ken's idea that the origin is not in any quadrants, and Matie's idea that the origin is in all four quadrants. The following questions can help frame the viewing and discussion.

What do you see going on here?

How do Ken and Matie seem to be reasoning about the question of where the origin is located?

What does Bethell do with Matie 's use of the box around (0,0)?

How does Bethell use what Ken and Matie have talk ed about earlier?

Bethell's Reflections.

The way Matie was talking, I just thought that was really interesting. She had that idea—to start with a square, a box, and make it smaller and smaller. And no matter how small you make it, that point will be in the center of the box. She wouldn't push herself to think about, "Oh, what if that box **was** that point?" She seemed to be thinking that no matter how small you make the box, it still has size to it. Ken was arguing that eventually, in making the box smaller and smaller, there is "nothing there."

In other classes, students have made different arguments for the origin to be in all four quadrants. One I have seen is where a student takes the quadrants and splits them apart. Then a corner of each would still be (0,0), so it's in all four quadrants. In an algebra II class, a student once used $y = 1/x$ to argue that (0,0) is in no quadrant. He reasoned that as x approaches positive infinity, the range would take on all values closer and closer to zero but y could never equal zero. And likewise, x could take on increasingly smaller values, but it could never equal zero. He made a similar argument for the behavior of the function in the third quadrant. Since the graph would never include a point on the axes because neither $x = 0$ or $y = 0$ would satisfy the rule, it seemed reasonable to conclude that the origin was not in any quadrant, that (0,0) is different.

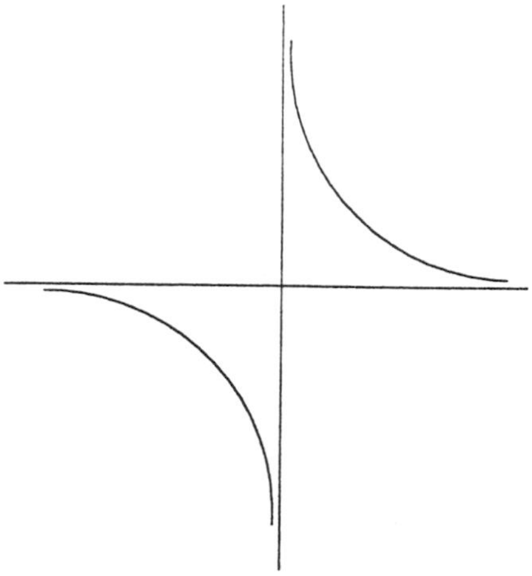

$y = 1/x$

Segment Three

About 6 minutes has elapsed between segments two and three. During that time, several students press Bethell to "tell us who is right." She resists and instead probes a bit more for how Ken and Matie and others are thinking about points on the plane. In this third segment, Jeremiah, Nicole, and Scott, who have been silent to this point, join the conversation. Jeremiah asks a new question: Are the ax es in the quadrants?

Two additional questions can be posed for discussion.

What do you think is the source of Jeremiah 's question and how does it influence the discussion?

What sense do the others, including the teacher, seem to be making of his question?

Bethell's Reflections.

Jeremiah's question was a pleasant surprise, although it has come up before in other classes a couple of times. "What is that axis?" I thought that was really cool. I couldn't have planned it better. Scott said, "If it's in both quadrants, then it doesn't make any sense. There wouldn't be any quadrants then." I thought that was kind of interesting, that point where you change from one quadrant to another.

Matie is reasoning about Jeremiah's question in a way consistent with her position on the origin. She thinks any point on the axes, except (0,0), is located in two quadrants. And Kyle is being consistent with his previous arguments about the origin by calling the axes "neutral territory," and that any point on the axes is in no quadrant. It's interesting that they are trying to reconcile a new idea with their earlier thinking.

Segment Four

At this point, the discussion has been continuing for about 25 minutes. In this segment, Ken challenges Matie's idea that a line passing through the origin is in four quadrants. Matie persists with her representation of drawing circles around the origin suggesting that a point has a size. Jake has been relatively silent since early in the conversation when he, perhaps to be contrary, said that he thought (0,0) was in three quadrants. The notion of a point having size provok es Jake to enter the conversation again.

A further discussion question may be useful.

To what extent and in what ways are any of the students revising their thinking about the original question?

Bethell's Reflections.

I thought it was interesting to see Jake reenter the conversation. He was saying that if you're going to make an argument based on making the point (0,0) bigger, then to be consistent you need to make the axes thicker. But I don't know where this was leading him.

Segment Five

The question, How big is (0,0)? that came from a comment Matie made earlier, is the starting point for this segment.

What sense do you have about where Ken, Matie, and Kyle are in their thinking about the origin?

How does Bethell leave the discussion?

Bethell's Reflections.

Ken was saying, "Zero is nothing, it's not there, it's not like a quantity." Matie was saying, "Well, (6, 0) is a place; (0, 0) is a place." She's saying that it is an assigned location. She didn't say that, but that is what she was referring to. It has a name, just like every other point. I don't know if Ken was convinced of that or not. But initially, I think any other point that you drew, Ken would say, "Yeah, it's there." He would have said, "In this quadrant, that quadrant." But if it was on a line—an axis—he would have probably said both. "(0, 0) is not there because it is not a number."

Activity 2: Taking Up Issues of Definitions and Right Answers

In this activity, participants pursue additional important issues that the case raises. You will need to distribute the following to each participant.

- *Questions for Discussion: Taking Up Issues of Definitions*
- *Questions for Discussion: Taking Up Issues of "Right" Answers*

In this activity, it may be useful to have small groups tackle the questions before having a whole group discussion.

The Nature of Definitions in Mathematics

One set of issues concerns how a teacher portrays to students the nature of definitions in mathematics.

If mathematics is an abstract, theoretical endeavor, not constrained to fit the natural world, how do definitions arise?

When does it become important to set a definition?

Is it important that students understand the sorts of dynamics which lead to the development of definitions?

In the classroom, can students make definitions for use by their class, or should they always look to mathematics texts and teachers to tell them what definitions have been accepted by mathematicians?

"Right" Answers in Mathematics

Mathematics is often thought of as a subject of right and wrong answers, yet there are times when teachers come across places where there is not a strong press to choose between different approaches.

Is there a right answer to the question of whether (0,0) is in four quadrants or none?

On what does the answer depend?

Is the question more important than the answer? Why or why not?

What other examples are there of topics where there is not a strong press to choose between contradictory views?

Should such examples be highlighted in the curriculum?

What purposes might be served by highlighting or avoiding such examples?

Activity 3: Viewing Bethell's After-Class Reflections

In this final piece of video that was recorded after the lesson, Bethell reflects on this particular class discussion and sets it in the context of her stance on teaching and learning for all students. In her conversation with graduate student Melissa Dennis, Bethell makes reference to the writings of Joseph Schwab[4] as she talks about her goal of fostering a disposition of inquiry in her students. The Questions for Discussion are in-

[4]In two essays, Joseph J. Schwab writes about the semantics and syntax of a discipline. See Schwab (1964a, 1964b).

tended to have participants consider Bethell's teaching philosophy and how that might influence her actions in this class.

You will need to distribute the following to each participant.

- *Questions for Discussion: After-Class Reflections*

In what ways and to what extent does the issue of who has "authority for mathematical knowledge" underpin teacher and student actions in this classroom?

What purposes might a teacher have in eliciting students' intuitions about the origin and the axes?

Why do you think this might be important?

How might such discussion effect future discussions in this class?

Bethell's Reflections.

Some may question my comment about developing consensus, wondering whether "anything goes" in my class. My stance is something like this: I think that mathematical rigor is something to strive for with my students, but I think about this developmentally. I think my role as a teacher is to first try to uncover the intuitions my students bring to the study of new ideas. How are they reasoning, what do they draw upon to think about new ideas? Where is there agreement, where is there disagreement? But my role also is to devise activities that will push them further, to create some dissonance with their currently held views with the aim of helping them develop more mathematically powerful views. And I think about this not just in terms of my class, but in terms of their mathematical studies over several years.

DELIBERATIONS WITHIN THE PROJECT

In our conversations about this classroom event, we moved back and forth between a consideration of content—the mathematical ideas the students were discussing—and process—how they were engaging the mathematics, how they were engaging each other, and how Bethell was using assessment to facilitate the conversation. Our conversations seemed to converge around a set of analytic questions, which we consider next.

What Are the Big Mathematical Ideas in This Lesson?

We posed this question because we had a hunch that some teachers, particularly the preservice teacher candidates with whom some of us work, might judge that the questions under consideration in this case are really not worth the time Bethell had taken. On the contrary, we think the students were investigating some very important mathematics. We found it interesting to consider what Bethell had intended and what actually took place.

Intended Big Ideas

Students were completing the worksheet, which asked them to decide whether a line always, sometimes, or never passes through exactly two quadrants. The question has several intentions. As students make arguments about their ideas, they must give three examples for an "always" situation, an example and a counterexample for a "sometimes" situation, and three counterexamples for a "never" situation. Although three examples certainly are not proof of an always situation, the activity helps students come to understand that an example and a counterexample show that a statement is sometimes correct. Later, students will be asked to explore the conditions under which the statement, "A line passes through exactly two quadrants," will be true and the conditions under which the statement will be false. For example, students may conclude that the line $y = 5$ is an example of a line which passes through exactly two quadrants and the line $y = 2x + 3$ is an example of a line which passes through more than two quadrants. The interesting question then is, What would be true about a rule that goes through exactly two quadrants? A follow-up question is, What is it about rules in the form $y = c$ that would make them go through exactly two quadrants?

Bethell has found that some students think something like $y = 50(x - 2)$ is a vertical line because of the image it produces on their graphing calculator. However, other students suggest that they broaden their window, so the class learns something about an appropriate window, and they come to understand that any given window does not show the entire relationship between the independent and the dependent variable. Often, students keep trying to make the slope bigger and bigger. This leads to a conjecture that they really could never get a number big enough to mak e a vertical line.

The investigation is extremely important in developing concepts central to the study of linear functions: the relationship between the constant in front of the x and the steepness of the line; that a constant function results in a horizontal line; that an appropriate window on the graphing calculator is important so that overgeneralizations are not made; that the graph shown on a given window does not represent the entire relationship defined by the function.

The Actual Ideas that Emerged Through the Investigation

In Which Quadrants Does (0,0) Lie? As students tried to make lines that go through two quadrants, some of them came up with a line that passed through the origin. Then the conversation shifted to whether the point (0,0) is in no quadrants or four quadrants. Mathematicians probably believe that this is really a moot point. In mathematics, we define the axes and points and then consider the ramifications of our definitions. But these students did not have this luxury. They had no experience with setting definitions. They had no experience with considering how deciding on a particular definition has consequences for meaning making of interrelated ideas. In short, they did not have any way yet of understanding the ramifications of setting a particular definition about boundaries in the plane.

One option would have been for Bethell to just tell her students that the point (0,0) represents a relationship between the independent and the dependent variable, which would show up on the table as $x = 0$ and $y = 0$. But the point itself could be a boundary between the quadrants, depending on how quadrants are defined. The students in this class did not yet have the experience to understand all of the relationships among the graph, rule, and table; that was the point of this lesson. So the definition would have meant nothing. Students had not yet explored *boundary* as a concept, nor did they really understand that lines on the coordinate plane are *continuous*. It is important to remember that these students had not had a formal geometry course (and may never).

Bethell is a perceptive teacher who takes into account what is interesting to students. A result in this case was that the students started to make arguments that were very near to the argument made about what it means to be continuous (for an arbitrarily small interval around a function value, there exists an interval d around the independent variable such that all function values of $x + d$ and $x \_ d$, fall within the original interval). Students were asking each other to consider a neighborhood around (0,0) that was becoming arbitrarily small.

What is a Point? At the same time, the conversation revealed that some students were struggling with what a point is. Ken seemed to distinguish (0,0) from other points with nonzero coordinates. For him, the point (0,0) was "nothing" because "zero is nothing." We wondered if Ken was drawing on some earlier discussions about quantities and that he was thinking that zero is not a quantity (see Segment Five) and therefore it is nothing. Kyle argued that (0,0) "is just a point." He agreed with Ken that (0,0) was in no quadrants. He disagreed with Ken's reasoning that (0,0) was different from all other points, yet in his interchange with Ken, Kyle's own sense making was not apparent. We were left wondering how he understood what a point is.

Matie seemed to hold to a notion that a point has size or that a point takes up space. Her particular representation of "putting a box around the circle" meant for her that no matter how small the box, it would still be in all four quadrants and therefore the circle at (0,0) would be in all four quadrants. Later in the conversation, Matie argued with Ken that his line that passed through the origin and quadrants one and three was really in all four quadrants, because if he drew a circle around (0,0) on the line, the circle and its center would be in all four quadrants.

What are the axes? Again there were different stances taken on this idea. Nicole said the axes were in all four quadrants although she did not provide much elaboration, except to say, "It's, well, it's there." Matie used a particular point on the positive x-axis to argue that it (and all points on the positive x-axis) would be in two quadrants, noting that this was similar to her reasoning about the origin being in all four quadrants. We wondered if Nicole was thinking about the question in much the same way as Matie except that Matie made a distinction among the positive and negative portions of the axes.

Jeremiah, Kyle, and Scott thought the axes were in no quadrants. Kyle called the axes "neutral territory." Scott argued that if the axes were in all quadrants, "then there wouldn't be any quadrants ... It'd all run into each other." He saw the axes as boundaries (a term that Bethell introduced) separating but not belonging to the quadrants. We noted that Bethell introduced a notion of picking points in quadrant one closer and closer to the x-axis (see Segment Five) and that "all of a sudden we would be switching to quadrant two and that doesn't make any sense." Scott seemed a bit unsure of this line of thinking, saying this was "sort of" what he was saying.

What Does It Mean to Listen to Students?

Using assessment in the moment-to-moment of a whole-class discussion demands that a teacher listen carefully to what students are saying, to try and make sense of what they might be thinking. For Bethell, this meant engaging in what she called a "different kind of listening." It is not about posing a question and then listening for the right answer. It is about listening for the intuitions, the nuances, the tentative formulations, the new insights that students contribute to the conversation. It demands trying to figure out in real time just what ideas are in the conversation and to what extent these ideas are in harmony or tension. It involves attending not only to the words that are spoken, but the tone in which they are uttered. It entails making judgments about the usefulness of a discussion in advancing her mathematical agenda. It calls for being flexible, ready to pursue students' ideas, rather than be held to a predetermined script. Bethell described her listening:

> It is a kind of mind reading. I try to interpret what they are saying and bring it back to the table. This gives them an opportunity to say whether they agree with my interpretation. They are struggling to say what they want and I'm trying to help them articulate that.

It seemed that as Bethell listened to students on this occasion, she was ever conscious of wanting them to be okay, to feel they could take intellectual risks and that she was in their corner. When Matie became frustrated, Bethell tried to be her "cheerleader." When Ken told Matie, "Now see, that's where she's wrong," Bethell reminded them that their comments needed to be in the form "I disagree" or "I have something different." It seemed that one of the norms of this classroom was that they could challenge people's ideas, not the people themselves.

Bethell's teaching involves what Davis (1997) called hermeneutic listening, "a title intended to reflect the negotiated and participatory nature of this manner of interacting with learners" (p. 369). In this kind of teaching, "learning [is] a social process, and the teacher's role [is] one of participating, of interpreting, of transforming, of interrogating—in short, of *listening*" (p. 371). It is a kind of pedagogy that takes into account the context in which teaching and learning are taking place including who the students are and what are their histories.

How Does a Teacher Act on Her Belief that *All* Students Can Learn and Do Mathematics?

At the beginning of the school year, students in this course typically are hesitant to talk about how they are thinking or reasoning about a problem. They generally are not respectful of what others say and respond to those who are participating by name-calling. This event took place about the middle of the school year and demonstrated, from Bethell's vantagepoint, how much progress had been made in establishing norms for engaging in mathematical discussions.

This change occurred, in part, because Bethell acted consciously to acknowledge the contributions of all students to the discussion. But the nature of her acknowledgment varied. This is not a classroom where anything goes or where all contributions are treated equally or with the same level of seriousness. For example, Bethell was quite certain that Jake's comment that the point (0,0) is in three quadrants was his attempt to be somewhat contrary—something he does often. Her strategy was not to dismiss him out of hand but to ask for his reasoning. When his response was simply "Don't know. I just do," Bethell moved on while keeping the door open that if he did have a reason, the class would consider his idea.

Part of deciding what to do is connected to having a history with students, collectively and individually, knowing who the students are, and recognizing their patterns of interaction. Bethell knew that if she had seriously pursued Jake's comment, she would have lost credibility with the others. However, she also wanted to reaffirm that she was giving him a chance to make a reasoned contribution to the discussion. Bethell characterized some of her interactions with Jake as "a kind of bantering" that kept him in the conversation. Later in the discussion, Jake pushed his idea again even though Bethell was quite sure he knew his idea was absurd. But he entered the discussion seriously in response to Matie's notion of giving size to the point (0,0). Jake did not have a problem articulating his position and his contrariness did not get in the way of his thinking about what others were saying. Bethell's choices about how to respond to Jake seemed to have the effect of keeping him engaged with the discussion.

This event was significant because it was the first sustained discussion about a hard idea that had engaged the class. There were times when Bethell wondered whether most of the students had "checked out." But just when she was about to move on, someone added a new idea. As Bethell commented later, "Students find the question compelling."

REFERENCES

Davis, B. (1997). Listening for differences: An evolving conception of mathematics teaching. *Journal for Research in Mathematics Education, 28* (3), 355–376.

Schwab, J. J. (1964a). Problems, topics, and issues. In S. Elan (Ed.), *Education and the structure of knowledge*. (pp. 4–47). Chicago: Rand McNally.

Schwab, J. J. (1964b). The structure of the disciplines: Meanings and significance. In G. W. Ford & L. Pugno (Eds.), *The structure of knowledge and curriculum*. (pp. 1–30). Chicago: Rand McNally.

Schwartz, J., & Yerushalmy, M. (1992). Getting students to function in and with algebra. In G. Harel & E. Dubinsky (Eds.), *The concept of function: Aspects of epistemology and pedagogy* . (pp. 261–289). Washington, DC: Mathematical Association of America.

MATERIALS FOR MAKING PHOTOCOPIES AND TRANSPARENCIES

- *Transcript and Questions for Discussion: Segments One, Two, Three, Four, Five.* Prepare one copy for each participant. Prepare transparency of Questions for Discussion.
- *Questions for Discussion: Taking Up Issues of Definitions*. Prepare one copy for each participant. Prepare transparency of Questions for Discussion.
- *Questions for Discussion: Taking Up Issues of "Right" Answers*. Prepare one copy for each participant. Prepare transparency of Questions for Discussion.
- *Transcript and Questions for Discussion after Class Conversation with Bethell.* Prepare one copy for each participant. Prepare transparency of Questions for Discussion.

TRANSCRIPT

Segment One: (Length: approximately 3 min.)

We join the class discussion about 6 minutes into the lesson. The students had been investigating if increasing lines always, sometimes, or never pass through exactly two quadrants. Kyle had provided an example of a line that goes through three quadrants. Bethell then asked for an example of a line that goes through just two quadrants. Ken pointed to a line that passes through the origin.

Bethell: Okay. What's an example of one that goes through just two quadrants? Let's look at that, how does that look? It goes through two quadrants.

Ken: Same as most of them. [Pointing to an example.] Left, down, bottom, three x.

Bethell: Yep. Going like this. Okay. So it's in Quadrant 1. Here it's in Quadrant 3. Does everybody agree with Ken? That's two quadrants? What are you thinking Jenny? [Jenny shrugs] You don't know?

Matie: I say it goes through all four instead.

Bethell: This point's [indicating origin] a problem, isn't it? That's a question, when it goes through the point zero, zero. What do we think about that point? Is that in two quadrants, one quadrant, zero quadrants, what is that?

Matie: It looks like it's in all four. [Other students are mumbling.]

Bethell: The way that you described it Ken you weren't counting that, right? The point zero, zero and I understand that. If we don't think about zero, zero Ken's right, isn't he? It's two quadrants. And if we think about the point zero, zero, do you think that makes it in all four quadrants or still two, or three?

Ken: I think it makes it two, still.

Bethell: Do you? Cause you say let's not count that.

Ken: No I just say it does anyway even if it does cause it's nothing. It's not something, something, something, it's just zero.

Matie: But on question three it says "does it exactly go through two quadrants." But zero, zero is in four, I think.

Bethell: Uh-huh. Matie say a little more cause I didn't follow you exactly.

Matie: I don't think it never goes through just two on the zero, zero axis. I think it goes through four.

Bethell: You think the point zero, zero is in all four quadrants?

Matie: Yeah.

Bethell: And Ken, you're saying.

Ken: I disagree.

Bethell: zero, zero is in no quadrants?

Ken: Exactly.

Bethell: Okay, ahh.

Ken: Cause it's like not point something. Out there one, something. I mean it's just goes right through the zero.

Bethell: Now this is an example of what I was talking about before. How do we know? Sarah can you write these down for me please, because I'm standing up here.

Write Matie says zero, zero is in all four quadrants. Ken says zero, zero is in no quadrants. How many people agree with Matie? That zero, zero is in all four quadrants? How many people agree with Ken it's not in any quadrants? How many people?

Jake: I think it's in three out of the four.

Bethell: Okay that's another option. How many don't know? Okay, all the hands go up. And Jake you think in three out of the four.

Jake: Hmm-hmm.

Bethell: Why?

Jake: Don't know. I just do.

Bethell: You just want to disagree. (Jake: Hmm-hmm) Okay. If you had a reason I think we'd consider it, but you could say anything. All right. I think that's a real important point. Is zero, zero in no quadrants or in all four quadrants.

QUESTIONS FOR DISCUSSION: SEGMENT ONE

- What do you see going on here?
- How does the point (0,0) get introduced into the conversation?
- What initial ideas do Ken, Matie, and Jake seem to have about how many quadrants a line goes through if it goes through (0,0)?
- How are the ideas of individual students treated by Bethell and by the other students?
- Why might this be an important question for Bethell to pursue with her students?
- What might be a direction Bethell could take at this point and why?

TRANSCRIPT:

Segment Two: (Length: approximately 2 min.)

Bethell: Ken you were saying zero, zero, it's not like point anything, it's not a number?
Ken: Right.
Bethell: That's your reasoning?
Ken: Hmm-hmm
Bethell: And , what's your reasoning for its all four?
Matie: Cause in eighth grade we learned it. If you put a box around the circle it will be in all four corners.
Bethell: Put a box there. The box is in all four quadrants and you are saying since that point's in there it is in all four quadrants.
Matie: Hmm-hmm.
Bethell: Okay
Matie: If the box is smaller it'd be in all four quadrants.
Bethell: Right?
Matie: Yeah
Bethell: How small do you want to make the box?
Matie: Well, we make it, we make, we make the circle the square, in ours.
Bethell: You made this dot.
Matie: The center, the center, yeah, the center.
Bethell: Okay.
Matie: is all four. So it lies in all four quadrants.
Bethell: So it's kinda like if you picture a square and it's getting smaller, smaller, smaller. Is that what you are saying?
Matie: Hmm-hmm.
Bethell: Then that point no matter how small you got it, it would still be in there? [Matie: Hmm-hmm] What' ya think about that, class? Matie, picture the point zero, zero okay
Matie: Hmm-hmm.
Bethell: and that box is getting smaller, smaller, smaller, smaller. How about when that box is just that point?
Matie: [pause] Then it's the center.
Bethell: Still in all four?
Matie: Yeah.
Bethell: And Ken, you would say no cause you're not around any numbers anymore, right?
Ken: Right.
Bethell: Do you agree with Matie that as small as we got the boxes [pause] it would be in there, right?
Ken: Yeah.
Bethell: Until we got to it, is that how you think?
Ken: Yeah, but it still wouldn't be in all four quadrants.

Bethell:	Okay.
Ken:	I disagree all along.
Bethell:	All right.

QUESTIONS FOR DISCUSSION: SEGMENT TWO

- What do you see going on here?
- How do Ken and Matie seem to be reasoning about the question of where the origin is located?
- What does Bethell do with Matie's use of the box around (0,0)?
- How does Bethell use what Ken and Matie have talked about earlier?

TRANSCRIPT

Segment Three: (Length: approximately 3 min.)

About 6 minutes has elapsed since the second segment. At one point Bethell appeared ready to leave the conversation for the moment, letting the disagreement hang around for a while. She told them that they would return to the idea from time to time. But she got drawn back into the conversation when Jake and Ken wanted to know who was right. Ken asked, "So who was right out of this conversation?" Kyle, in a more insistent tone, called on Bethell: "Why don't you just tell us who's right so we would know." But rather than give them her answer, she responded by referring back to the ways in which they were reasoning about the question: "But the two of you both sound like you have good reasoning, right?"

In this segment, Jeremiah poses a new question about whether the axes are in the quadrants.

Ken: Who's right?
Bethell: Jeremiah?
Jeremiah: Would you count the axis as being in the quadrants?
Ken: That's all I care about.
Bethell: Oooh! Listen to Jeremiah. I love that question.
Student: What'd he say?
Jeremiah: Would you count the axis as being in the quadrants?
Bethell: This is a great question.
Kyle: Like zero, one.
Bethell: Okay Jeremiah's question was this. I'll go ahead and draw
Kyle: This the point right there, right?
Bethell: He said are the axes. This is the x-axis. This is the y-axis. Say it again Jeremiah, the way you put it.
Jeremiah: Would they be, would they be in the quadrants? Would the axis be in any of the quadrants?
Bethell: So let's look at the x-axis. What would you say is it? What quadrants is the x-axis in? I know you have a question, but I'm just asking what do you think?
Jeremiah: I, nothing. I just think …
Nicole: It's all of them.
Jeremiah: It divides into quadrants.
Bethell: You think it's in no quadrants?
Jeremiah: Yep.
Bethell: Why?
Jeremiah: Cause that's the dividing line that makes them into quadrants.
Bethell: Okay. It's just the divider. It's like the boundary …
Kyle: Neutral territory.
Bethell: between Canada and the United States the boundary wouldn't be in either one?
Jeremiah: Yeah.
Bethell: That's what you think. Nicole, what were you saying?

Kyle: It's just like neutral.
Nicole: It's in all quadrants.
Bethell: Why?
Nicole: Because it's, well it's there.
Kyle: I say it's just neutral.
Bethell: So you're saying Quadrant 1 you go down here and there's that line. Quadrant 2 you go back in there's that line.
Scott: Miss if that's true then there wouldn't be any quadrants. There just be a whole big quadrant.
Jeremiah: Yep.
Scott: Cause that line wouldn't even exist.
Bethell: This is the point. [inaudible] What are you saying ?
Matie: That if you put, if you put one right there. I don't know, you had us do a paper …
Bethell: Uh-huh.
Matie: where the quadrants were on zero and then you had one or something, zero, one and then the dot would be right there cause …
Bethell: One, zero, yeah, yeah
Matie: Well not one, but whatever that is, six or whatever.
Bethell: Six, zero. Okay so what are you saying that that's in both quadrants or that's in no quadrants?
Matie: in two.
Bethell: A, a point over here is in these two quadrants?
Matie: Yeah.
Bethell: You're agreeing with Nicole?
Matie: Yeah, cause basically the same thing that I'm saying that about the center. It's four quadrants.
Scott: [hard to understand something about *y* and *x* axis in all four quadrants]
Bethell: Why?
Scott: Because it'd just be a big whole quadrant. Cause it'd have to be [inaudible] It'd all run into each other.
Bethell: As we get closer and closer and closer to this line. You're saying that every, that all these points are in Quadrant 1. If this was in Quadrant 1, it would be Quadrant 1, but all of a sudden we would be switching to Quadrant 2 and that doesn't make any sense. Is that kind of what you are saying?
Scott: Yeah, sort of.
Bethell: That that line is kinda of a boundary. It doesn't belong to it.
Scott: Yeah, yeah.
Bethell: Okay

QUESTIONS FOR DISCUSSION: SEGMENT THREE

- What do you think is the source of Jeremiah's question and how does it influence the discussion?
- What sense do the others, including Bethell, seem to be making of his question?

TRANSCRIPT

Segment Four: (Length: approx. 2 min.)

Ken: Draw a line going from Quadrant 1 to Quadrant 3, please.
Bethell: Okay.
Ken: Right through the zero.
Bethell: Okay, right through here.
Ken: Yes, it's in two quadrants. [Laughter]
Bethell: Okay, Why? Cause you're saying let's not count this.
Ken: It doesn't count anything.
Matie: Now make a bigger circle around it and prove it.
Ken: It's still in two quadrants.
Matie: See it's in four.
Ken: The circle is, but not the line.
Matie: The center, the center.
Jake: What?
Ken: Now see that's where she's wrong.
Matie: The centers in four.
Bethell: Your comments need to be in the form I disagree or I have something different, remember? We're not going to say right or wrong cause I, I certainly haven't told you and these people haven't told you and we don't have the father of mathematics here, whoever that is so we don't know.
Jake: Hold on, Miss Bethell. Look see how Matie, er, yeah, she made that middle point bigger, right?
Bethell: Uh-huh.
Jake: If that gets bigger shouldn't these lines get bigger? And if those lines get bigger, then maybe even with the size of that to make that a black spot, where two things cross? Phew!
Bethell: Um, Jake. I think I understood what he said.
Ken: I got it. I got it too.
Jake: Kenny understands.
Bethell: Let me compare what you were saying.
Jake: Except for in one of the three quadrants where it's smaller still so it doesn't touch there.
Bethell: Okay
Matie: I just got lost there. I did not get any of that.
Bethell: Jake's come. You just came up with a different reason. Let me compare what you said to what Matie said. Cause I think what you're saying is a little different from what she was saying. He's saying, Matie, and then you can respond, okay. He's saying if you make that point bigger. See Jake, you thought she was saying if you made this point bigger it's in all four quadrants, right?
Jake: No, she put that circle around it and then she put the next one around it.

Bethell: Yeah.

Jake: So she's saying that that middle circle or the smaller one is the very middle?

Bethell: Yeah.

Jake: And she's saying see how there's triangles in all the four corners and she's saying that's how it's touching it cause going through that.

Bethell: That's what you're saying, right?

Matie: I'm just saying zero is in all four quadrants. Zero, the center. It doesn't get bigger, it doesn't get smaller, zero.

QUESTIONS FOR DISCUSSION: SEGMENT FOUR

- To what extent and in what ways are any of the students revising their thinking about the original question?

TRANSCRIPT

Segment Five: (Length: approximately 2 min.)

Bethell: Here's a question that came up from something Matie said. How big is zero, zero?
Kyle: It's a point.
Ken: Zero is zero, that's exactly how big it is.
Bethell: How big is it?
Kyle: It's just a point.
Ken: It's as big as nothing. Zero, nothing.
Bethell: You're saying it has no size at all. It is nothing.
Ken: Well it is bigger than negative something, but I mean it's nothing, really.
Bethell: Okay. How big is, if … Kenny's saying there is no point there cause it's nothing.
Ken: There is a point there because you have to have …
Matie: But if you're graphing six, zero.
Ken: zero. You have to have it, but it's not like a number or something.
Bethell: It's not an amount?
Ken: Yeah.
Bethell: How big is that point, Ken?
Ken: [pause] Just as big as any other point on the graph where it doesn't have any value or not [inaudible] just, just nothing. Where that …
Matie: Miss B, six, zero that's nothing? Where that is? That's what I'm trying to prove. There is …
Ken: Six is, zero.
Bethell: I think he's agreeing with you. He's saying this doesn't have a number like a quantity. So he's saying it's not, everybody says, well there is a point there just like here, right?
Matie: But can it be graphed?
Bethell: Yeah.
Matie: Zero, zero can be graphed and it's in all four quadrants.
Ken: But it's not in a …
Bethell: How big is that point?
Ken: It's on the x-axis, zero is. Sooo … This is getting out a hand.
Matie: No one cares anymore, can we just drop it.
Bethell: We can go on in just a second.
Kyle: The point may be in all four quadrants, but the line is not.
Bethell: Which line?
Kyle: The line that's going like through it. Yeah that …
Bethell: So.
Kyle: The point's in all four but the line isn't.
Bethell: Does, does the line contain that point?
Kyle: Yeah

Bethell: But you're disregarding that point.

Kyle: The point is there, but the line is just heading on through that. I mean it's just ...

Bethell: It's coming along. It's going "Nope I'm not in all four quadrants, I'm just a going."

Kyle: Yep. Cause if it was in all four quadrants it would have to be bigger or something.

Bethell: Okay.

Kyle: So it's in two.

Bethell: So we still have a difference in opinion. Some people think two, some people think four and Jake thinks three.

Jake: Three.

QUESTIONS FOR DISCUSSION: SEGMENT FIVE

- What sense do you have about where Ken, Matie, and Kyle are in their thinking about the origin?
- How does Bethell leave the discussion?

QUESTIONS FOR DISCUSSION: TAKING UP ISSUES OF DEFINITIONS

- If mathematics is an abstract, theoretical endeavor, not constrained to fit the natural world, how do definitions arise?
- When does it become important to set a definition?
- Is it important that students understand the sorts of dynamics which lead to the development of definitions?
- In the classroom, can students make definitions for use by their class, or should they always look to mathematics texts and teachers to tell them what definitions have been accepted by mathematicians?

QUESTIONS FOR DISCUSSION: TAKING UP ISSUES OF "RIGHT" ANSWERS

- Is there a "right" answer to the question of whether (0,0) is in four quadrants or none?
- On what does the answer depend?
- Is the question more important than the answer? Why or why not?
- What other examples are there of topics where there is not a strong press to choose between contradictory views?
- Should such examples be highlighted in the curriculum or not?
- What purposes might be served by highlighting or avoiding such examples?

TRANSCRIPT

After Class Conversation With Sandra Bethell

Dennis: But Ken and Jake started riding you at one point.

Bethell: Just tell us.

Dennis: Just tell us. And once again how did you, what were you thinking?

Bethell: Wouldn't that be great if I could just tell you. But I, The bottom line for me is I think of zero, zero as a limit. I think of all those boundaries of the quadrants as being limits. On the other hand, I can imagine a geometric system, finite, where it's not. So it could be both.

Dennis: So you're saying you don't really know. You don't really think there is a correct answer.

Bethell: Right, I think it depends how you define the situation whether you have infinite or finite.

Bethell: The um, the inquiry itself is a disposition I want to foster and I think this is a good example to do that. You know, if you think of knowledge, attitude, disposition or you know, if you think about Schwab's way of thinking about subject matter as the semantic piece, the syntactic, and then the dispositional or whatever goes in that bottom one (a reference to a graphic she remembered in an essay by Schwab that she had read sometime earlier). I want to push toward that. The disposition of "That's okay to leave this not together yet. This is something where we disagree about. We can think about it more." [I want to] Leave that dissonance there for as long as I possibly can. Cause I think that's where math is.

The semantic piece—as they're arguing about or thinking about that they're becoming clear about what they mean about a point, a locus. How are lines? You know, they know that a line can be horizontal. If it's not quite vertical, it's not quite vertical. You know, it's pushing them that you know that the table on their calculator isn't, I mean, the face on their calculator isn't the whole picture that we consider a line to be in. They're putting a lot of facts together as they go. So you know that piece is going on.

And then the syntactic piece "Well how do we know when we come to consensus?" And I think, I vary from what a mathematician would say. If you have the four basic ways of proving something. I think that most people rely on more subjective means and so sometimes that's okay. If everyone agrees, I let it go. You know, I think the Bonneville is the best car made. It doesn't matter — black, white, numbers, anything. Quantities don't matter in that case. And I think sometimes that kind of truth is okay.

You know that's part of the dispositional piece, but I do want to push them. If we all agree does that mean it's actually true. I think a couple of people, I don't know how many, would think "well, no we're just going to accept it for right now." And, you know, that's okay too. We have axioms.

Dennis: Yeah, but why didn't you choose to tell them that, that you yourself don't necessarily feel that there is a right or a wrong. Well that would be telling them.

Bethell: Yeah. That would be saying there's no right or wrong … hmm … I continue to struggle with that question and you know I have ways I could describe it or explain it in mathematical terms, but just thinking about that point zero, zero. I enjoy playing around with it in my head. Like what if we had ten points in our geometric system. What might that point zero, zero signify. You know or you know I would rather have them doing that than to know that I do it.

Dennis: Okay, because?

Bethell: Cause their experiences are a lot more real to them than mine. I don't think I'm the authority and what is important in this world to them naturally, you know, they don't. Some classes, you know, like pre-calc, maybe calc, they would wonder what I think and I would be part of the conversation and.

Dennis: But more on a level.

Bethell: Yeah, yeah.

Dennis: But you still think in this class you are viewed as the authority?

Bethell: In a way, in a way, yes. I'm the authority for mathematical knowledge, maybe. Maybe that is changing. But what I say and do and the way that I verify it. It's not valued by them. They would enjoy it [telling them the "right" answer" because then it would put closure on it, but it's not like they say "I want to do what she does." They don't identify with me necessarily. Pre-calc, or calc kid would identify with me because of our social class or our mutual interest or they're going to college, they see themselves in that role. But someone who, I don't know, who wants to work construction may not see me as a model for what's good or right or language is appropriate. So it might make the situation more comfortable, but in the long run, they haven't experienced it themselves nor do they identify. I don't know if I made that clear, but. I know that language has an alienating effect in that as soon as they start to use those terms that either unfamiliar or not in their regular use, I think I separate myself from them. I mean, I could have said, you know, I think about it the point zero, I don't know, three, three and zero, zero. There's an infinite number of points there. Now as soon as I said that, Kyle, Matie, and Ken wouldn't have anything else to say about it.

Dennis: Right.

Bethell: See, so

Dennis: But in the pre-calc or the calc where they had a concept of those things then you could …

Bethell: Uh-um, we share the language and it would just be part of the situation. Now, that's not to say that I think it's okay to, um, never use mathematics terms or to coddle these kids in a way that they never have access to a more academic, mathematical community. I'm trying to pump them in that direction.

QUESTIONS FOR DISCUSSION: AFTER CLASS REFLECTIONS

- In what ways and to what extent does the issue of who has "authority for mathematical knowledge" underpin teacher and student actions in this classroom?
- What purposes might a teacher have in eliciting students' intuitions about the plane?
- Why do you think this might be important?
- How might such discussion effect future discussions in this class?

Case 3: Learning Children's Understandings of Algebra

From the classroom of Danise Cantlon in collaboration with Kara Suzuka, Sandra Wilcox, and Perry Lanier

OVERVIEW

This case provides opportunities over two sessions to:

- *Explore children's early algebraic thinking*: The ideas young students bring to the study of algebra; the ways they represent real problem situations that involve patterns; the patterns they see in abstract tables of numbers and the ways they describe those patterns; the differences among children's abilities to find patterns, to generalize, and to create algebraic number sentences;
- *Investigate the mathematics in the unit*: Conceptions of the mathematical territory within algebra that are appropriate for young students; the selection of tasks that explore this territory—how and what they might contribute to building students' ways of knowing and reasoning; the relation between pattern formulation with natural language and the translation to an algebraic expression;
- *Consider goals for student learning*: Balance across the multiple goals a teacher has for her students; the tensions often inherent in multiple and competing goals; the implications for instructional decision making.

Mathematical Content: Observing, describing, representing, and generalizing patterns.

Case Materials: Samples of student work from the mathematics notebooks; video segments of students presenting their pattern descriptions to the whole class; reflective commentary from the teacher and some notes from her teaching journal.

Suggested Time: Two sessions, each 2–3 hours.

INTRODUCTION

This case is drawn from the classroom of Danise Cantlon and her third- and fourth-grade students who spent several weeks working with a unit on algebra. Cantlon chose to explore algebra with her students for several reasons. Since the beginning of the school year, a few students had expressed with some persistence an interest to "learn algebra." Cantlon knew it was a topic typically overlooked in elementary classrooms, even though the National Council of Teachers of Mathematics and her state's curriculum guidelines urged that patterns and relationships be a key content strand in the elementary grades. She thought that teaching algebra would provide another way for her students to communicate about mathematics, by generalizing patterns with algebraic sentences. And she wanted to learn more herself—about the topic and what younger students could do in this area.

We include this case because it provides a glimpse into an elementary classroom where the teacher is exploring new territory—in her teaching and learning, and the learning of her young students. Given the experimental nature of the unit, ongoing assessment is a central activity. The case lends itself to having participants examine their own beliefs about working with these ideas in elementary classrooms as they question how the students were thinking, what kinds of tasks the teacher had posed, and what a teacher would need to know about algebra to teach it to young students. The case raises a number of issues that teachers of older students also encounter in teaching algebra.

The Case Materials

The materials for this case consist of samples of students' written work taken from their mathematics notebooks, an edited video recording of class discussions near the middle of the unit where students presented their reasoning about patterns in tables and got feedback from others, some of the teacher's planning notes, and her reflection and commentary on particular events. The materials are drawn from lessons on several of the days that the class explored ideas about algebra.

Given the extensive set of case materials and the nature of the work that engaged the students, this case should be explored over two sessions. Our rationale is three-fold. There is much going on in this case and this classroom—with tasks; with children's thinking; with a teacher's beliefs, knowledge, analysis, interpretations, and actions; with mathematics for teaching; with assessment. Participants need time to dig deep into the various issues of teaching, learning, and assessment that the case will raise. The case will engender conversations about participants' own beliefs about teaching algebra to young students. The interaction of their beliefs with analysis of the case materials is likely to extend the time spent on any one activity. Finally, we believe that professional development is most useful when it is carried out over time within a community of learners. If local circumstances permit, participants might gather some information between the two sessions about their own students' algebraic thinking.

USING THE CASE MATERIALS

Introduction to the Case

Danise Cantlon began team-teaching in a multi-age classroom in 1991. In that year she joined some of her colleagues and Pamela Schram, a mathematics educator at Michigan State University, in a Math Study Group. The teacher preparation program that led to her certification involved some study in mathematical content and pedagogy, but her concentration had been in reading instruction. The opportunity to work with others in the Math Study Group had pushed her thinking about mathematics education and what young children could learn and do.[5] Cantlon consistently works at creating a classroom environment, instructional and discourse practices, learning activities, and assessment strategies that embody her interpretations of the reform agenda in mathematics education. A typical routine in her classroom involves students working on mathematical problems—sometimes individually, sometimes in small groups—writing solutions in their notebook, and then presenting their strategies and solutions to the class using the overhead projector. As students present their solutions, others are encouraged to ask questions, to say whether they agree or disagree and why, and to offer suggestions for ways in which work might be revised. During these whole-class discussions, students often offer conjectures about new ideas they are formulating (e.g., "If you add two odd numbers, you always get an even number ").

Cantlon's 23 students had already done some work on number theory (especially even and odd numbers and prime numbers), integers, and operations. Immediately preceding the algebra unit, they had been working on multiplication: using tiles for an area representation; using calculators for repeated addition; decomposing numbers for multiplying double-digit numbers mentally [e.g., for 27 x 3 they might do (25 x 3) + (2 x 3)]; finding patterns in multiplication, and formulating conjectures about those patterns (e.g., an even number times an even number is always even).

[5]A product of the Math Study Group is a book titled *Nurturing the Freedom to Wonder: Vignettes from Elementary Mathematics Classrooms* (Schram, Cantlon, Hunt, Scholten, & Seales, 1994). Danise authored a chapter in the book entitled, "Toward Authentic Assessment: Two Case Studies," in which she described strategies she developed to assess and report on students' growth in content, process, and attitudes. She provided cases of two students to highlight ways in which reporting forms and narratives that she used to supplement the district's report card gave a more robust picture of her students' strengths and weaknesses.

Planning the Unit. One of the first things Cantlon did on deciding to create the unit was to research algebra as a school subject. She sought out ideas and resources from university faculty with whom she had studied and collaborated. She read articles on algebra to develop her own understanding. She looked through curriculum guides including the NCTM *Curriculum and Evaluation Standards* and the *Michigan Essential Goals and Objectives*. She also spent time trying to learn what kinds of understandings children might have of algebra. She thought that having students use tables to record data from problem situations would help them look for patterns among changing quantities. She wanted to explore their efforts at describing patterns using natural and symbolic language.

Cantlon has a framework for student learning goals that guides her planning, instruction, and assessment. The goals fall into three categories: attitude outcomes, process outcomes, and content outcomes. Using that framework, she created a concept map (Fig. C3.1) that outlined a set of possible student outcomes for this exploration of algebra.

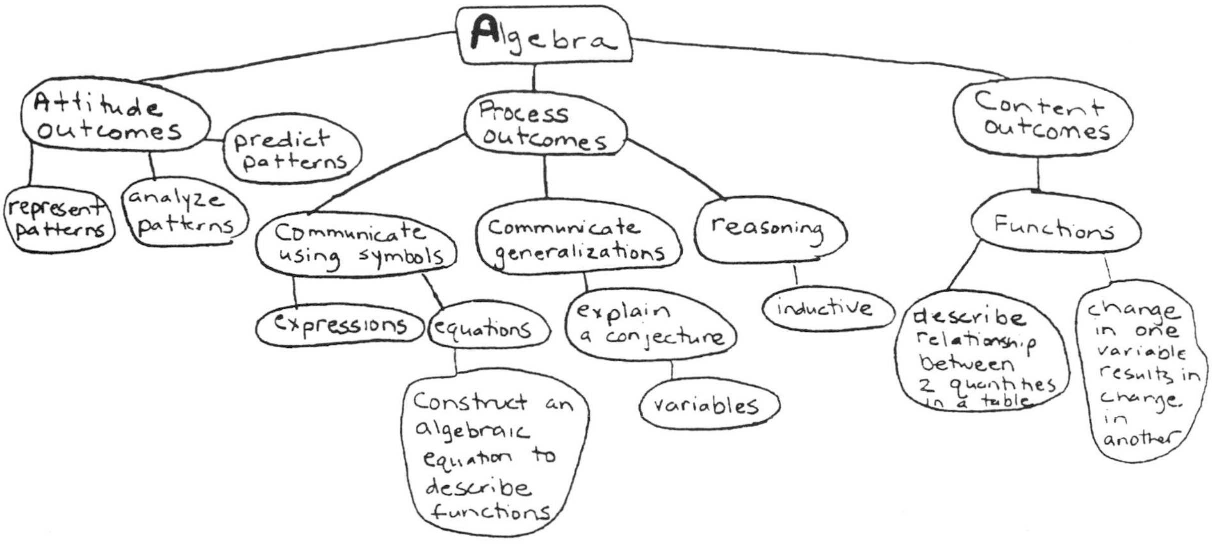

FIG. C3.1.

As a pre-assessment activity, Cantlon posed the question, What is algebra?, and had students write their ideas in their math notebook. From there, she launched them on a series of lessons that ranged from using tables to generate data from real problem situations to extending and generalizing patterns in decontextualized mathematical tables.

Working With the Materials

Using the Case Over Two Sessions. Session One is built around two events. Cantlon began the unit with a pre-assessment activity in which she posed the question, What is algebra? She had students write their ideas in their math notebook. From there she launched them on a series of lessons that involved generating data from real problem situations, using tables to record the data, looking for and describing patterns within the table, and generalizing the patterns with algebraic number sentences. The materials for the first session are primarily selections of students' written work from their notebooks. In addition, some student work is annotated with a transcript of how the student described her or his solution to the whole class and the discussion that followed. These annotations highlight the various ways in which students used tables to solve the problem and what patterns they found.

Session Two is built around student engagement with a new problem type: decontextualized tables with two variables. Here, students were to find patterns in the tables, complete the tables, and represent the patterns with algebraic number sentences. The materials for the second session include selections of students' written work from their notebooks. In addition, there is a video recording of a whole-class discussion about two of the tables in the lesson.

Investigating Sudents' Thinking. There can be several strands of investigations in these materials. One strand involves an investigation into students' thinking. What did these young learners bring with them to this unit on algebra? What did they think algebra is? Where might these ideas have come from? What were the different ways that they considered the values in the tables they constructed? Were some more helpful in trying to move toward algebraic representations than others? What were the different ways they had for representing symbolically the relationships among changing quantities in a problem? What understandings did students need to come up with their solutions?

Investigating Mathematics for Teaching. A second strand involves investigations into mathematics for teaching. To begin, it has proved useful to explore how the participants themselves conceptualize algebra as a mathematical domain, and what they think young children might explore in this domain. What does a teacher need to know to work with these ideas in a class of young learners? What kinds of difficulties might students experience? Then participants can turn to the case materials to consider how Cantlon conceived the domain and how it shaped choices she made about learning activities.

Exploring Different Problem Types. A third strand involves investigations into the types of tasks that Cantlon posed for her students. How does a teacher choose tasks? What makes some tasks harder than others to complete? What makes some relationships among quantities harder to represent algebraically? What do different tasks reveal about students' thinking about relationships among quantities?

You and the participants will probably find yourselves moving across the strands, particularly when you investigate students' solutions to different problem types. In these instances it is almost impossible, even unwarranted, to try and separate a consideration of students' reasoning about a problem from the nature of the problem itself.

SESSION ONE: USING REAL PROBLEM SITUATIONS TO EXPLORE ALGEBRAIC IDEAS

Activity 1.1: Exploring What There Is to Learn and Teach About Algebra

Participants' Representations of Algebra. You will need to have large sheets of paper and marking pens at hand. You will need to prepare a transparency of the following material.

- *Cantlon's Concept Map of Algebra*

We suggest you begin by having participants make a representation of what they think there is to learn and teach about algebra at the elementary level. This might be a concept map, a list of ideas, or some other personally meaningful representation. A way to carry this out is to have people work individually to get down their own ideas first. Then have them get into small groups of four or five and create a "consensus" representation that they can share with the whole group. Putting it on large paper and taping it to a wall for everyone to view facilitates a whole-group discussion. When small groups present their product, have them talk about two things: What they included in their representation and how they decided what to include and what not to include.

Invite the whole group to discuss some of the similarities and differences across the representations. Have them talk about the process of moving from the representation of an individual's ideas to that of a larger group's collective ideas. Listen for and draw out their comments on whether coming to consensus increased the complexity and depth of their representation, whether they had difficulty integrating others' ideas, learning others' ways of seeing and thinking, as well as creating "space" for people to share their ideas.

Conclude this activity by displaying the transparency of Cantlon's concept map so participants can see how her thinking about the topic maps onto the group 's representations.

Participants' Lists of Understandings of and Difficulties With Algebraic Formulations. Have participants generate a list of the different kinds or levels of understanding they think young children might have about algebra. Also, have them consider what difficulties elementary students might have when trying to move toward algebraic formulations. Allow some time for a discussion about their lists. During the conversation, ask whether some of the issues they are raising in relation to elementary students might also apply to the teaching and learning of algebra with older students.

The final activity in this case has participants revisit both lists—about what there is to learn and teach about algebra in the elementary grades, and about young children's understanding of these ideas—to see whether they might revise either in light of their investigation of this case.

Activity 1.2: Finding Out What Children Are Bringing

You will need to distribute the following materials, one copy for each participant.

- *What is Algebra*? These are pages from the notebooks of several students in response to the question Cantlon had posed at the beginning of the unit. We have included the responses of Cameron, Victoria, Amanda, Tyler, Lauren and Chris B.
- *Discussion Questions* What ideas do the children have about algebra? Where might their ideas come from? How might the teacher build on those ideas? What challenges might a teacher face?

Allow time for participants to examine students' responses to the task. Then engage them in a discussion about the questions. When you feel they are ready to move on, you might want to share this additional insight from Cantlon.

Cantlon's Reflections. After the children had written in their notebooks, Cantlon asked them to share their ideas. Her summary of the discussion follows.

> I was surprised as I looked at their pre-assessment thoughts on algebra. I incorrectly predicted that the students would have little to say about the initial question, What is algebra? Almost everyone had some idea written down in their notebooks. When I asked the kids to share their ideas, they were very verbal and listened hard to one another's ideas. Some interesting ideas came up. For example, Kevin asked "Can you use a negative *y*?" Chris B. replied that you could but "You would have to know what the *y* is. Like negative *y* equals negative 5." Michael agreed and said the number could be a negative one. A second idea that I had not thought of was when Patrick asked if you need two letters if it is a double-digit number. A misconception came up with the a, b, c meaning a correlation to 1, 2, 3. I was pleased with some of the kids thinking. For example, Jake brought up the commutative property, $a \times b = b \times a$. Also, Jesserae noticed "If you are using the same numbers like $5 + 5 = 10$ then you need to use the same letters, $a + a = 10$."

Activity 1.3: Early Explorations of Algebra

You will need to distribute the following materials, one to each participant.

- *Early Explorations of Algebra: Problems and Discussion Questions*. These are the first two problems the students worked on in the unit that Cantlon created. The questions can help frame an examination of the two tasks. How are these problems alike and how are they different? What do you think students might find difficult about either of the problems?

As participants begin to look over the problems, you can set the context in which the problems were posed by drawing on the following information. Invite participants to consider the two problems, using the Discussion Questions as a frame. As they discuss their thinking about the problems, you might begin to collect and record a list of new questions that are raised in the conversation.

For their first problem, Cantlon presented the class with a chart that had "students" in one column and "shoes" in another.

students	shoes
1	2
2	4

The class did a few examples together, filling in the chart: If there were two students then there would be four shoes altogether. If there were three students then there would be six shoes altogether. Cantlon then had students work on the problem independently, filling in the chart for up to 10 students. As she typically does, Cantlon pressed students to think about any patterns they might see in the chart. Some students drew from one to ten stick figures for each row in the table, whereas others noticed that "they are going up by twos" and stopped drawing stick figures after a few rows.

The next day Cantlon posed several follow-up questions: How does this problem relate to multiplication? Will the number of shoes ever be the same as the number of students? Why? Will the number of shoes ever be 3 times the number of students? Why?

On the third day she asked them to create their own question using the problem. The questions that Amanda (Fig. C3.2) and Clint (Fig. C3.3) wrote were fairly typical.

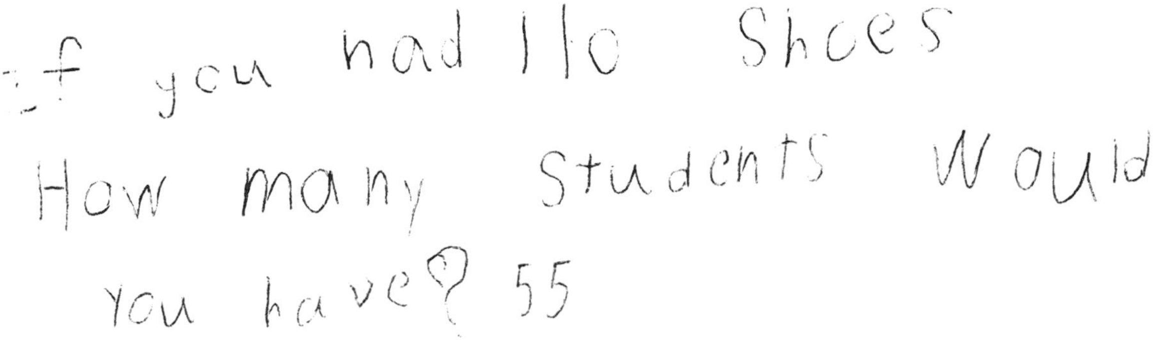

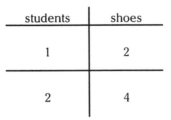

FIG. C3.2. Amanda's problem.

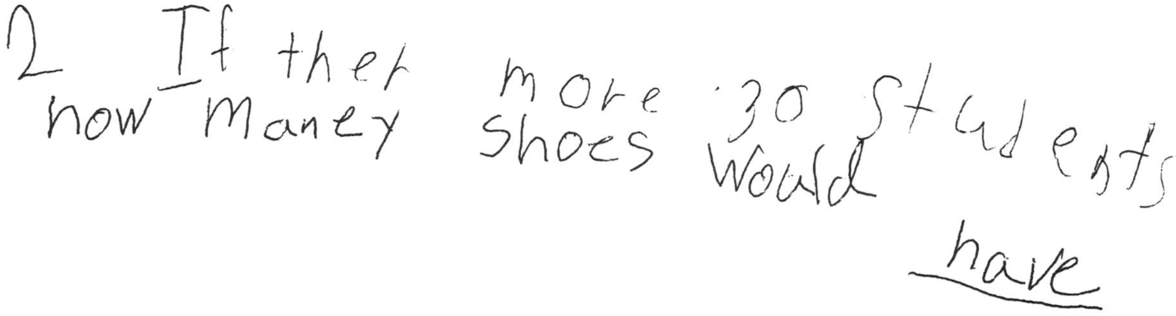
2 If ther more 30 students
how maney shoes would
have

FIG. C3.3 Clint's problem.

Keegans' responses were different from the other children (Fig. C3.4).

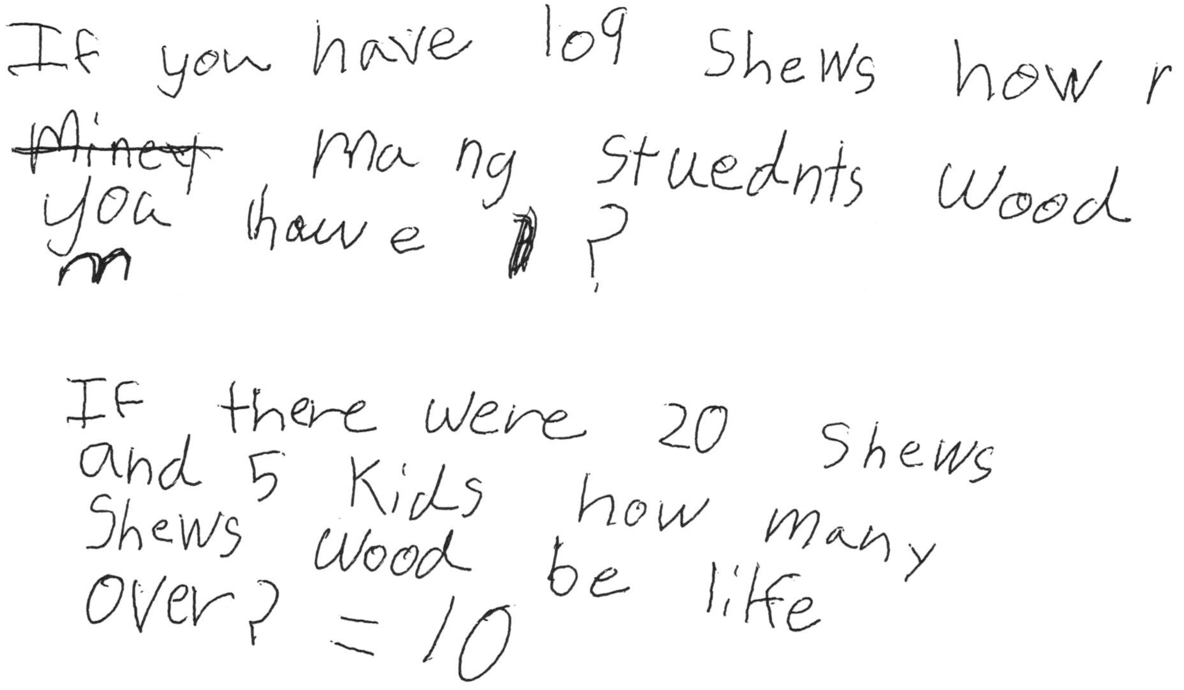
If you have 109 Shews how r
ma ng stuednts Wood
you have ?
If there were 20 Shews
and 5 Kids how many
Shews Wood be life
Over? = 10

FIG. C3.4 Keegan's problem.

The second problem they worked on involved filling in a chart of square numbers. They used tiles to make square arrays and figure out the area of each square. They then filled in a chart that looked something like the following.

1	1
2	4
3	9
4	16
5	25

Cantlon's Reflections. It seems important to share Cantlon's thoughts about the second problem that she wrote in her journal. It is an instance of a teacher talking with herself about her own uncertainty as to what made the problem less engaging and more difficult for her students. We suggest that you read this portion of Cantlon's journal and ask participants to consider Cantlon's interpretation of students' difficulties with the second problem and whether there might be other plausible interpretations.

> The second problem I felt wasn't as engaging for the students. They used one through ten tiles and recorded the total number of tiles, or the area. I was curious to see if they could extend the pattern and make a connection to the student/shoes problem. I also asked them to describe the pattern in words. Lastly, I wanted to see if they could describe the pattern of the chart using an algebraic number sentence. They really had difficulty with that. I think that algebra is so vague to them, or so restricted to thinking about letters for the variable that it makes the task hard. I don't think many of them knew what I was asking them to do. What I wanted them to notice was that when you double the factors you get the product.

Activity 1.4: Bobby's Cookies Problem

The next problem that Cantlon posed was one she created called "Bobby's Cookies Problem." Display a transparency of *Problem of the Day* and provide some context from the description that follows.

> Problem of the day: December 11
>
> Bobby was getting ready for Christmas. He could decorate 3 cookies in 1 minute. Use a table to show how many cookies were finished from 1 minute to 9 minutes.

Students worked independently for about half an hour on the problem and then they had a whole-class discussion about their solutions to filling in the table. The next day, Cantlon extended the work with Bobby's Cookies Problem.

> Problem of the day: December 12
>
> If x = number of minutes, how can you write an algebraic number sentence to show the relationship between minutes and cookies?

You will need to distribute the following materials, one set for each participant.

- *Students' Annotated Work on Bobby's Cookies Problem*. We have selected the written responses of Stacey, Michael, Keegan, Bobby, and Chris B. Their work represents a range of strategies that students used to solve the problem—filling in the table and then writing an algebraic sentence to describe the relationship among the quantities in the table. Stacey, Michael, Keegan, Bobby, and Chris each presented their solution to the class. Their written work is annotated with a transcript of the whole-class conversation that took place around their presentation.
- *Discussion Questions: Solutions for Algebraically Representing the Bobby's Cookies Problem*. What are the similarities and differences among students' approaches? How do these various approaches

lend themselves—or not—to algebraic representations? For each of the students' approaches, what kinds of understandings did the student need to have to come up with their solution? What questions do you have that looking at students' written work alone does not allow you to answer with much certainty? What does the annotation contribute to interpreting the written work? If you were the teacher, what might be your next instructional moves? What are you taking into account as you consider various actions?

Have participants carefully examine students' written responses to each problem in light of the Discussion Questions. You might plan in advance to have a separate large sheet of paper for each student and have groups write their comments about each student's way of representing the problem, their hunches about the student's reasoning, and what they are using as evidence to support their hunches.

BEYOND THE CASE

If you will be using the second part of this case at a subsequent session, you might want to have participants carry out some activities in their own classrooms between sessions to learn about their students' algebraic thinking. The next meeting could begin by looking at the tasks teachers gave to their students, how they decided on particular tasks, and what they learned.

SESSION TWO: MOVING FROM PROBLEM SITUATIONS TO ABSTRACT TABLES

The next investigation that Cantlon gave her students represented a shift in problem type. To this point, students had been exploring problems that were embedded in some context—real-life situations or concrete materials. The next set of problems was decontextualized, pure mathematical investigations. Students were given tables like the one following and asked to find patterns in the table, fill in the table, and describe "the relationship between the numbers that are on top and the numbers that are on the bottom." These tables are sometimes called "input–output tables," although Cantlon did not use this language.

x	0	1	2	3	4	5	6
y	0	10	20	30			

We suggest you begin by having participants work individually on a few problems of this type themselves before they examine students' written work and the edited video recording of the whole class conversation about these problems.

Activity 2.1: Finding Patterns in Tables, Describing Them Algebraically

You will need to distribute the following, one copy for each participant.

- *Figuring Out Algebraic Representations from Tables*. This set of problems includes the four tables the students were given (1–4) plus an *additional one* (5), intended to engage adult participants in a more challenging exploration of patterns. Together the five problems should raise important issues about figuring out patterns, figuring out algebraic representations, and whether tables have unique "solutions."
- *Discussion Questions: Figuring Out Algebraic Representations*. How are these problems similar to and different from the first set of problems the children worked with? What makes some of these tables harder (which ones) or easier (which ones) than the others to complete? What makes some of these tables harder or easier to represent algebraically? What kinds of difficulties might students' experience?

Have participants work on the five problems, following the set of directions. Then engage them in a conversation about their work on the problems and the questions. When you think you have spent sufficient time discussing these problems and raising issues, move on to the ne xt activity.

Activity 2.2: Getting Started With Tables

Cantlon and her students had spent the majority of class on December 12 finishing up the Bobby's Cookies Problem.

About 10 minutes before lunch, Cantlon introduced the next set of problems they would be working on. She displayed a table at the overhead and asked students to think about "what's going on between, the relationship between the numbers on the top and the numbers that are on the bottom."

To engage participants in this activity, you will need to show the short video clip of December 12.

- *Video: Getting Started with Tables*. This segment, in which Cantlon launches work on a new set of problems, is approximately 7 minutes in length.

Before showing the video, you will need to distribute the following, one to each participant.

- *Transcript of the Video: Getting Started with Tables*. Participants may want to jot down some notes on the transcript as they view the video. Alert them that it is often a temptation to simply "read" along the transcript as the video plays and not watch the video. Encourage them to only use the transcript to support watching the video.

You may want to make a transparency of the questions to guide the viewing and subsequent discussion.

- *Questions For Viewing The Video: Getting Started With Tables*. What are the different ways that children who share in the video clip are thinking about the table? Are some of these ways more helpful than others when trying to move toward algebraic representation? Are some of these ways more helpful for other purposes?

Allow some time to discuss the questions following the viewing of the tape.

Activity 2.3: Sharing Work on the Table Problems

Cantlon gave her students about 20 minutes at the beginning of class on December 13 to work independently on the table problems she had assigned the day before. Then she had the whole class come together to share the work they had done with the tables.

To engage participants in this activity, you will need to show the edited video recording of December 13.

- *Video: Sharing Work on Table Problems*. This segment is approximately 25 minutes in length. It records the children's discussion about two of the tables—the c/d table and the m/n table. One helpful way to view a long video like this is to show the students' discussion about *one of the tables at a time*, then stop the video and give people a chance to jot notes on the transcript and discuss the students' solution to that one table. Then proceed on to the next table. The video has been edited so that the place to pause is easily identified.

You will need to distribute the following, one for each participant.

- *Transcript of the Video: Sharing Work on Table Problems*. As participants view the video, have them consider the same set of questions that framed your discussion of the earlier video segment.

Activity 2.4: Examining Students' Written Work on Tables

You will need to distribute the following materials, one set for each participant.

- *Students' Written Work on Table Problems*. We have included pages from the notebooks of Cameron, Bobby, Lauren, Billy, Keegan, Stacey, Michael, Clint, and Victoria.
- *Discussion Questions: Students' Written Work on Table Problems*. Which aspects of the work are easier or harder for the student? If there are things the student has done incorrectly, is there a pattern to what she or he seems to be thinking and doing? Is there a pattern within a given table, is there a pattern across all the tables or a subgroup of tables? How does the students seem to be making sense of moving from the tables to constructing and algebraic number sentence? Can you generate more than on plausible interpretation? Which explanation seems most likely and why?

After the students had an opportunity to discuss their solutions to the table problems, Cantlon asked them to represent each table with an algebraic sentence that showed the relationship between the top and bottom numbers in each table. The pages from the notebooks of the nine students show a range of solutions across the class and their attempts to write an algebraic relationship. Have participants examine closely the work of each individual student, with the Discussion Questions as a lens.

Activity 2.5: Looking Across the Unit

You will need to distribute the following, one to each participant.

- *Discussion Questions: Looking Across the Unit*. What might be said about these young children's learning of algebraic ideas? What kinds of ideas or thinking seems to come easily to them and what is the evidence? What kinds of things less so? What are some of the subtle and not-so-subtle differences among the children's abilities to find patterns, generalize, and move toward algebraic representation? What are common things they do/think when given a certain kind of problem conte xt?

In this final activity, participants are asked to consider the entire set of case materials—the various problems, students' written work on the problems, students' discussions about how they thought about and solved problems, and Cantlon's reflections on some of the events. As they look across collection of materials, have them consider the Discussion Questions.

As a culminating activity, have participants revisit the representations they created in the first activity—about what there is to learn and teach about algebra in the elementary grades, and about young children's understanding of these ideas. Have them discuss revisions they might make in either list now. Then discuss the *process* of moving from the initial ideas they had to those that have been developed through the study of practice in this classroom. How might the investigation of these case materials help them think about planning and teaching an algebra unit for elementar y students?

DELIBERATIONS WITHIN THE PROJECT

Algebra for All. The Algebra Working Group, established by the National Council of Teachers of Mathematics in 1994, stated that "all students can learn algebra" and that "children can develop algebraic concepts at an early age" (NCTM, 1994, p. 5). It is a statement of beliefs and commitment, grounded in research and underpinned by a set of values about developing the mathematical power of *all* students. But what is meant by "algebraic thinking" in the elementary grades, and what should constitute algebra in the elementary curriculum is currently under intense debate.

A number of researchers and practitioners, as groups and individuals, are conducting empirical and theoretical studies, creating new curricular materials, and experimenting with new instructional practices to shape a foundation for helping young children develop algebraic reasoning. Some of these efforts are focused on what algebra content should be included in the elementary grades. Other efforts are focused on the nature of children's thinking and reasoning—their observations of patterns and relationships, the conjectures they make that grow out of their observations, the ways they test their conjectures, and the ways in which they represent and generalize these patterns and relationships (see, e.g., NCTM, 1994, 1997). Cantlon is one of a growing number of adventuresome teachers who are individually experimenting with this content area in their elementary classrooms.

As we examined the materials from Cantlon's classroom, our analysis seemed to focus on three aspects of her practice: the tasks she posed for students and the reasoning of the students that they prompted; the classroom environment she created and how it supported mathematical discourse and student sense making; and the goals she had for her students, the challenge in balancing attention to competing goals, and how attending to multiple goals can shape instr uctional decisions.

Mathematical Tasks and Student Reasoning

Task Types and Representations. Cantlon developed two distinct types of tasks for students to explore. At the beginning of the unit, she presented students with real situations to see what patterns they observed, what conjectures they had about generalizing about the patterns, and what further questions they might pose about a situation. Several of the children used drawings (stick figures to show the number of shoes worn by a classroom of students, drawings of cookies grouped by threes to show how many could be decorated each minute) to represent the situations, even when Cantlon had explicitly asked them to "use a table" on the cookie problem. We were amused by Michael's interpretation of table, as evidenced by his drawing of nine individual four-legged objects, each holding three cookies. (Michael's drawings led to a whole-class discussion about what is meant by a mathematical table).

The second type of task involved looking for patterns in tables. These tasks differed from the first type in that they were not presented in some real problem situation. They involved decontextualized, pure mathematical investigations. They did not lend themselves to students' earlier ways of using drawings to explore and reason about a situation. We wondered what sense students made of these abstract formulations. In fact, Kevin asked about the first table, "Why is it the x and y are there?"

Deciding about mathematical tasks can pose some real challenges for teachers who are charting new territory. It is not surprising that teachers might draw, in part, on their own experiences of learning algebra, which was likely dominated with writing symbolic expressions for abstract number relationships involving two variables. They may not appreciate that this represents a huge conceptual leap for young learners. Even at the middle grades, students require a lot of experiences with real problem situations before being able to abstract some general principles that they can apply to pure mathematical investigations of functions and relationships.

Pattern Recognition and Description. In tasks that involved real situations, students had a variety of ways to describe the patterns they saw. In the cookie problem, some saw a recursive additive pattern—"You add three to the number before." In this case, students seemed to focus on a single variable—how the number of cookies decorated was growing—and did not appear to look at the relationship between the number of minutes Bobby had been decorating cookies and how many he had decorated. A few saw a multiplicative pattern—"You can just multiply the number of minutes by three." In this case, students seemed to be looking at both variables and the relationship between them as they changed. In each instance, students were observing and describing patterns in the situation and in their tables.

This dual way of looking for patterns—within variables and across variables—was apparent when tables were presented as abstract objects. For example, in describing patterns in the (x, y) table of December 12, students offered a variety of descriptions. Josh said, "It's going up by ten." Kevin said, "X might mean like going up one and y might read, I mean, mean tens, going up by tens." Here both students appeared to be looking for patterns in how each variable was changing and not how one was changing in relation to the other.

The whole-class conversation about the (c, d) table elicited a number of descriptions of patterns.

- It goes one up.
- Like whatever the number is you put it in front of the 10.
- I just timesed it once. I went 1 times, 1 times 13, 1 times 14, 1 times 15.
- I knew it was going odd, even, odd, even so I just put the 13, 14, 15, 16.
- You could use like the 10 mainly. Like 10 plus 0 is 10. Ten plus one is eleven. Ten plus two is twelve. Ten plus four is fourteen and etcetera, etcetera.

Most were accepted by teacher and students as valid ways of talking about patterns in the table. And although the descriptions varied, they all led students to complete the table with the same set of values.

The (m, n) table proved to be more challenging. Most students tended to consider only a subset of the numbers in the table. One strategy was to focus on the second and third values for n (1 and 4), noting that the difference was 3, and then complete the table by adding 3 for each subsequent entry. Some appeared to focus on the relationship between the third entries for m and n, noting that n was two times m, or n was m plus m, and then completed the table using one of those rules. Only two students observed a pattern in which n was "m times m." With this table, the various descriptions led to the table being filled in with different sets of values. The written work of the (s, t) table indicated that it, too, produced different ways of seeing patterns that led to completing the table with quite different values (see Cameron, Lauren, Stacey, and Clint).

Generalizations With Algebraic Number Sentences. Moving from describing patterns with natural language to describing patterns with symbolic language appeared to be extremely challenging. With Bobby's cookie problem, when students did try to write an algebraic number sentence, they tended to write a statement about a particular instance (e.g., $X \times \Delta = 27, X = 9,\ \Delta = 3$). Chris B. was the only student who generated a statement that showed the general relationship: X = any number of minutes, C = cookies, $X \times 3 = C$.

Writing algebraic number sentences seemed to be even more problematic in the case of the abstract tables. It looked like Cameron wrote a similar sentence for each table in which the sum of the two variables equaled the last entry in the table (e.g., $x + y = 24$). Lauren appeared to have three sentences for the (x, y) table: $X = 4; X \times 4 = Y; X \times Y = 4$. We were unable to make any sense of Clint's number sentences: $X \times Y = 18; c \times d = 11; m \times n = 4$.

We also considered how the ways students described a pattern made writing an algebraic number sentence easier or harder. For example, the rule *whatever the number is you put it in front of the ten* is not easily translated into an algebraic number sentence. Nor are any of the recursive patterns such as *you just keep adding ten*.

We wondered whether having students generalize with algebraic number sentences was a reasonable expectation at this point. Their initial notebook entries about what they thought algebra was indicated a common notion of variable as a place holder for an unknown in a number sentence (e.g., $12 \times 2 = m; 2 \times \Delta = 8$). We suspect that few of these students were ready to make the considerable conceptual step to writing symbolic statements about the patterns they observed. There seemed to be much to pursue just in students' ways of describing patterns with natural language.

Environment, Discourse, and Sense Making

We were struck by the willingness of students to get up in front of their classmates to describe the patterns they observed. And we were struck by the interaction among the students, particularly during the discussion of the (m, n) table. Several different ways of describing a pattern and then filling in the table became a part of the conversation. And with each new pattern, there was some discussion, almost always initiated by individual students, about whether the pattern "worked."

The pattern of "*going up three*" raised several questions. If a table went up by threes, did it always have to go zero, three, six? If so, then some saw that there was a problem because the (m, n) table started 0, 1, 4. Victoria seemed to be suggesting that the numbers didn't necessarily have to start with zero when she commented "Yeah but you can still count by threes with other numbers." Samantha disagreed with the "plus three" because "if you put zero plus and then you plus it three it wouldn 't equal one."

Keegan described a different pattern that involved adding the top number to itself—"three plus three equals six and four plus four is eight." This was met immediately with a response from Michael that he had tried that too but he ran into a problem: "But one and one is two. Not one ."

When Michael presented his pattern of "We did zero times zero is zero. One times one is one. Two times two is four," Victoria reacted, "Yeah, but see we didn't do that on all the other ones. We, we took the top number and multiplied it by *one* number." The students seemed to be trying things that had worked before even if it meant disregarding some of the numbers in the table.

The students seemed to be working hard at making their own sense of the (m, n) table. They were not shy about disagreeing with others when new ideas did not make sense to them or did not fit with the patterns they saw.

Goals, Balance, and Instructional Decisions

Cantlon holds a complex set of goals for her students in this unit, as evidenced by her concept map. We speculated that it could be possible for attitude, process, and content goals to be in tension in this classroom. For example, in the whole-class conversation about the tables, Cantlon encouraged students to describe their patterns and question each other about whether the patterns worked. At the same time, some student conjectures went unchallenged, and quite different descriptions and extensions of patterns went unexamined. This seemed to fit with her attitude goals—predict patterns, represent patterns, and analyze patterns. She seemed to emphasize communication as a significant dimension of the attitude and process outcomes.

What appeared to be underemphasized was attention to the content outcomes. Cantlon's content outcomes specified "describe relationship between 2 quantities in a table" and "change in one variable results in change in another." But there were many occasions in which students persisted in looking at change within a variable rather than across variables. There were places in her own interaction with the students when it appeared that she, too, was looking at how one variable in a table was changing and not at the relationship between the variables.

We continually kept at the fore that Cantlon was taking a first stab at working with these ideas with students. She had not talked with students before about these ideas, so much of what happened was unanticipated. She could anticipate that students would see different patterns, but she had little idea of the particular formulations they might make. And in the moment-to-moment of teaching she may have concentrated on promoting the disposition to make conjectures without realizing the implications for developing misconceptions. For example, for the (c, d) table, one student described the pattern as "putting a one in front of the number." This description allowed the student to complete the table with the same numbers as those students who described other patterns. But something interesting happens if the table is extended to $c = 10$. All the other patterns would have generated 20 for d but the rule of "putting a one in front of the number" would have generated 110 for d. This would have been an interesting mathematical situation to pursue and one that might have pushed the students to develop further understanding of generalizing.

REFERENCES

National Council of Teachers of Mathematics. (1994). *A framework for constructing a vision of algebra*. Reston, VA: Author.

National Council of Teachers of Mathematics. (1997, February). *Teaching children mathematics, 3* (6). A focus issue on Algebraic thinking. Reston, VA: Author.

Schram, P., Cantlon, D., Hunt, K., Scholten, B., & Seales, P. (1994). *Nurturing the freedom to wonder: Vignettes from elementary mathematics classrooms*. Lansing, MI: Michigan Council of Teachers of Mathematics.

MATERIALS FOR MAKING PHOTOCOPIES AND TRANSPARENCIES

- *Cantlon's Concept Map of Algebra.* Prepare a transparency of the map.
- *What is Algebra: Pages from Students' Notebooks. Cameron, Victoria, Amanda, Tyler, Lauren, Chris B.* Prepare one set for each participant.
- *What is Algebra: Discussion Questions.* Prepare one for each participant; prepare a transparency.
- *Early Explorations of Algebra: Problems and Discussion Questions.* Prepare one for each participant; prepare a transparency.
- *Problem of the Day: December 11; Problem of the Day: December 12.* Prepare a transparency.
- *Students' Annotated Work on Bobby's Cookies Problem—Stacey, Michael, Keegan, Bobby, and Chris B.* Prepare one set for each participant; prepare a set of transparencies (optional).
- *Discussion Questions: Solutions for Algebraically Representing the Bobby's Cookies Problem.* Prepare one for each participant; prepare a transparency.
- *Figuring Out Algebraic Representations from Tables.* Prepare one set of problems for each participant; prepare a transparency.

- *Discussion Questions: Figuring Out Algebraic Representations*. Prepare one for each participant; prepare a transparency.
- *Questions for Viewing Video: Getting Started with Tables.* Prepare a transparency.
- *Transcript of Video: Getting Started with Tables.* Prepare one for each participant.
- *Transcript of Video: Sharing Work on Table Problems.* Prepare one for each participant.
- *Students' Written Work on Tables—Cameron, Bobby, Lauren, Billy, Keegan, Stacey, Michael, Clint, and Victoria.* Prepare one set for each participant; prepare transparencies (optional).
- *Discussion Questions: Students' Written Work on Tables.* Prepare one for each participant; prepare a transparency.
- *Discussion Questions: Looking Across the Unit.* Prepare one for each participant; prepare a transparency.

CANTLON'S CONCEPT MAP OF ALGEBRA

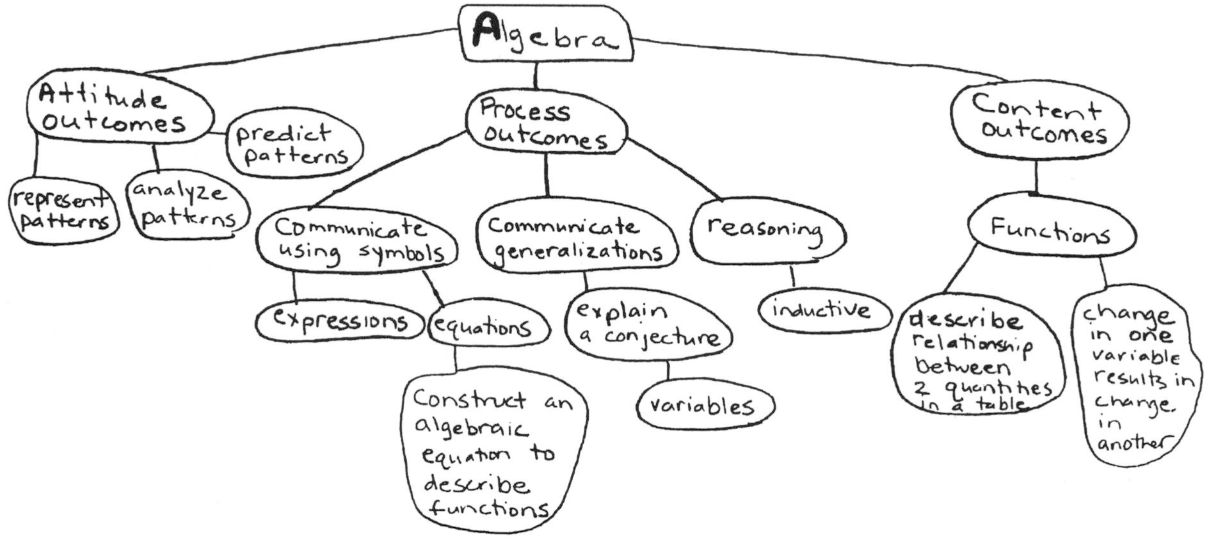

Cameron

What is algebra? 12-4-95

algebra is a type of math that uses ~~pictures~~ shapes or letter for the factor or product.

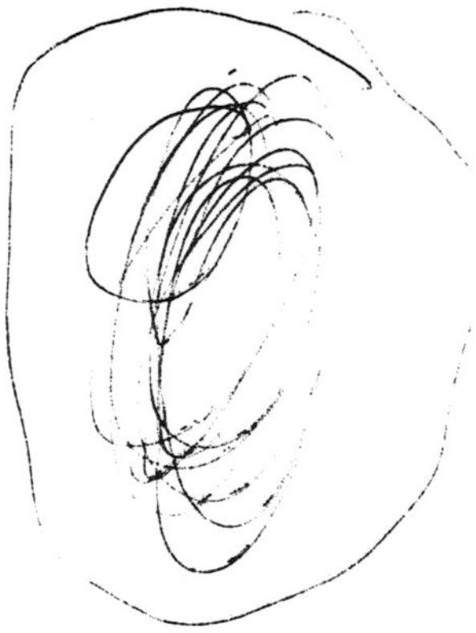

forver

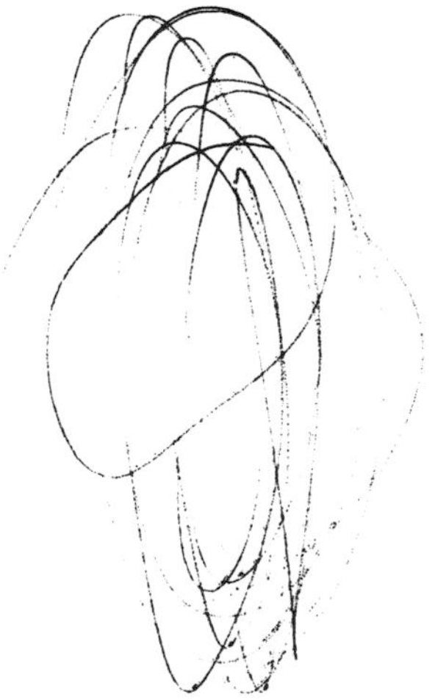

fyle

al Einstine

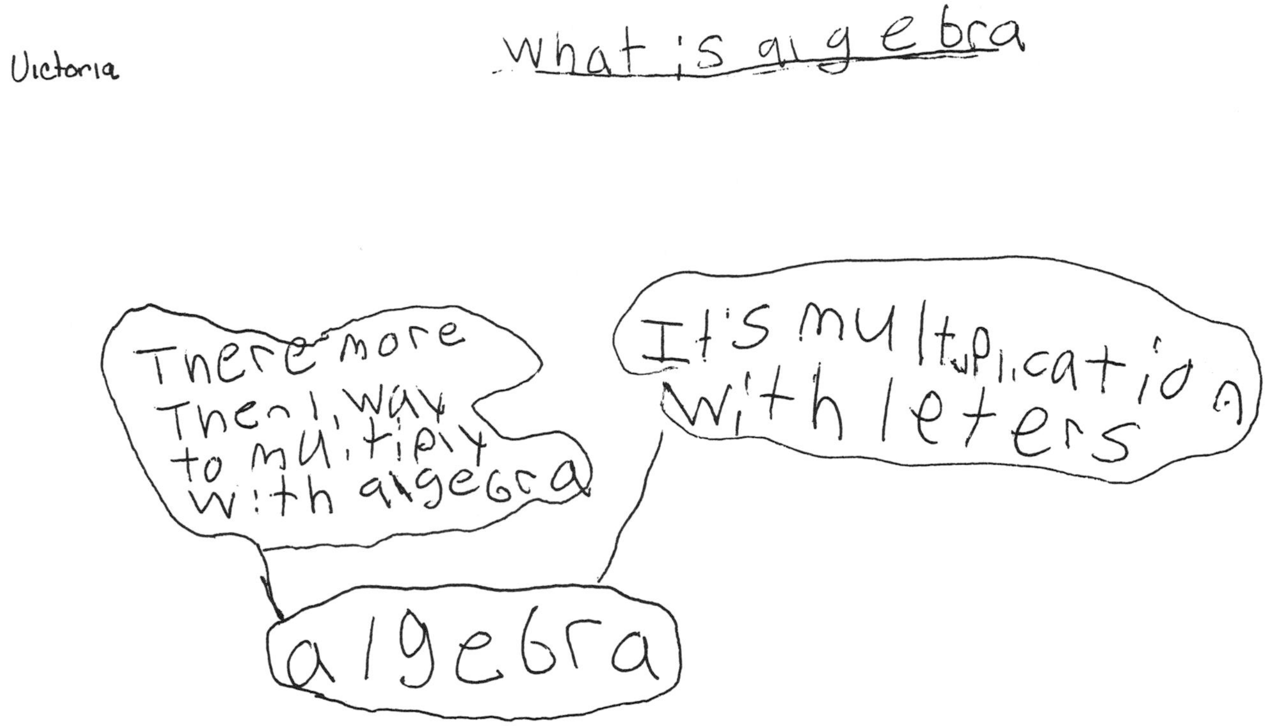
Victoria
what is algebra
There more Then 1 way to multiply with algebra
It's multuplication with leters
algebra

[redacted]

12-4-95

Amanda

Algebra
[redacted]

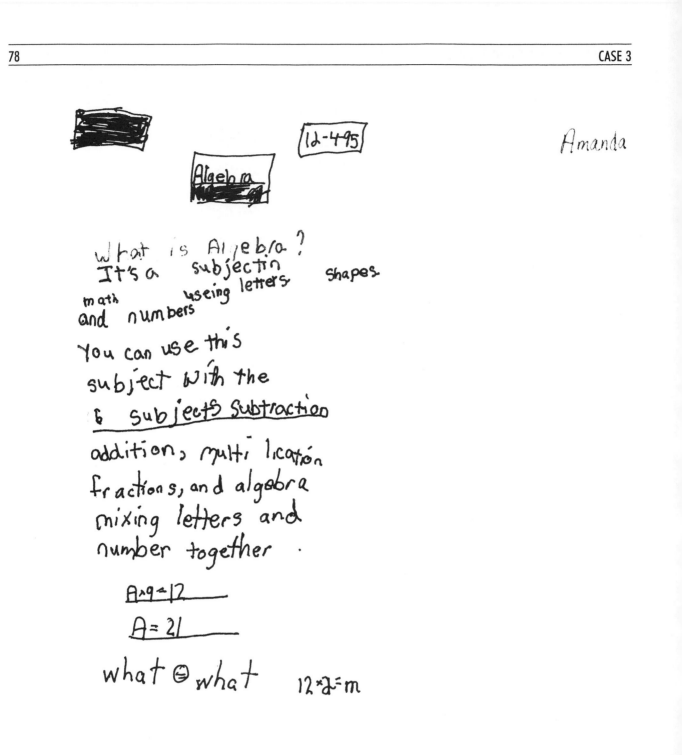

What is Algebra?
It's a subjectin math useing letters shapes and numbers

You can use this subject with the 6 subjects subtraction addition, multilication fractions, and algebra mixing letters and number together.

A×9=12
A=21

what ⊖ what   12×2=m

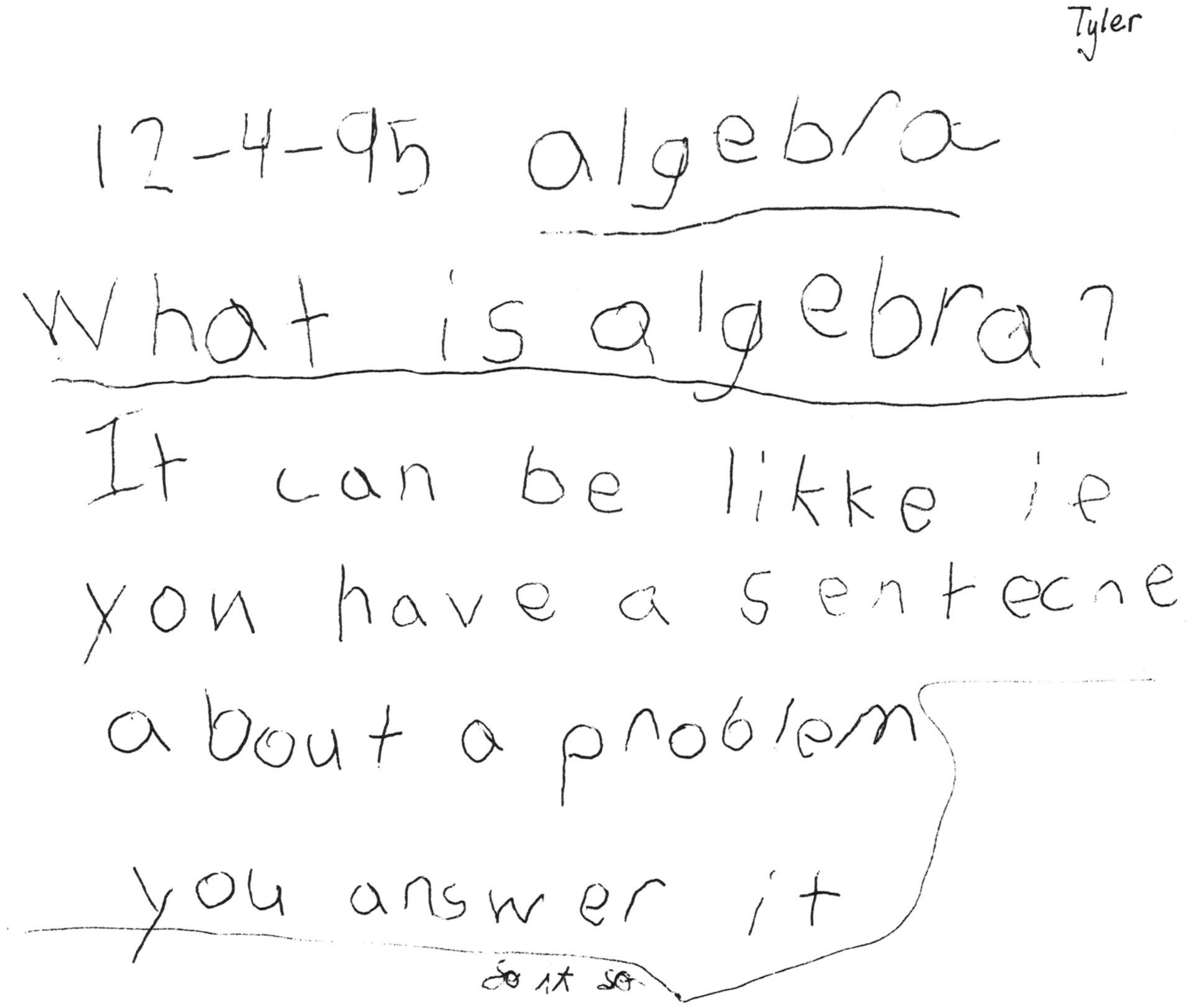

Tyler

12-4-95 algebra

What is algebra?

It can be likke ie
you have a sentecne
about a problem
you answer it
so it so

12-4-95

Lauren

What is Algebra?

Algebra is adding and using letters to get your answer

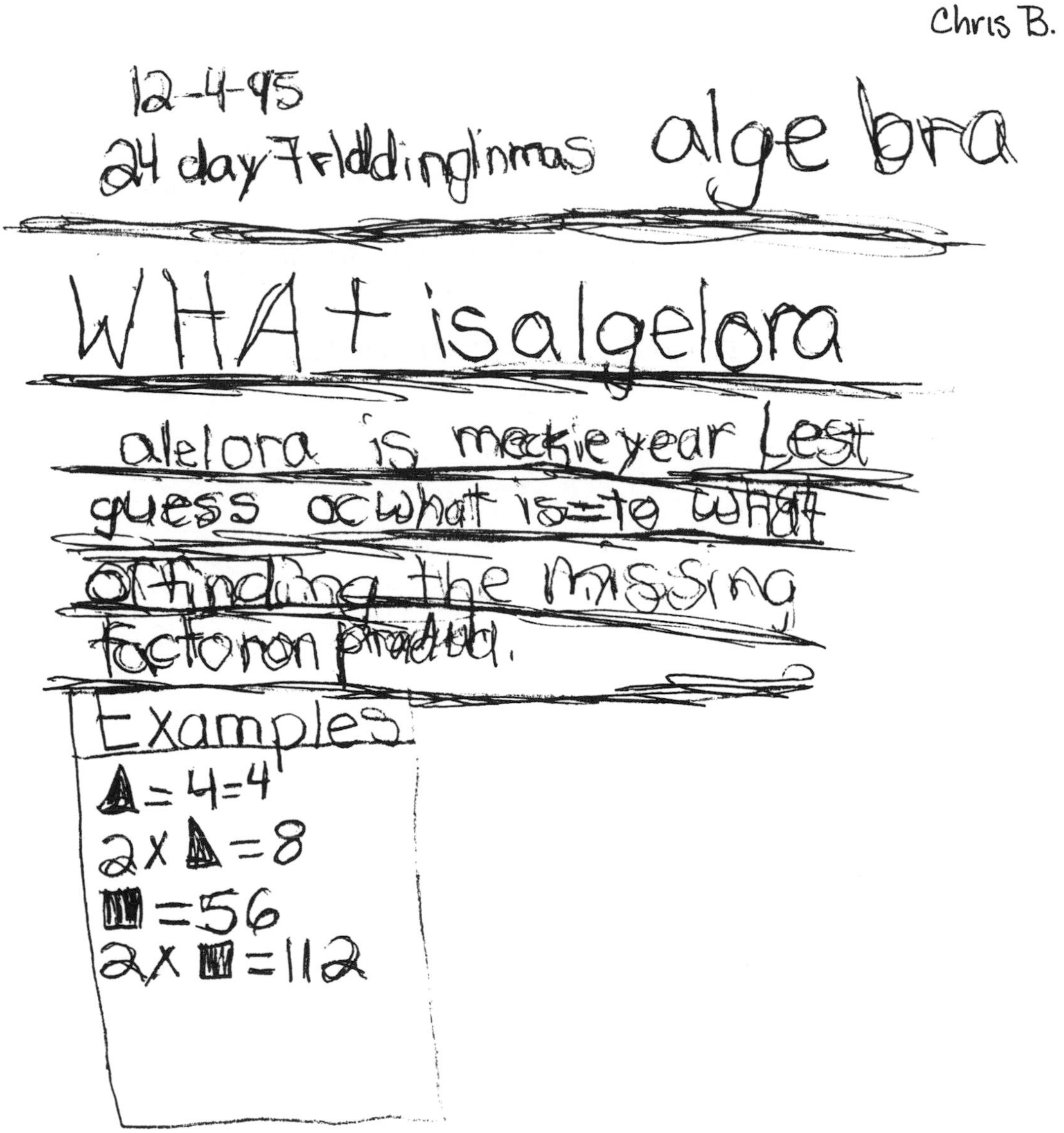
Chris B.
12-4-95
algebra
WHAt is algelora
alelora is meckie year Lest guess ocwhat is=to what orfinding the missing factoron
Examples
= 4=4
2x = 8
=56
2x =112

WHAT IS ALGEBRA: DISCUSSION QUESTIONS

- What ideas do the children have about algebra?
- Where might their ideas come from?
- How might the teacher build on those ideas?
- What challenges might a teacher face?

EARLY EXPLORATIONS OF ALGEBRA: PROBLEMS AND DISCUSSION QUESTIONS

Problem 1: Use a chart to show how many shoes the students are wearing. Fill in the chart for up to 10 students.

students	shoes
1	2

Problem 2: Use tiles to make squares. Then fill in the chart of square numbers.

1	1
2	4
3	9

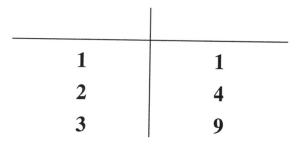

- How are these problems alike and how are they different?
- What do you think students might find difficult about either of the problems?

PROBLEM OF THE DAY

Problem of the day: December 11

Bobby was getting ready for Christmas. He could decorate 3 cookies in 1 minute. Use a table to show how many cookies were finished from 1 minute to 9 minutes.

Problem of the day: December 12

If x = number of minutes, how can you write an algebraic number sentence to show the relationship between minutes and cookies?

Stacey

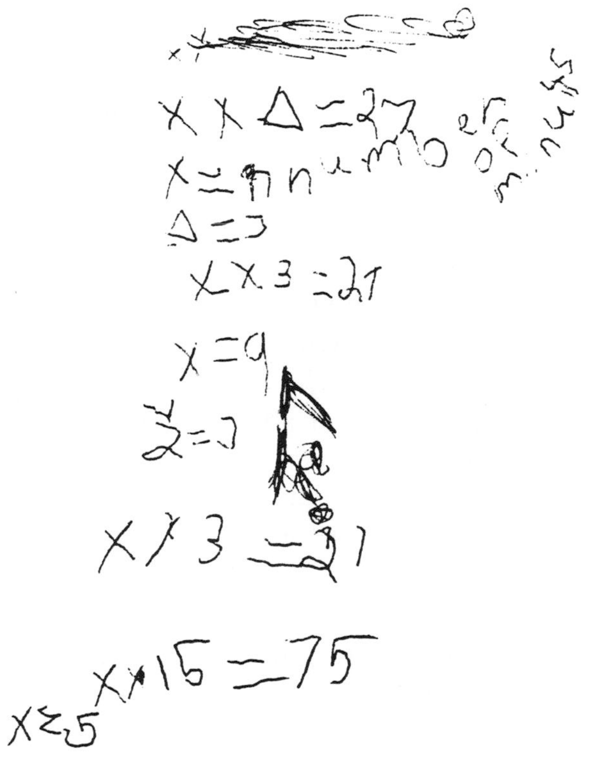

Conversation with Stacey

Cantlon: The first person I'd like to have come up and share would either be Stacey or Samantha. I don't know if you worked on it together or did you work on it separately?

Stacey: Together.

Cantlon: Okay. then why don't you two girls come on up, and you can write down on the overhead um, what it is you did.

$$X + \square = 27$$

$$x = 9 \quad \square = 3$$

Samantha: Well. Okay. One of 'em was x times square equals—wait a sec.[Writes on the transparency.] And, the X equals nine—wait a minute—x equals nine and square equals three.

Cantlon: Tyler, what do you think of the way that Samantha wrote her algebra number sentence?

Tyler: She used um, the x for any number between one and nine which right now is nine. And then she used square to equal three.

Cantlon: Okay. So she—and she showed you that down below. did that make sense to you? Amanda, do you have something to add?

Amanda: I agree with Tyler, Stacey, and Sam 'cause um, it said um, x is—if x was the number of minutes, and the number of minutes totally is nine. I did x times 3 equals 27 and x equals the total minutes which is 9. So I did it like you but I didn't have the square. You can do all sorts of things with …

Victoria: This problem could go on forever.

Student: Yeah.

Cantlon: Stacey did you have anything you wanted to add? Anything um, different or—

Stacey: We got, we got some more … actually.

Cantlon: Did you use the same idea where you have *x* equals the time and then you had a shape to show … Okay. that's one way that people were thinking about an algeraic number sentence.

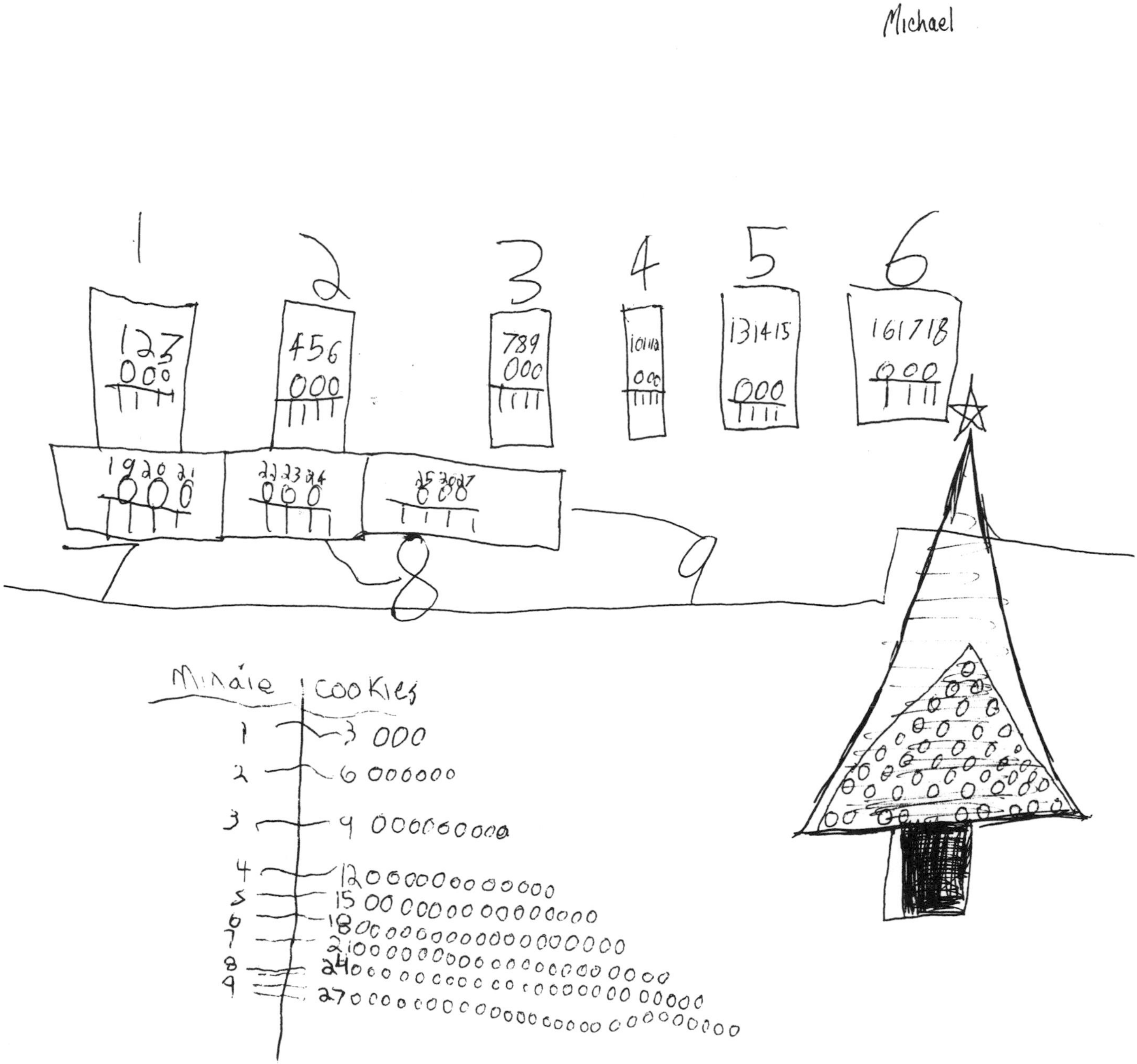
Michael
1
2
3
4
5
6
8
9
Cookies

Conversation with Michael

Michael: Um, I just times all the numbers by three. One times three is three, one—two times three is six, and so on.

Cantlon: What are the dots on the side?
Michael: That's just to show how many there are.
Student: How many cookies?
Michael: Yeah.

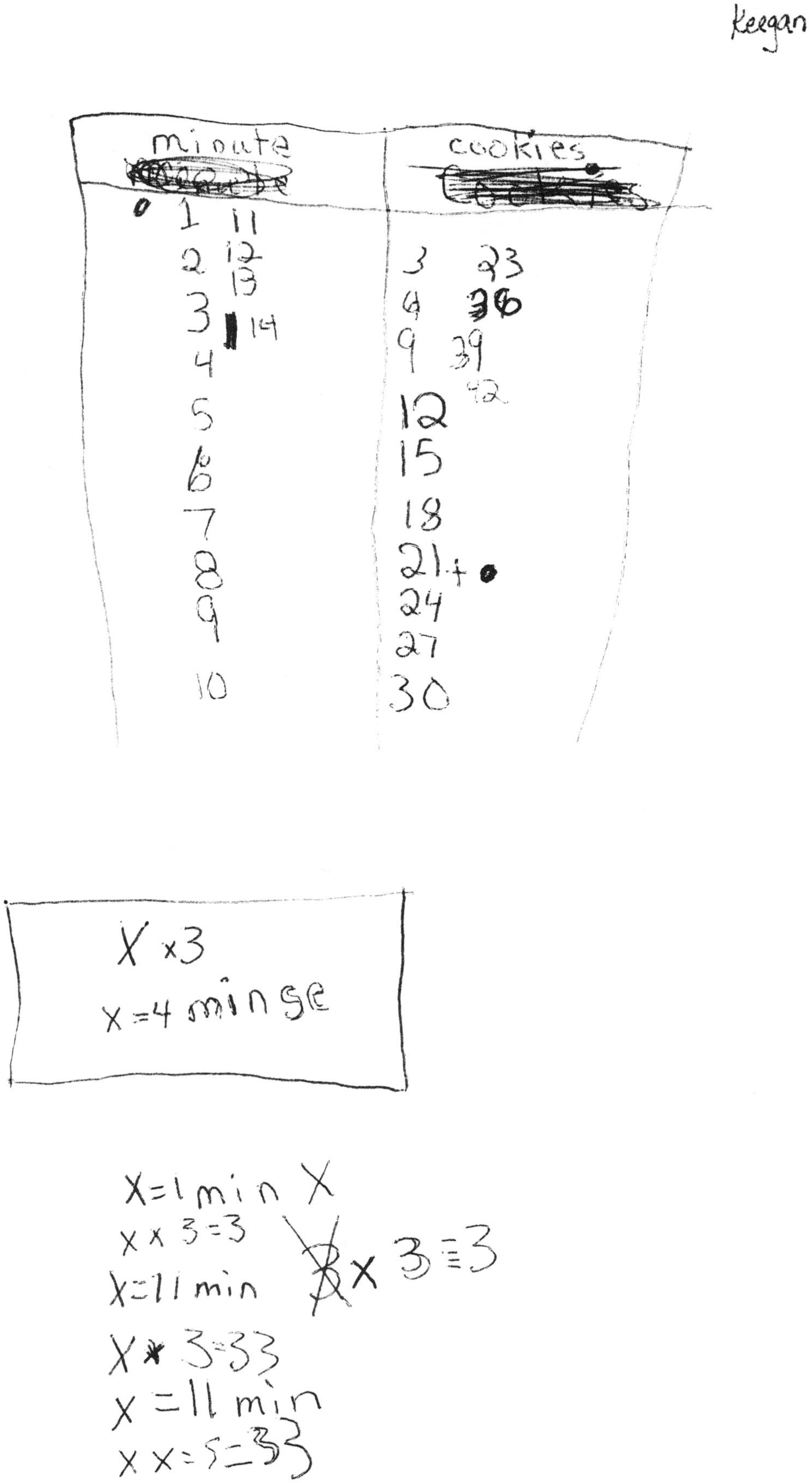
Keegan
minute
cookies
X x3
x =4 minge
X=1 min X
x x 3=3
X=11 min
X 3=33
X =11 min

Conversation with Keegan

Keegan: Okay, how we solved this problem was. Um, see, um—what we did is we, we counted by threes and we go—

Cantlon: Just a second Keegan. People are talking and not listening to Keegan.

Keegan: Well, what we did is we counted by three and we figured out like, okay, h—what minute is this going to bee an we did that and we go one—and we put, we put one, two, three, four, five, six, seven, eight, nine, ten, eleven, twelve, thirteen, fourteen and like we counted by threes on this side. Three, six, nine and on and on … Okay, any questions? Amanda?

Amanda: But—

Keegan: You disagree?

Amanda: Well, with your example. What do you mean … In the problem it didn't have only *three* minutes, it had *nine* minutes.

Keegan: But, well, we couldn't fit that all on there …
[Amanda and Keegan talk softly together.]

Cantlon: Amanda, if you're—Amanda, if you're up here speaking can you talk so that we can all hear you, please?

Amanda: Okay, well I just—cause, there wans't just three minutes but they said that they didn't have the time to put it in but it would be helpful if they would put all the minutes and all the cookies. Because then it would be—

Cantlon: Because the problem asks for how many minutes?

Student: ... or cookies

Amanda: Or how many minutes or wh—and how many cookes you end up with adfter nine minutes... could decorate.

Cantlon: Okay, so you've got this way of using the table where the girls, basically you wer going up counting by three as a way to do it.

Bobby: I was adding but until—buy, but I started multiplications until ...

student: Huh?

Bobby

minute cookes

1 3

2 3+3=6

3 3+3+3=9

4 3+3+3+3=12

5 3+3+3+3+3=15

3×6=18

6 3×7=21

7 3×8=24

8 3×9=27

9 3 [crossed out]

X×3=27

1=9

Conversation with Bobby

Cantlon: Take a look at what Bobby did. The way he was solving the problem.

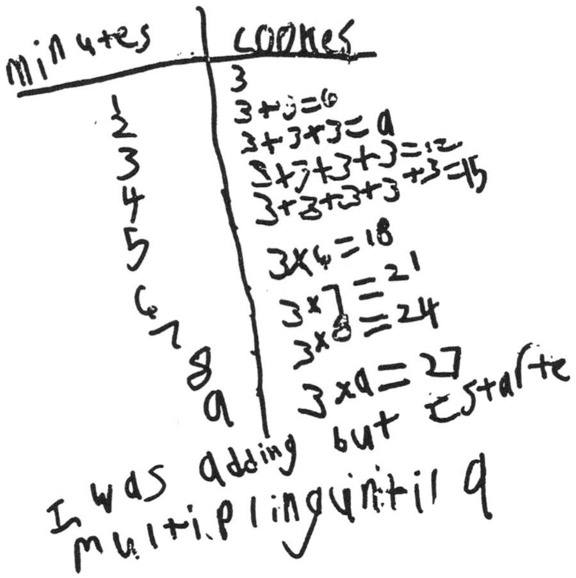

Amanda: It's the same thing. 'Cause he could have used multiplication, just addition is—

Victoria: Easier.

Amanda: Easier—

Victoria: And it's longer than doing …

Amanda: Actually, um—

Cantlon: I was wondering Bobby why did you switch over to multiplication from addition?

Bobby: It was—um, because it was going to the other page. Going to another page.

Cantlon: You mean your number sentence was getting so long—

Bobby: Yeah.

Cantlon: —You thought it would go on to the other page?

Bobby: Yeah.

Chris B.

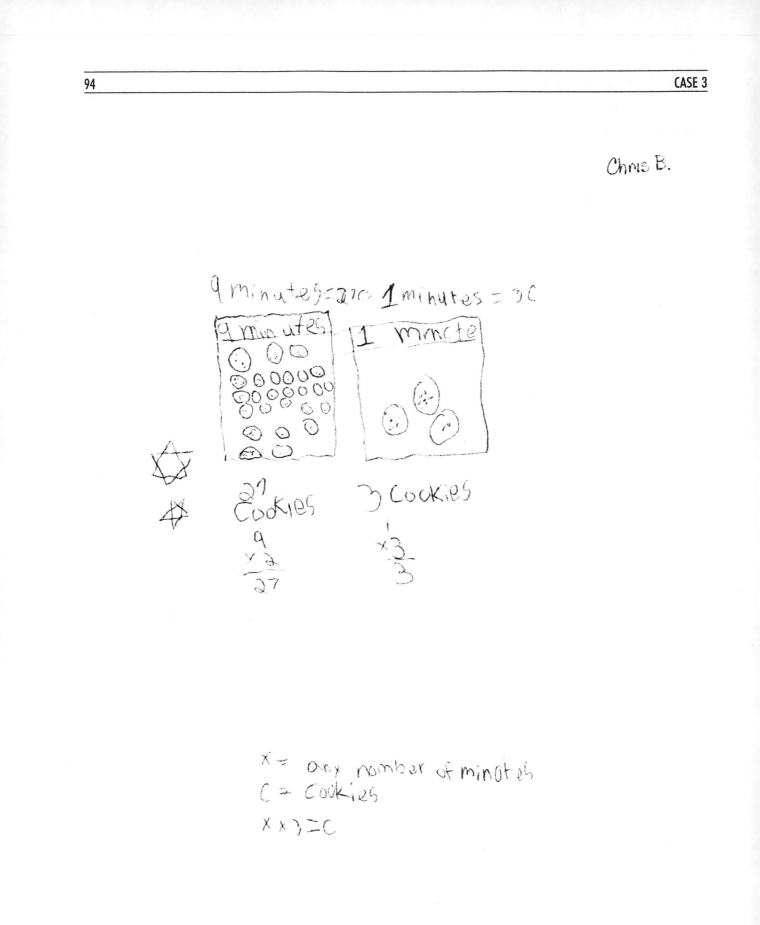

9 minutes = 27c 1 minutes = 3C

27 Cookies 3 Cookies

$$\begin{array}{r} 9 \\ \times 2 \\ \hline 27 \end{array} \qquad \begin{array}{r} 1 \\ \times 3 \\ \hline 3 \end{array}$$

x = any nomber of minotes
C = Cookies
x × 3 = C

Conversation with Chris B.

Cantlon: The last person I'd like to have share then would be Chris B. He wrote his a different way.

$$x \times 3 = c$$
$$9 \times 3 = 27$$

Cantlon: Can you explain what you have up here please?

Chris B: Yeah, *x* could be um, like, nine minutes times three. The is the *c*, is the cookies, the *c* would be 27. That like … This is … That's the way you write it with *not* algebra. That's just, that's just a example. There's—it can be possible for like, all for one through nine.

Cantlon: Could you help us out? Could you write underneath what you mean by what the *x* represents and what the *c* represents: what you just said. Just write it on the overhead so we can look at it.

c = Cookies
x = number of minutes

Chris B: Billy?

Billy: I like the way how you write what it would look like …

Cantlon: Clint, can you hear him over there?

Clint: I can't.

Cantlon: Could you speak up a little bit please?

Billy: I like the way he—that you wrote it with the way …

Chris B: Clint.

Clint: I like how um, you eq—you made it equal—when it equaled a letter.

Chris B: Alright.

Cantlon: What's different abou the way Chris wrote his algebraic number sentence? *x* times three equals *c* compared to like what um—oh, for example Samantha and Stacey started off with? Tyler?

Tyler: Instead of Stacey and um, um and Samantha's way um—how they used um, a, a square, Chris used a number and he used a letter at the end …

Cantlon: Do you understand what Tyler's saying between the difference of these two? Michael, can you say it back in your own words, what was the a—what was the meaning by that? What's the dirfference? The way Tyler's looking at it, do you understand what he's saying?

Michael: I think he's saying that if you do *x* times … I don't know.

Cantlon: Do you want him to say it again? Okay, Tyler, you want to give it another try?

Tyler: Instead of um, using a number at the end he used a letter so that—what's kind of make it, makes it difference from um, Stacey and Samantha's. And Stacey and Samantha, for the second number, instead of using three or any other number they used a square.

Canton: Michael?

Michael: Um, I think, I think that's true. You could use a square … instead of a number to represent three or … something.

Cantlon: Other ideas about that question? Billy?

Billy: Um, I was just going to explain what Tyler's saying.

Cantlon: Sure, go ahead.

Billy: He's saying like—He's—He put a, a number for the answer, and he put a letter for the answer and he's saying like he—they switched around. They ha—they have a squre for the second number …

Cantlon: If the *c* is a the other side of the equal sign for our—Chris B.'s number sentence can the *c* equal any number? Or does it have to—is it something specific more like what Samantha and Stacey did? Where they've given you a real specific answer.

Billy: yeah, they're giving an specific answer.

Cantlon: So what does the *c* mean?

Billy: Any number. He, he wrote …

Cantlon: That's just one of his examples?

Student: Yeah.

Cantlon: Victoria?

Victoria: My, uh—You really can't do it with Stacey's but I noticed a way that Chris is different than everybody else's.

Cantlon: How's that?

Victoria: I going to be using Lauren's example? Because—

Cantlon: You're using what as an example?

Victoria: Lau—Lauren's.

Cantlon: Lauren's example? Okay.

Victoria: Um, because that's the one that works here. Um, *x* equals number of minutes in Chris' and ususally in all the other ones tha—remember "a" equals uh any number on minutes. It, it doesn't equal an exact minute. It ju—doesn't say a number of minutes. It says like uh, like four minutes something. It has an exact number. And Chris' just says a number of minutes. Any—That way it could be any number to represent the whole chart. So,

Cantlon: Alright, so I hear you sayign that the way Chris has written this is a way to use the whole chart with. You could just plug in whatever a number of minutes, whatever number of cookies, if you needed to know that specifically but the way he's got it written you could use it for any of the one through nine?

Victoria: Hm, hm.

Cantlon: Other thoughts about that?

Keegan: I have a comment about that.

Cantlon: Do you have a question for Chris? Okay.

Keegan: I, um—right here um—but even though it's down here, could you write like what this equals and what this equals? Even though it's right here?

Student: he did—

Chris B: I did. *X* equals the number of minutes.

Student: No, I mean like—I mean like *x*, *x* equals that.

Student: He did ...

Student: He did.

Keegan: Yeah, but he didn't put an example ...

Victoria: ... Like this is one thing. This is just an example that shows what ...

Cantlon: Keegan, do you see what he's done? He's—with these? *X* times three equals c. That's his number sentence, he says it can explain any of the time or amount of cookies on the entire chart and underneath it he's just given you one example. One way of doing that would be the nine minutes times the three cookies he could make in a minute which would give you 27 cookies total. Do you see that connection, Keegan? Okay.

DISCUSSION QUESTIONS: SOLUTIONS FOR ALGEBRAICALLY REPRESENTING THE BOBBY'S COOKIES PROBLEM

- What are the similarities and differences among students' approaches?
- How do these various approaches lend themselves—or not—to algebraic representations?
- For each of the students' approaches, what kinds of understandings did the student need to have to come up with their solution?
- What questions do you have that you can't be sure of answering by looking at students' written work alone?
- What does the annotation contribute to interpreting the written work?
- If you were the teacher, what might be your next instructional moves? What are you taking into account as you consider various actions?

FIGURING OUT ALGEBRAIC REPRESENTATIONS FROM TABLES

- Fill in the tables below, describe the patterns you see in each.
- Write an algebraic sentence for the patterns you see.
- Try to write at least one other algebraic expression that would also work. Do more if you can think of more.
- Find other "patterns" a child might see for each table (even if it may not be what you would consider to be a "pattern").

1.

x	0	1	2	3	4	5	6
y	0	4	8				

2.

c	0	1	2	3	4	5	6
d	10	11	12				

3.

m	0	1	2	3	4	5	6
n	0	1	4				

4.

s	0	1	2	3	4	5	6
t	0	1/2	1				

5.

a	0	1	2	3	4	5	6
b	0	1	3	6			

DISCUSSION QUESTIONS: FIGURING OUT ALGEBRAIC REPRESENTATIONS

- How are these problems similar to and different from the first set of problems the children worked with?
- What makes some of these tables harder (which ones) or easier (which ones) than the others to complete?
- What makes some of these tables harder or easier to represent algebraically?
- What kinds of difficulties might students' experience?

QUESTIONS FOR VIEWING VIDEO: GETTING STARTED WITH TABLES

- What are the different ways that children who share in the video clip are thinking about the table?
- Are some of these ways more helpful than others when trying to move toward algebraic representation?
- Are some of these ways more helpful for other purposes?

December 12, 1995: Getting Started With Tables

X	0	1	2	3	4	5	6
Y	0	10	20	30			

Cantlon: Okay, the last thing that I'd like to have us think about today for math before we go to lunch is that—I want to think a little bit more about tables. I want to think about what's going on—just a second—what's going on between, the relationship between the numbers that are on top and the numbers that are on the bottom. If someone would like to come up—looks like Josh is interested in coming up. Could you explain a little bit about what's going on here? With this particular chart?

Josh: Well, uh, it's going up by ten and it's like, it's like ten times one, ten times two it's—

Cantlon: Did you want to fill in what would be our numbers that are in those blank spots?

Josh: And uh—and it, um—there's going to be a zero at every answer. Every— no. Every one down here.

X	0	1	2	3	4	5	6
Y	0	10	20	30	40	50	60

Cantlon: Go ahead and fill it in?

Student: This is just for this one isn't it?

Cantlon: Yeah.

Student: 'Cause there's other ones too.

Cantlon: Sure. This is just a relationship between the table with the *x* and *y*.

Josh: And it could go on forever.

Student: I know.

Student: You said that, Josh.

Cantlon: How do you know it could go on forever, Josh? Josh? Josh, how do you know it could go on forever?

Josh: Because, um … maybe um …

Cantlon: Josh, if you were to predict what the next two numbers would be what would you say they'd be?

Josh: I'd say the next two numbers on here, the next two numbers on here and up here?

Cantlon: Right. What would come after the six?

Josh: Seven and—

Cantlon: And what would come after the sixty?

Josh: Seventy.

Cantlon: Alright.

Josh: The um, number up here is going to be the fir—the first number in the tens place down here.

Cantlon: Katie, did you have something to say?

Katie: … I forgot …

Cantlon: You forgot?

Josh: Keegan.

Keegan: I have a pattern.

Cantlon: You see a pattern?

Keegan: Yeah. Er, it's not really a pattern it's just s—er, see? All right. See? Zero, one, one, zero, zero, three, three, four, four, five, five, six, six.

Student: I know!
[Several comment at once]

Cantlon: Other questions? Dan you ready? Could we extend this table the other way? Could it go to the left? What would it be if we extended it?

Student: Negative.

Students: Well, I'm not really su—
Negative what?
I'm not really sure but. …
[Several commenting at once]

Cantlon: I heard Billy say negative one and negative ten if it went the other way. Kevin?

Kevin: Why is it the x and y are there?

Cantlon: Why are the x and y there? Who can answer that question? What are th—what is the x showing on this table? What numbers? As you read across?

Student: Umm, negative.

Student: Zero, one, two, three, four, five, six?

Students: I have a question.
… hear, hear what … said?

Cameron: They're *positive* numbers.

Cantlon: There just happens to be positive numbers on this one, sure. And what about the y? What's happening, what's the pattern for—

Josh: It's—can I say it?

Cantlon: Sure.

Josh: It's adding by tens. It's like, …

Cantlon: It's adding by ten? Okay, that's one way to ex—explain it. Good.

Josh: Or it could be a zero, and then you have the numbers …

Cantlon: Can you talk so they can here you? What did you say Josh?

Josh: I said it could be a zero too because like maybe that could be a zero, zero, zero, zero, zero, zero.

Kevin: I've got something …

Josh: Kevin

Kevin: Um, I've got something … X might mean like going up one and y might read—I mean, mean tens, going up by tens.

Cantlon: So Kevin's idea on this particular table is that the *x* represents numbers that are going up by one and the y represents numbers that are going up by ten.

Josh: Keegan.

Keegan: I, I have a, another pattern or something that ... Well, it's really not a pattern, but ... But see, he had similar answers, agreeing with um, Kevin but I can describe what more he's saying. He's try—he's sort of saying that it's—he doesn't have to use it all with letters—er, I mean words. He can use it like letters, like we learned, where we're counting up by ones and then the *y* we were counting up by tens.

Cantlon: Okay, that's helpful.

Keegan: ...

Cantlon: Okay. Thank you both very much.

Josh: And uh, it, it kind of works with adding too but only you would have to do it ten plus ten. You would have to add with ten, not timing one time ...

Cantlon: Okay, so Josh is reminding us that we can use addition or multiplication with it. Now,

Josh: ... Or with Algebra too.

Cantlon: I know we're not going to get done with all of these today but I'd like us to get started so could you please copy these four different tables into your notebooks and start working on the pattern relationships between numbers.
[Several people talking at once]

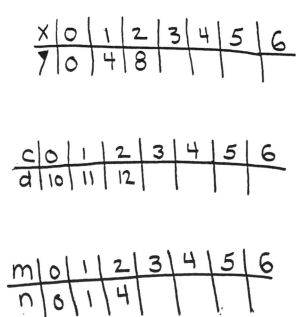

x	0	1	2	3	4	5	6
y	0	4	8				

c	0	1	2	3	4	5	6
d	10	11	12				

m	0	1	2	3	4	5	6
n	0	1	4				

s	0	1	2	3	4	5	6
t	0	½	1				

Cantlon: Boys and girls if you have all four of the tables at least copied down into your notebook then start getting ready for lunch. We'll talk about it tomorrow. [Several people talking at once]

December 13, 1995: Sharing Work With Tables

PROBLEM OF THE DAY

—Finish your tables

—Discuss

—Write an algebraic number sentence

—Discuss

—New problem if time

c	0	1	2	3	4	5	6
d	10	11	12				

Cantlon: All right if there aren't any other comments about this first table, I'd like to move on to the second one. Thank you, Michelle; thanks, Lauren. Our second table is the one with c and the d and it starts off with the zero, the one, and the two. Chris S., what do you have for that?

Chris S.: Where?

Student: See—

Cantlon: Our second table that's up there. Can you go up and fill in what you, uh—yeah. Put on your own table.

Chris S.: I put, uh ...

Cantlon: In a really loud voice so we can all hear you, please.

Chris S.: I put, um, ten here and eleven because of the ... ten, eleven, twelve, thirteen, fourteen ...

Student: Like you add to 'em.

Chris S.: It goes one up ...

Student: 'Cause you're adding one all the time, right?

Cantlon: Can you point out, ... write in the numbers that you came up with, please, so we can look at that?

c	0	1	2	3	4	5	6
d	10	11	12	13	14	15	16

Cantlon: For this one, I think Chris explained nicely that the relationship between the numbers that are represented by the *c* and the ones that are represented by the *d* are going up by ten. Or going up by—if you look at the pattern, Jake also added it, that it goes up by one each time. Got some hands up, Chris.

Chris S.: Michael?

Michael: ...

Cantlon: Okay, let's hear it.

Michael: Um, I just made the um, zero on the end and just keep going ... twenty ... Like one, like whatever the number is you put it in front of the ten, you put in front of the ... on top.

Chris S.: Jesserae.

Jesserae: Um, I, I did a different way 'cause all I, all I did I just timesed it once. I went one times, one times thirteen, one times fourteen, one times fifteen.

Cantlon: Could you say that again a little bit louder so we can hear you, please?

Jesserae: I went to one times fourteen, one times fifteen, one times sixteen. And that's how I ...

Cantlon: I guess I'm not understanding what you're saying.

Jesserae: Michael?

Michael: I have something ... I think I disagree ... Cause what about the zero?

Student: Zero? What about zero times zero?

Student: 'Cause you'd have to do zero times ...

Student: ... Anything times zero equals zero.

Student: Zero times one is equal to zero.

Student: ... We already have those ...

Cantlon: Does everybody understand the question that Michael's raising? He's saying that—he's reminding us of the conjecture from before that any number times zero is zero. And he's asking Jesserae to explain how in relationship up there on the table would work with that.

Chris S.: I sort of agree with Jesse too. I sort of agree with him and, and sort of ... Well, it *can* go—you can add the zero, and zero times one and ...

Student: 'Cept that's not what I said. I'm saying it starts at the one.

Students: ...

Student: I know but ...

Student: ... but that—how's that work?

Student: What would happen if you didn't know—what would happen if ...

Kyle: I kind of did it a different way. I, once I looked at it, it was going ten, eleven, twelve. And then I thought it was—I thought—I knew it was going odd, even, odd, even so I just put the thirteen, fourteen, fifteen, sixteen. That's how I got my answer.

Student: ...

Kyle: On the first three alone—odd, even. I thought that's how it goes through the whole thing.

Chris S.: … It's probably one of these should be zero and this should be eleven, twelve, thirteen, fourteen …

Amanda: Um, no, I didn't do mine—I just thought of a way that you could do it but I didn't do it that way. I u—I—you could use like the ten mainly. Like ten plus zero is ten. Ten plus one is eleven. Ten plus two is twelve. Ten plus four is fourteen and etcetera, etcetera.

Cantlon: So then you're thinking a relationship between those two numbers is you're *adding* ten to each one

Amanda: Actually adding … yeah.

Jake: I have a different way to do it. You could go like whatever number it is on the top you could put that number on the bottom. And you put a one on the left side.

Cantlon: Isn't that kind of what Michael was saying earlier?

Jake: Hm, hm. I was adding on the number.

Cantlon: You were adding, you were … any more?

Keegan: I, um— how I did it. If you were um, doing like— okay. If you were doing like ten and it would get … Here they put ten, eleven, twelve and how I thought I could get it a different number but you couldn't— it wouldn't like, go very good with it. Like it wouldn't go ah, try putting fourteen there. It wouldn't go with the ten. Like—

Cantlon: Are you saying that the 14 doesn't fit the pattern?

Keegan: No, I mean like if you would leave ten, eleven, twelve and I put a 14 and a 13 there then it wouldn't really match the pattern—er, it will … match the pattern because if you were to know that there was a one …

Student: I don't get it.

Keegan: What do you don't get about it?

Student: You said it wouldn't match the pattern.

Keegan: No, I said if I put—see, if I put … if I put, like—if you put—[she starts writing 0,1,2 on the overhead transparency] wait …

Cantlon: Laure— er, Keegan, uh is this a different table that you're creating or are you talking about the same one?

Keegan: Yeah, … The same.

Cantlon: Can you work from the table so that we can look at it then? Alright?

Keegan: Wait. What I was going to say—if you put, if you put this like right here. If you put the, the thir—if you put 14 here [points to where the 13 currently is on the chart], it wouldn't really match the pattern.

Cantlon: But the 14 is not there, it's 13.

Student: Yeah—

Keegan: I know but …

Student: —that's what I'm worried about.

Keegan: If I put the 14 there than it wouldn't …

Student: Are you talking about Jake's? What he said?

Keegan: … it's about how I figured the pattern out. How I figured it out. If I put, okay—you had 10, 11, 12. And I put that down under that … and I was thinking for a second—and I was saying well, if I put—well, if I put one number, like, if I put—see I put 14 here and 13 there than it wouldn't match like how it could go one, two, three. It would go one, two, four, three.

Cantlon: So, Keegan, you're saying this was your strategy to *check* to make sure that your pattern was making sense to you?
[PAUSE]

m	0	1	2	3	4	5	6
n	0	1	4	7	10	13	16

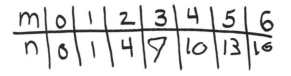

Cantlon: Sam, could you take care of that please?

Kyle: Chris?

Chris S.: Um, …

Cantlon: Wait, before you ask questions, can you explain what you've done? So we can understand your thinking?

Kyle: Okay, what I did was I—since there was zero, one, and four. I um, took the one and the four and I counted from the one up to four and that gave me—I had count up three so I just went on and um, and did the rest of 'em counting, counting up three.

Kyle: Chris?

Chris S.: I got um, a question.

Kyle: Okay.

Chris S.: Um, I did the same way but—it's like going up three and it's like the same thing except they're like all odd numbers except for two.

Cantlon: They're all odd numbers except for what, Chris?

Chris S.: Two.

Cantlon: Cameron has his hand up

Kyle: Okay, Cameron?

Cameron: Um, I know that like, um two and two is four, um; four, four and three is seven; and four and four is eight and …

Victoria: But there's not eight up there.

Cameron: I know.

Student: This is *m* and *n*.

Student: … doesn't matter what …

Cantlon: Think Cameron's saying that instead of ten he got an eight?

Cameron: Yeah.

Kyle: … three, I thought there's four, ten, and sixteen. It's kind of like in the first, middle, and last

Chris S.: And I see another pattern. One, um—it goes even, odd, … Zero's even, one is odd …

[Several students comment at once about zero]

Victoria: Zero is even because if you divide it in half, both people get nothing,

Kyle: Keegan?

Keegan: Um, I have something to say. I don't get you quite clearly 'cause you added one and you added four. If you add one—

Kyle: I didn't add both of them. I said I took the three—I took one and I counted two, three, four …

Cantlon: There's a—Billy and Michael also had a question about your numbers that you filled in with your table.

Michael: We did it a little bit differently. Um, we did zero, one—we did zero times zero is zero. One times one is one. Two times two is four. Three times three is nine. Four times four is … Four times four is 16. Five times five is 25. Six times six is 36 and seven times seven, 49.

Victoria: Michael, I disagree with you because seven and ten equals three and one and four equals three. One and—one and four in between equals three. And seven and ten in between …

Amanda: …

Victoria: Never mind.

Student: … you can only write three more …

Kyle: Sam.

Samantha: The thing I—my question is—it's—part of the … I disagree because zero—if you put zero plus and then you plus it three it wouldn't equal one. It would be zero, one, …

Kyle: But that's the way it went and then from one on it just went up three.

Students: Yeah.

Cantlon: Is it important to be able to use any of the numbers along the top and do the exact same thing to the number along the bottom? Have you been doing that all along? So Samantha's raising a question. There seems to be a discrepancy in what Kyle is showing up there saying with the lower numbers that what he's saying doesn't work for those.

Kyle: Victoria?

Victoria: Uh, but if you did—if you were counting by fours then you wouldn't have a one in it. If you were counting by fours they'd only be going zero, four, eight.

Kyle: I wasn't counting by four.

Victoria: I know I was talking to Michael about that and counting be threes you have a one in there so aft—so that—you start off with zero or you could—or you could go like this.

Cantlon: Michael … Michael, though, Victoria he wasn't saying you were just multiplying by four. Maybe you couldn't hear the first part of what he said since he was speaking kind of softly? Would you like him to repeat his idea? Michael, do you want to—Michael, why don't you come up and write what you have so they can look at it. That might make it easier to see.

Michael: I think it goes, um—I think it goes—I think this should be a, a nine. A nine. This should—

Cantlon: Could you just write down below so we can look at it all the way across?
Michael: Okay. Zero … [Michael seems to be thinking about how to write it on the overhead transparency] I don't know if I can write this.
Student: … the other side of the board.
Students: He's left-handed
Billy: I'll do it. I'll write it. [Billy comes up to the front]

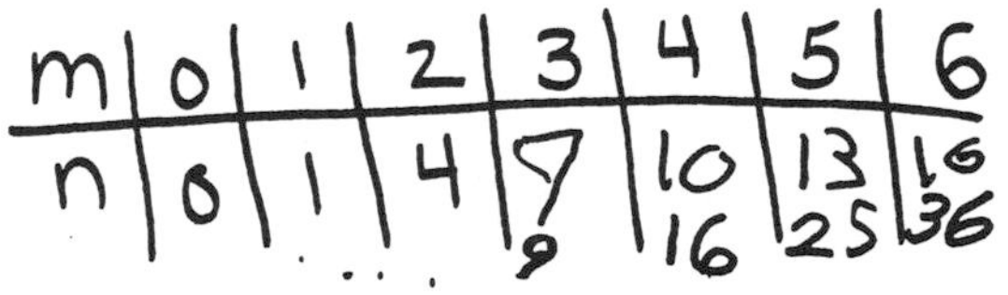

Michael: …Um, we think it was this since it—we can't—and because I wasn't talking about the fours. If you were counting up by threes you'd go zero, three, six.
Cantlon: Michael, can you go or Billy—one of you go up and explain what the relationship is between the two so people have an idea what it is you're referring to?
Michael: If it was counting by threes like the, the second one was counting by four it would be going zero, three, six, nine.
Victoria: Yeah, but Michael, when you're counting with threes, you don't always have to start out with three. Three can be in th—just …
Cantlon: Michael, can you explain the way you've written the numbers, what's the relationship between the two?
Michael: It's, it's just kind of like you—usually you would have to start out with um, zero then to go three. But—
Victoria: Yeah but you can still count by threes with other numbers.
Michael: If you counted by threes, you go zero, three, six.
Victoria: I know but—
Michael: One is … for three, seven …
Cantlon: Michael. Michael. Michael!
Michael: Hm?
Cantlon: What's the relationship between the zero and the zero? What did you do? What did you think about? What is that?
Michael: Zero times zero is zero.
Cantlon: What about the next one. One times what is one?
Michael: One times one is one.
Cantlon: And the next one.
Michael: Two times two is 4. And three times three is 9. And four times four is 16. [Several students comment at once]
Victoria: Yeah, but see we didn't do that on all the other ones. We, we took the top number and multiplied it by *one* number.
Michael: May I use this to show her?
Cantlon: Sure.
Michael: This is counting by fours. Right? It goes zero, four, eight.

Student: …

Michael: No, I'm not talking—look, okay, if it was talking about threes, it would kind of go zero, three, …

Student: Yeah, but it always starts out zero, one …

Student: I know what you're talking about in this one but …

Kyle: I think it could be both ways.

Michael: It can be both ways. There could be more than one answer to a problem.

Keegan: I disagree with both of them because—see, with this one, right here. See, what I did … because if you, if you did—

Cantlon: Shh! Concentrate on Keegan, please.

Keegan: … but if I did threes—if I did three plus three equals six, that … and four plus four is eight …

Michael: That's what I tried once, but it didn't work. It wouldn't work. Watch. Look, it wouldn't have worked. Zero and zero is zero, right? But one and one is two. Not one.

Keegan: Well, you could— well, I mean even though you have— you have …

Michael: Zero and zero is zero. One and one is two.

Students: And two and two is four …

Victoria: So your pattern doesn't work.
[Several students talk at once]

Keegan: What, what I was saying is even if—well, if we didn't use from here.

Amanda: Yeah but that is there so it don't matter.

Keegan: I know, but if we didn't use like right here like—if we didn't use for, like, right here.

Michael: That wouldn't work. That's not going to happen.

Keegan: I know but, but if—if,

Michael: It's not.

Keegan: It would be two plus two is four, three plus three is six.

Student: Keegan, I don't know why you're thinking that because it's …

Cantlon: Michael. It has to have all that Michael's saying in the chart. I think this is a good opportunity for us to stop right now with your talk and this is what I'd like you to do. I think this will help me understand what each one of you is thinking about these tables. On the first three. Could you sit down, Kyle so we can … On the first three tables I'd like you to create like we did the other day when we were talking about … an algebraic number sentence for this chart. Cameron, are you, are you looking up here so you know what to do? One for this one—algebraic number sentence. And the third one for this third table. You all understand these aren't together. These are three separate number sentences that you're going to be creating. Do you have any questions about what I'm asking you to do? I'm asking you to look at the relationship between these numbers on these different tables. Like we did this with the cookies, and the time.

Student: Ah, how many do we put?

Cantlon: Well, you have—I'd like you to do one number sentence for here, one number sentence for here, and the third one for that.

Student Do we have to finish before lunch?

Cantlon Ah, I'd like you to work on it for a little bit.

Cameron

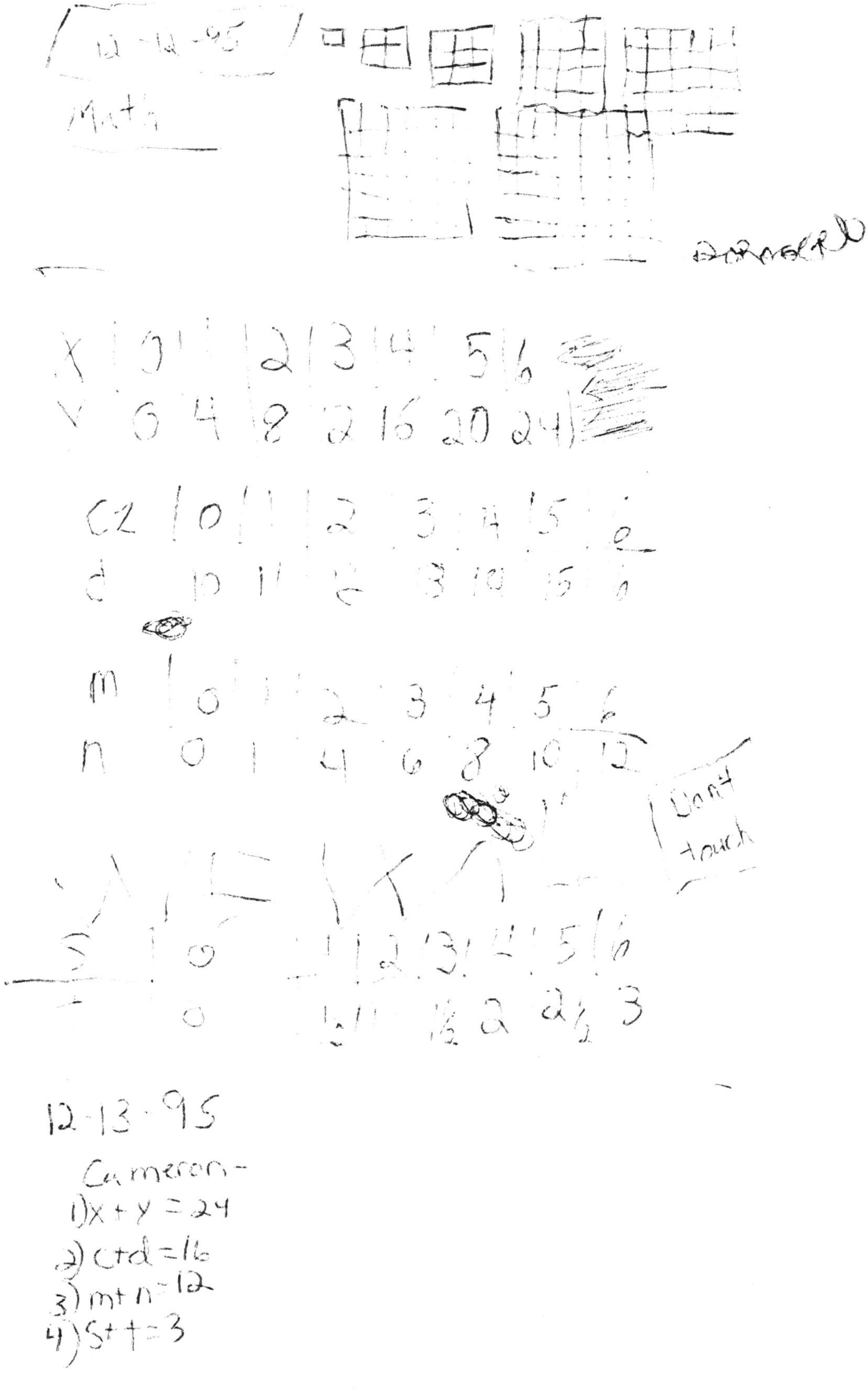
12-12-95
Math
x | 0 1 2 3 4 5 6
y 0 4 8 12 16 20 24
c | 0 1 2 3 4 5 6
m | 0 1 2 3 4 5 6
n 0 1 4 6 8 10 12
Don't touch
s | 0 1 2 3 4 5 6
t 0 1/2 1 1 1/2 2 2 1/2 3
12-13-95
Cameron-
1) x + y = 24
2) c + d = 16
3) m + n = 12
4) s + t = 3

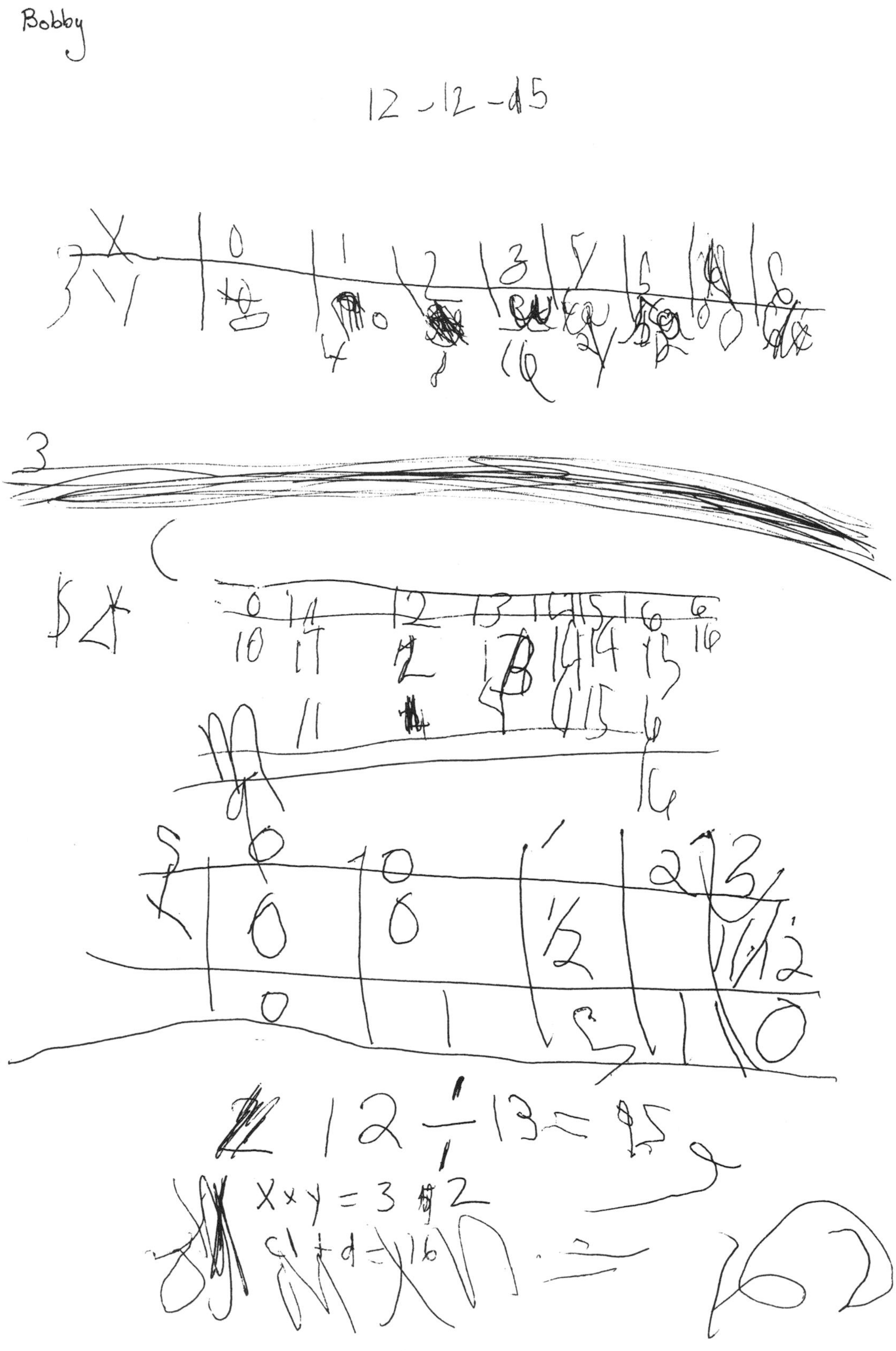

Lauren

12 13 14 15

x	0	1	2	3	4	5	6
y	0	4	8	12	16	20	24

C	0	1	2	3	4	5	6
D	10	11	12	13	14	15	16

B	0	1	2	3	4	5	6
b	0	[illegible]	4	6	8	10	12

d	0	1	2	3	4	5	6
t	0	1/2	1	2	3	4	5

✓ 1¼

12 – 18

x = 4

x4 = y

x9 = #

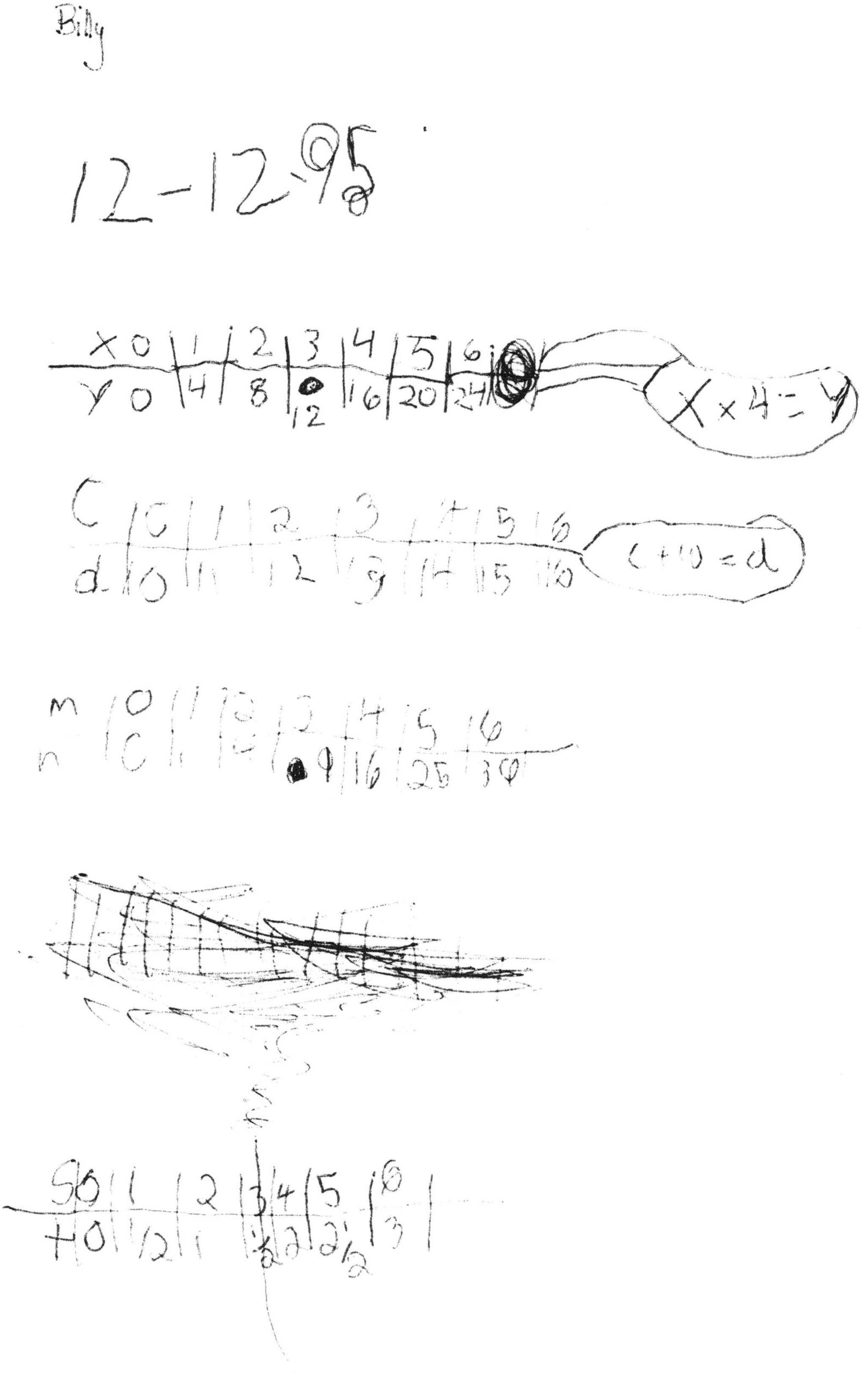
Billy
12-12-95
X × 4 = Y
c+10 = d

Keegan

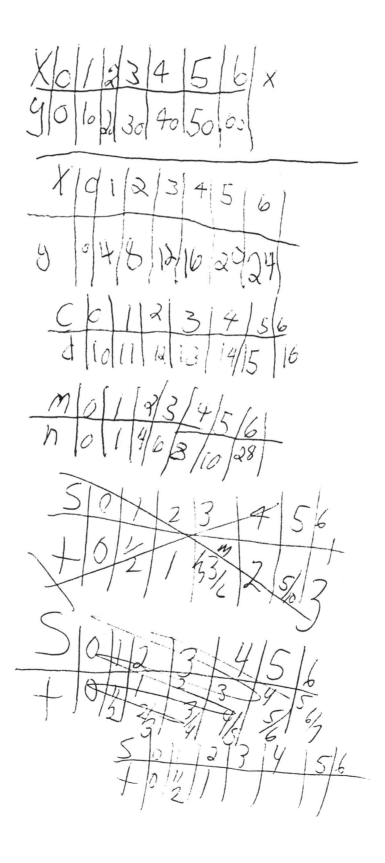

X	0	1	2	3	4	5	6	x
y	0	10	20	30	40	50	60	

X	0	1	2	3	4	5	6
y	0	4	8	12	16	20	24

c	0	1	2	3	4	5	6
d	10	11	12	13	14	15	16

m	0	1	2	3	4	5	6
n	0	1	4	6	8	10	28

s	0	1	2	3	4	5	6
t	0	1/2	1	3 3/2	2	5/10	3

s	0	1	2	3	4	5	6
t	0	1/2	1, 2/3	2, 3/4	3, 4/5	4, 5/6	5, 6/7

s	0	1	2	3	4	5	6
t	0	1/2	1				

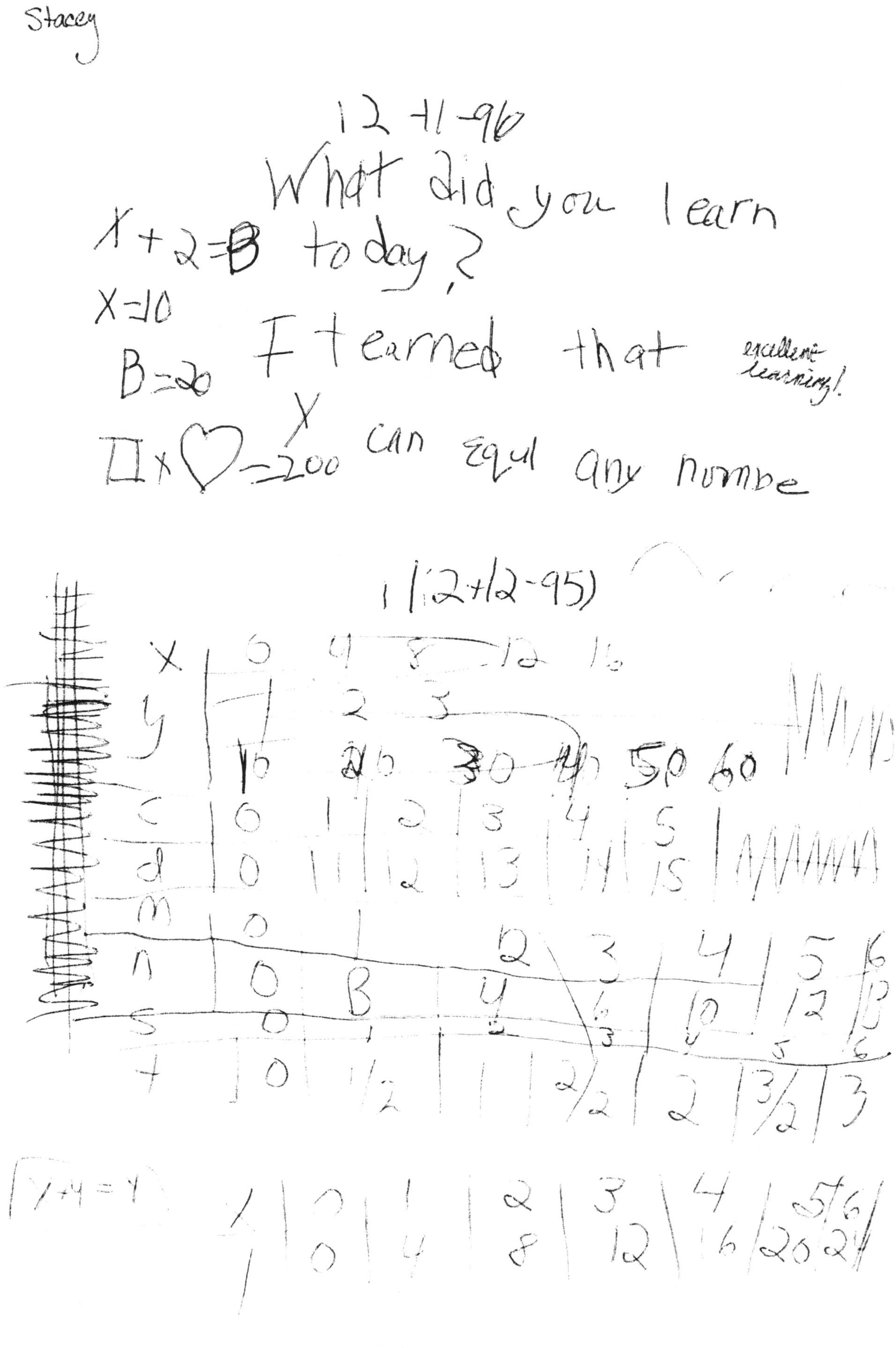
Stacey
12-11-96
What did you learn today?
I learned that
x can equl any numbe
excellent learning!
x + 2 = B
x = 10
B = 20
□ x ♡ = 200
1-12-12-95
y + 4 = y

Michael

Write an algebra
X = students

x	0	1	2	3	4	5	6
y	0	4	8	12	16	20	24

4x

c	0	1	2	3	4	5	6	7	8	9
d	10	11	12	13	14	15	16	17	18	19

1t

m	①	1	2	3	4	5	6
n	0	1	2	3	4	5	6

s	0	1	2	3	4	5	6
t	0	1/2	1	1 1/2	2	2 1/2	3

X/Y

✓

x	0	1	2	3	4	5	6	7
y	0	4	8	12	16	20	24	28

✓

c	0	1	2	3	4	5	6
d	**10**	11	12	13	14	15	16

✓

m	0	1	2	3	4	5	6	7
n	0	1	4	9	16	~~10~~ 25	~~12~~ 36	~~14~~ 49

s	0	1	2	3	4	5	6
t	0	1 1/2	1	1 1/2	2	2 1/2	3

12-18-95 12/18/95 12-18-95 #
12/18/95 December, 18. 1995

Stacy

x	1	2	3	4	5	6	7	8	9	10
y	4	8	9	16	20	24				

X = munuts
Y = cookies

X × 4 = Y

x = any number
y = 45 multiples

c + 10 = d

Clint

12-12-95

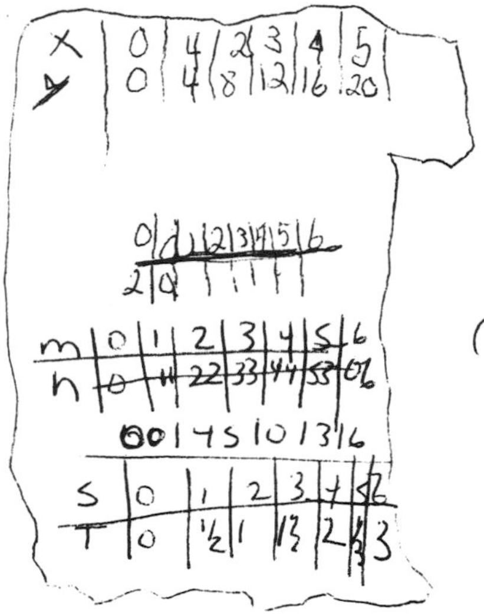

$x \times y = 18$

$c \times d = 11$

$m \times n = 4$

① The frist one goes by 8.

2 goes ~~ee~~ by 1

~~3~~

12-13-95

① The realashonsipp with all them have ~~ones in them.~~

② All of them have the same number in each row. examed the frist row.

Victoria

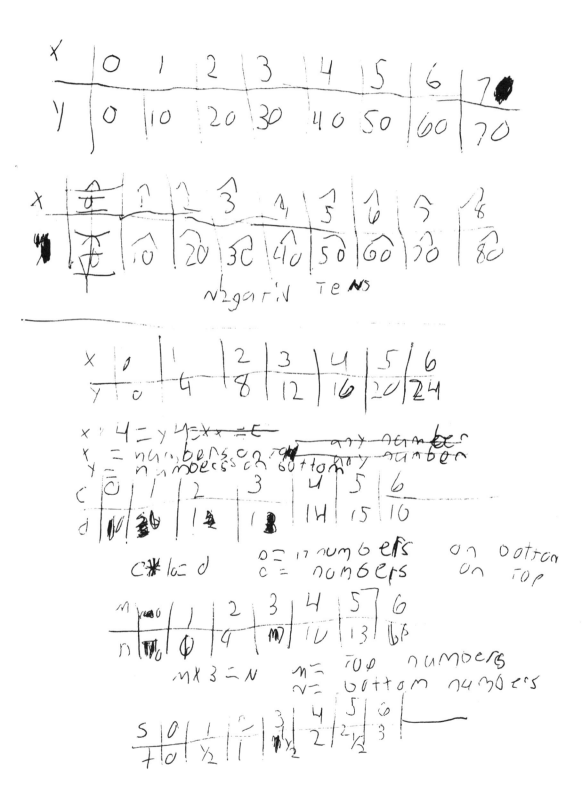

x	0	1	2	3	4	5	6	7
y	0	10	20	30	40	50	60	70

x	0	1	2	3	4	5	6	7	8
[redacted]	0	10	20	30	40	50	60	70	80

n2gativ Tens

x	0	1	2	3	4	5	6
y	0	4	8	12	16	20	24

x × 4 = y ~~4 = x x = E~~ ~~any number~~
x = numbers on top ~~any number~~
y = numbers on bottom

c	0	1	2	3	4	5	6
d	[redacted]	[redacted]	1[redacted]	1[redacted]	14	15	16

c + 10 = d d = numbers on bottom
c = numbers on top

m	0	1	2	3	4	5	6
n	[redacted]	ϕ	4	[redacted]	10	13	16

m × 3 = n m = top numbers
n = bottom numbers

s	0	1	2	3	4	5	6
t	0	1/2	1	1 1/2	2	2 1/2	3

DISCUSSION QUESTIONS: STUDENTS' WRITTEN WORK ON TABLES

- Which aspects of the work are easier or harder for the student?
- If there are things the student has done incorrectly, is there are pattern to what she or he seems to be thinking and doing?
- Is there a pattern within a given table, is there a pattern across all the tables or a subgroup of tables?
- How does the student seem to be making sense of moving from the tables to constructing and algebraic number sentence? Can you generate more than on plausible interpretation? Which explanation seems most likely and why?

DISCUSSION QUESTIONS: LOOKING ACROSS THE UNIT

- What might be said about these young children's learning of algebraic ideas?
- What kinds of ideas or thinking seem to come easily to them and what is the evidence? What kinds of things less so?
- What are some of the subtle and not-so-subtle differences among the children's abilities to find patterns, generalize, and move toward algebraic representation?
- What are common things they do/think when given a certain kind of problem context?

2

ASSESSING THE POTENTIAL OF TASKS

The two cases in this chapter are constructed around classroom events in which the nature of the assessment activity is a key aspect of learning what students understand and using that information to make instructional decisions. As you read the cases, consider the following questions. They are intended to extend your thinking beyond the specifics of each case, to reflect on and reconsider your own classroom and assessment practices.

- What makes a good assessment task?
- How do I think about the strengths and limitations of any single assessment activity?
- How do the specific formal assessment activities that I create support the learning goals that I have for my students?
- How can I design a classroom-based assessment system that gives me information about multiple dimensions of student understanding?

CASE 4—Students' Knowledge of Linear Relationships as Represented in Concept Maps—is built around a particular assessment tool—concept maps. The case is unique in several respects. It presents a provocative way of doing pre-unit and post-unit assessments. And it contains data from 2 school years. The case invites an evaluation of concept-maps as an assessment tool. A key question raised is whether a concept map can be more than just a vocabulary list re-presented as a map. The data from the second year come from the use of an augmented concept map activity. The case provides the occasion to consider the value of this kind of task beyond demonstrating knowledge: its contribution to empowering students; its power to communicate students' accomplishments to interested others.

CASE 5—Geometric Construction: The Contributions of Context—presents students' written work on two distinct assessment events following a unit on geometric constructions. The first assessment was a traditional set of exercises that called upon students to reproduce compass and straightedge constructions. The second assessment was a real-world situation that involved some of the ideas about location of points that students had been studying. The case highlights problems associated with a traditional approach to teaching and learning about locus of points. It raises issues of what understanding entails in this domain, particularly whether proficiency at a technical skill level indicates a conceptual understanding of the mathematics embedded in construction tasks. The case illustrates a teacher, whose practice has been quite traditional, taking tentative but important first steps in helping his students develop a richer understanding of the mathematics of locating points.

Case 4: Students' Knowledge of Linear Relationships as Represented in Concept Maps

From the classroom of Marie Sahloff in collaboration with the Project Team

OVERVIEW

This case provides opportunities to

- *analyze students' written work*: examining students' concept maps of "analytic geometry" and "linear relationship," what the concept maps indicate about students' understanding, what counts as evidence of what students know and how they know it;
- *generate instructional options based on analysis of case materials*: analyzing concept maps for the purpose of deciding where to go next in instruction or assessment;
- *evaluate an assessment tool*: considering strengths and weaknesses of concept maps as a tool for assessment; redesigning and/or augmenting concept maps to give a richer, more detailed picture of students' understanding;
- *explore the potential of concept maps*: using concepts maps as a means for students to do self-assessment; as a means for empowering students; as a way to communicate students' mathematical accomplishments to others.

Mathematical Content: Functions and relations.

Materials: Pre- and postunit concept maps from 1993–1994. Pre- and postunit concept maps from 1994–1995.

Suggested Time: Minimum of 2.5 hours to investigate the case.

INTRODUCTION

The Role of Concept Maps in our Project

This case is built around a specific assessment strategy that proved extremely useful in our project. Our team of teachers, teacher educators, and graduate students worked in small groups to produce concept maps as a representation of a particular content domain to learn what each of us considered important for middle-grades youngsters to learn within that domain. A key resource for this work was a chapter entitled "Concept Mapping" in *Probing Understanding* (White & Gunstone, 1992). Following the guidance of these authors, we sought to show relations between ideas and objects with attention to the structure and the linkages among them.

The maps as objects were enlightening because they revealed interesting similarities and differences in our conceptions of a domain, what we identified as "big ideas," and what kinds of connections we made among the ideas. But even more valuable were the discussions we had as we constructed and shared the maps. We had intense conversations about what to include and what not to include and why. Often our discussions revealed ways in which we might be tied to outmoded ways of conceiving the domain (e.g., sets of isolated skills, decontextualized ideas and processes). We include two maps constructed early in our project from our exploration of handling data and statistics (Figs. C4.1 and C4.2).

Most of us found it extremely challenging to select words to write along connecting lines that adequately communicated how we saw linkages among ideas. We puzzled about how to include process dimensions—problem solving, reasoning, and communication. We sometimes seemed headed toward con-

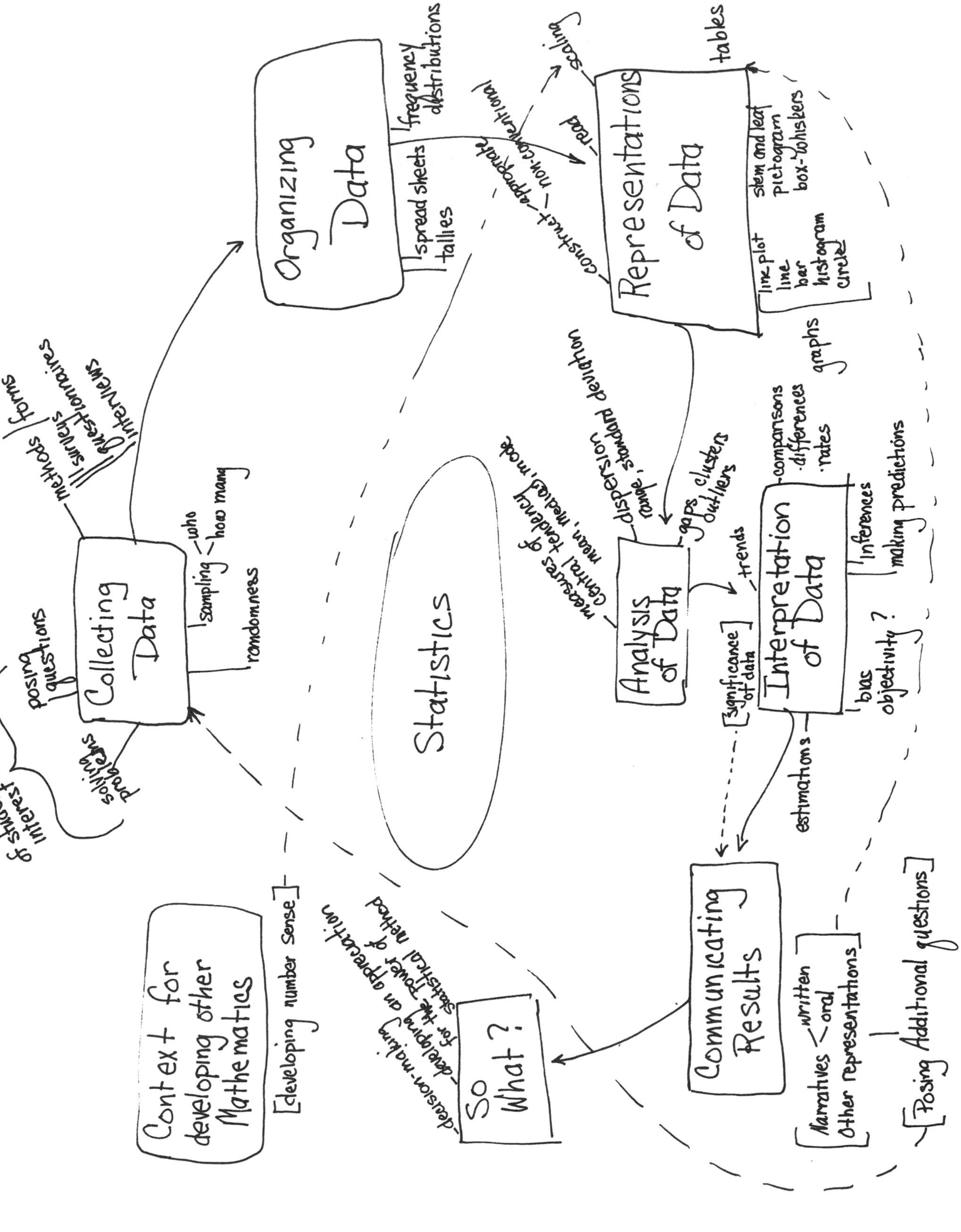

FIG. C4.1. Concept map.

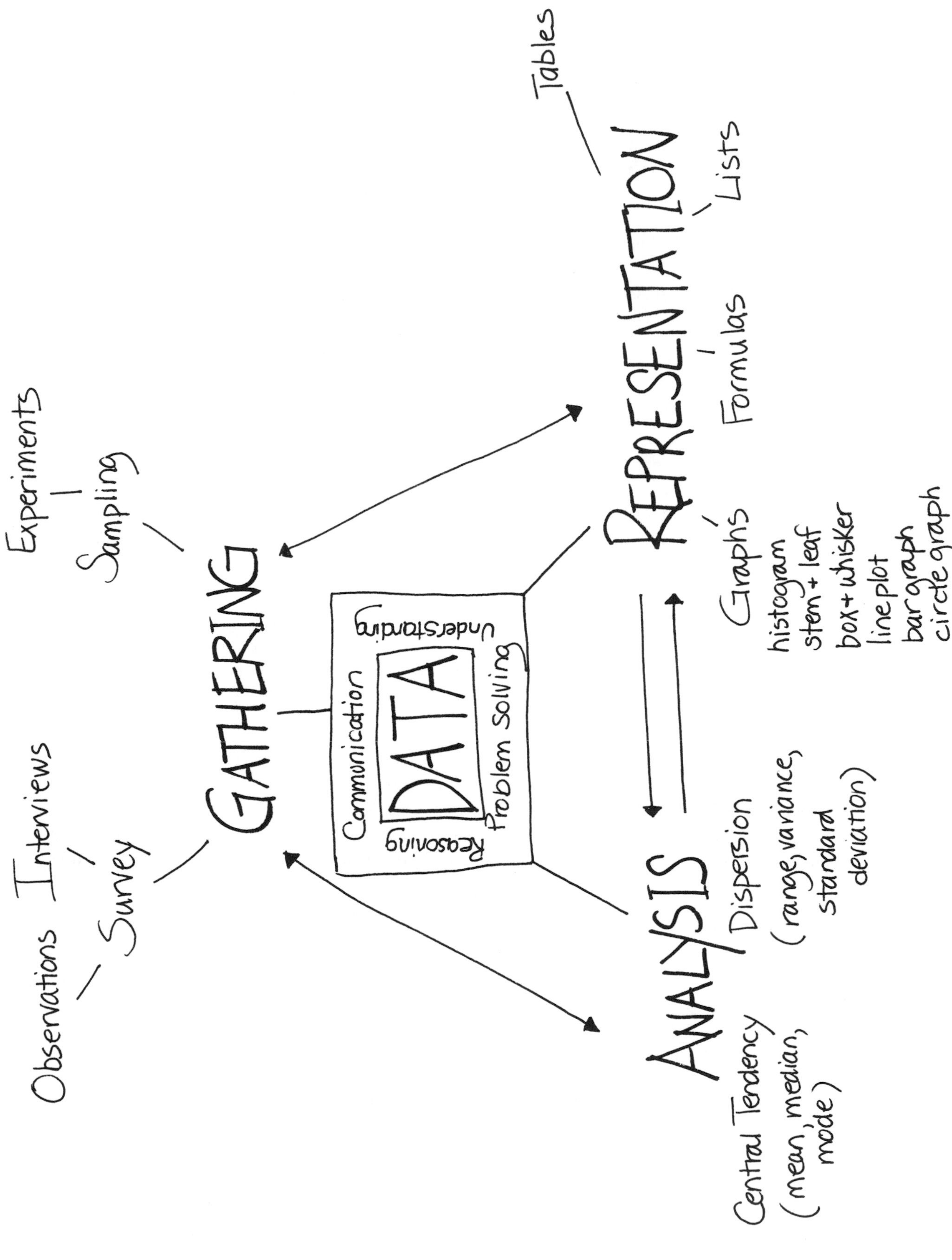

FIG. C4.2. Concept map.

structing something so complex, with multiple connections, that the maps obscured rather than clarified how we conceived the domain. The most important benefit was that the process helped us become clearer as a professional community about what we valued (and how that varied across the team), what we ought to value, and to think more consistently about connections—within and across domains, to other school subjects, and to the real-world lives of young adolescents.

The Role of Concept Maps in the Middle Grades Mathematics Classroom

White and Gunstone (1992) cited several purposes for using concept maps in the classroom (pp. 30–35). Concept maps provide a tool to

- explore understanding of a limited aspect of a topic;
- see whether students relate distinct topics;
- probe appreciation of which concepts are the key ones;
- identify relations that students perceive between concepts;
- promote discussion.

They argued that concept maps provide teachers with insights into what individual students have learned from a unit of instruction. This information can help them assess not only students' understanding but also the effectiveness of their own teaching.

> The way in which students conceive the structure of a topic tells much about the quality of their learning. A poor concept map coupled with reasonable performance on a test of detail suggests that this student's learning may be rote, and hence that the knowledge will soon be lost ... [T]he maps reveal the understanding present in the whole class, and hence tell much about the effectiveness of the teaching. If many omit a relation that the teacher saw as crucial, ... then the teacher has failed and must reconsider how to develop an understanding of this point (White & Gunstone, 1992, pp. 36–37).

As a result of our own use of concept maps within the project team, some teachers decided to try them as a way to learn about how their students conceived the important ideas in a domain and the connections they made after a unit of study. Marie Sahloff was the first to try this task in her classroom. She adopted a particular assessment strategy of having students construct a concept map at the beginning of a unit of instruction and then again at the end of the unit. Her instructions were simple: "Tell all you can about what you know about ... "

Introducing concept maps in the mathematics classroom. Sahloff's students brought some experiences with mapping from their language arts classes although their language arts textbook called it *clustering*. To introduce concept mapping in the mathematics class, Sahloff began with a non-mathematical idea. She asked students what they thought of when she said *house* and as they listed words, she wrote them as offshoots from her map where "house" was the center bubble. After students had generated a lengthy list, she asked them to look at the map and decide if there were some bigger categories that described several of the words. Students identified *rooms* as a larger category and so Sahloff began to construct a second map with "rooms" as a first level offshoot bubble and then specific rooms as second level offshoots from it. Students identified *people* as another big category and had words such as *mother* and *sister* as offshoots. After they had together constructed this second map, using all the terms on the first map, Sahloff moved on to a mathematical idea.

Sahloff wanted to work with a mathematical topic that she thought students would not find too difficult. The class had worked earlier on a unit on integers, so she asked them to list all the things they knew about integers. As they called out specific ideas, she constructed a map with *integers* as the center bubble. Again she made every word the students gave an offshoot of this single bubble. When she judged that students had pretty much exhausted all the terms they could think of, she had them look for bigger categories. Students noted that they had included "addition," "subtraction," "multiplication," and "division," and that these were *operations*. So Sahloff began a second map with "operations" as a first-level bubble with the specific operations as second-level offshoots. They continued with the process until they had reconstructed the ideas in the first map to show big categories of ideas within the domain of integers.

Sahloff's style of mapping had big ideas in circles or ovals, with lines connecting the bubbles to show that ideas or objects were linked in some way. Unlike the White and Dunstone approach to concept-mapping, Sahloff did not stress writing words or phrases along the connecting lines to describe the nature of the linkage.

In the case that follows, we have drawn from Sahloff's experiences over 2 years of using pre-unit and post-unit concept maps with units on functions and relations.

USING THE CASE MATERIALS

Levels of Working With the Materials

The richness of the data in this case provides the opportunity to pursue several levels of exploration. At one level, participants can have direct experience in analyzing students' written work. They can analyze the information contained in the concept maps, what the information suggests about students' understanding of the domain of functions and relations, and what counts as evidence of what they know and how they know it. From this analysis, participants can consider how this information might help a teacher decide where to go next in instruction.

At another level, participants can evaluate concept maps as a tool for assessment. What are their strengths and weaknesses? How can concept maps be redesigned or augmented to give a richer, more detailed picture of students' understanding?

At yet another level, participants can explore the potential of concept maps as a means for students to do self-assessment and the ways this might contribute to empowering students as learners of mathematics. They can also explore the potential of concept maps to communicate students' mathematical accomplishments to interested others.

Because of the richness of the data and the fact that they were collected in two school years, we suggest that the conversation with participants be structured in three parts. In the first part, we suggest a careful analysis of the pre- and post-unit concept maps from 1993–1994. Here the work with the materials focuses on analyzing the information contained in students' maps. As participants consider the maps, they are likely to raise issues about what they can not tell from the maps. This then becomes an occasion to consider how this assessment activity might be reshaped or augmented to provide additional kinds of information that would be useful to a teacher.

In the second part, we suggest a similar careful analysis of the pre- and post-unit concept maps from 1994–1995. In this instance, Sahloff had augmented the activity, drawing on our own analysis within the project team of the previous year's maps. She asked students to pick one part of their map that they felt pretty sure about and elaborate on all they knew about that piece. And she asked them to select a part of their map that they were struggling with and to write about that. Participants can consider what this contributes to the teacher who wants to use this assessment activity to think about and plan ne xt instructional moves.

In the third part, participants move from the analysis of students' written work to consider the potential power of concept maps in three respects: as a tool for student self-assessment, as a means of empowering students and as a way to communicate students' mathematical accomplishments to others.

Activity 1: The Concept Maps of 1993–1994

You might want to begin by describing this as a case that centers on a particular assessment strategy—concept maps. Inquire of the group whether any have used concept maps. Some teachers may be more familiar with clustering, webbing, or webs, terms that are frequently used in language arts classes. You will need to distribute the following materials, one set to each participant.

- *Sahloff's description of using concept maps*. This is optional. You may decide simply to read Sahloff's description to the group.
- *1993–1994 pre- and postunit concept maps on analytic geometry*. There are maps for Greg, Katie, Toby, La'Keshia, and Jenny.
- *Discussion Questions for 1993–1994 Maps*

Read Sahloff's description of her classroom setting and how the concept map task was introduced to her grade 8 students in November, 1993.

> This was not the first concept map that my students had done. They had previously done one on integers and one on statistics. Therefore, we didn't have to go into detail about what a concept map was and what they were expected to do. But this was the first time I asked them to make a map before we studied the topic. Prior to starting the topic, in this case analytic geometry, I assigned the concept map as a "pre-test." I gave them the term "analytic geometry" and asked them to tell me anything they knew about it. The concept maps with the November, 1993, date are the students' original maps. They show what the students thought about analytic geometry before starting the unit. They had already learned that there were no right answers and so if they put down something that did not apply, it would not count against them.
>
> I collected their pre-unit maps and then we worked on a unit on analytic geometry. I used a variety of materials including the textbook and some problem solving materials that I have. We made extensive use of the graphing calculator. Approximately 5 weeks later, we had completed the unit. As a "post-test" I had them construct a concept map on the reverse side of the one they had done several weeks earlier. The directions were the same as before.
>
> There were a couple of neat things about having the original and final maps back-to-back. First, the students were amused to see how little they were able to write on the topic in their first map. Second, it was extremely powerful to see that all of the students were able to write considerably more about the topic than they did initially. One student's comment was, "Boy, I've really come a long way in just a month."
>
> In doing their concept maps, students were not allowed to use their notes, the textbook, or any other materials. They had to rely on their knowledge and understanding of analytic geometry from the class discussions and assignments.
>
> This was not the only assessment that was done for this unit. It was used more for their self-assessment and it was not graded. It also provided me the opportunity to make some inferences for myself, such as noticing similarities and differences between individual maps. I also looked for items that were consistently omitted or incorrectly included to help me reexamine my instruction. I used this information to plan future lessons.

Urge participants to use the first two discussion questions to examine closely the concept maps. These questions and the maps engage participants in a lively conversation about inferences they feel they can make about what students know—and what counts as evidence—and what they feel uncertain about. In our field trials of this case, we found that some participants focused on what they *cannot* tell about student knowledge and understanding from the concept maps. You may want to emphasize that, initially, they consider what claims they can make about what students *do know*.

> What can you learn about a student's understanding of analytic geometry by looking at her or his concept map?
>
> What do you think these students understand about this topic and what counts as evidence of understanding?
>
> What does the comparison across students' maps reveal about differences and similarities in how they conceive the domain and what they seem to know about it?

After participants have had some time to examine the maps closely, they will likely express a desire to know more about student understanding than they can infer from the maps. You might then pose the additional two questions: In looking at an individual concept map, what more would you like to know about what the student knows and how the student is thinking about the topic? How might you augment this assessment task to learn more about students' understanding?

Typically, a range of interesting suggestions is offered about how a concept map might be enhanced by some additional activities. After you think participants have had sufficient time to consider the first set of maps, move on to the maps from 1994–1995.

Activity 2: The Concept Maps of 1994–1995

You will need to distribute the following materials, one set for each participant.

- *1994–1995 pre- and postunit augmented concept maps on linear relationships*. There are maps and written responses of Ryan, Sarah, Todd, and Eric.
- *Discussion Questions for 1994–1995 Concept Maps.*

As you distribute these maps, explain that the following year Sahloff added a new component to the concept map assessment.[6] This additional activity resulted from discussions within our project about how to learn more about what students thought they knew with confidence and with what they were struggling. Sahloff asked each student to elaborate in writing on one portion of their map:

- Select an idea on your map that you think you know a lot about and write all you know about that idea.
- Select an idea on your map that you think you don't know much about and tell why you think you are having trouble with that idea.

Have participants use the Discussion Questions for 1994–1995 Concept Maps as a lens for examining this set of augmented maps. What can you learn about a student's understanding of linear relationships by looking at her/his augmented concept map? What do you think these students know about this topic and what counts as evidence of understanding? What are you able to learn about students' understanding that the map alone does not reveal? How might a teacher use the analysis of the information in the maps and the written elaborations to decide where to go next in instruction?

Encourage participants to consider other forms of elaboration that would provide more information about what students are coming to know about this important part of the middle grades curriculum. For example, another way of constructing concept maps is to write on the lines that link different nodes or bubbles of the concept map to describe the relationship that connects these ideas or objects.

Some teachers might consider whether and how to adapt this self-assessment activity for students with special learning needs. In one field trial, a teacher who works with "learning disabled" youngsters thought he might need first to generate a list of some of the key ideas with his class and then ask them to arrange them in their own map, drawing linkages, and adding other ideas as they thought of them.

Activity 3: The Potential Power of Concept Maps

You will want to distribute the following materials, one set for each participant.

- *Discussion Questions: Potential Power of Mapping.*
- *Discussion Questions: Stepping Back.*

This seems to be an appropriate time to move outside the specific materials of this case to consider the potential of this assessment strategy to serve multiple purposes. The following questions are intended to frame a discussion about the potential of concept maps beyond eliciting what students know about a domain.

---

[6]In 1994–1995, Marie was field-testing curriculum units from the *Connected Mathematics Project*. The unit for this case was the draft unit, Walking a Straight Line, (Lappan et al., 1994), an investigation into linear relationships. Many of the ideas were similar to ones she taught the previous year in the analytic geometry unit.

To what extent can the use of concept maps serve as a means for students to do self-assessment?

Does mapping—and the intellectual demands required—become part of the curriculum?

In what ways can using self-assessment serve to empower students?

What can concept maps communicate to interested others about student's mathematical accomplishments that more traditional forms of reporting fail to capture?

Finally, ask participants to step back for a moment and consider a more general query. Why would a teacher want to engage in deep analysis of students' written work on concept maps? How might this kind of deep analysis and conversation among a group of professionals contribute to enhancing teaching and learning in mathematics classrooms?

BEYOND THE CASE

Several in our project used concept maps following Sahloff's experience. Cindy Simon had her grade 8 students make a post-unit map at the conclusion of an extensive unit on geometry. She brought the maps to a project meeting and as we examined them closely, Cindy noted that not one student had included "Pythagorean theorem" on his map. She was quite puzzled because she thought they had spent quite a bit of time on the idea. We suggested that she return the maps to her students, noting this absence, and ask them to add it to their maps where they thought it was most appropriate. Cindy did return the maps and she added a further task. She asked the students to write why they had not included Pythagorean theorem on their initial map. Whereas a few students wrote that they just forgot, most wrote that they really had not understood the theorem. Quite simply, it was not yet a meaningful concept for them.

Participants can be encouraged to try this strategy with an upcoming unit. They might consider other ways to augment concept maps. Some may want to experiement with having students write along the connecting lines to describe more explicitly the nature of the connections.

The editors of this volume have used concept maps in a number of professional development settings as an initial activity to learn what ideas participants have about assessment. Recently we had teachers at the first meeting of a graduate course on alternative assessment in mathematics construct a map of how they conceived assessment. Teachers pinned their maps on the wall and we discussed similarities and differences across the maps.

In our conversation, we noted that common entries tended to link assessment to goals and objectives, and to types and uses of assessment. Only one teacher made explicit reference to teaching or teachers, linking assessment to the "evaluation" of "teachers, methodology, and curriculum." There was no evidence in either the maps or in our discussion of them that the teachers were thinking about how assessment might be used to help them make instructional decisions. John, a high-school science-department chair and sometimes mathematics teacher, had an interesting insight during our conversation. He said that even though he might use different forms of assessment (e.g., group projects, demonstrations, and presentations), he was using them in just the same way he used traditional tests. That seemed to bother him. He thought that alternative assessments should contribute something else but he wasn't sure what or how. John's initial map is presented here (Fig. C4.3).

At the end of the 3-week course, we asked each teacher to construct a second concept map as a representation of how they were now thinking about assessment. Three things were prominent in the end-of-course maps that had been absent in the initial ones. First was the matter of evidence for making claims about student learning. The maps showed an awareness of the need to gather information about student learning in multiple ways, not just relying predominantly on students' written work. The second was about when to assess. The teachers had come to see the value of using assessment as an ongoing activity, not just as an end-of-unit evaluation. The third was about how to use assessment. The maps provided evidence that teachers were beginning to make linkages between teaching and assessment and that a good instructional task is also a good assessment task. John's end-of-course map is presented here (Fig. C4.4).

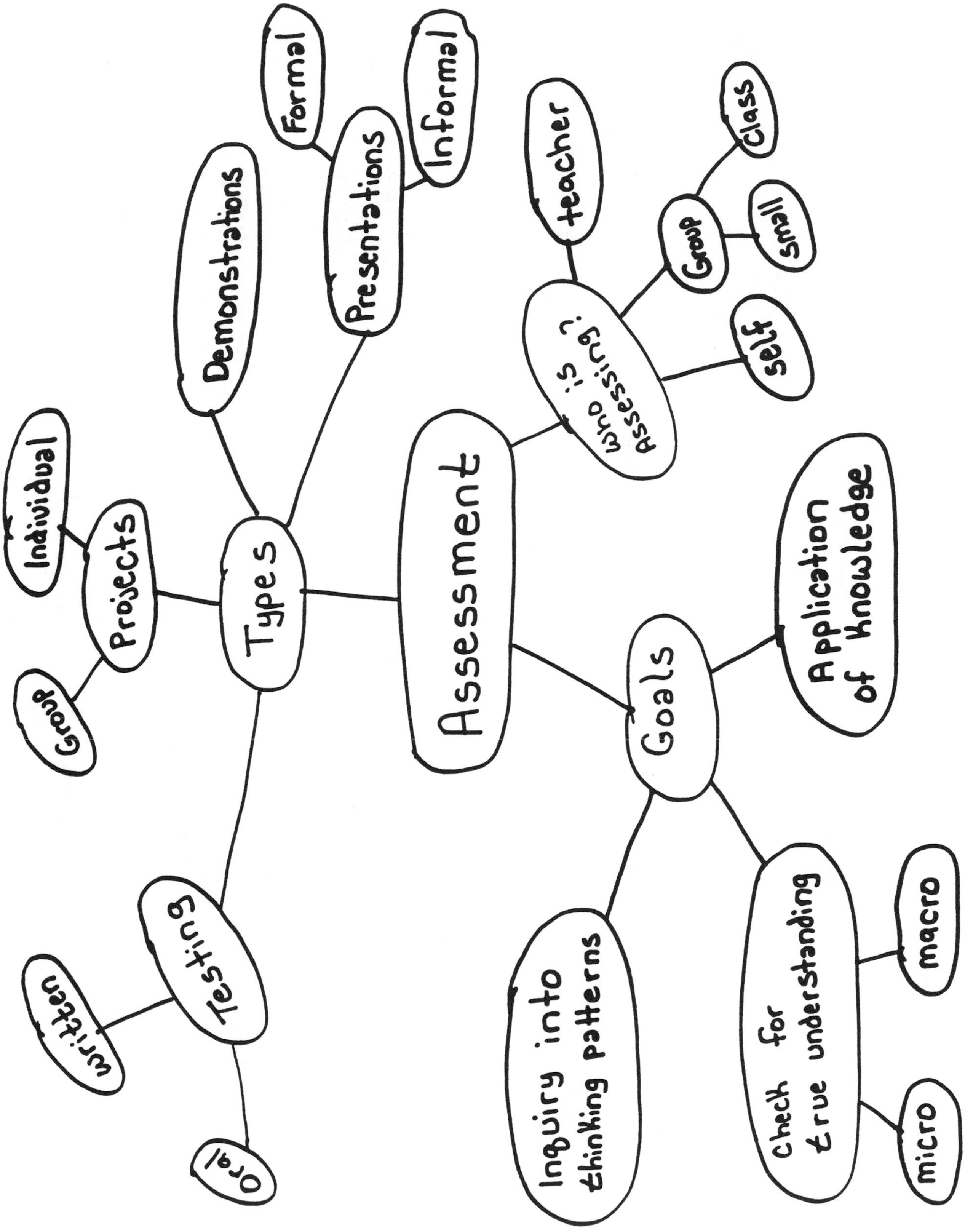

FIG. C4.3. John's initial concept map.

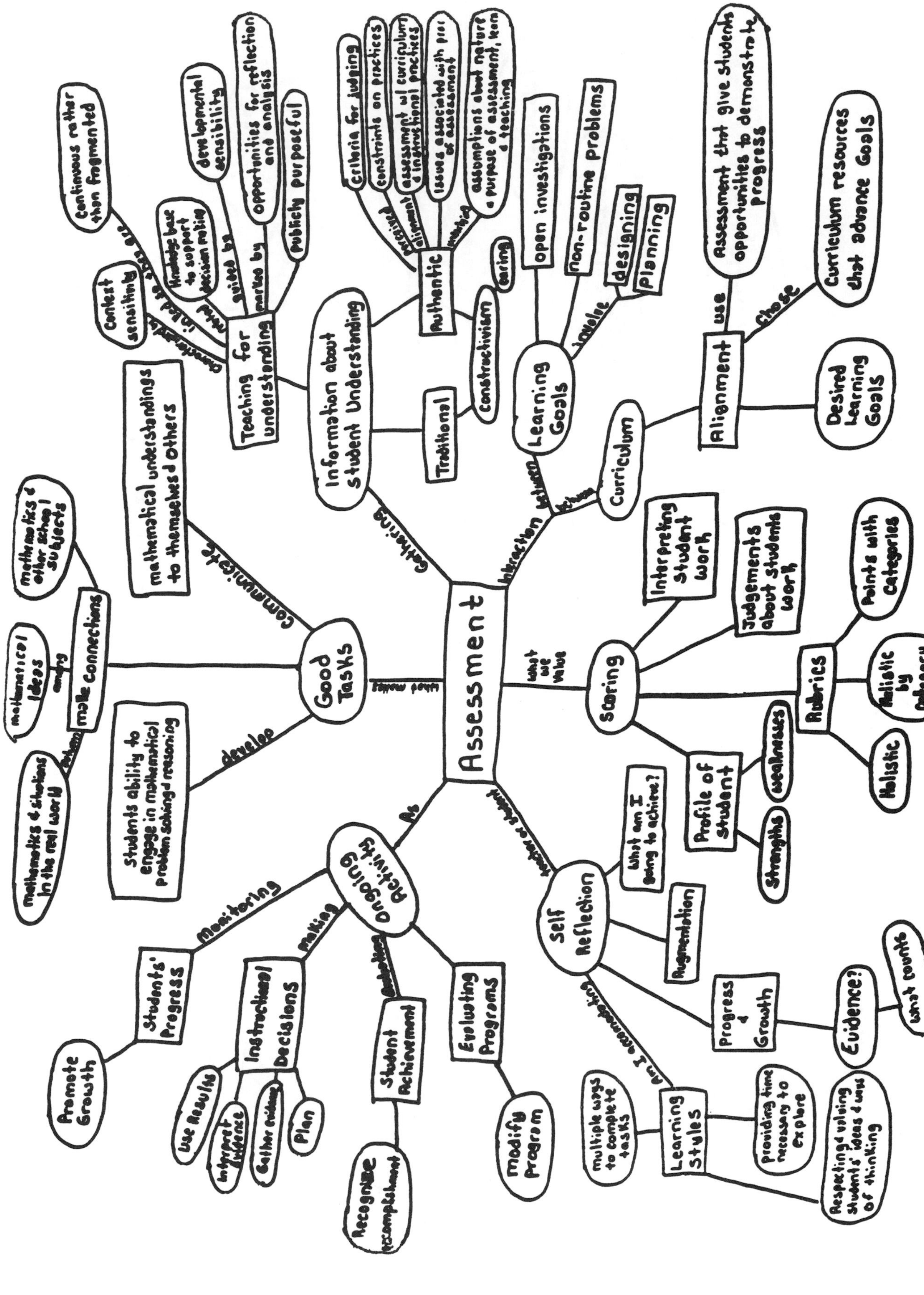

FIG. C4.4. John's after-course concept map.

In every instance where we have used concept maps, the act of making the representation is only part of the experience. The activity is enriched by the conversation the maps generate, by the questions that get raised about what is and is not included, about the meaning of linking various elements on the map. And as an initial activity, it provides us with important early assessment information about current conceptions of the domain.

DELIBERATIONS WITHIN THE PROJECT

Analysis of Students' 1993–1994 Maps: Making Sense of What Students Understand

It is common for educators to be skeptical of what student-constructed concept maps actually reveal about students understanding of a mathematical topic. Some think that what students produce is nothing more than a vocabulary list. The focus is often on what the maps do not tell When Sahloff presented the first set of maps at a project meeting in early 1994, we first looked at students' written work, trying to make inferences about their understanding from what they included on their maps. There was a tendency on the part of some of us initially to focus on what was not on the maps or the limitations of what any particular entry revealed. We decided to examine the 1993–1994 post-unit maps by drawing inferences about what we thought students *did* understand and what we could point to as evidence of that understanding. We looked carefully at individual papers and we looked across the papers as a whole.

The pre-unit maps were meager. We could not be sure what this meant. One plausible interpretation was that this content was new, students knew little about it, and wrote things that they associated with geometry. But one of our team members wondered if students might not know more than the maps revealed but were not familiar with the term *analytic geometry*.

As we examined the post-unit maps, we were intrigued by how students made linkages—what they included in their bubbles, how they connected bubbles on their maps. We noted interesting similarities across the maps. Every map presented a hierarchy of ideas, terms, or concepts. Of the first level terms, three were common across all the maps; equations or systems of equations, variation, and grids. At the next level, there were further similarities. Equations branched into terms about degree, standard forms, and details about linear equations, particularly slope. Branches from systems included references to what equations and graphs would look like and the number of possible solutions. Variation was linked to direct and inverse and in some instances students included text about what distinguishes these two in terms of relationships among variables or the general form of a symbolic expression. The maps presented their knowledge of some mathematical conventions—dividing the Cartesian plane into four quadrants, labeling the axes, using coordinates to describe a point in the plane.

There were also notable differences. Greg's map included some terms with reasonable links but we thought it looked a lot like a vocabulary list simply re-presented as a map. Some of the links were questionable. For example, from "systems of equations," he had a running link from "parallel" to "intersect" to "# of solutions" to "y-intercept." We wondered whether Greg thought of these ideas as hierarchically ordered. We noted that none of the second-level terms was connected to another at that level. For example, *systems of equations* was not linked to *equations*. And we puzzled about what his entry "$x + y$" was intended to represent.

Katie's post-unit map contained considerably more detail than Greg's. Katie organized her presentation about systems of equations into a matrix, revealing the elements she understood as distinguishing different systems of linear equations (e.g., the graph, slope of the lines, the y-intercept, and the number of solutions). Whereas Greg had listed "direct" and "inverx" [sic] as linked to "variation," Katie went further in her map to describe both direct and inverse variations by giving the general equation and a written description of each situation and what the graph of each would look like.

Toby's map also included not just terms but some further elaboration (e.g., "Linear: when graphed it forms a line"; "Line of best fit is line that connects coordinates on a graphic [sometimes all coordinates won't be connected]"). Unlike Greg, Toby had multiple linkages at the same level. For example, he had a loop from analytic geometry to equations, to slope, to graphing, and back to analytic geometry.

Although Sahloff had not stressed writing along the linking lines, Jenny and La'Keshia did make an attempt to do so. It looked like they were trying to elaborate on or give an example of a term within a bubble, something Toby had done but with a different method. That additional information helped us see that Jenny appeared to be thinking that linear equations were functions but that nonlinear equations were not functions.

At the same time, we wanted to know more. We wondered about the depth of their understanding. What did students really understand about linear regression? What did students really understand about function? Could they provide examples of situations that involved direct and inverse variation? Did they have a sense of where any of the ideas on their map apply in the real world? What use could they make of any of these ideas? How did they see and how would they describe the nature of the connections between bubbles that they linked?

Evaluating an Assessment Tool: Augmenting Concept Maps

We considered a number of ways to enhance the power of the maps to reveal student understanding: taking a piece of the map and writing about it; providing some examples of where a particular idea is used or situations that give rise to particular kinds of relationships; using words to give a language for linking the bubbles on the map.

From our conversation, Sahloff developed the idea of extending the task by asking the students two questions after they completed their post-unit maps:

- Select an idea on your map that you think you know a lot about and write all you know about that idea.
- Select an idea on your map that you think you don't know much about and tell why you think you are having trouble with that idea.

When Sahloff taught a similar unit the following year, she incorporated this into the concept map assessment.

Analysis of Students' 1994–1995 Maps: Making Sense of What Students Understand

What caught our attention as we first looked at these maps was students' use of drawings as well as words on their maps, something that was not common on the maps the previous year. Sahloff thought that the curriculum she used the second year had encouraged drawing more so than previous materials. We also thought the additional question Sahloff posed may have prompted students to use drawings as a further elaboration of an idea they felt they understood.

Ideas that appeared across most maps as a bubble directly connected to "linear relationships" were *equation*, *table*, *graph*, *expressions*, and *slope*. *Variables* appeared on most maps, sometimes as a first-level bubble, sometimes as a second level bubble. For example, Sarah had "variable" branching from "tables," and from "equations." The idea of "two lines" appeared across many maps, sometimes as a first-level bubble (see Todd and Eric), sometimes as a branch from another idea (see Sarah's branch from "graphs"). We found evidence to feel confident that most students understood the relationship between the numerical value of the slope of a line and its direction when graphed on the coordinate grid (although we noted that Ryan had written $y = 6x$ for a horizontal line).

The written responses to the two additional questions that Sahloff posed were particularly interesting. Nearly every student wrote about graphs or slope or both as ideas they thought they knew a lot about. Ryan used a considerable amount of symbolic language, drawing a coordinate grid, using a table to generate sets of points for two equations he had chosen (one with a positive slope, the other with a negative slope), graphing the points on his grid, then using the graphical representation to point out certain features (e.g., slope, y-intercept, coordinate pairs, point of intersection of the two lines). Sarah used natural language almost exclusively to write about aspects of graphs of linear functions and how graphing can allow for comparison of different equations.

Todd and Eric wrote about the slope of an individual line as an idea they thought they knew a lot about. We noted that in their written elaborations, neither connected their thinking about the slope of an individual line to their thinking about systems of two lines. We went back to their maps and found where Todd had represented the three possible relationships between the slopes of two lines and their graphs. Eric's map showed some relationships ("same slope" connected to "parallel lines") but he did not comment on the relationships between the slopes of two lines that intersect in a single point.

More than half the students indicated they were struggling with expressions and manipulating variables in expressions. The unit Sahloff had been using introduced students to solving systems of equations algebraically. But it was a brief detour, largely unconnected to the considerable graphing work on which they had spent much of their investigations. Students appeared to be reasonably sure about using tables and graphs to find the intersection of linear equations, but they were struggling to make sense of what Sarah called the "symbolic method." Ryan too wrote that "I can't do the equation solvings." Another student (whose map we have not included with the case) wrote: "The variables would be the part I don't know that much about because I know it has to do with the letters that represent numbers, equations, and $mx + b$. I don't know that much about it because I don 't understand what else has to do with it."

Todd wrote that he knew the least about expressions. Yet a look at his map showed he had written a number of things about expressions (e.g., "like terms," "monomials" with "$5x$" connecting it to "expressions"). We wondered why he judged that he didn't know much about expressions. One speculation was that everything else on his map was in some way connected to graphing and the part on "expressions" looked like a self-contained, disconnected piece on his map. So it seemed reasonable that if he couldn't connect it to one of the big ideas in the unit—graphing—then he thought he didn't have a good grip on understanding expressions.

Working with signed numbers also appeared to be a problem area for a number of students. Ryan wrote that he had trouble adding and subtracting integers. Another students (whose map we have not included with the case) wrote: "I don't know very much about integers. I get the number line but not adding and subtracting them."

There was one thing noticeably absent from the maps across the class. Students did not give examples of real situations that can be modeled by linear relationships. This was a surprise, in part, because much of the work students had done in the unit involved real-world contexts. We puzzled about what might account for their not giving any examples of where these ideas apply in real-world situations.

Using Assessment in the Service of Instruction

The set of maps constructed by students in 1994–1995 provided enormously useful information for Sahloff as she considered where to go next in instruction. The maps coupled with the responses to the two questions disclosed important data about what students knew, how they knew it, how they applied it, and of what they were unsure.

It seemed that in the weeks to come, students needed to revisit some of the key ideas from this unit, to build on the fragile knowledge they had about expressions, variables, and integers. They appeared to have a pretty sound understanding of graphing linear relationships. They knew that the point where two lines intersected gave them a coordinate pair that worked in both equations. It seemed reasonable that Sahloff could build on that understanding to help students make connections between the graphs and the symbolic statements, particularly how to represent symbolically the situation at the point of intersection. For example, consider the two equations $y = 2x + 1$ and $y = x + 3$. Students could find the point (2,5) where these two lines intersect by graphing and generating a table of coordinate pairs. Sahloff could help them describe this point as the place where $2x + 1$ and $x + 3$ have the same value, and that can be found algebraically by solving $2x + 1 = x + 3$. But Sahloff knew that she still faced the challenge of helping students make sense of various symbolic maneuvers, and they needed much time and many experiences to develop this procedural understanding and proficiency. And she realized that this was complicated by the fact that many of the students were struggling with making sense of operating on signed numbers.

The maps also provided an unexpected insight. In some cases, students furnished a personal reflection on their understandings and what contributed to different levels of knowing. Eric wrote, "I think I know the most about slope because I found this the most interesting and payed [sic] more attention;" and " think I don't know much about variables because I didn't take very good notes and didn't study enough." Sarah thought a reason she didn't understand expressions was that "I wasn't here for one of the days of explanation."

Assessing the Strengths and Limitations of Concept Maps

Any single mode of assessment and any single form of reporting students' accomplishments has its strengths and limitations. Concept maps alone cannot reveal to a teacher all that she or he would like to know about students' understandings. As we examined the maps closely from both years, we always wanted to know more than the maps alone could tell us. At the same time, we increasingly came to value this assessment tool for how it could show growth over time that other forms of assessment might not. Next we share our own assessment of the potential of concept maps and further ideas we have had about augmenting them.

Empowering Students Through Self-Assessment. Typically, most classroom assessment activity is controlled by the teacher. The teacher decides which problems to pose, which questions to ask, and what kinds of responses to accept. What a student is able to demonstrate about her/his learning over a unit of study is conditioned, in part, by the teacher's decisions about what to assess and how to assess it.

We were struck by the level of autonomy and control that resided with students in this assessment activity. It gave them control over the situation by inviting them to construct their own personal representation of what they knew and how they knew it. They decided how to show the connections that they had made among the various ideas within a domain. The maps gave a panorama, a sense of the whole as perceived by students. By augmenting the map with a set of questions about their level of understanding, students could communicate to their teacher what they were finding troublesome. We have a hunch that this kind of activity can contribute to empowering students. Sahloff reported that the students were quite amused when she returned their pre-unit maps. The two maps were a powerful visual representation to the students themselves of how much they had learned in the unit.

Communicating Students' Accomplishments to Others. Sahloff uses the concept maps at parent–teacher conferences. For parents who are typically provided with little but a grade, a record of attendance, and occasionally a piece of written work, the concept maps are a powerful document. Parents are struck by the differences in what students are able to include in their pre-unit and post-unit maps. They are amazed, in terms of sheer quantity, at the growth over several weeks. Sahloff reported that parents also noticed the degree to which a map seemed to have some kind of order, structure, or apparent organization. In one instance of what was judged to be a rather disorderly and disorganized map, the parents commented on how this was characteristic of other aspects of their child's behavior.

An area we have only begun to explore is developing nontrivial ways of describing the nature of the connections among items on a map. For example, how could we help Ryan, Sarah, Todd, and Eric figure out a way to describe the linkage between "linear relationships" and "slope." This is a very challenging aspect of concept mapping. As White and Gunstone (1992) remarked, "constructing involves intellectual effort" (p. 42). But helping students learn this more complex process could provide the teacher with an even wider lens into the ways in which they are making connections. This added dimension can be a strategy to push some students beyond producing a kind of map that is little more than a superficial listing of ideas remembered.

We think we have much more to learn about how to use this strategy as a way for students to show growth in understanding over time. We have only begun to capitalize on its potential to communicate a much richer picture of students' achievements in mathematics to interested others.

REFERENCES

Lappan, G., Fey, J., Friel, S., Phillips, E., & Fitzgerald, W. (1994). *Walking a straight line: Linear relationship* (Pilot Edition). E. Lansing: Michigan State University, The Connected Mathematics Project.
White, R., & Gunstone, R. (1992). *Probing understanding*. London: Falmer Press.

MATERIALS FOR MAKING PHOTOCOPIES AND TRANSPARENCIES

- 1993–1994 Concept Maps—Greg, Katie, Toby, LaKeshia, Jenny. Prepare one set for each participant; prepare a transparency of each map.
- Discussion Questions for 1993–1994 Concept Maps. Prepare one for each participant; prepare a transparency.
- 1994–1995 Concept Maps—Ryan, Sarah, Todd, Eric. Prepare one set for each participant; prepare a transparency of each map.
- Discussion Questions for 1994–1995 Concept Maps. Prepare one for each participant; prepare a transparency.
- Discussion Questions: Potential Power of Mapping. Prepare one for each participant; prepare a transparency.
- Discussion Questions: Stepping Back. Prepare one for each participant; prepare a transparency.

Greg

11-15-93

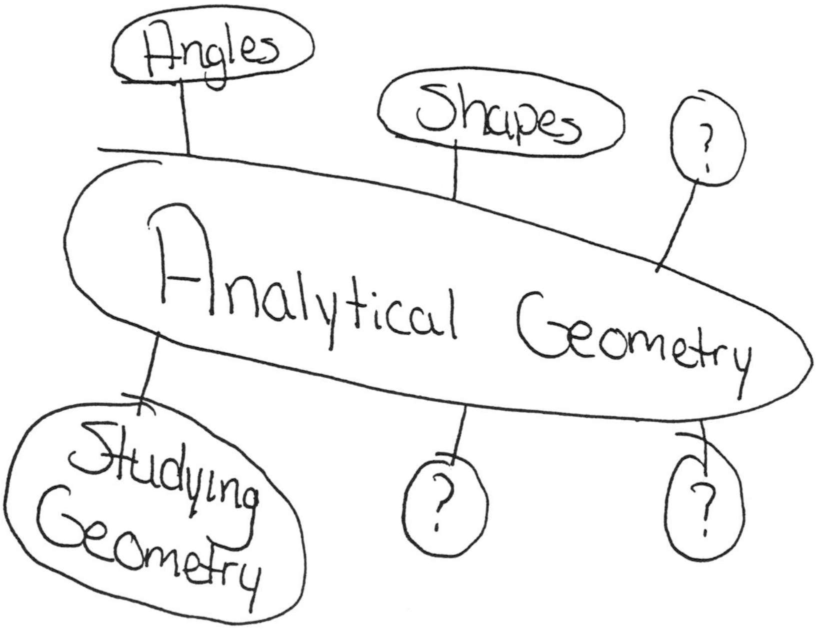

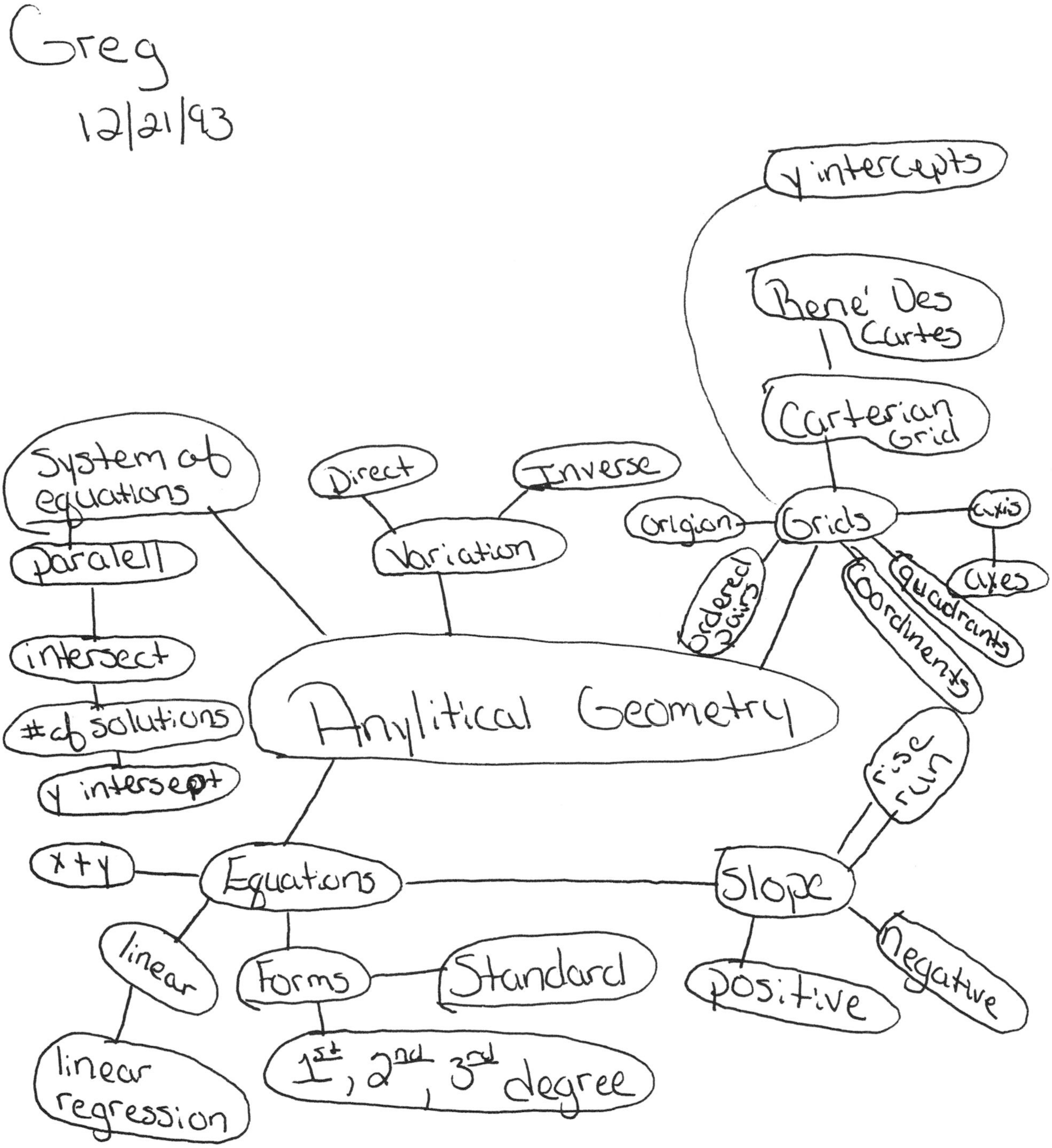
Greg
12/21/93
y intercepts
René Des Cartes
Carterian Grid
System of equations
Direct
Inverse
Origion
Grids
axis
axes
paralell
Variation
ordered pairs
quadrants
Coordinents
intersect
Anylitical Geometry
# of solutions
y intersept
rise run
x+y
Equations
Slope
linear
Forms
Standard
positive
Negative
linear regression
1st, 2nd, 3rd degree

11/15/93
Katie
Concept
Map

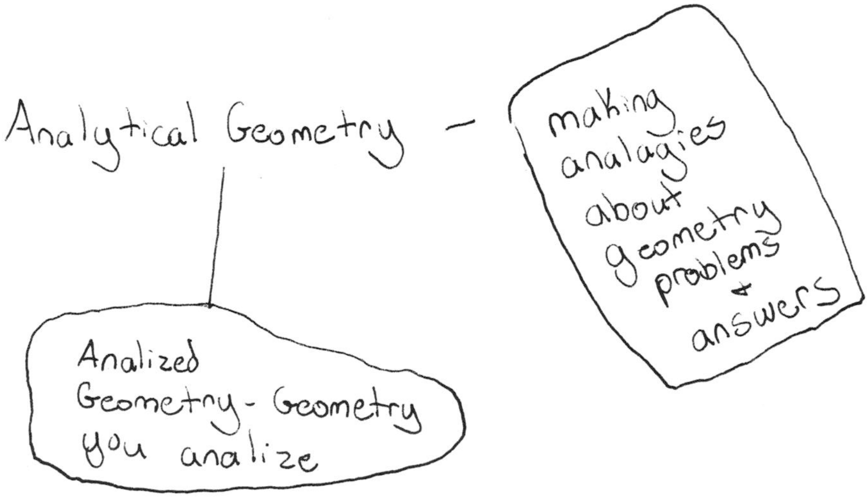
Analytical Geometry
making analagies about geometry problems + answers
Analized Geometry - Geometry you analize

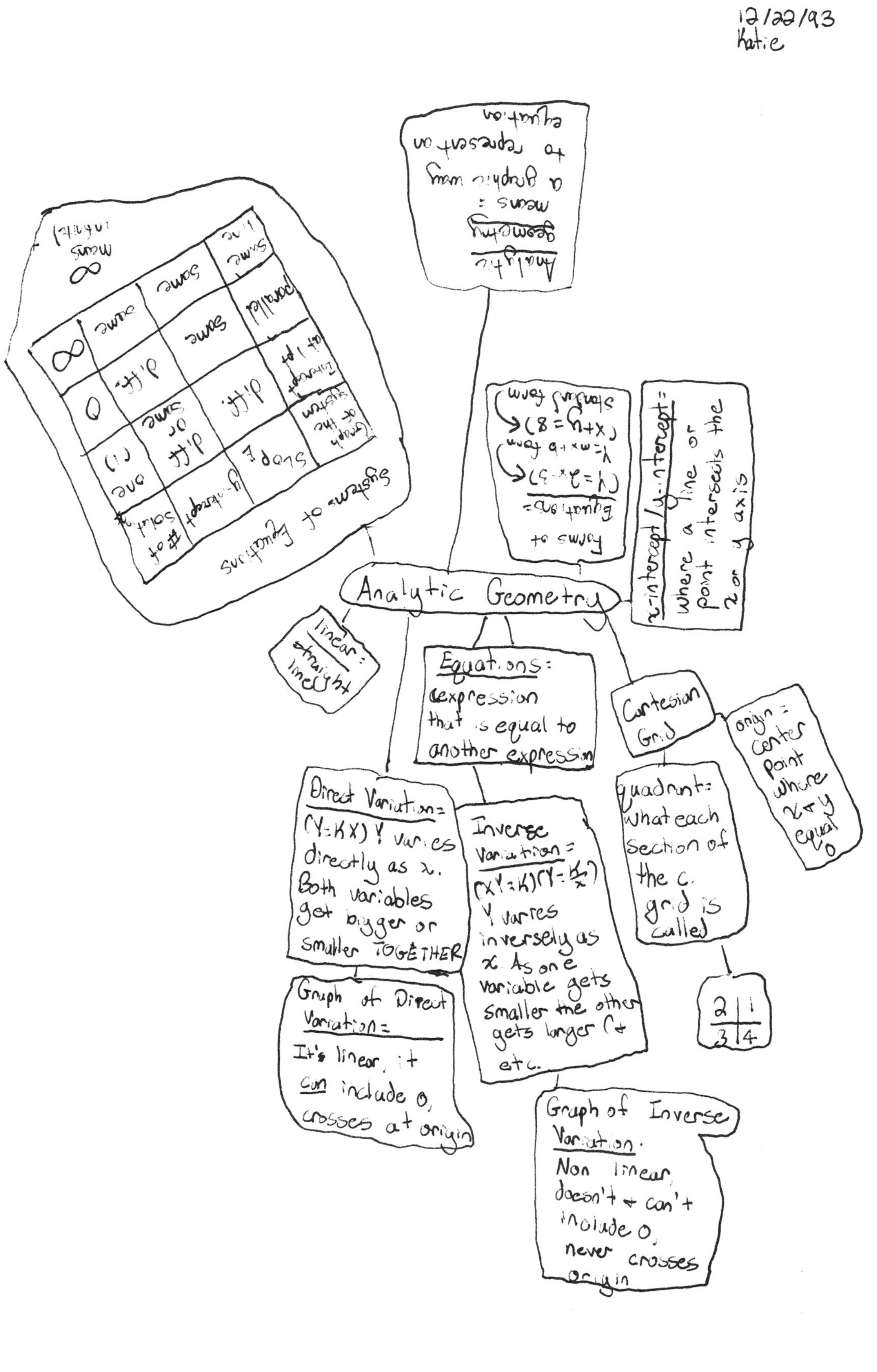
12/22/93
Katie
Analytic Geometry
Analytic geometry means = a graphic way to represent an equation
Forms of Equations:
(Y=2x-3) y=mx+b form
(x+y=8) standard form
x-intercept/y-intercept = where a line or point intersects the x or y axis
Systems of Equations
linear = straight line
Equations = expression that is equal to another expression
Cartesian Grid
origin = center point where x + y equal 0
Direct Variation = (Y=KX) Y varies directly as x. Both variables get bigger or smaller TOGETHER
Inverse Variation = (XY=K)(Y=K/x) Y varies inversely as x. As one variable gets smaller the other gets larger & etc.
quadrants = what each section of the c. grid is called
2 | 1
3 | 4
Graph of Direct Variation = It's linear, it can include 0, crosses at origin
Graph of Inverse Variation. Non linear, doesn't & can't include 0, never crosses origin

Toby
11/15/93

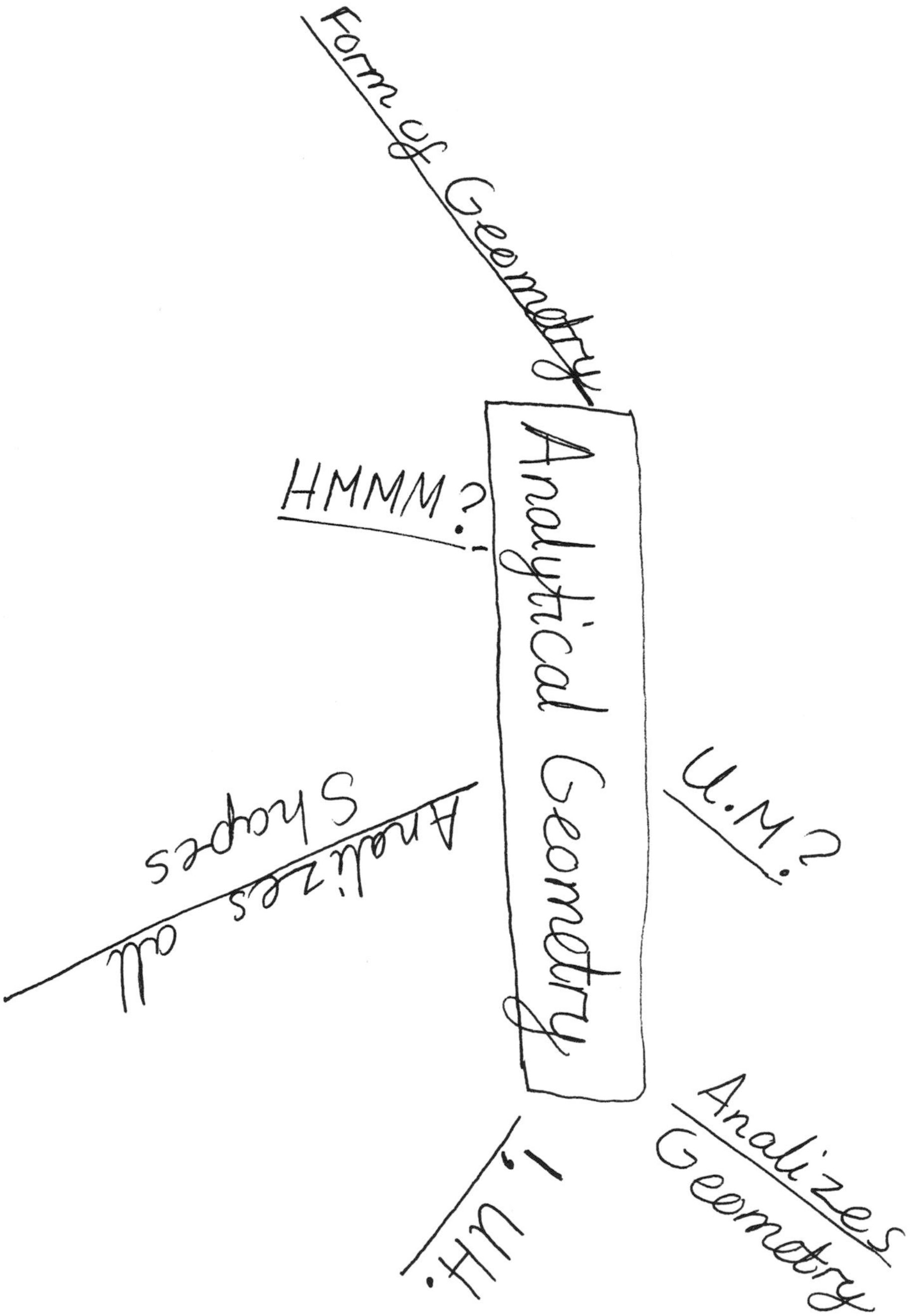
Analytical Geometry
Form of Geometry
HMMM?!
U.M.?
Analizes all Shapes
Analizes Geometry
!U.H.

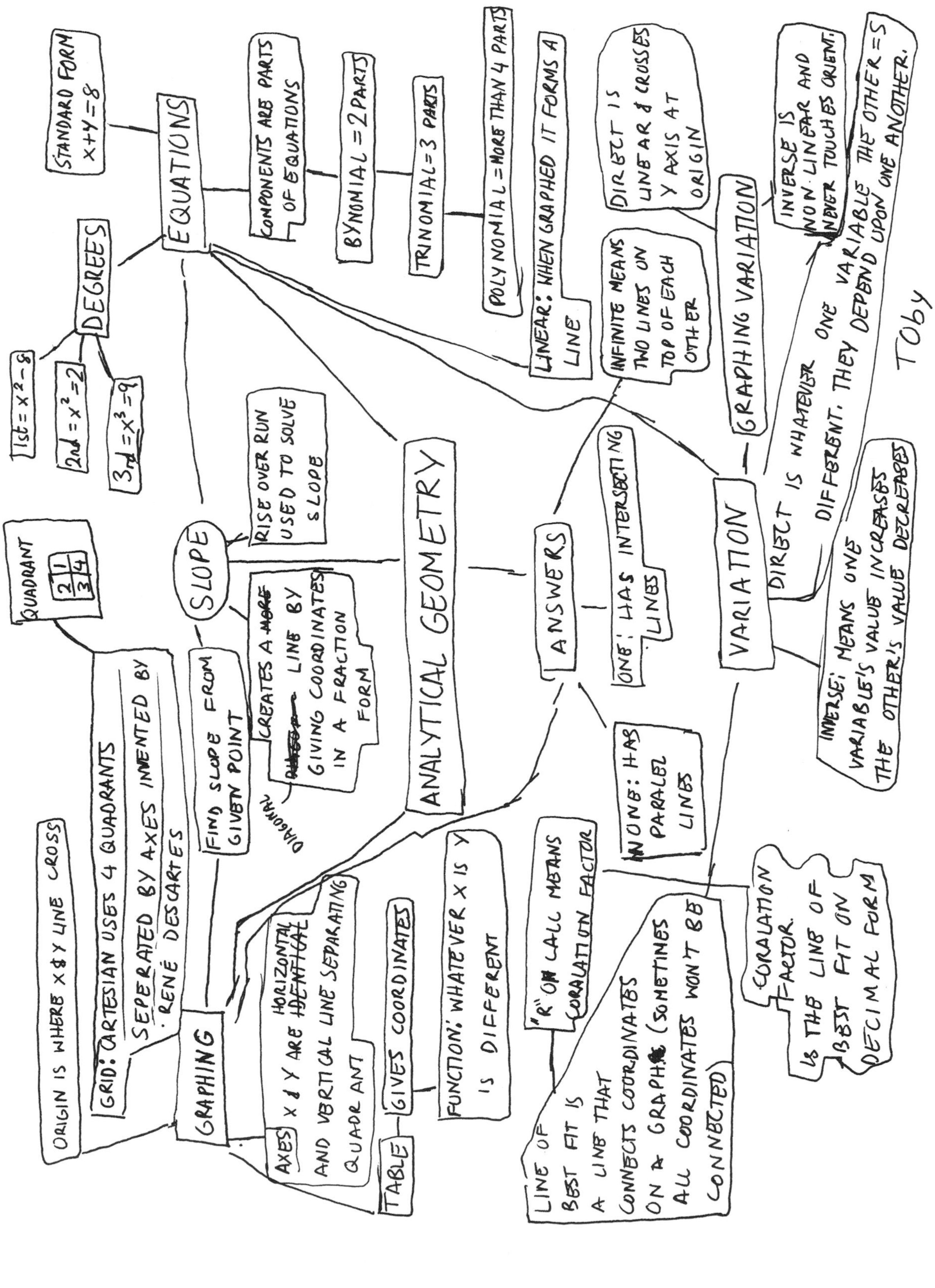
EQUATIONS
STANDARD FORM x+y=8
COMPONENTS ARE PARTS OF EQUATIONS
BYNOMIAL = 2 PARTS
TRINOMIAL = 3 PARTS
POLYNOMIAL = MORE THAN 4 PARTS
LINEAR: WHEN GRAPHED IT FORMS A LINE
DEGREES
1st = x^2 - 8
2nd = x^2 = 2
3rd = x^3 = 9
SLOPE
RISE OVER RUN USED TO SOLVE SLOPE
FIND SLOPE FROM GIVEN POINT
ANALYTICAL GEOMETRY
ANSWERS
ONE: HAS INTERSECTING LINES
NONE: HAS PARALEL LINES
INFINITE MEANS TWO LINES ON TOP OF EACH OTHER
VARIATION
GRAPHING VARIATION
DIRECT IS LINEAR & CROSSES Y AXIS AT ORIGIN
INVERSE IS NON-LINEAR AND NEVER TOUCHES ORIGIN.
INVERSE: MEANS ONE VARIABLE'S VALUE INCREASES THE OTHER'S VALUE DECREASES
QUADRANT
GRAPHING
ORIGIN IS WHERE X & Y LINE CROSS
GRID: CARTESIAN USES 4 QUADRANTS SEPERATED BY AXES INVENTED BY RENÉ DESCARTES
TABLE
GIVES COORDINATES
FUNCTION: WHATEVER X IS Y IS DIFFERENT
"R" OR CALL MEANS CORALATION FACTOR
CORALATION FACTOR IS THE LINE OF BEST FIT ON DECIMAL FORM
Toby

La'Kheshia

11-15-93

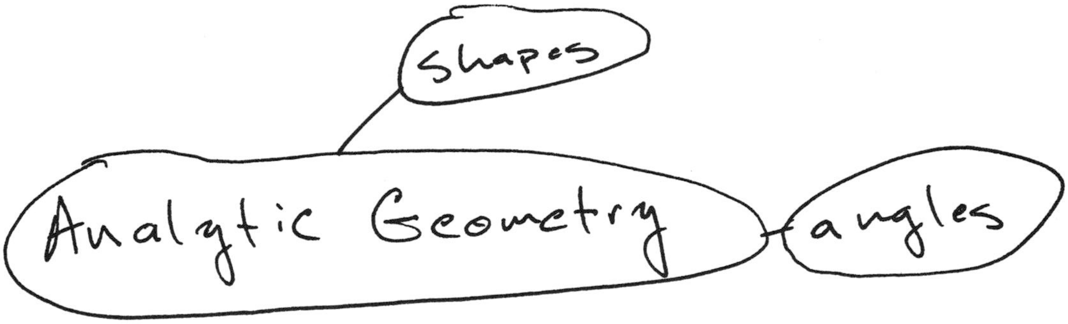

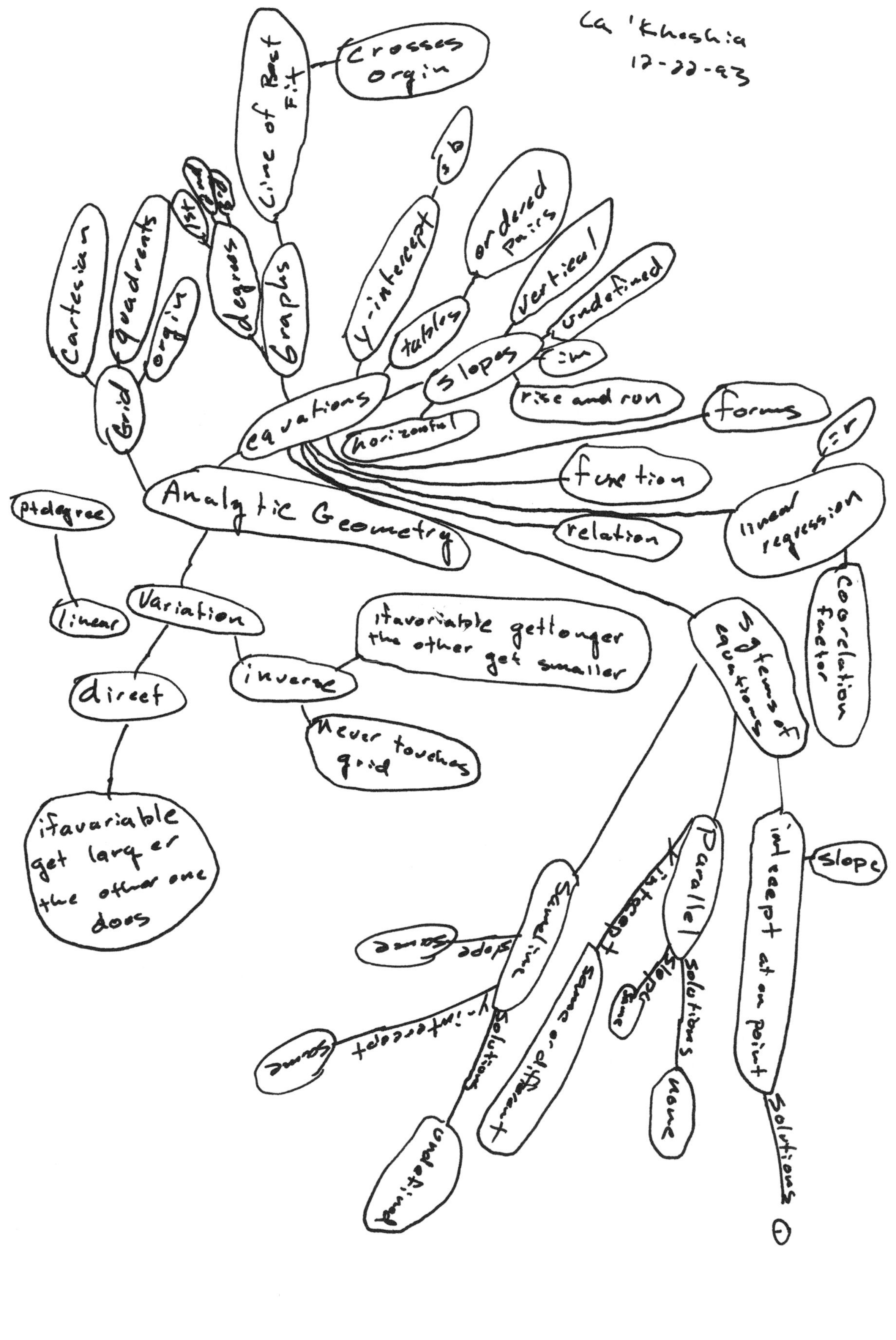
Ca'Khoshia
12-22-93
Crosses orgin
Line of Best Fit
y-intercept
ordered pairs
vertical
undefined
tables
slopes
rise and run
forms
equations
horizontal
function
Analytic Geometry
relation
linear regression
Coorelation factor
Grid
Cartesian
quadrents
orgin
degrees
Graphs
ptdegree
linear
Variation
inverse
direct
Never touches grid
Systems of equations
Parallel
Same line
intercept at on point
slope
Solutions
None

Nov. 15, 1993
Jenny

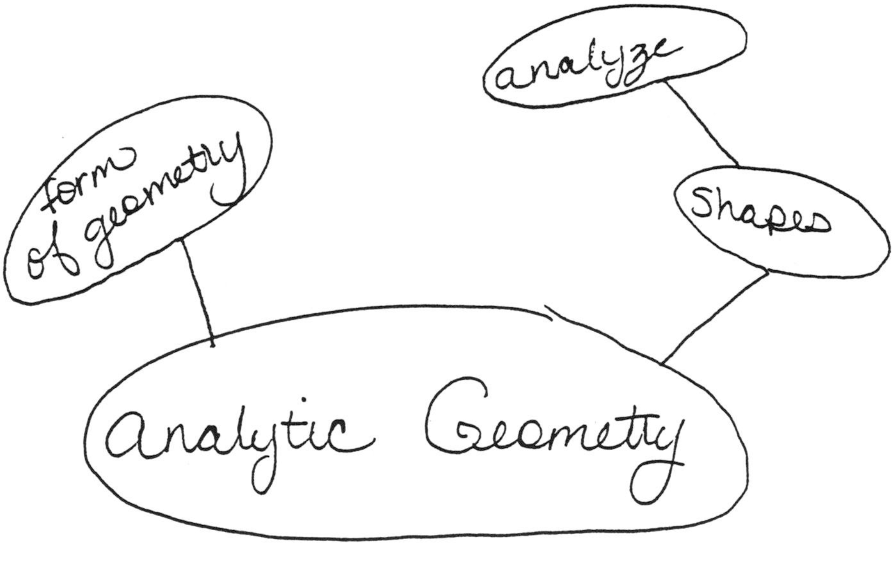

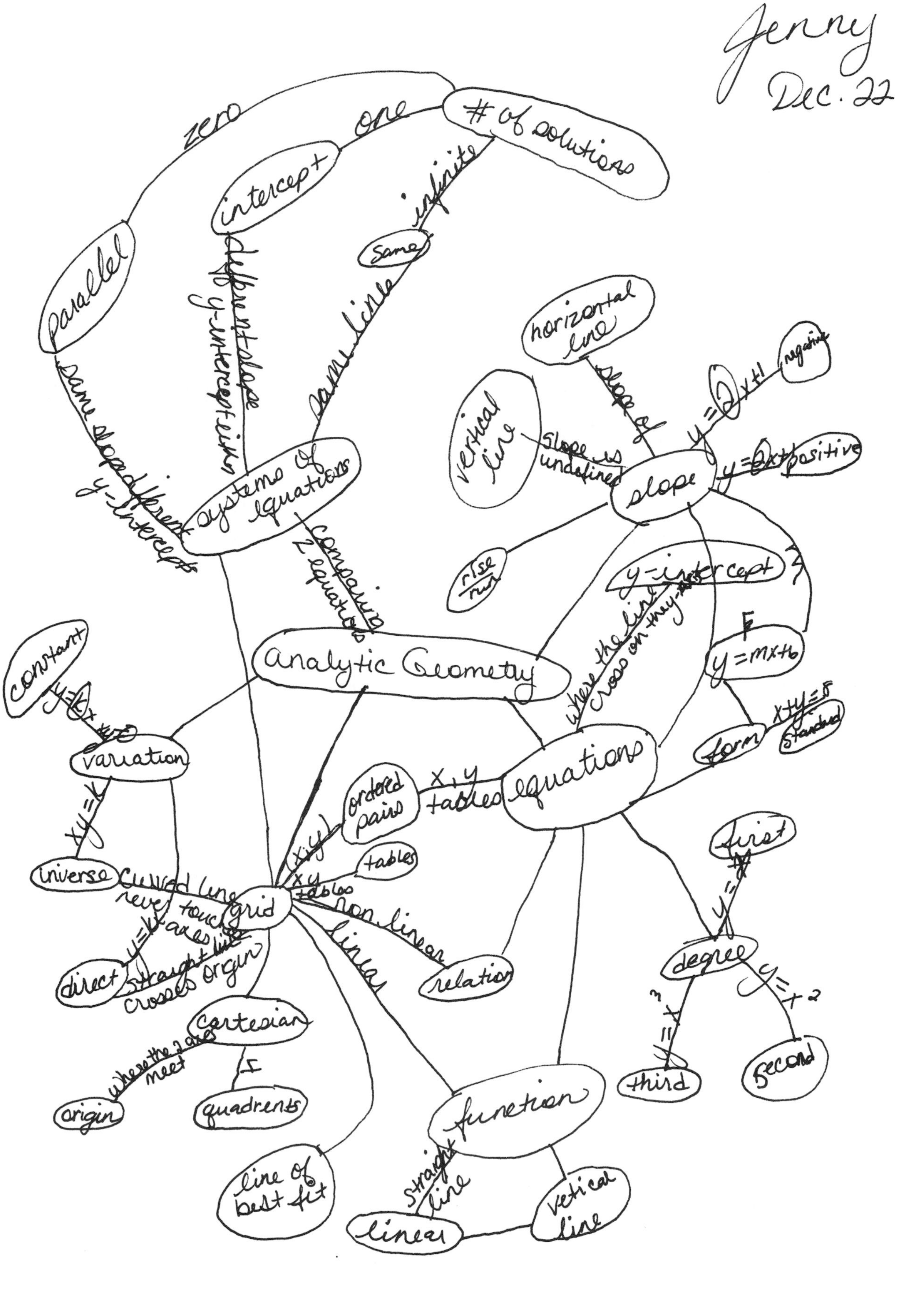
Jenny
Dec. 22
# of solutions
zero
one
intercept
infinite
same
parallel
different slope
same line
same slope
systems of equations
comparing 2 equations
horizontal line
slope of
vertical line
slope is undefined
slope
negative
positive
rise/run
y-intercept
where the line cross on the y-axis
y=mx+b
form
standard
analytic Geometry
constant
variation
xy=k
inverse
curved line
never touch axes
grid
y=kx
direct
straight line
crosses origin
ordered pairs
x, y tables
equations
tables
non linear
relation
linear
first
degree
y=x²
second
third
cartesian
where the 2 axes meet
origin
quadrents
function
line of best fit
straight line
linear
vetical line

DISCUSSION QUESTIONS FOR 1993–1994 CONCEPT MAPS

- What can you learn about a student's understanding of analytic geometry by looking at her or his concept map?
- What do you think these students understand about this topic and what counts as evidence of understanding?
- What does the comparison across students' maps reveal about differences and similarities in how they conceive the domain and what they seem to know about it?
- In looking at an individual concept map, what more would you like to know about what the student knows and how the student is thinking about the topic?
- How might you augment this assessment task to learn more about students' understanding?

Ryan 9/14

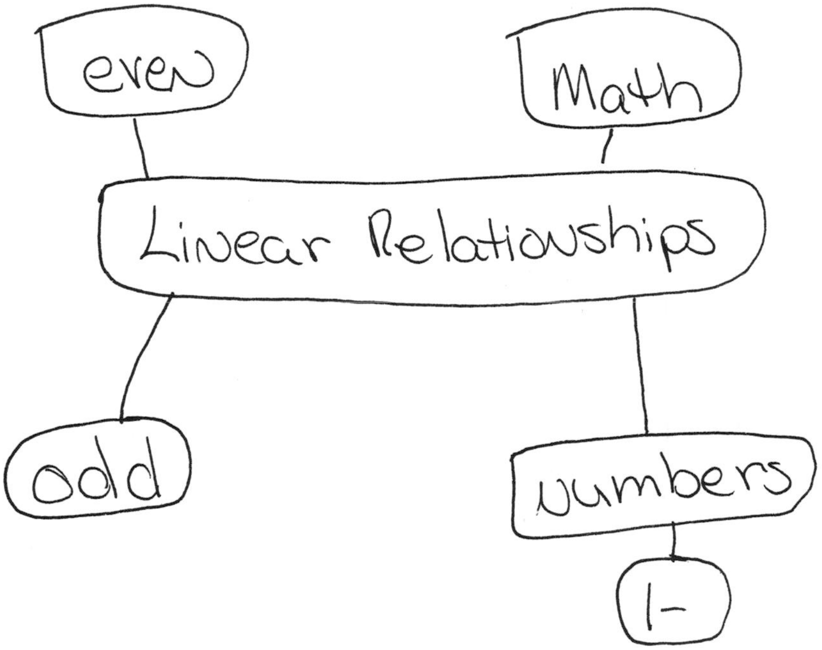

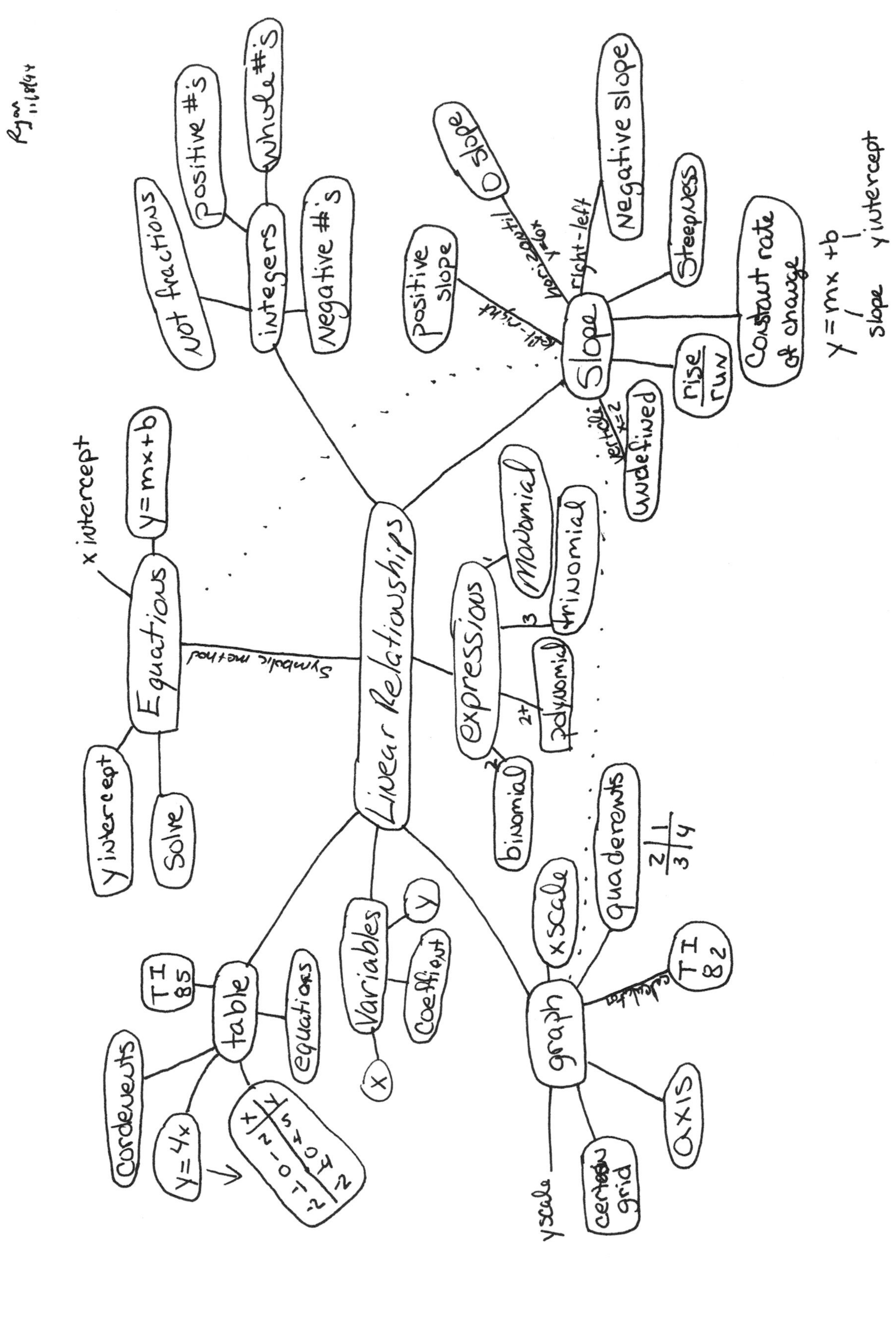
Linear Relationships
Equations
symbolic method
x intercept
y=mx+b
y intercept
Solve
integers
not fractions
positive #'s
whole #'s
Negative #'s
Slope
positive slope
left-right
0 slope
right-left
Negative slope
Steepness
Constant rate of change
rise
run
undefined
y=mx+b
slope
y intercept
expressions
Monomial
trinomial
polynomial
binomial
graph
x scale
quaderents
TI 82
AXIS
grid
y scale
Variables
y
Coefficient
x
table
TI 85
equations
Cordenents
y=4x

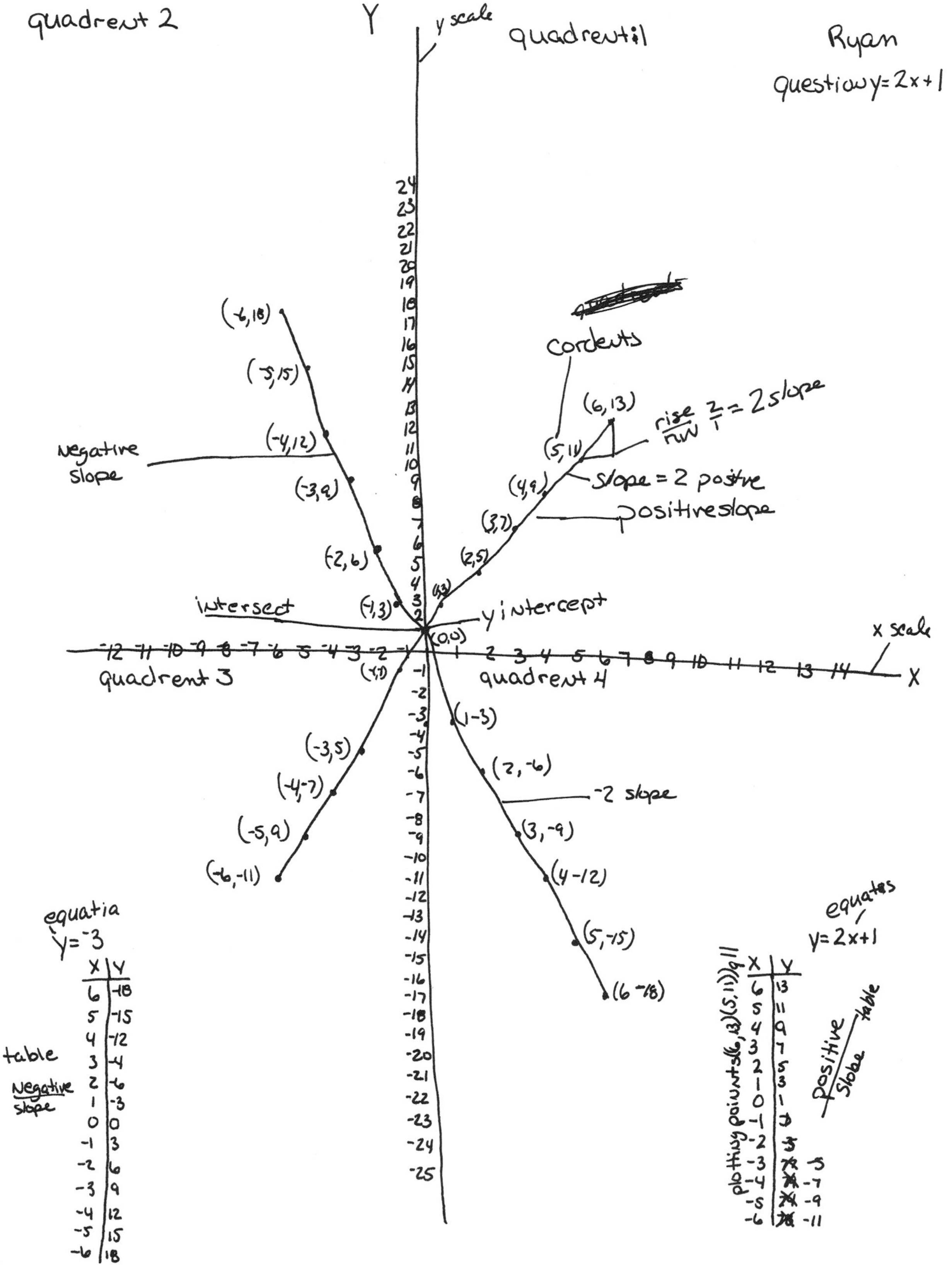
quadrent 2
Y
y scale
quadrentil
Ryan
questiow y=2x+1
cordents
(6,13)
rise/run 2/1 = 2 slope
(5,11)
slope = 2 postive
positiveslope
Negative slope
(-6,18)
(-5,15)
(-4,12)
(-3,9)
(-2,6)
(-1,3)
intersect
y intercept
(0,0)
x scale
X
quadrent 3
quadrent 4
(1-3)
(2,-6)
-2 slope
(3,-9)
(4-12)
(5,-15)
(6-18)
(-3,5)
(-4,-7)
(-5,9)
(-6,-11)
equatia
y=-3
table
Negative slope
equates
y=2x+1
plotting points (6,13)(5,11)(9,11)
Positive slope table

1 The part of the cocept map I fell I really Know is the graph and slope. I understand rise over run and all the + and negative slopes. I Know how to put all these things on a graph.

2. I don't really Know about integers. I have trouble adding them and subtracting them. I am getting better though. Also I can't do the equation solving is.

Ryan
1st
11/8/94

On the graphpaper it shows the steps to make a graphline. It shows mentions about things on the concept map

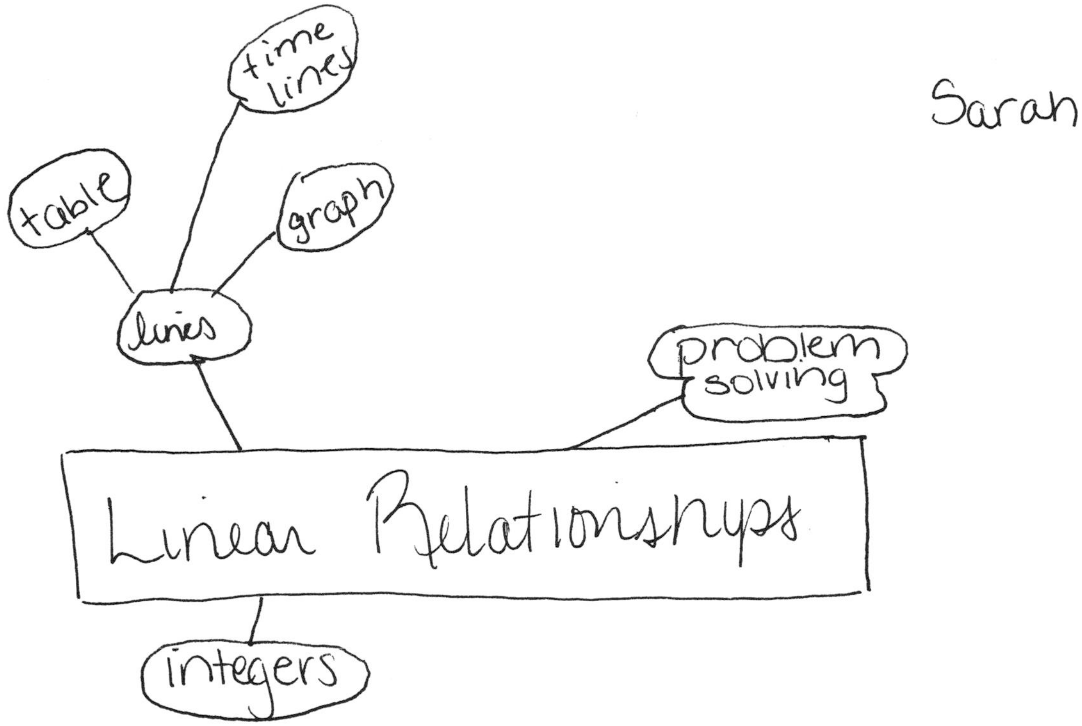
time lines
table
graph
lines
problem solving
Linear Relationships
integers
Sarah

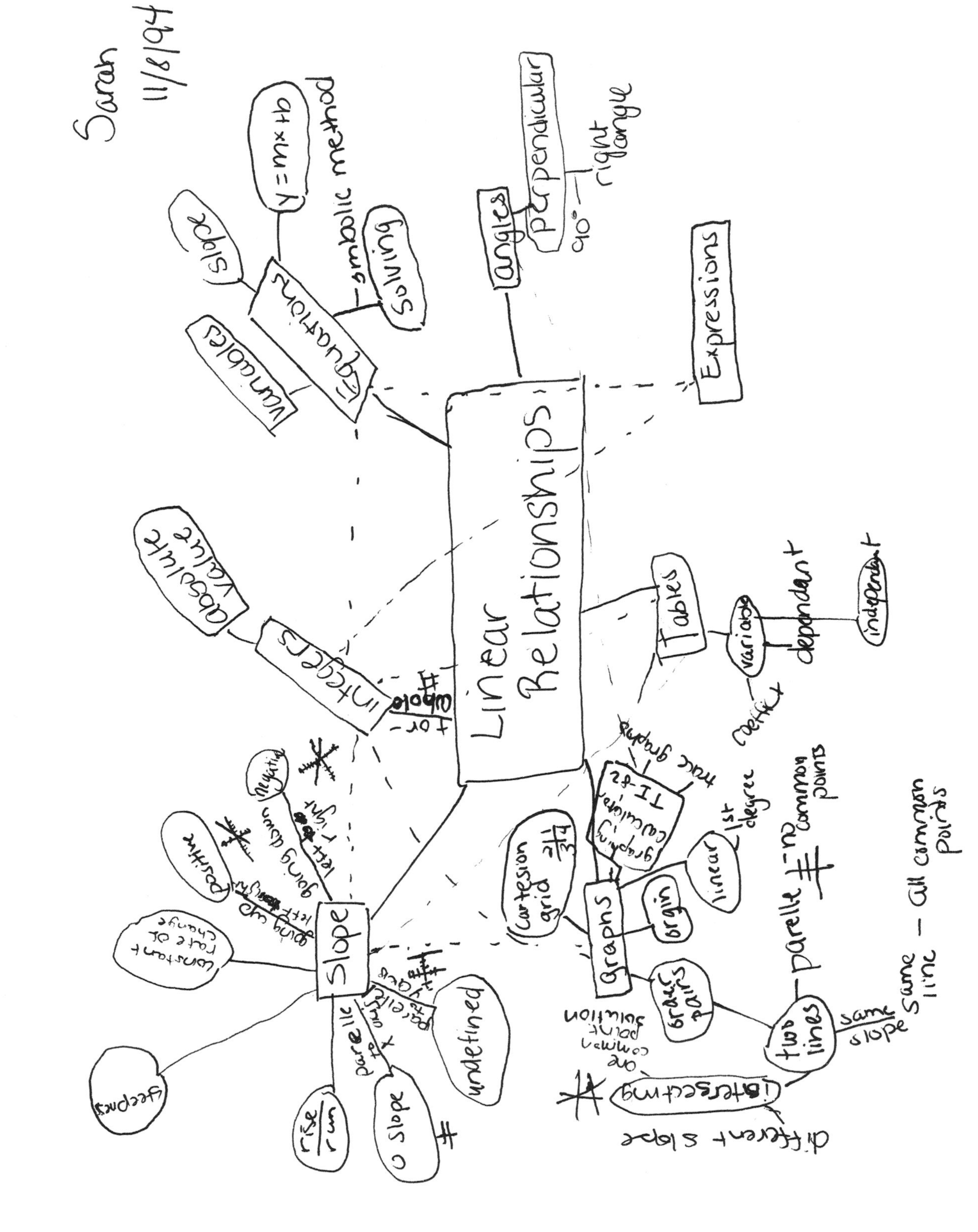
Sarah
11/8/94
Linear Relationships
Equations
variables
slope
y = mx + b
symbolic method
Solving
angles
perpendicular
90°
right angle
Expressions
Tables
variable
dependant
independent
Graphs
cartesion grid
origin
linear
1st degree
graphing calculator TI-82
trace graphs
ordered pairs
two lines
intersecting
different slope
same slope
same line — all common points
parelle — no common points
Slope
constant rate of change
steepness
rise/run
0 slope
undefined
positive
negative
Integers
absolute value
whole #

Sarah
11/8/94

Questions

① Something I know alot about are graphs. That's the one thing that clicks with me the most. Basically, there are the two axis -y axis which is the dependent one, and the x axis which is the independent one. The point where these two axis meet is the origin. A graph shows how a line or "subject" increases and/or decreases in relationship to the "subject's variables. Graphs can also show the relationship between two different things by putting them both on a graph and comparing the slopes.

Most of the time, you need a table to figure what to do on a graph Or an equation will do just fine. To put points on the graph you must take two cordinates such as (3, 6) and plot them on the graph. In an equation, take the number 3 and do what the equation says to do. For example. if the equation says to do. was y = 2x you would multiply 3x2=6 so you cordinates are 3,6 (and remember to always start on the x axis for 3.)

All in all graphs work best for giving presentations fine an equation or to compare two different things

Sarah

2. Something I feel I don't know much about is expressions and the symbolic method It's not that I don't understand expressions, it's just that I don't remember it to well since I wasn't here for one of the days of explanation. The symbolic method, on the other hand, is completly different. It's like I understand what their doing and why they do that but when it come to working out a problem, - I just draw a blank.

11/9/94 (1)

Guess what! I have more to say about graphs! Let's start with two lines on a graph. These two lines can be parellel - in which case they have no common points, intersecting - in which they have have one common point. (which is called the solution) or they are the same line - in which they have the same slope and all common points.

also diff slope

A cartesion grid is most common grid which looks like this: + and numbered looks like this II | I / III | IV

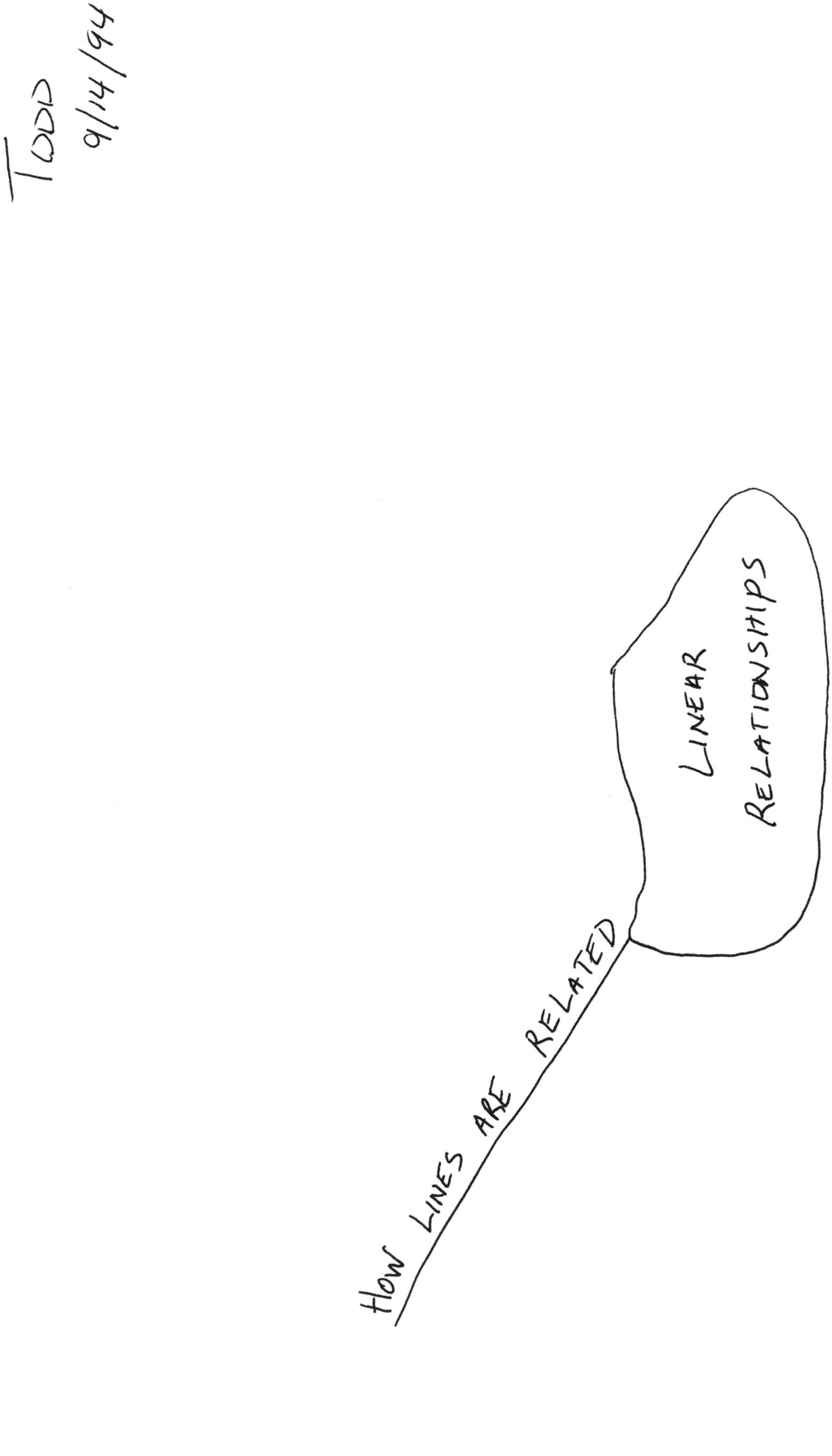
TODD
9/14/94
LINEAR
RELATIONSHIPS
HOW LINES ARE RELATED

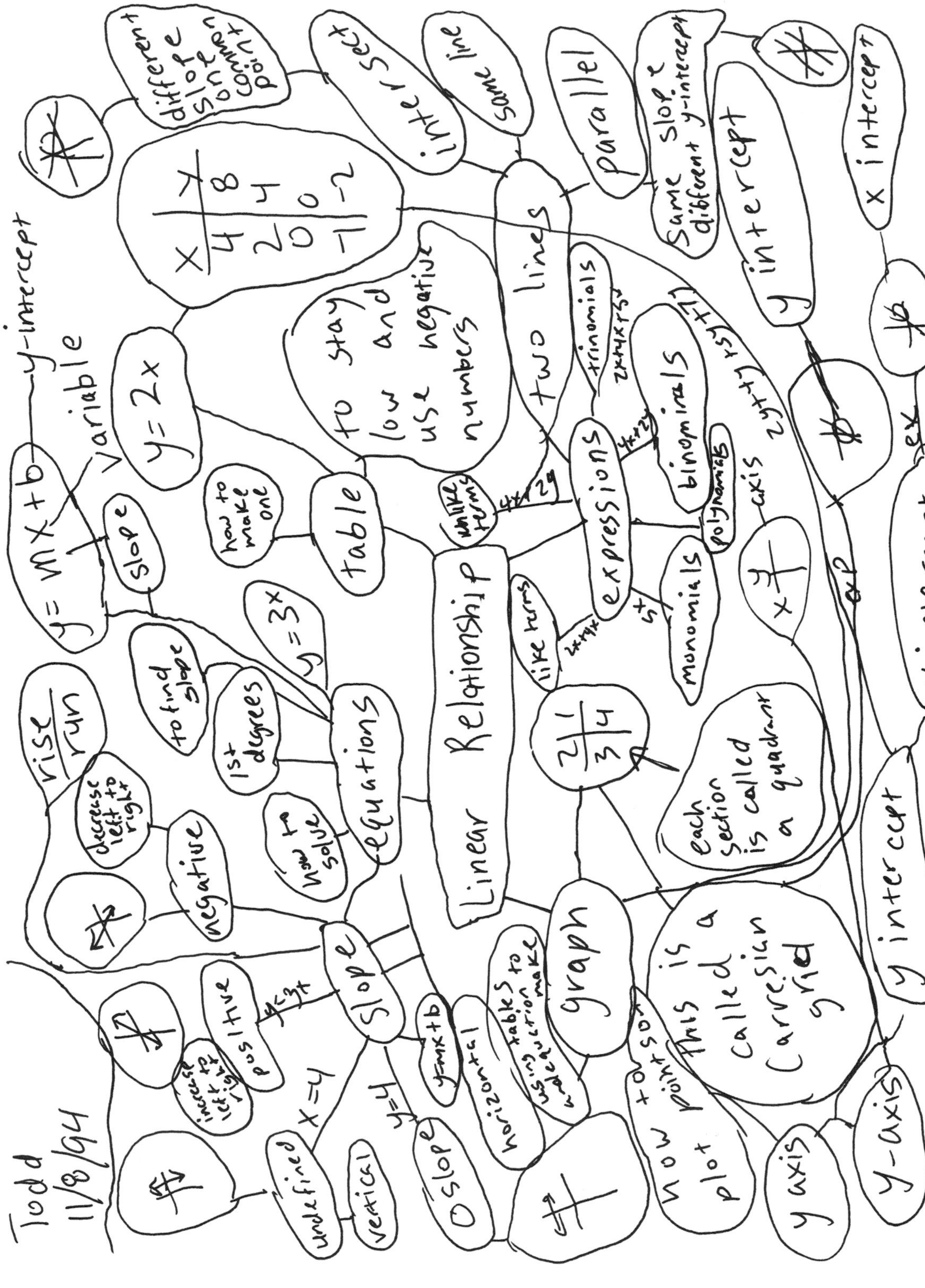
Todd
11/8/94
Linear Relationship
equations
slope
graph
table
expressions
two lines
y = mx + b
variable
y-intercept
rise/run
negative
decrease left to right
positive
increase left to right
undefined
vertical
x = 4
0 slope
y = 4
horizontal
how to solve
1st degrees
to find slope
y = 3^x
y = 2x
how to make one
to stay low and use negative numbers
intersect
same line
parallel
different slope one common point
same slope & different y-intercept
y intercept
x intercept
y axis
y-axis
how to plot points
this is called Cartesian grid
each section is called a quadrant
using tables to make an equation
like terms
unlike terms
monomials
binomials
trinomials
polynomials
axis

Todd

11-8-94

---

1. I feel slope is the thing I learned most about you can have a 0 slope $y=4$

parallel horizontal line to x axis

---

you can have an undefined slope $x=4$

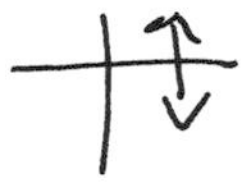

vertical line parallel to y axis

you can have a positive slope $y=3x$

which increases from right to left.

You can have a negative slope $y=-3x$

which decreases from right to left

To find slope there are 2 equations

$y=mx+b$ or $m=\frac{y1-y2}{y1-y2}$

Todd

7. I feel I Know The least about expressions becaus I forgot what They were. If I looked in my notebook I would probably be able to remember

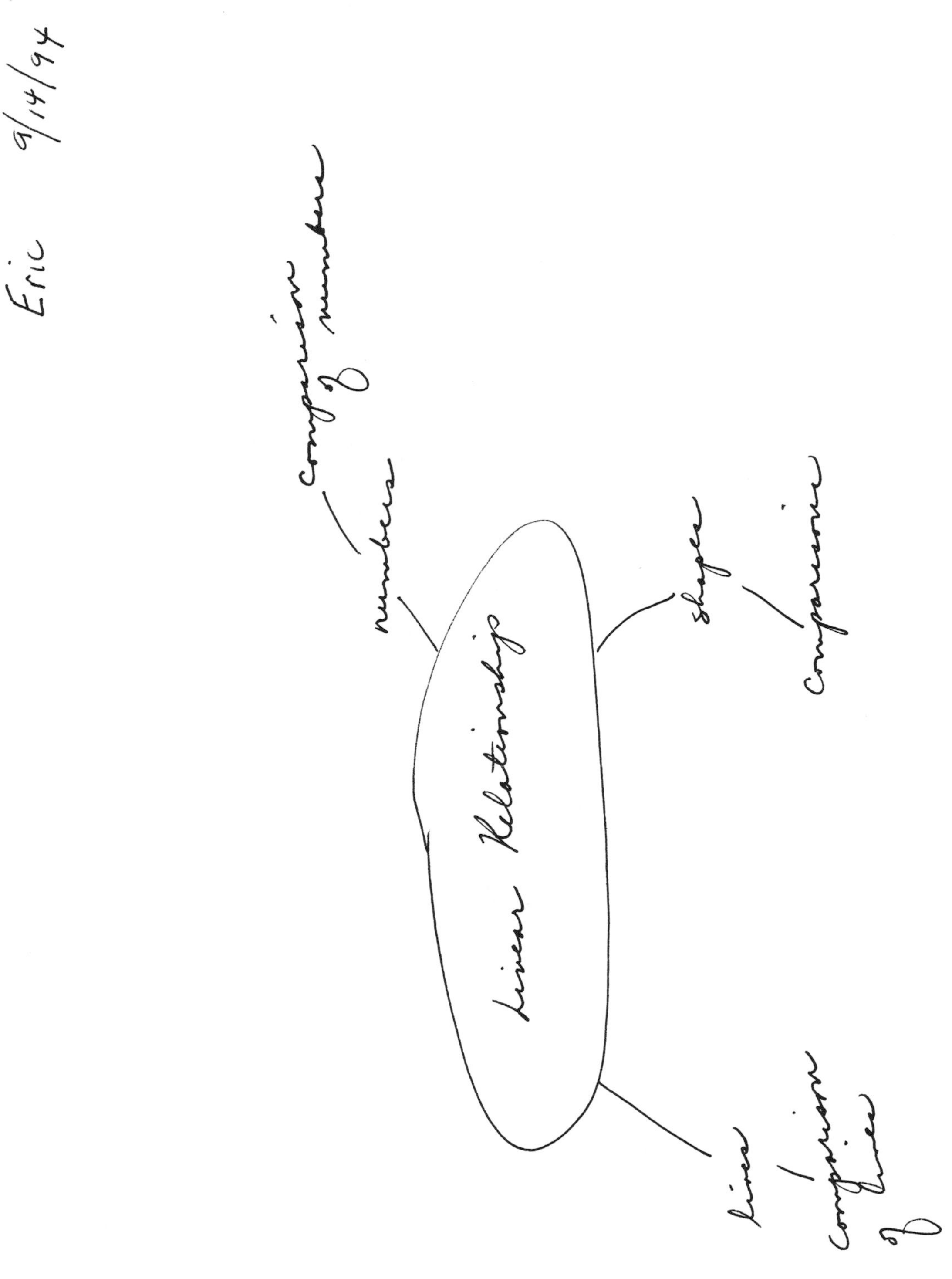
Eric
9/14/94
Linear Relationships
numbers
comparison of numbers
shapes
comparison
lines
comparison of lines

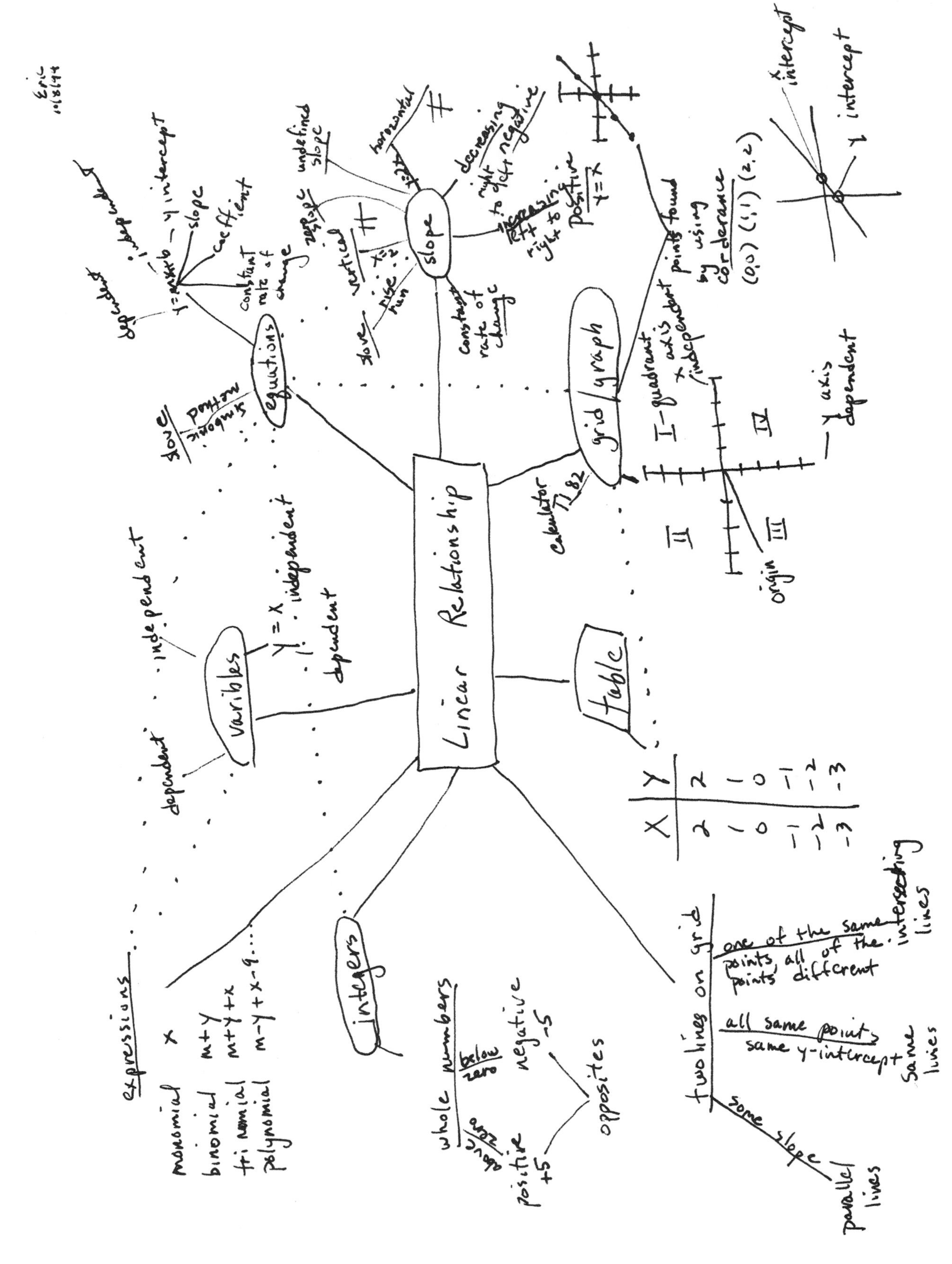
Linear Relationship
variables
dependent
independent
Y = X
equations
slope
constant rate of change
rise/run
vertical
horizontal
zero slope
undefined slope
decreasing
negative
positive
grid/graph
calculator TI 82
I-quadrant
II
III
IV
origin
x axis independent
Y axis dependent
points found by using cordinance
y intercept
x intercept
table
X
Y
expressions
monomial
binomial
trinomial
polynomial
integers
whole numbers
negative
positive
opposites
two lines on grid
intersecting lines
same lines
parallel lines
same slope

Eric
11/9/94

Questions

1. Slope - is the make of the line of the graph. Slopes can be positive, ($Y=2$) inc. left to right, negative, decreasing ($y=-2x$) right to horozontal, ($y=2$) which has a zero slope, or ($x=2$) vertical which has an undefined slope. Linear slopes have a straight line which is call constant rate of change. (coefficient and slope) We can find the slope of a line by using $\frac{rise}{run}$.

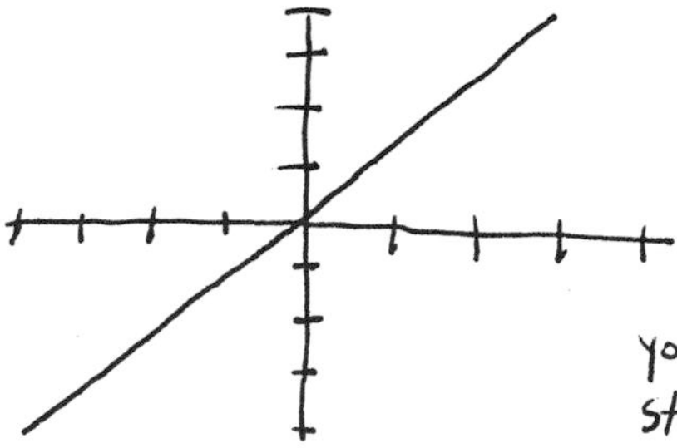

$m = \frac{rise}{run}$

$m = \frac{2}{2} = 1y = X$

you run on the y-intercept stop any place move up and two the line again. Divide the number of space traveled on the y-intercept and how many it took to reach line.

I think I know the most about slope because I found this the most interesting and payed no attention.

2. I think I don't know much about variable because I didn't take very good notes and didnt study enough.

DISCUSSION QUESTIONS FOR 1994–1995 CONCEPT MAPS

- What can you learn about a student's understanding of linear relationships by looking at her or his augmented concept map?
- What do you think these students know about this topic and what counts as evidence of understanding?
- What are you able to learn about students' understanding that the map alone does not reveal?
- How might a teacher use the analysis of the information in the maps and the written elaborations to decide where to go next in instruction?

DISCUSSION QUESTIONS: POTENTIAL POWER OF MAPPING

- To what extent can the use of concept maps serve as a means for students to do self-assessment?
- Does mapping—and the intellectual demands required—become part of the curriculum?
- In what ways can using self-assessment serve to empower students?
- What can concept maps communicate to interested others about student's mathematical accomplishments that more traditional forms of reporting fail to capture?

DISCUSSION QUESTIONS: STEPPING BACK

- Why would a teacher want to engage in deep analysis of students' written work on concept maps?
- How might this kind of deep analysis and conversation among a group of professionals contribute to enhancing teaching and learning in mathematics classrooms?

Case 5: Geometric Constructions: The Contributions of Context

From the classroom of Ron Zielinski in collaboration with Sandra Wilcox and Melissa Dennis

OVERVIEW

This case provides opportunities to

- *analyze students' written work*: how they carry out several geometric constructions on several tasks, what they seem to understand, how they make connections and apply knowledge of compass and straightedge constructions to a real-world situation;
- *analyze learning/assessment tasks*: what they have the potential to reveal about different aspects of understanding about locus of points, why a teacher might choose to use any of these tasks, how the tasks are aligned with the teacher's learning goals for students;
- *consider what a teacher might do next in instruction*: what kinds of activities might develop students' conceptual as well as procedural knowledge about locus of points.

Mathematical Content: Locus of points, compass and straightedge constructions.

Case Materials: Samples of student work on several learning/assessment tasks.

Additional Materials Needed: A compass and straightedge for each participant.

Suggested Time: Minimum of 2 hours.

INTRODUCTION

This case is built around several learning and assessment tasks given to an eighth-grade class during a unit on geometric constructions. Most of the work involved students in learning, reproducing, and practicing decontextualized, compass, and straightedge constructions (e.g., angle bisector, perpendicular bisector, tangent to a circle at a point on the circle, circles inscribed in and circumscribed about a triangle). At the end of the unit, students assembled their collection of work into a notebook. This included a final worksheet that covered the range of constructions they had been taught and had practiced during the unit. Several weeks after the conclusion of the unit, the teacher gave the students another task. This task involved the application of some of the ideas in the unit to a real situation where students had to use a map drawn to scale and ideas from geometry to reason about times and distances involving lightning and thunder.

We include this case because it raises important questions about what it means to know mathematics and what different types of tasks have the potential to reveal about students' knowledge at conceptual and procedural levels of understanding. The case highlights the limitations of relying solely on an assessment of students' procedures in carrying out a task to make claims about their conceptual understanding of the mathematics embedded in the task. The case also raises questions about the extent to which learning and assessment tasks are aligned with a teacher's learning goals for students.

USING THE CASE MATERIALS

The Case Materials

The materials for this case consist of samples of completed tasks from the notebooks of four students whose work the teacher judged to be quite strong. We have selected pieces of work to show the range of constructions they had been taught. The case also includes samples of student work on the application task, including the four students whose notebook work is featured earlier.

The case has been constructed so that participants first consider student work from the notebooks on traditional construction tasks, what claims they can make about what students understand, and what they can point to as evidence to support the claims. At the heart of this analysis is what can be said about students' understanding of the mathematical ideas embedded in these kinds of tasks.

Trying to make sense of what students understand raises the issue of what knowledge participants themselves bring to a consideration of this mathematical domain. To pursue this, we have crafted an activity that will bring to the fore procedural and conceptual aspects of knowing and doing mathematics. At the heart of this activity is considering whether proficiency at a technical skill level assures that one has a robust conceptual understanding of the mathematics embedded in a task.

Finally, the focus shifts to a different kind of task involving some of the ideas students had been working on in the unit on geometric constructions. Here, participants consider how students are making connections between the construction work they had been doing and a real-world situation and how they are applying that knowledge to the situation.

Introduction to the Case

Ron Zielinski teaches mathematics in an urban junior-high school. One of the courses he teaches is Integrated Math, an honors-level course in which a considerable amount of time is spent on topics in algebra and geometry. One of Zielinski's favorite topics to teach in this course is compass and straightedge Euclidean constructions. This is a part of the curriculum that he and his students have fun with and where his students are more actively engaged. Zielinski has several goals for his students in relation to this topic. He wants them to be able to "demonstrate skills in geometric construction with the appropriate sequence of steps." He wants them to "analyze and develop relationships between various constructions and to draw conclusions." And he wants them "to make connections to other ideas."

The curriculum materials that Zielinski typically uses for this topic are a series of worksheets that he assembled from a variety of sources. He likes being able to "provide an alternative to the traditional textbook." Zielinski's instruction typically follows this format. He shows the students a sequence of moves with a compass and straightedge that locates particular points and segments, and then students practice these moves on similar exercises. Usually he provides an explanation or a formal proof to demonstrate that the resultant figure does indeed satisfy the conditions of the required construction.

On some occasions, the steps of a new construction are given on a worksheet. For example, students were given the following steps on a worksheet to construct an equilateral triangle with one side given (Fig. C5.1).

Students kept their work in a notebook. After the completion of the unit, Zielinski brought several student notebooks to one of our project meetings. He selected them as examples of strong work on the topic. As we examined students' work on the tasks, we began to ask ourselves what we thought students really understood and what counted as evidence of their understanding. And we wondered whether the nature of the tasks provided information relative to all the learning goals Zielinski had for his students.

Activity 1: Analyzing Student Work on Construction Tasks

In this first activity of the case analysis, participants examine student work from the notebooks. You will need to distribute the following, one set for each participant.

- *Student Work on Tasks in Notebook*. We have included a sample of the tasks from the notebooks of Linda, James, Angela, and Anthony. We selected these particular papers because they show the range of constructions that students had been taught. Because Zielinski brought only notebooks of students whose work he judged to be rather strong, the samples are not representative of his class as a whole.

A______________________B

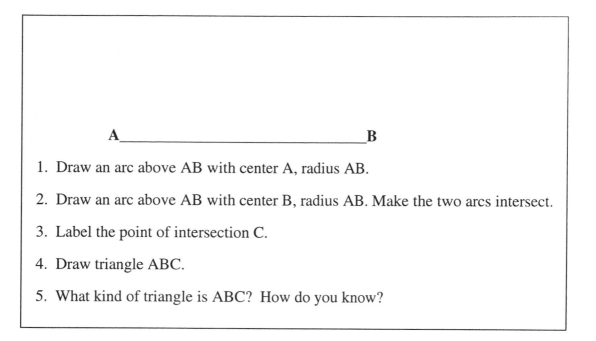

1. Draw an arc above AB with center A, radius AB.
2. Draw an arc above AB with center B, radius AB. Make the two arcs intersect.
3. Label the point of intersection C.
4. Draw triangle ABC.
5. What kind of triangle is ABC? How do you know?

FIG. C5.1. Steps to construct an equilateral triangle.

- *Questions for Discussion: Tasks in Notebook*. The following questions are intended to help you facilitate a discussion in which participants analyze students' written work on the construction tasks, consider what students know about the topic, what counts as evidence, and to what extent Zielinski's students have achieved the goals he has for them. To what extent do students seem to be able to carry out the appropriate steps that result in a correct figure being constructed and to what extent does this vary across different constructions? What does this work reveal about what students understand? What does it mean to understand this topic? What does being able to carry out a set of procedures indicate about students' conceptual understanding of the mathematics embedded in a construction task? Zielinski has several goals for his students including (a) demonstrating skills in geometric construction with the appropriate sequence of steps, (b) analyzing and developing relationships between various constructions and drawing conclusions, and (c) making connections to other ideas. What evidence is there in students' written work about their accomplishments in relation to these goals?
- *Compasses and straightedges*. Participants may want to use these tools to check on the accuracy of student work on the tasks. In Activity 2, participants will need these tools to do a specific construction.

In looking closely at student work, participants are likely to notice that most students carried out the correct sequence of steps, as indicated by arcs that appear to be appropriately placed and figures that seem to be accurately drawn. It is also likely that they will have a lively conversation about what understanding entails in this domain. Some may think that carrying out the correct procedures indicates sufficient understanding. Others may wonder what sense students make of the various marks and whether they can make an argument to themselves and others about why a specific set of moves produces a particular figure. This is a central issue in this case and grounds the next activity.

Activity 2: Understanding the Mathematics in a Construction

What does being able to carry out a set of procedures indicate about students' conceptual understanding of the mathematics embedded in a construction task? A useful way to engage this question is to have participants consider a specific construction. We have found the angle bisector to be especially intriguing. For this activity you will need to distribute the following.

- *Steps to Construct the Angle Bisector*. This is the sequence of steps that students in Zielinski's class were given to carry out the construction of the bisector of an angle. Have participants do the construction by following the steps and then consider the discussion questions.
- *Questions for Discussion: The Angle Bisector*. These questions are intended to push participants to consider what is entailed in understanding the mathematics of geometric constructions and locus of points. What does each of the arcs in the angle bisector construction represent? What argument could I make to myself about why this particular set of moves produces the angle bisector? What condition(s) does the set of points of the angle bisector satisfy? What sense does it make to construct bisectors of the angles of a triangle as a first step in inscribing a circle within the triangle? What connection do I see between the intersection of the angle bisectors of a triangle and the center of a circle that is tangent to each side of the triangle?

We have experienced that many middle-grades teachers find this activity quite challenging. Many do not remember constructions from their high-school geometry classes. They usually are able to carry out the steps of the construction but then are quite puzzled about how to describe the set of points that make up the angle bisector. They may describe the angle bisector as a line that they could fold along so that the two sides of the angle match up, coincide, or lie on top of each other. But they may not understand that their construction is built on the idea that the angle bisector is the set of points equidistant from the sides of the angle and that the distance of any point from the side of an angle is measured along the perpendicular from the point to the side of the angle. They are often at a loss to make sense of why constructing an inscribed circle in a triangle involves constructing the angle bisectors of the triangle. This may also be the case for high-school teachers who themselves have learned and teach only a set of steps.

Facilitating this activity demands a special sensitivity to the different levels of knowledge and experience that participants will bring, to help them come to grips with the rich mathematics involved in geometric constructions, and to support them in taking risks in revealing what, for some, will be partial knowledge at a mostly procedural level.

Activity 3: Making Connections to Real Situations

Participants' close analysis of students' work on the notebook tasks and their own efforts on the angle bisector activity will likely leave them with questions they will find difficult to answer about the depth of students' understanding. They are apt to begin to question whether tasks of this kind can reveal information in relation to some of Zielinski's goals (e.g., making connections, analyzing relationships, drawing conclusions). Our own inquiry among the project team shifted to looking for tasks that we thought had the potential to assess more than students' technical skill.

One such task, *Lightning*,[7] seemed promising. In this task, students consider questions that arose in the context of a real situation involving lightning and thunder. The task involves working with a map that is drawn to scale, using a rate to convert between distances and times, and reasoning about distances and times using perpendicular bisectors and circles. Two of the questions were directly related to the work students had been doing on constructions. We thought this task would provide an opportunity to see to what extent students could make connections between the constructions they had been practicing and

---

[7]An elementary grades version of this task appeared in *Measuring Up* (MSEB, 1994) and has been adapted for the secondary level by the *Balanced Assessment for the Mathematics Curriculum* project.

questions posed in the context of a real situation. Zielinski took the task back to his classroom and gave it to his students.

In this activity, participants work on the task themselves. You will need to distribute the following materials.

- *The Lightning task*. Each participant will need a copy of the task. We have often found that participants want a clean copy of the task that they can take back to their classrooms to try with their own students, so you may want to make enough copies for each person to have two.
- *Questions for Discussion: The Lightning task*. These questions are intended to focus participants on the nature of this task and to compare it with the earlier tasks that dominated students' work in their notebooks. Why would a teacher want to use a task like this? What does this task have the potential to reveal about students' understanding of locating points that meet certain conditions? What is the potential of this task to provide information to Zielinski about students' accomplishments in relation to his three big goals?

Activity 4: Examining Student Work on Lightning

In this activity, participants examine the work of six students, including the four whose work they looked at earlier. You will need to distribute the following.

- *Student Work on Lightning*. We have included the work of Linda, James, Angela and Anthony, whose earlier work participants have examined. In addition, we have included the work of Johnny and Ben because they had interesting ways of reasoning about question #3.
- *Questions for Discussion: Student Work on Lightning*. These questions are intended to focus participants on how students are applying their work on constructions to a task that involves locating points that meet particular conditions. What are the ways in which students approach this task? To what extent do they seem to be drawing on their work with geometric constructions? What can Zielinski learn about his students' progress toward the three learning goals he has for them? How might student work on this task shape a teachers' decisions about next instructional moves?

DELIBERATIONS WITHIN THE PROJECT

Making Sense of What Students Know and Can Do

Examining Work in Students' Notebooks. Zielinski brought the notebooks of several students from his Integrated Math class as examples of learning and assessment tasks that he thought went well. He was pleased with what students had been able to accomplish and offered the tasks as resources to share with the team. As usually happens in our project meetings, we began by closely analyzing student work on the task. Our examination of the work indicated that most had mastered and applied the technical skills to accurately carry out many of the constructions. Points, arcs, and lines seemed to be accurately and appropriately located. In some instances, students wrote the method they used next to their construction. For example, in constructing a line through a point parallel to a given line, students wrote "rhombus method." Our analysis of their work suggested that they had constructed a rhombus with one side on the given line and a vertex at the given point yielding a figure whose opposite sides were parallel.

There seemed to be some evidence that these students might be making connections between the constructions they were carrying out and other things they knew about geometric figures. For example, to construct a parallelogram with given sides and an angle between them, students needed to draw on their knowledge that opposite sides of a parallelogram are equal. To construct a rectangle with two sides given, students needed to know that the angle between the sides of a rectangle is a right angle. To construct a rhombus with diagonals given, students needed to draw on their knowledge that the diagonals of a rhombus are perpendicular and bisect each other.

At the same time, we noticed that there were gaps in completely carrying out the sequence of steps in some of the more complex constructions. For example, Linda wrote "perpendicular bisector" next to #10, and she appeared to construct the perpendicular bisectors of XY and XZ accurately. But then she did not use an appropriate length for the radius of the circumscribed circle. Her resulting circle did not pass through the three vertices of given triangle XYZ. In attempting to construct the inscribed circle in #11, it appeared that Angela found the bisector of angle R of the triangle, but then swung an arc from Q and used the point where this arc intersected the bisector of angle R as the incenter. Her two attempts then to draw a circle tangent to all three sides of the triangle were futile.

What Does Understanding Entail in This Domain? Our close examination of student work led us to take up the question of what we thought students really understood and what counted as evidence of their understanding. Curiously, we had different views. Some, including Zielinski, thought that being able accurately to carry out a construction (as evidenced by an appropriate set of arcs, points, and segments) was an indication of understanding. Others argued that being able to carry out a sequence of steps indicated proficiency at a technical skill level but did not assure that students had a rich and deep understanding of the mathematics of the construction. Our own discussion of several specific constructions helped to clarify the distinction.

For example, the steps Zielinski taught for constructing an angle bisector are not complex and are easily memorized. In fact, every paper we examined closely had the appropriate set of marks for question #3 that asked simply for the angle bisector. However, we wondered whether students could describe the conditions satisfied by the ray they had constructed. Did they have any sense of this ray containing all points equidistant from the sides of the angle? Did they have any sense of measuring the distance from a point on the angle bisector to the side of the angle along the perpendicular from the point to the side? What sense did they make of constructing bisectors of the angles of a triangle to locate the center of the inscribed circle?

We noted that all four students whose work we examined closely had successfully completed #9, constructing a tangent to a circle from a point outside the circle. The method they used involved first constructing the perpendicular bisector of the segment joining the external point, R, and the center of the circle, O. The point where the perpendicular bisector intersected RO was used as the center of a circle that was then drawn through O. The intersection of the second circle with circle O gave two points. Lines were then drawn to each of the points through R. Angela, Anthony, and James further indicated that the tangent line and the radius that it intersected met at a right angle. Again, we wondered what sense students made of these moves. What would they answer if asked why this sequence of steps produced two lines that touched the circle in exactly one point? How would they respond if asked why the tangent line meets the radius at a right angle?

Assessing the Usefulness of Learning and Assessment Tasks. Our close analysis of student work on the learning and assessment tasks simply could not answer the questions we had about the depth of students' knowledge. We began to question to what extent these tasks could reveal information about students' progress toward Zielinski's goals for them to make connections, analyze relationships, and draw conclusions. We thought these tasks provided scant opportunities for students to demonstrate accomplishments along these dimensions. We began to look for tasks that we thought might have the potential to provide some of this kind of information.

The *Lightning* task seemed to be a kind of task that might provide information about some of these goals, particularly whether and in what ways students made connections between ideas from the construction unit and their application to a real situation. Zielinski took the task back to his classes and gave it to his students.

Examining Student Responses to Lightning. At our next project meeting, Zielinski brought work on the task from 41 students in his two Integrated Math classes. We found it interesting that most students were able to answer the questions in #2 correctly by applying the "divide by three" rule, but they had different ways of interpreting what the rule meant. Anthony interpreted the rule as "it takes 3 seconds for thunder to reach you if you are 1 kilometer away," Linda interpreted the rule as "lightning travels 3 times as fast as the sound," and James thought it meant that "sound travels 3 times slower than light." We were truly puzzled by Ben's response that "the sound of thunder travels at 3 seconds per hour."

But our attention was drawn to students' responses to questions #3 and 4. Responses to #3 revealed that students applied several different strategies. A third of the students located just one point in response to 3b. Some students identified only the midpoint of PQ. Some students marked a point that was incorrect and we were unable to make sense of how a student might have reasoned about the problem. Half the students located several points using one of three methods. Like Anthony, some drew arcs or circles with the same radius using P and Q as centers and marking the intersection of the circles. Some, like Johnny, measured like distances from P and Q with a ruler and found the approximate point of intersection. Others, like Linda, seemed to use visualization, "eyeballing" several points about the same distance from P and Q. Fewer than 10 students indicated, as Angela did, that the lightning could have struck anywhere along the line joining the points of intersection of congruent circles about P and Q. And of these, only two students specifically identified the line as the perpendicular bisector of PQ.

In response to #3c, nearly every student said it was impossible to tell whether P or R heard the thunder first. A typical response was something like James: "No, because you don't know exactly were [sic] it struck." Ben was one of only two students who seemed to have some sense that there was a point on the line drawn between P and Q where lightning could strike and the thunder be heard simultaneously at P and R. And Ben went further to suggest that if lightning struck on the line below that point, R would hear the thunder first.

Most students seemed to understand that #4 involved using the "divide by three" rule and then finding points 3 cm from P and 6 cm from R. All but nine students drew circles about P and R. Two who did not draw circles found a few distinct points satisfying the conditions for P and for R but were not successful in finding points where P and R would have heard the thunder simultaneously. Of those who did draw the two circles, they seemed to have different interpretations of where the lightning would have struck. Some, like Linda, did not identify specific locations where the lightning would have struck. Some, like James, marked the area of overlap of the two intersecting circles. Slightly more than a third of the students marked the two points where the circles intersected.

Zielinski was surprised that so few students made explicit reference to the geometric constructions that he had taught. At the same time, he was intrigued by the various strategies students used to engage the problems.

This case highlighted for us the problems associated with a traditional approach to teaching and learning about locus of points through compass and straightedge constructions. Even when a teacher explains why a set of moves produces a particular figure, the act of telling does not assure that students can or will make their own personal sense of the actions. In this kind of instruction, the development of procedural knowledge is privileged, the development of conceptual knowledge is shunted to the side, and students come to see their job as remembering numerous sets of moves, each in a particular order, and different for each kind of construction. Furthermore, the typical kinds of exercises that students practice are decontextualized. They become school tasks that seem to have no relation to real situations outside the mathematics classroom. We have come to believe that this kind of approach far too often has students carrying out mindless procedures rather than presenting them with interesting situations for their investigation.

Using Assessment to Consider Where to go Next in Instruction

Zielinski gave the *Lightning* task to his students near the end of the school year and brought the student work to one of our summer project retreats. Our discussion focused mostly on how Zielinski might make changes in teaching the unit to another group of students the following year.

Zielinski began to think about using the *Lightning* task as a "springboard" for the unit the next time he teaches it. He remembered the different ways we in the project approached the problem when we first saw it. Some of us immediately applied the same constructions that Zielinski had taught his students (e.g., constructing the perpendicular bisector of PQ for #3). But one of our teachers who did not remember geometric constructions from high-school geometry had an equally effective way of approaching the situation in #3. She reasoned that if she drew circles of the same radius around P and Q, then where the circles crossed should be a point where the lightning struck. Zielinski thought that beginning with this task could provide him with insights about the kinds of strategies his students would bring to solving the problem.

Zielinski's experience with an alternative task caused him to reconsider his own claims about what his students understood and to rethink his usual approach to teaching geometric constructions. He still planned to teach the typical constructions and have his students practice them because he wants them to develop a "fundamental proficiency with basic constructions." At the same time, he was making tentative but important shifts toward helping his students develop a richer understanding of the mathematics of locus of points. Toward that end, he hoped to provide them with tasks that cast the mathematics of locus of points in real situations so that students could see connections between school tasks and real-world contexts.

MATERIALS FOR MAKING PHOTOCOPIES AND TRANSPARENCIES

- Student Work on Tasks in Notebook—Linda, James, Angela, and Anthony. Prepare one set for each participant; prepare one set of transparencies.
- Questions for Discussion: Tasks in Notebook. Prepare one for each participant; prepare a transparency.
- Steps to Construct the Angle Bisector. Prepare one for each participant.
- Questions for Discussion: The Angle Bisector. Prepare one for each participant; prepare a transparency.
- The *Lightning* Task. Prepare one for each participant
- Questions for Discussion: The *Lightning* Task. Prepare one for each participant.
- Student Work on the *Lightning* Task—Linda, James, Angela, Anthony, Johnny, and Ben. Prepare one set for each participant.
- Questions for Discussion: Student Work on the *Lightning*. Prepare one for each participant; prepare a transparency.

CONSTRUCTION WORKSHEET #5

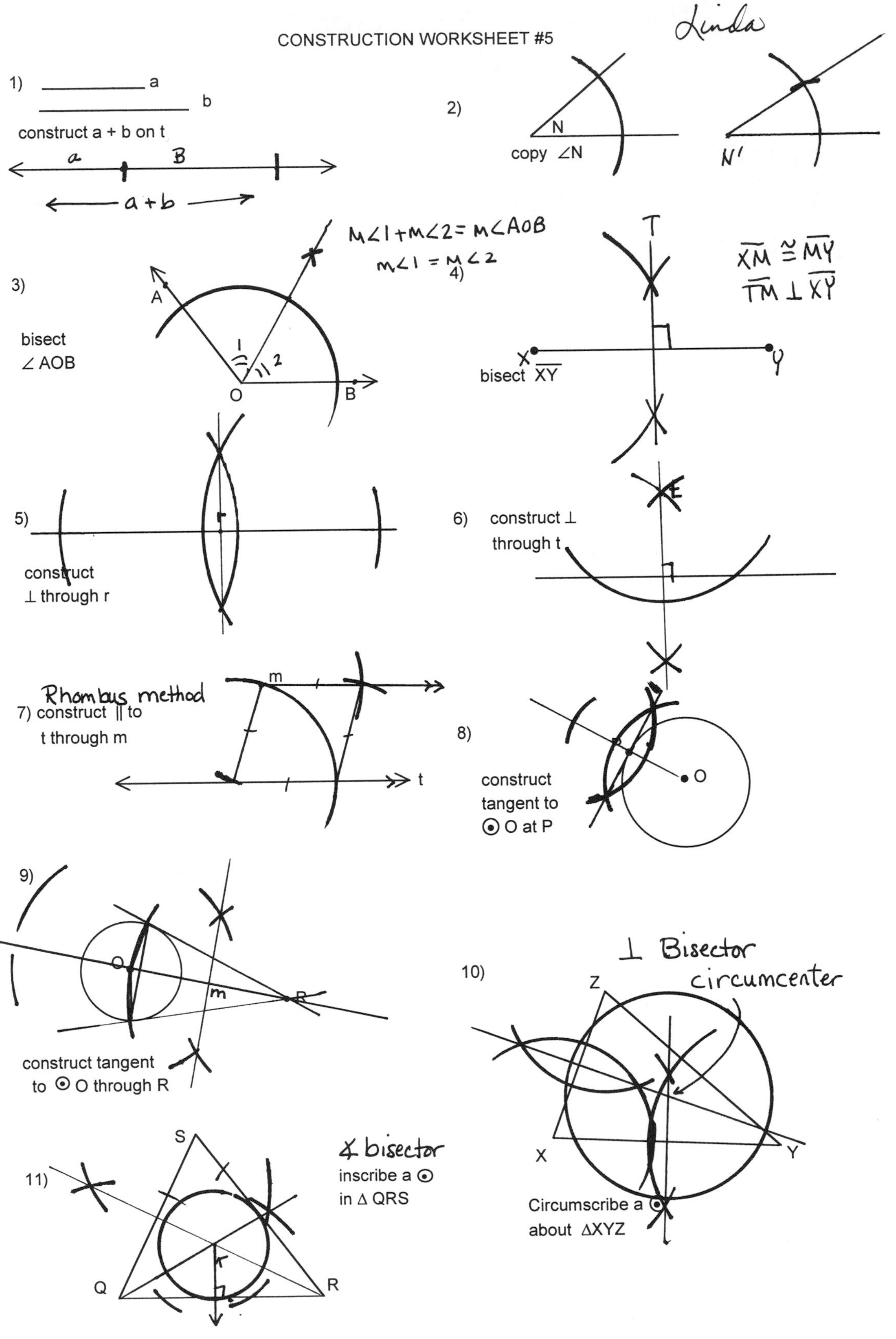

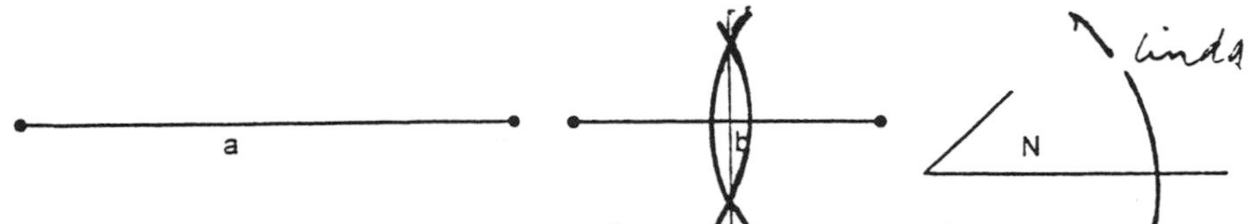

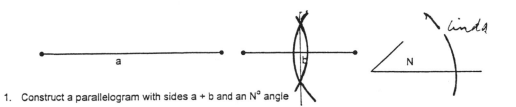

1. Construct a parallelogram with sides a + b and an N° angle

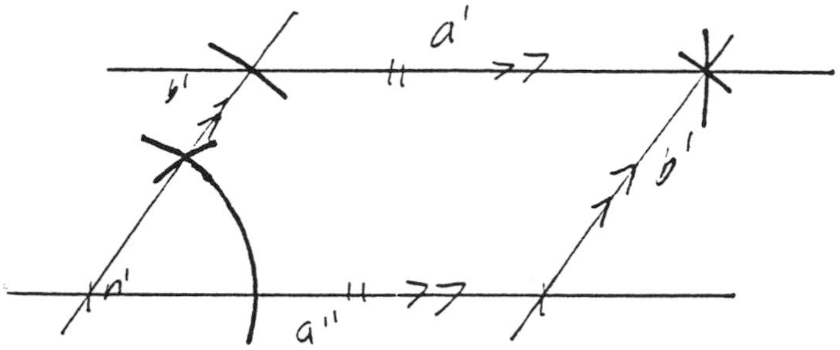

2. Construct a rectangle with sides a + b

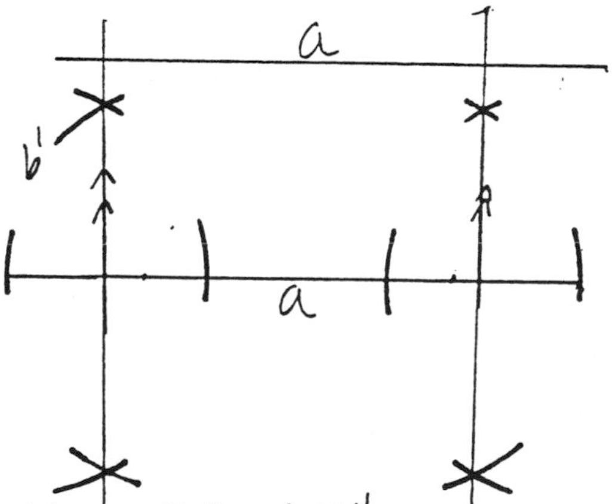

3. Construct rhombus with diagonals a + b

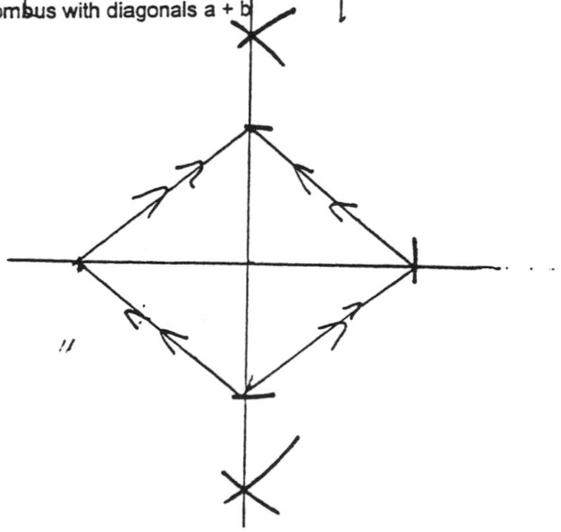

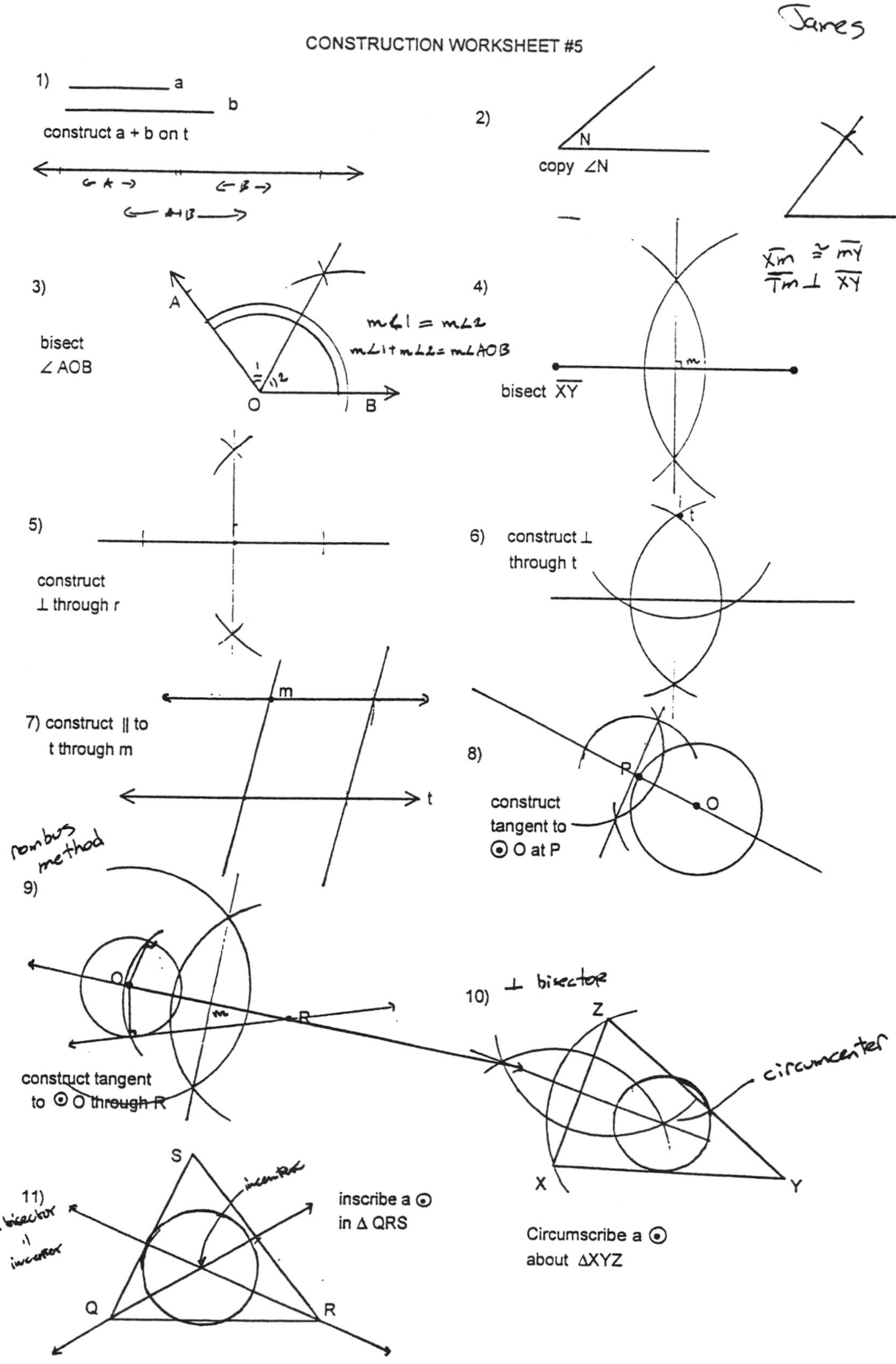
Jares
CONSTRUCTION WORKSHEET #5
1) a
b
construct a + b on t
2)
N
copy ∠N
3)
A
bisect
∠ AOB
O
B
m∠1 = m∠2
m∠1 + m∠2 = m∠AOB
4)
bisect XY
5)
construct
⊥ through r
6) construct ⊥
through t
t
7) construct ∥ to
t through m
m
t
8)
construct
tangent to
⊙ O at P
P
O
rombus method
9)
O
R
construct tangent
to ⊙ O through R
10) ⊥ bisector
Z
X
Y
circumcenter
Circumscribe a ⊙
about ΔXYZ
11)
∠ bisector
incenter
S
Q
R
inscribe a ⊙
in Δ QRS

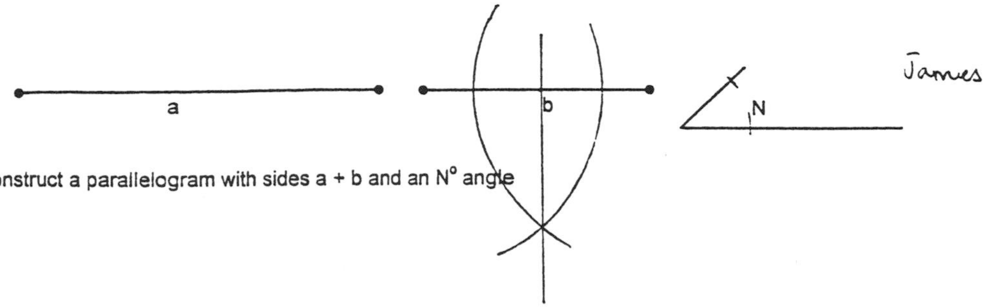

1. Construct a parallelogram with sides a + b and an N° angle

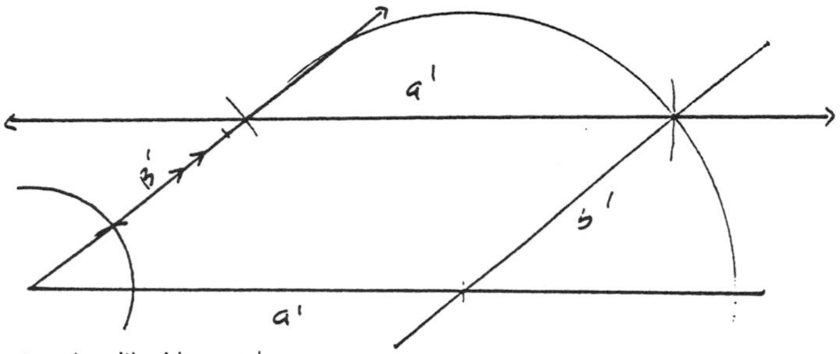

2. Construct a rectangle with sides a + b

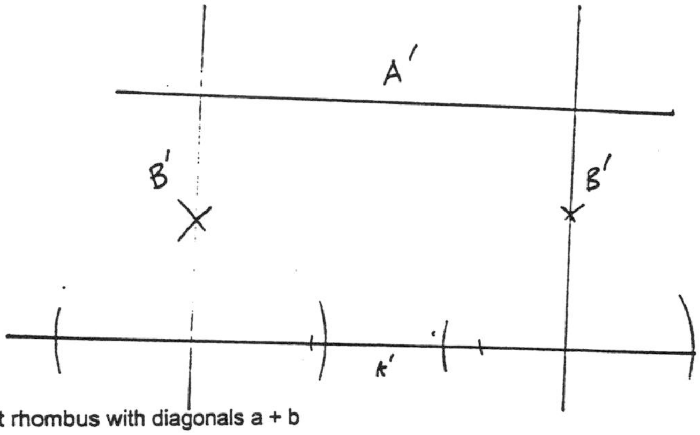

3. Construct rhombus with diagonals a + b

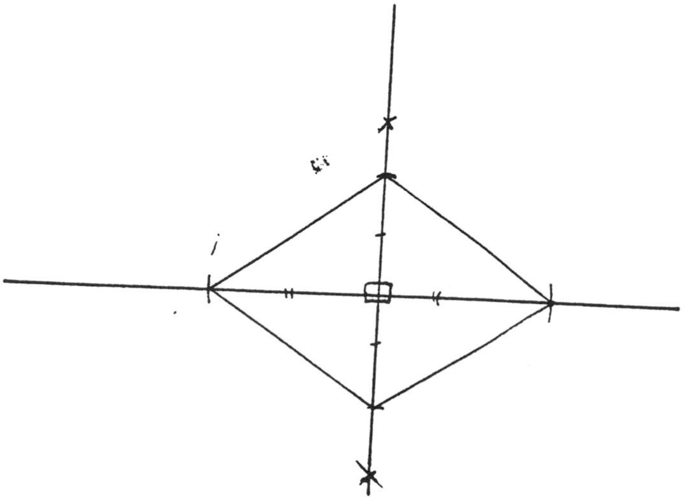

Angela

CONSTRUCTION WORKSHEET #5

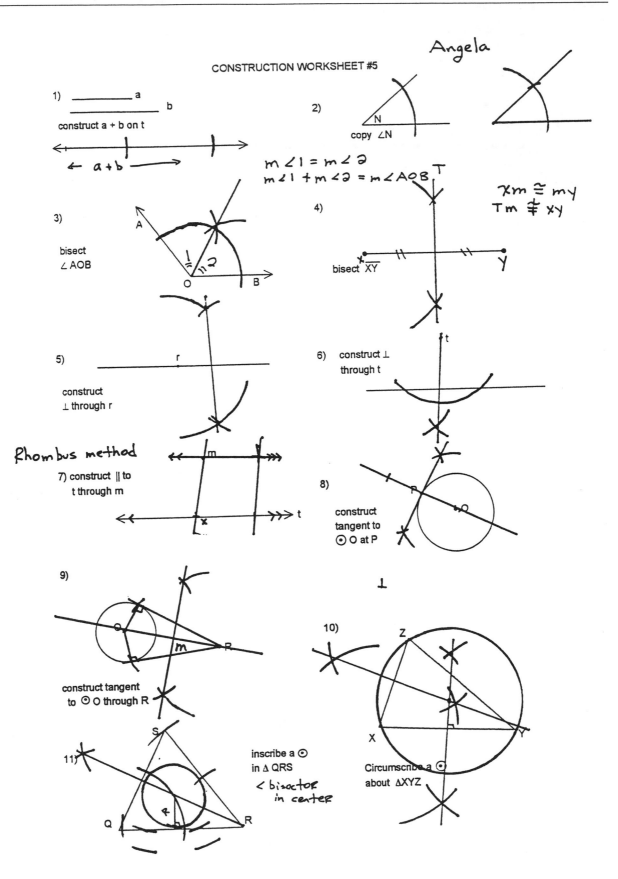

1) a b

construct a + b on t

2) copy ∠N

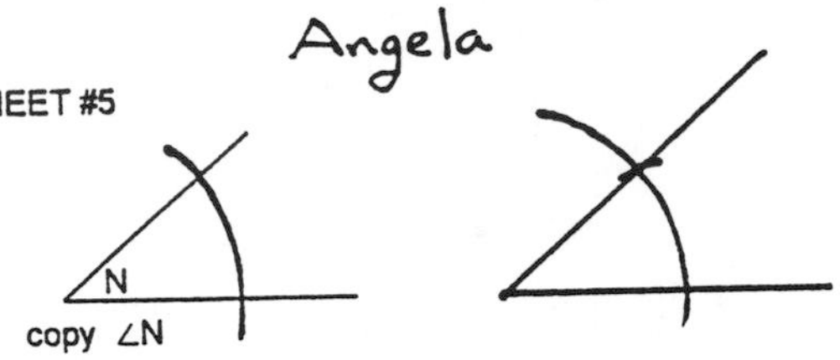

m∠1 = m∠2
m∠1 + m∠2 = m∠AOB

3) bisect ∠AOB

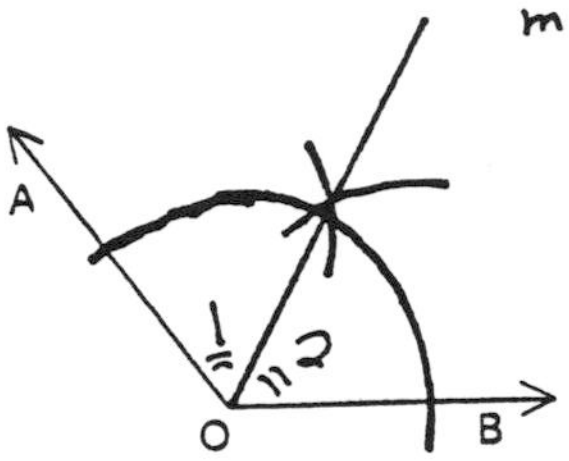

4) bisect $\overline{XY}$

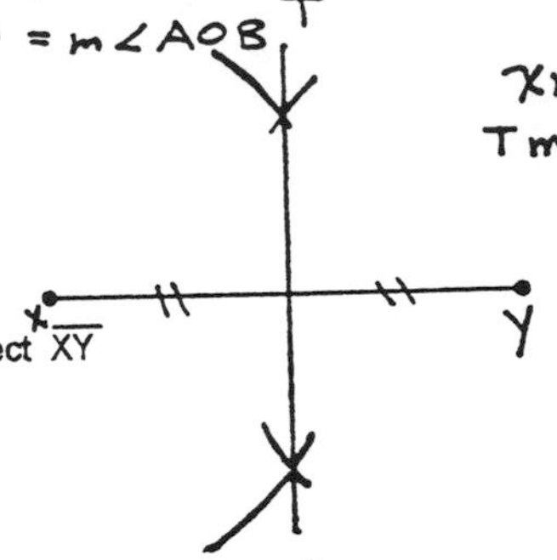

Xm ≅ mY
Tm ≇ XY

5) construct ⊥ through r

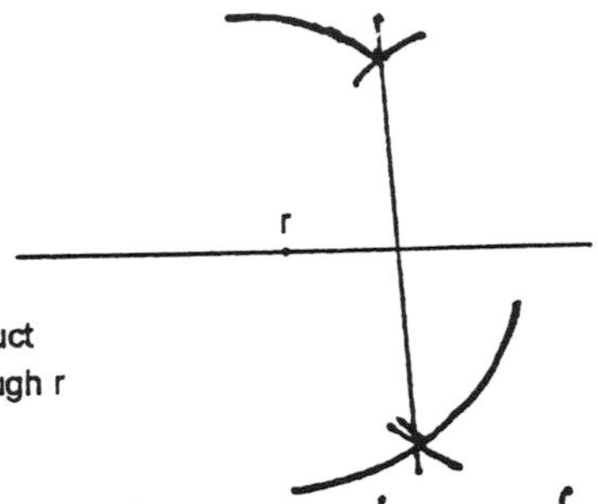

6) construct ⊥ through t

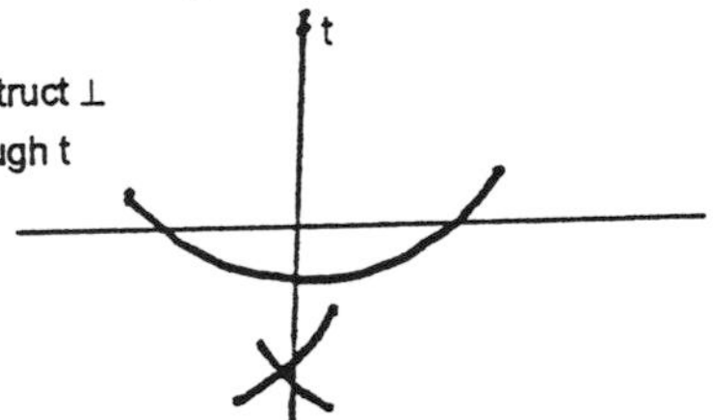

Rhombus method

7) construct || to t through m

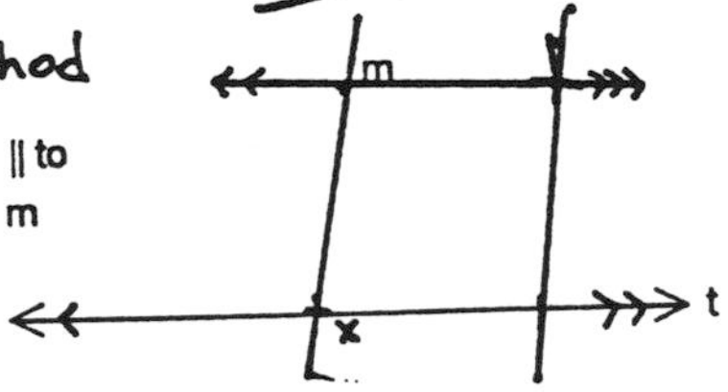

8) construct tangent to ⊙ O at P

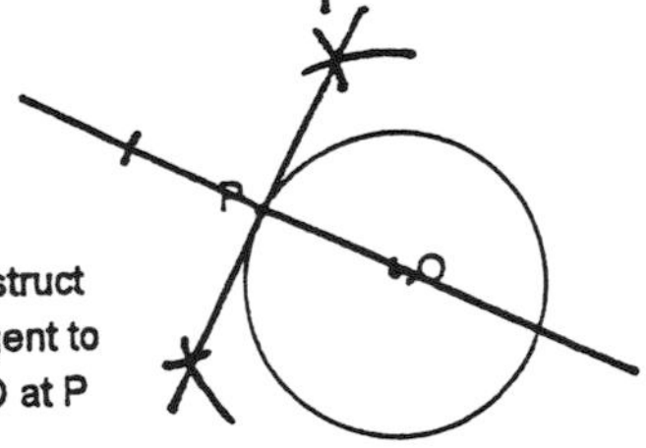

9) construct tangent to ⊙ O through R

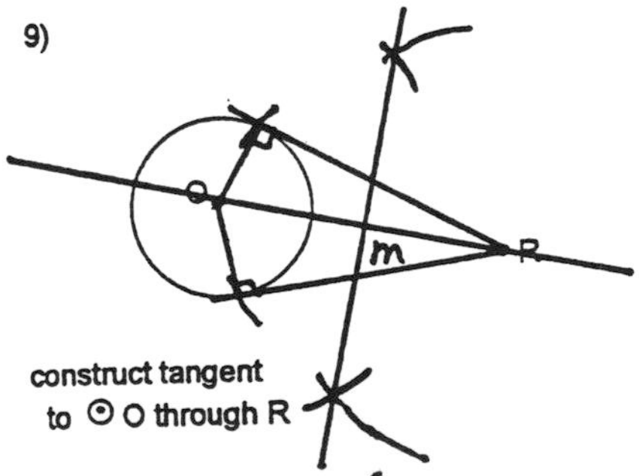

⊥

10) Circumscribe a ⊙ about ΔXYZ

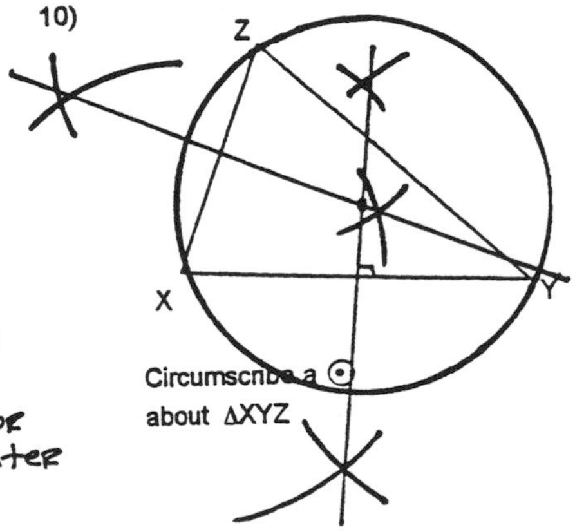

11) inscribe a ⊙ in Δ QRS

< bisector
in center

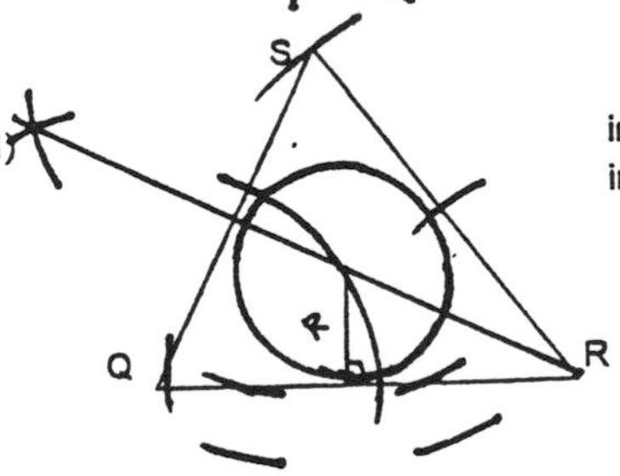

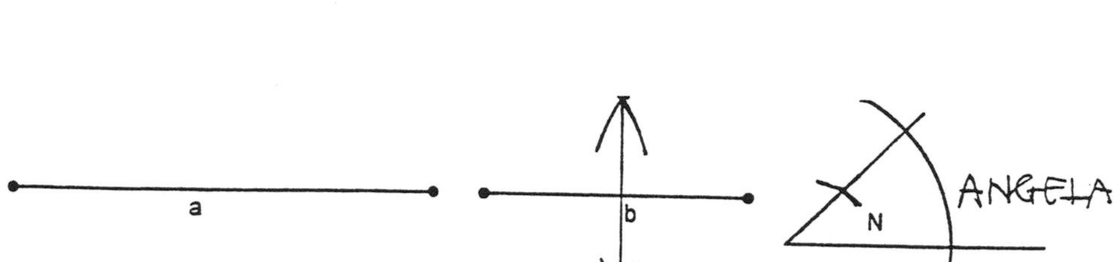

1. Construct a parallelogram with sides a + b and an N° angle

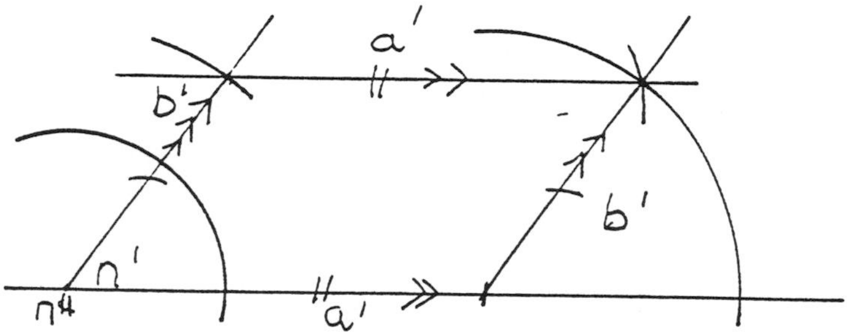

2. Construct a rectangle with sides a + b

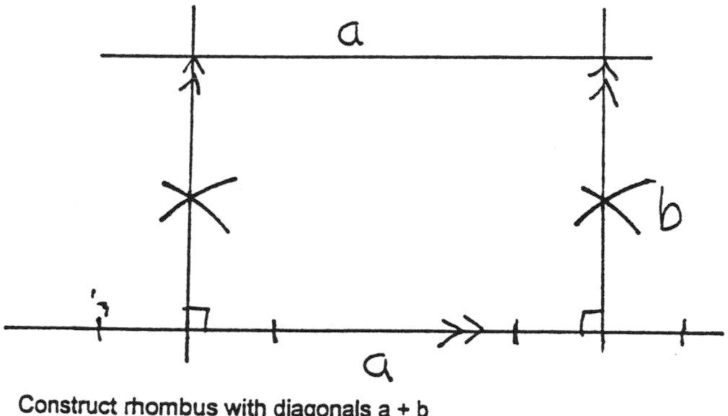

3. Construct rhombus with diagonals a + b

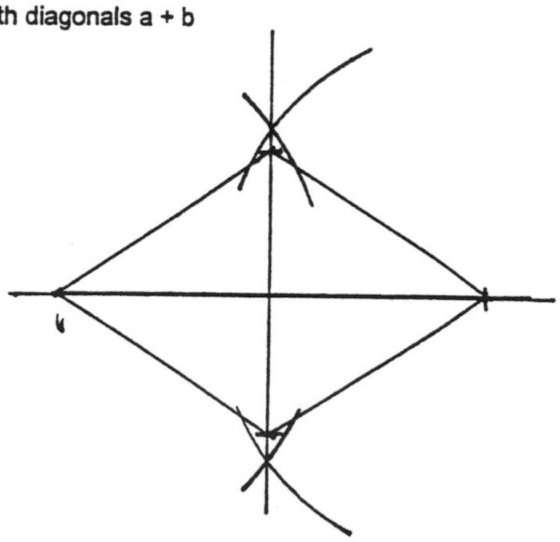

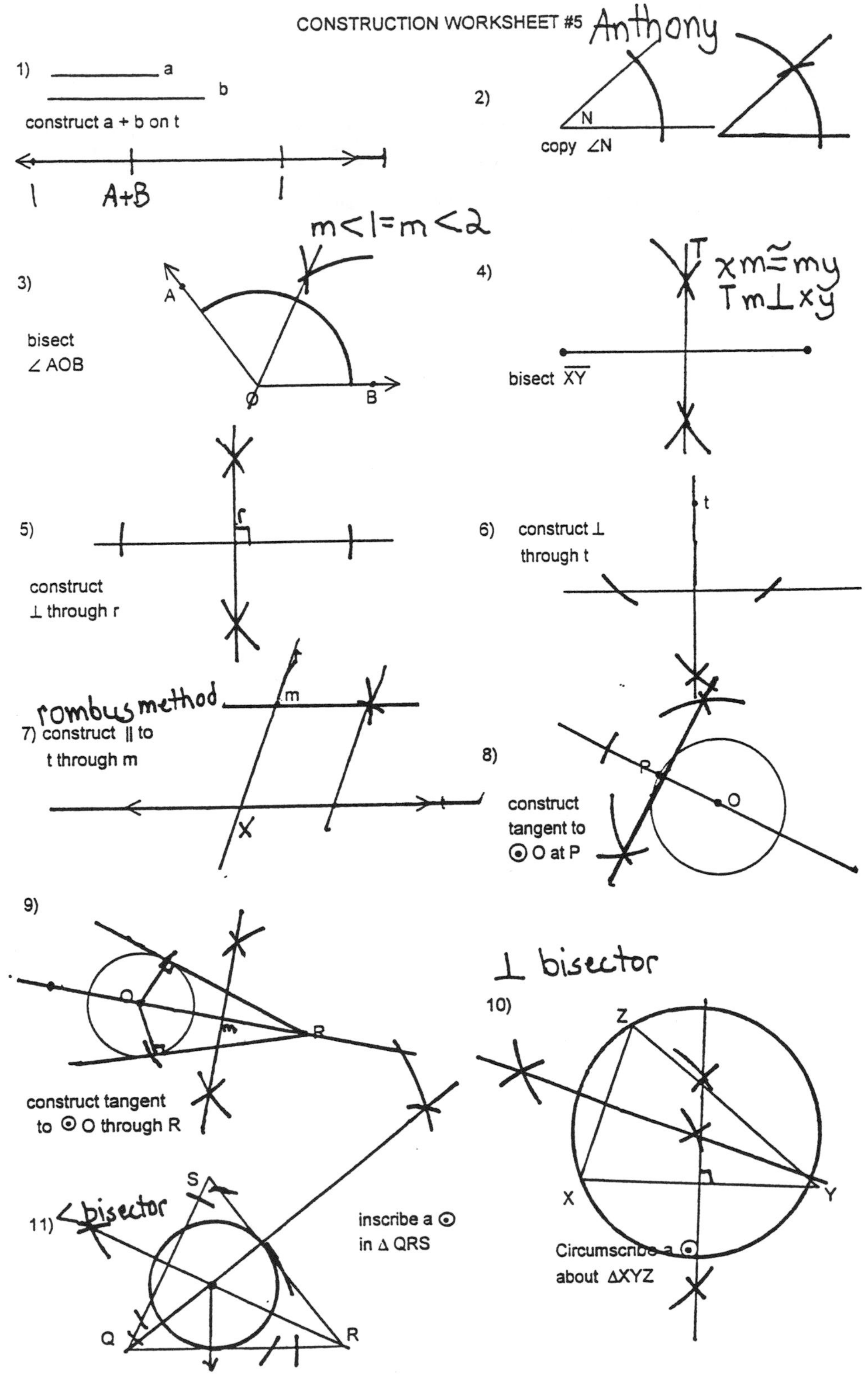
CONSTRUCTION WORKSHEET #5
Anthony
1)
a
b
construct a + b on t
A+B
2)
N
copy ∠N
m<1=m<2
3)
A
bisect
∠ AOB
O
B
4)
T
xm≅my
Tm⊥xy
bisect $\overline{XY}$
5)
r
construct
⊥ through r
6)
t
construct ⊥
through t
rombus method
m
7) construct ∥ to
t through m
X
8)
P
O
construct
tangent to
⊙ O at P
9)
O
m
R
construct tangent
to ⊙ O through R
⊥ bisector
10)
Z
X
Y
Circumscribe a ⊙
about ΔXYZ
S
11) < bisector
inscribe a ⊙
in Δ QRS
Q
R

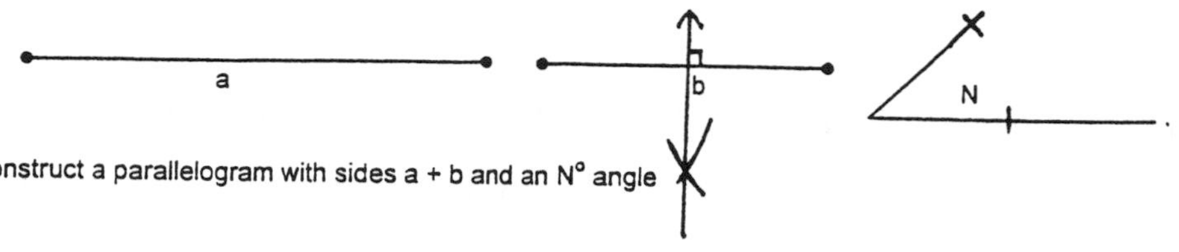

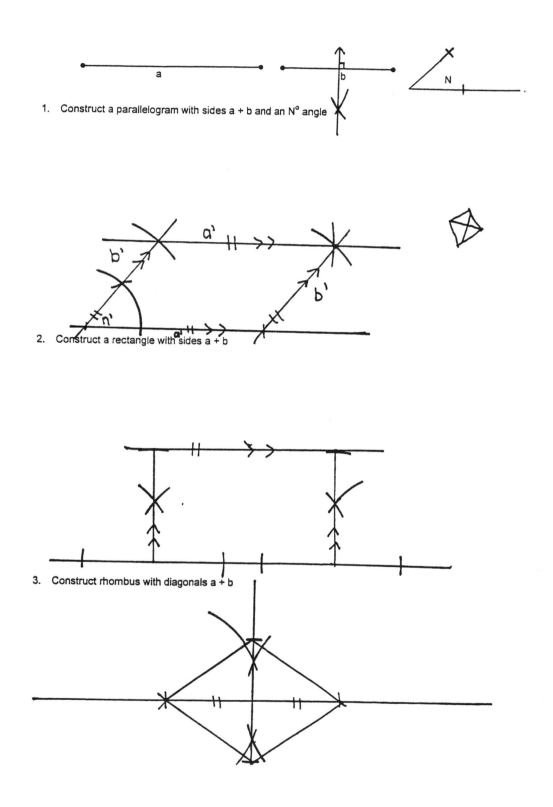

1. Construct a parallelogram with sides a + b and an N° angle

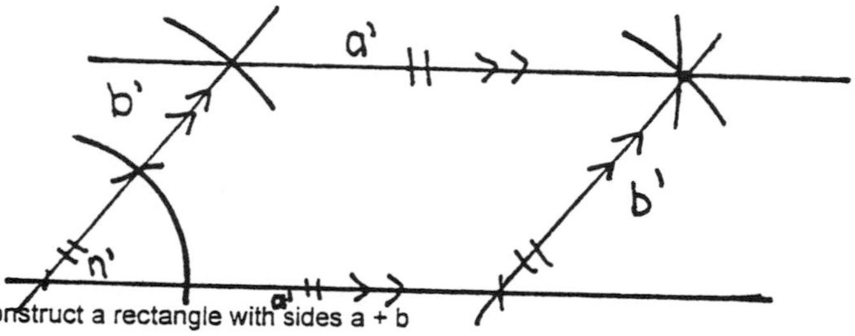

2. Construct a rectangle with sides a + b

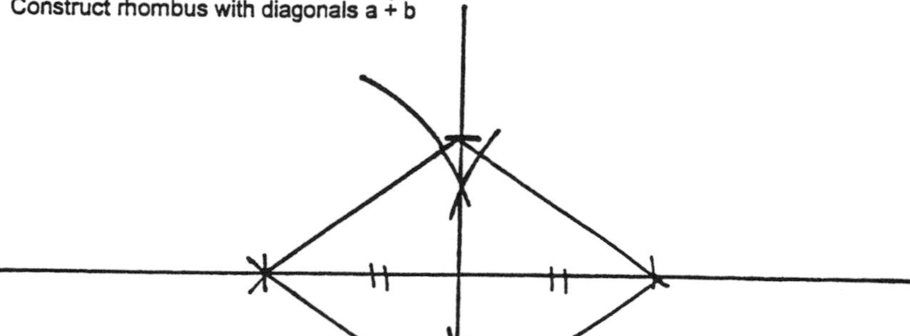

3. Construct rhombus with diagonals a + b

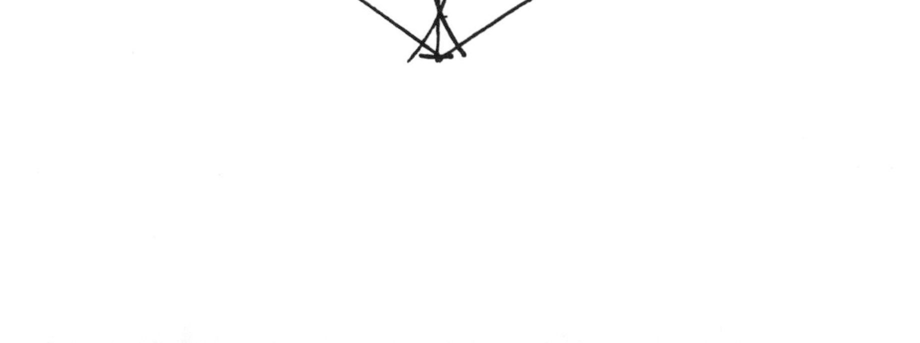

QUESTIONS FOR DISCUSSION: TASKS IN NOTEBOOK

- To what extent do students seem to be able to carry out the appropriate steps that result in a correct figure being constructed and to what extent does this vary across different constructions?
- What does this work reveal about what students understand?
- What does it mean to understand this topic?
- Zielinski has several goals for his students including (a) demonstrating skills in geometric construction with the appropriate sequence of steps, (b) analyzing and developing relationships between various constructions and drawing conclusions, and (c) making connections to other ideas. What evidence is there in students' written work about their accomplishments in relation to these goals?

STEPS TO CONSTRUCT THE ANGLE BISECTOR

1. Draw any angle ABC that is less than 180°.
2. Place the tip of the compass on vertex B of angle ABC.
3. Swing an arc so that it intersects each side of the angle.
4. Put the tip of the compass on the point where the arc you just made crossed side BA and swing an arc inside angle ABC.
5. Without changing the opening of the compass, put the tip of the compass on the point where the arc crossed side BC and swing an arc inside angle ABC so that it intersects the arc you made in step 4. Call that point D.
6. Line up the vertex B of the triangle with the point D and draw a ray from B through D. BD is the bisector of angle ABC.

QUESTIONS FOR DISCUSSION: THE ANGLE BISECTOR

- What does each of the arcs in this construction represent?
- What argument could I make to myself about why this particular set of moves produces the angle bisector?
- What condition(s) does the set of points on the angle bisector satisfy?
- What sense does it make to construct bisectors of the angles of a triangle as a first step in inscribing a circle within the triangle?
- What connection do I see between the intersection of the angle bisectors of a triangle and the center of a circle that is tangent to each side of the triangle?

Lightning

In this task you are asked to solve problems about real situations involving lightning and thunder. It also provides the opportunity for you to work from a map drawn to scale and use ideas from geometry to reason about distances.

In a thunderstorm, you see the lightning before you hear the thunder.

This is because the light travels essentially instantaneously, whereas the sound of the thunder may take a few seconds to reach you.

One way to estimate the distance from where you are to where the lightning struck is to count the number of seconds until you hear the thunder, and then divide by three. The number you get is the approximate distance in kilometers.

1. Suppose you see a lightning flash, and count 3 seconds before you hear the thunder.
   a) How far away was the lightning?
   b) What does the "divide by three" rule tell you about how fast the sound of thunder travels through the air? Explain.

2. People are standing at the four points P, Q, R, and S marked in the map below. They all saw lightning strike at point L.

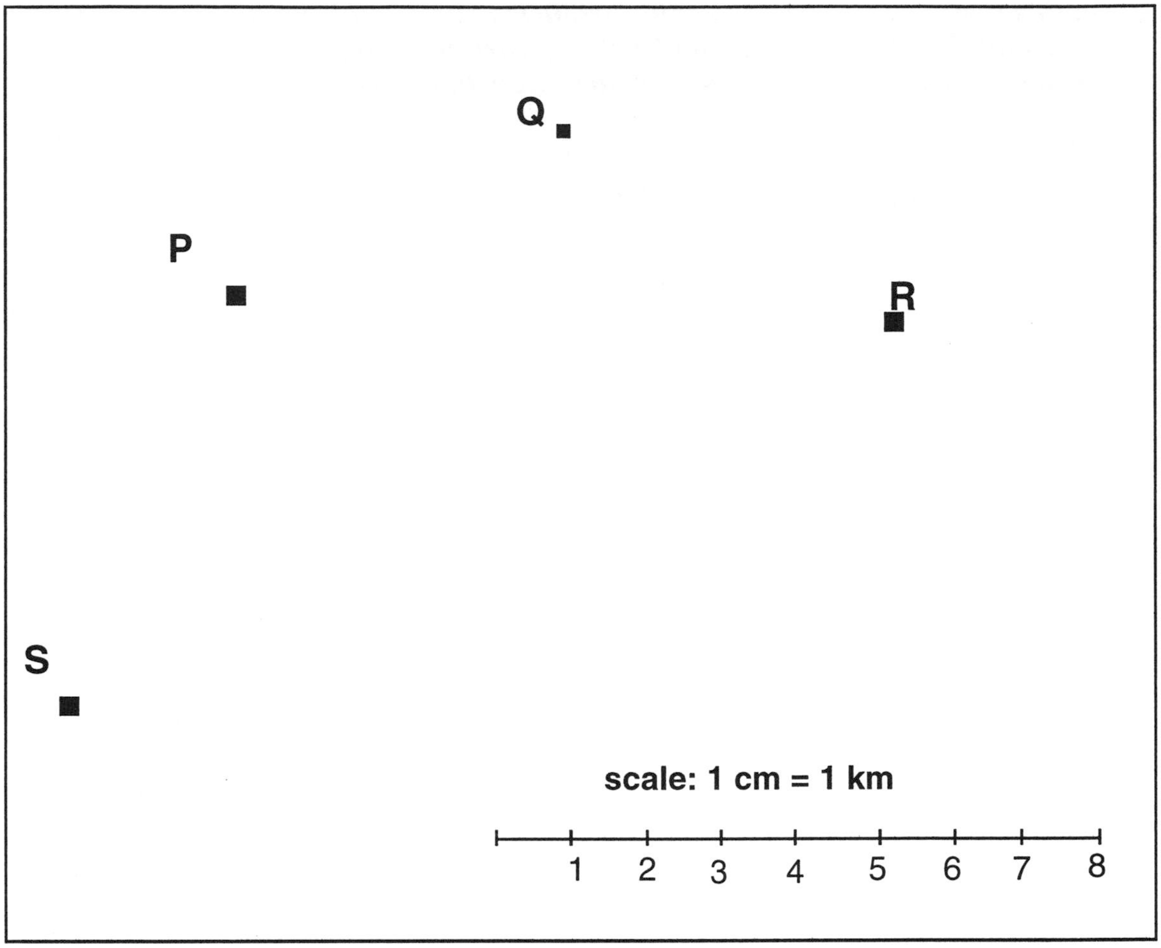

a) Who heard the thunder first? Why?

b) Who heard it last? Why?

c) One of the people heard it after about 15 seconds. Who was it? Explain.

d) After how many seconds did the person at P hear the thunder? Show how you know.

3. Now suppose lightning strikes again at a different place. The person at P and the person at Q both heard the thunder after the same amount of time.
   a) Show on the map below a place where the lightning might have struck.
   b) Are there other places where the lightning might have struck? If so, show as many of these places as you can.
   c) Can you tell which of P and R heard the thunder first? If so, say how. If not, say why not.

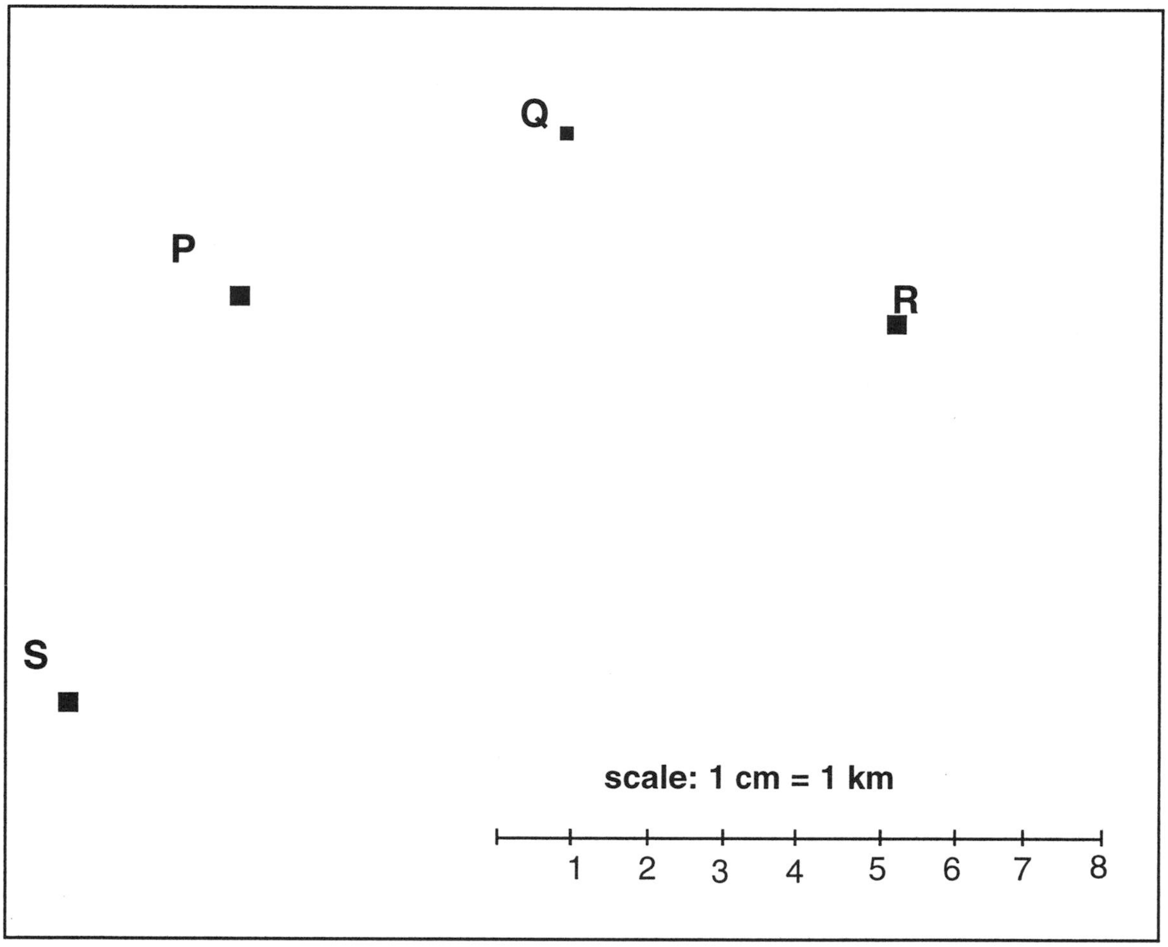

4. Now suppose lightning strikes once again at yet a different place.
   a) If you know that the person at P heard the thunder 9 seconds after she saw the lightning, show on the map as many points as you can where the lightning might have struck.
   b) If you learn that the person at R heard the thunder from this same lightning stroke 18 seconds after he saw the lightning, show on the map the places where the lightning might have struck.

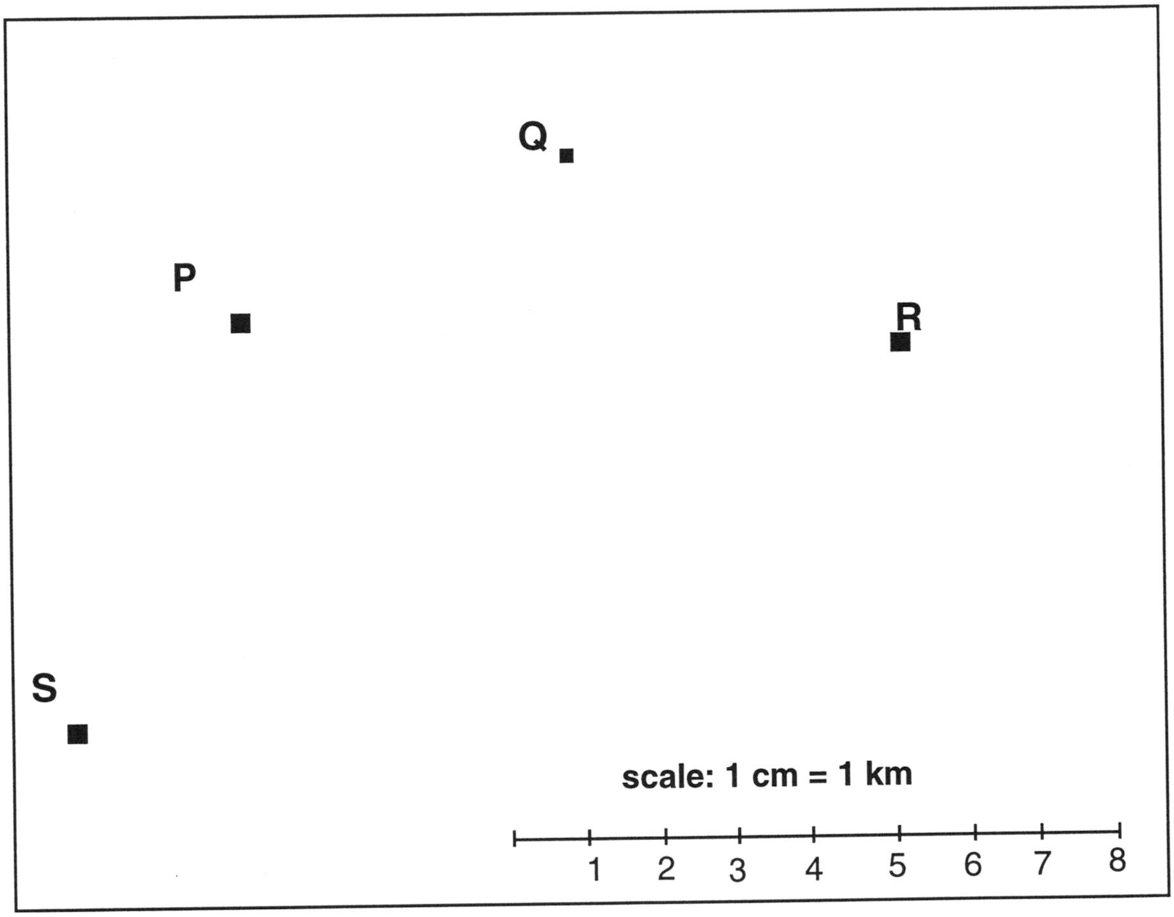

QUESTIONS FOR DISCUSSION: THE *LIGHTNING* TASK

- Why would a teacher want to use a task like this?
- What does this task have the potential to reveal about students' understanding of locating points that meet certain conditions?
- What is the potential of this task to provide information to Zielinski about students' accomplishments in relation to his three big goals?

STUDENT WORK ON THE *LIGHTNING* TASK

Name__________________ Date Linda

Lightning

The aim of this assessment is to provide the opportunity for you to:
• solve problems about real situations involving lightning and thunder;
• work from a map drawn to scale;
• use ideas from geometry to reason about distances.

In a thunderstorm, you see the lightning before you hear the thunder. This is because the light travels essentially instantaneously, whereas the sound of the thunder may take a few seconds to reach you.

One way to estimate the distance from where you are to where the lightning struck is to count the number of seconds until you hear the thunder, and then divide by three. The number you get is the approximate distance in kilometers.

1. Suppose you see a lightning flash, and count 3 seconds before you hear the thunder.

   a. How far away was the lightning?

   1 Kilometer

   b. What does the "divide by three" rule tell you about how fast the sound of thunder travels through the air? Explain.

   This tells us that lightening travels 3 times as fast as the sound

Name________________ Date Linda____________

2. People are standing at the four points P, Q, R, and S marked in the map below. They all saw lightning strike at point L.

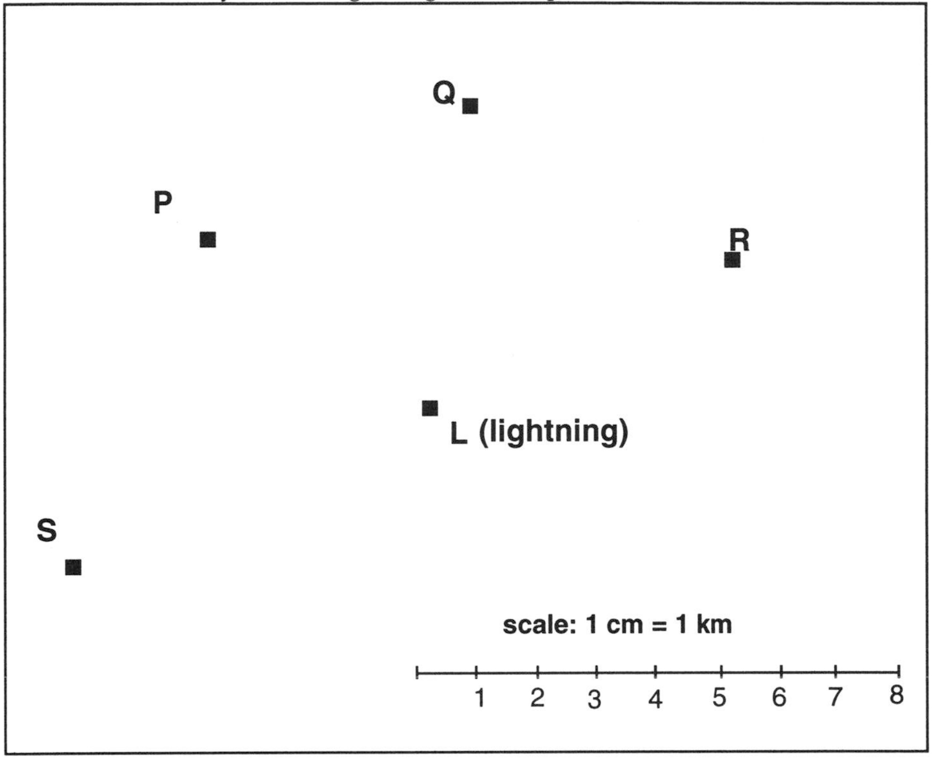

a. Who heard the thunder first? Why?

P/ heard it first because it is the closest.

b. Who heard it last? Why?

S/ heard it last because it is the further away

c. One of the people heard it after about 15 seconds. Who was it? Explain.

Q/ it has 5 Kilometers away and 5.3 is 15.

d. After how many seconds did the person at P hear the thunder? Show how you know.

About 14 1/2 seconds because it was just a little under 5 kilometers

Name____________________ Date____________________

3. Now suppose lightning strikes again at a different place. The person at P and the person at Q both heard the thunder after the same amount of time.

   a. Show on the map below a place where the lightning might have struck.

   b. Are there other places where the lightning might have struck? If so, show as many of these places as you can.

   c. Can you tell which of P and R heard the thunder first? If so, say how. If not, say why not.

   Yes/the closest one would have heard the noise first.

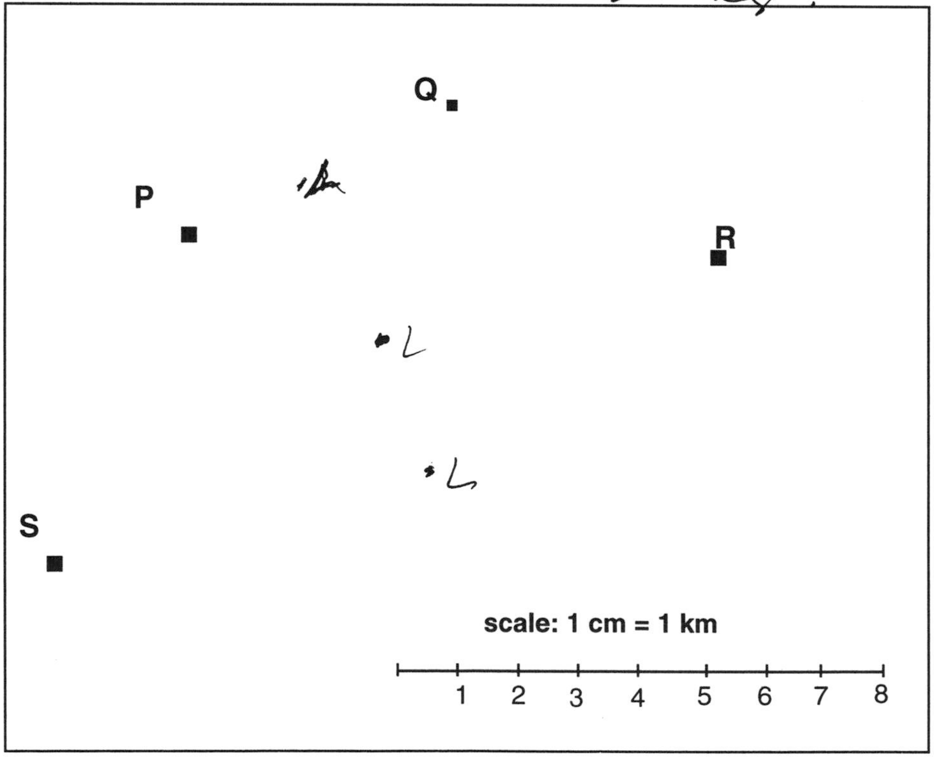

Name_________________ Date_________________

4. Now suppose lightning strikes once again at yet a different place.

a. If you know that the person at P heard the thunder 9 seconds after she saw the lightning, show on the map as many points as you can where the lightning might have struck.

b. If you learn that the person at R heard the thunder from this same lightning stroke 18 seconds after he saw the lightning, show on the map the places where the lightning might have struck.

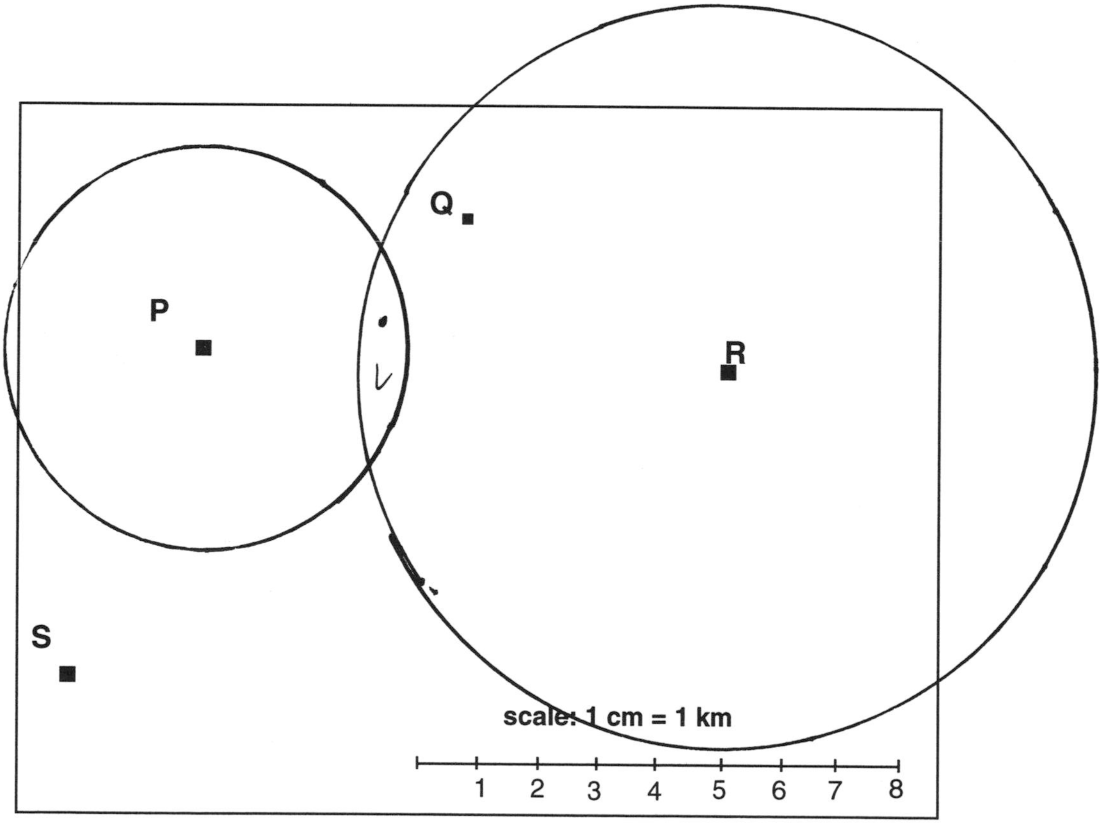

Name__________________ Date__________________ James

Lightning

The aim of this assessment is to provide the opportunity for you to:
- solve problems about real situations involving lightning and thunder;
- work from a map drawn to scale;
- use ideas from geometry to reason about distances.

In a thunderstorm, you see the lightning before you hear the thunder. This is because the light travels essentially instantaneously, whereas the sound of the thunder may take a few seconds to reach you.

One way to estimate the distance from where you are to where the lightning struck is to count the number of seconds until you hear the thunder, and then divide by three. The number you get is the approximate distance in kilometers.

1. Suppose you see a lightning flash, and count 3 seconds before you hear the thunder.

   a. How far away was the lightning?

   1 Km

   b. What does the "divide by three" rule tell you about how fast the sound of thunder travels through the air? Explain.

   Sound travels 3 times slower than light through the air

Name__________________ Date__________________

James

2. People are standing at the four points P, Q, R, and S marked in the map below. They all saw lightning strike at point L.

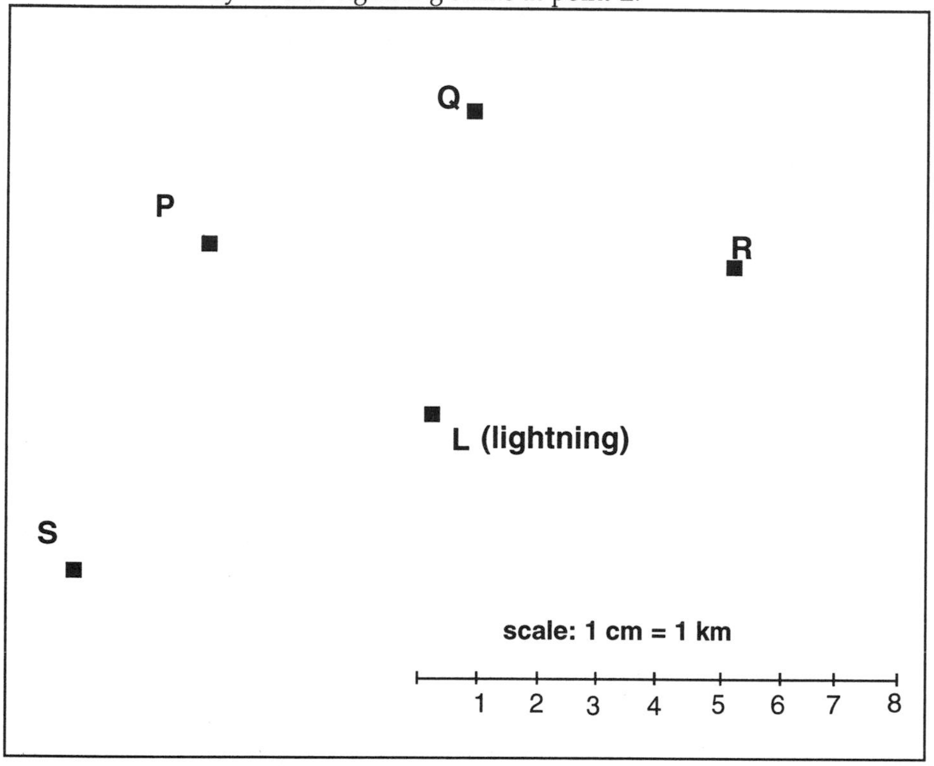

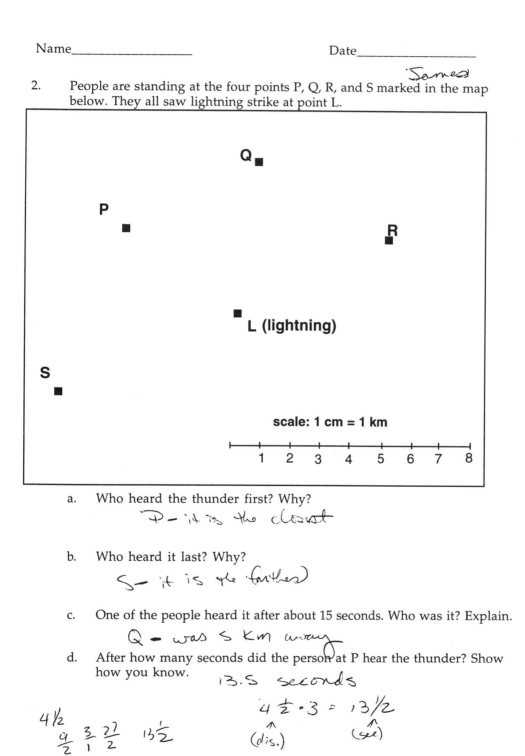

a. Who heard the thunder first? Why?

P – it is the closest

b. Who heard it last? Why?

S – it is the farthest

c. One of the people heard it after about 15 seconds. Who was it? Explain.

Q – was 5 km away

d. After how many seconds did the person at P hear the thunder? Show how you know.

13.5 seconds

$4\frac{1}{2} \cdot 3 = 13\frac{1}{2}$

(dis.) (sec)

$4\frac{1}{2}$

$\frac{9}{2} \cdot \frac{3}{1} = \frac{27}{2}$ $13\frac{1}{2}$

Name__________________ Date__________________

James

3. Now suppose lightning strikes again at a different place. The person at P and the person at Q both heard the thunder after the same amount of time.

a. Show on the map below a place where the lightning might have struck.

b. Are there other places where the lightning might have struck? If so, show as many of these places as you can.

c. Can you tell which of P and R heard the thunder first? If so, say how. If not, say why not. No, because you didn't know exactly were it struck

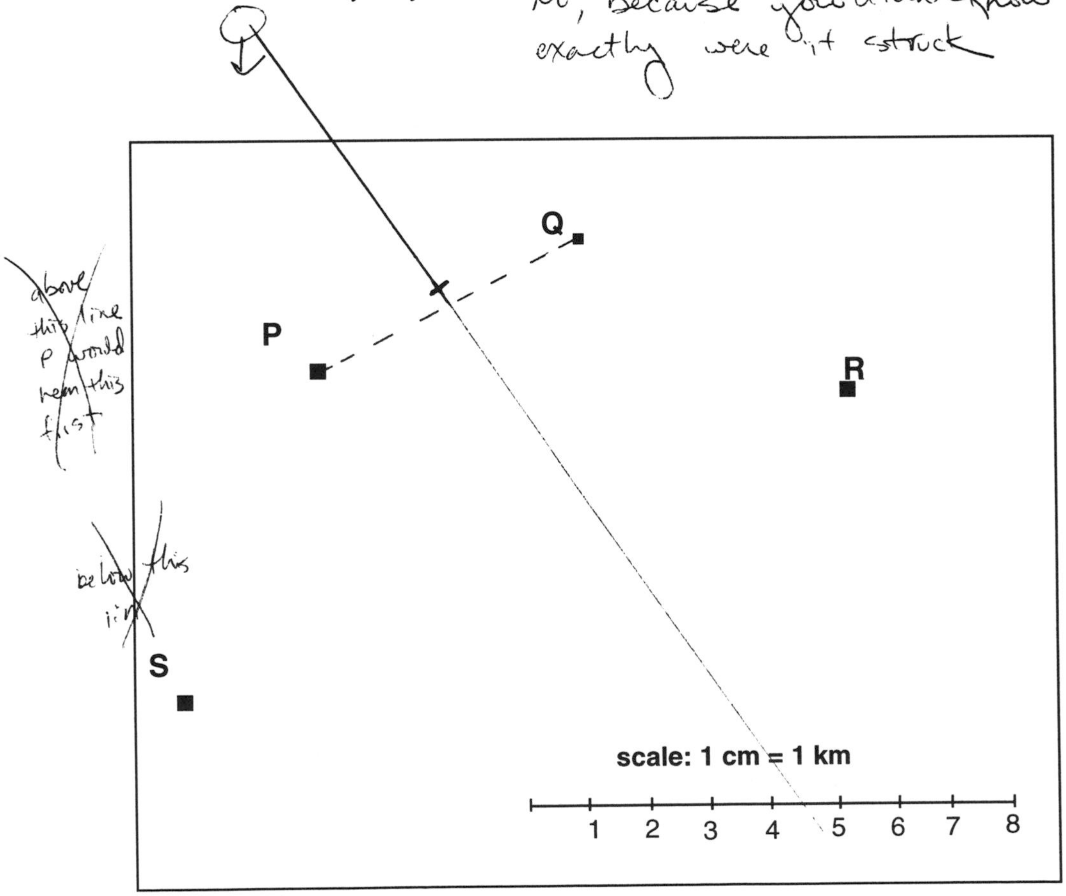

Name____________________ Date____________________

4. Now suppose lightning strikes once again at yet a different place.

a. If you know that the person at P heard the thunder 9 seconds after she saw the lightning, show on the map as many points as you can where the lightning might have struck.

b. If you learn that the person at R heard the thunder from this same lightning stroke 18 seconds after he saw the lightning, show on the map the places where the lightning might have struck.

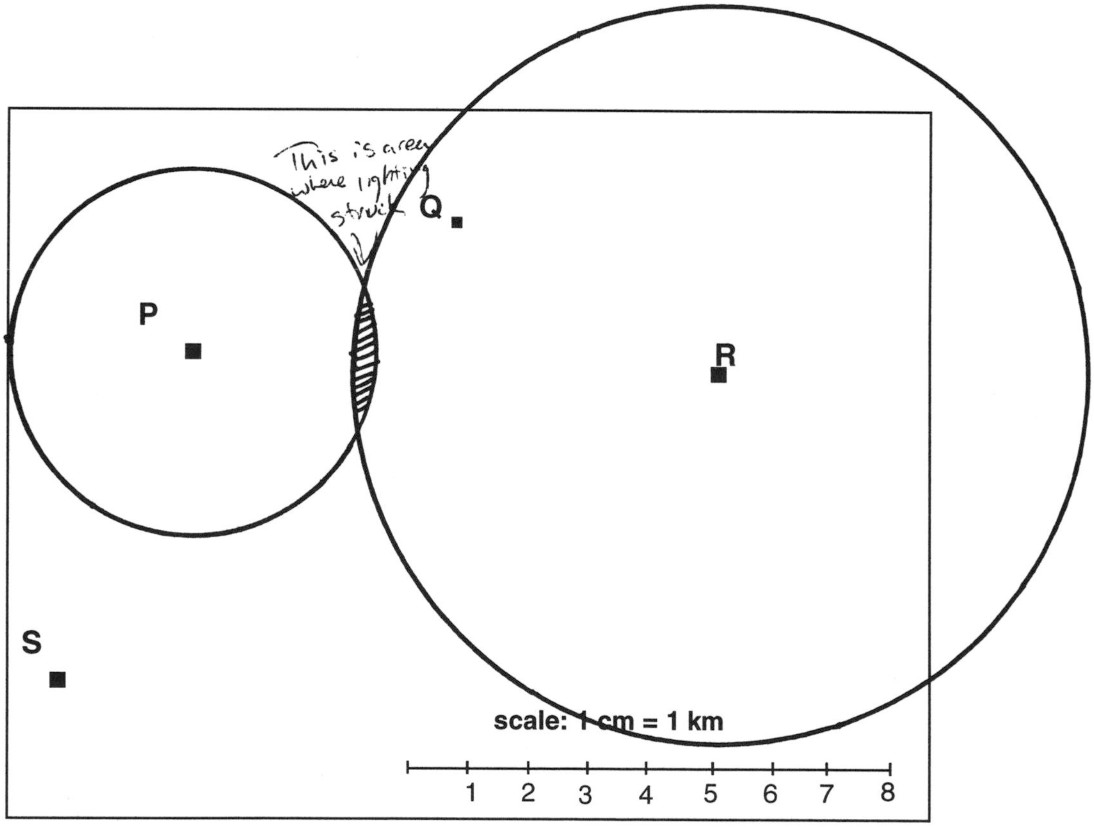

Name *Angela* Date

Lightning

The aim of this assessment is to provide the opportunity for you to: • solve problems about real situations involving lightning and thunder; • work from a map drawn to scale; • use ideas from geometry to reason about distances.

In a thunderstorm, you see the lightning before you hear the thunder. This is because the light travels essentially instantaneously, whereas the sound of the thunder may take a few seconds to reach you.

One way to estimate the distance from where you are to where the lightning struck is to count the number of seconds until you hear the thunder, and then divide by three. The number you get is the approximate distance in kilometers.

1. Suppose you see a lightning flash, and count 3 seconds before you hear the thunder.

   a. How far away was the lightning?

   1 Kilometer

   b. What does the "divide by three" rule tell you about how fast the sound of thunder travels through the air? Explain.

   Sound travel about 1km./per Seco
   That mean Sound travel Slower
   than light

Name *Angela* Date____________

2. People are standing at the four points P, Q, R, and S marked in the map below. They all saw lightning strike at point L.

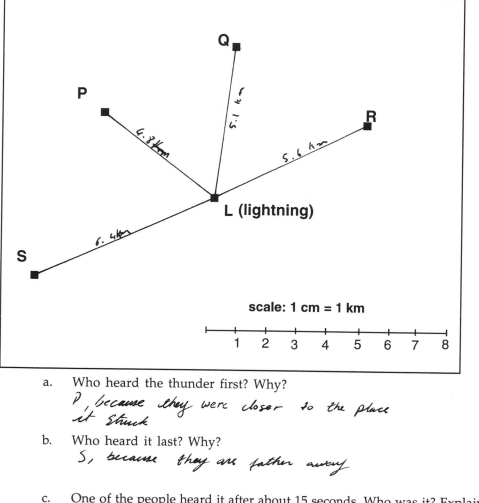

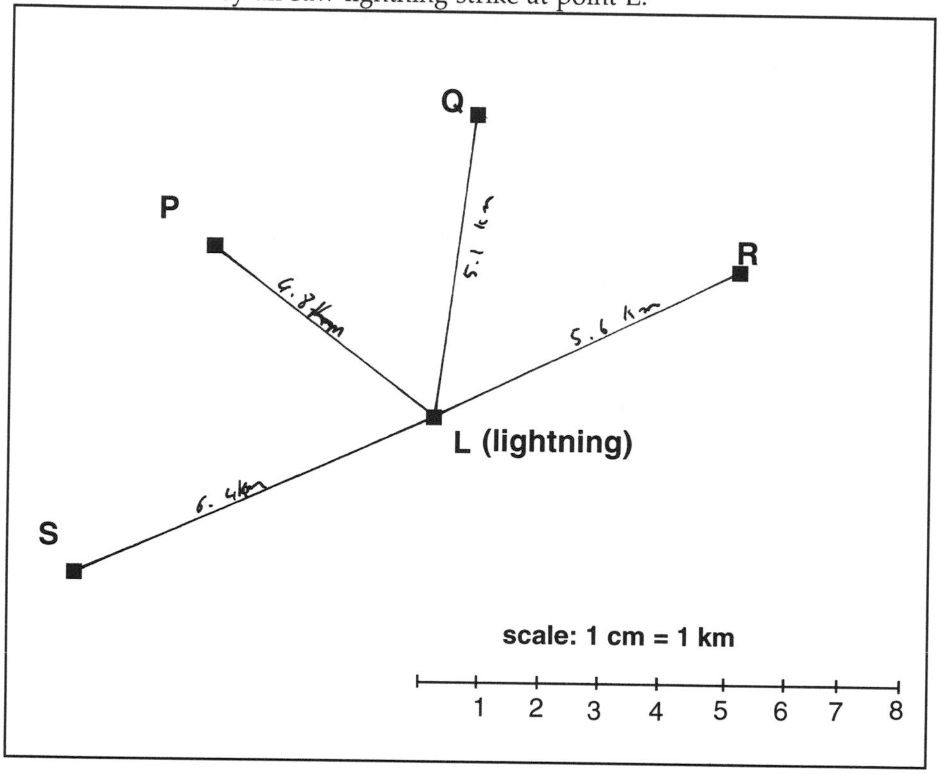

a. Who heard the thunder first? Why?

P, because they were closer to the place it Struck

b. Who heard it last? Why?

S, because they are father away

c. One of the people heard it after about 15 seconds. Who was it? Explain.

Q, because 15 divide by 3 is 5 and that is how far ~~it is~~ away from the lighting

d. After how many seconds did the person at P hear the thunder? Show how you know.

14.5 sec if sound travel at 3 sec/1km you take 4.8 and multiply by 3 and get approx. 14.5 sec.

Name Angela Date

3. Now suppose lightning strikes again at a different place. The person at P and the person at Q both heard the thunder after the same amount of time.

   a. Show on the map below a place where the lightning might have struck.

   look at the map

   b. Are there other places where the lightning might have struck? If so, show as many of these places as you can.

   yes, the lighting could have struck any where along line since this line travel exactly in between P and Q

   c. Can you tell which of P and R heard the thunder first? If so, say how. If not, say why not.

   No, because you cant tell the exact point of where the thunder hit. If you knew that you could answer this question.

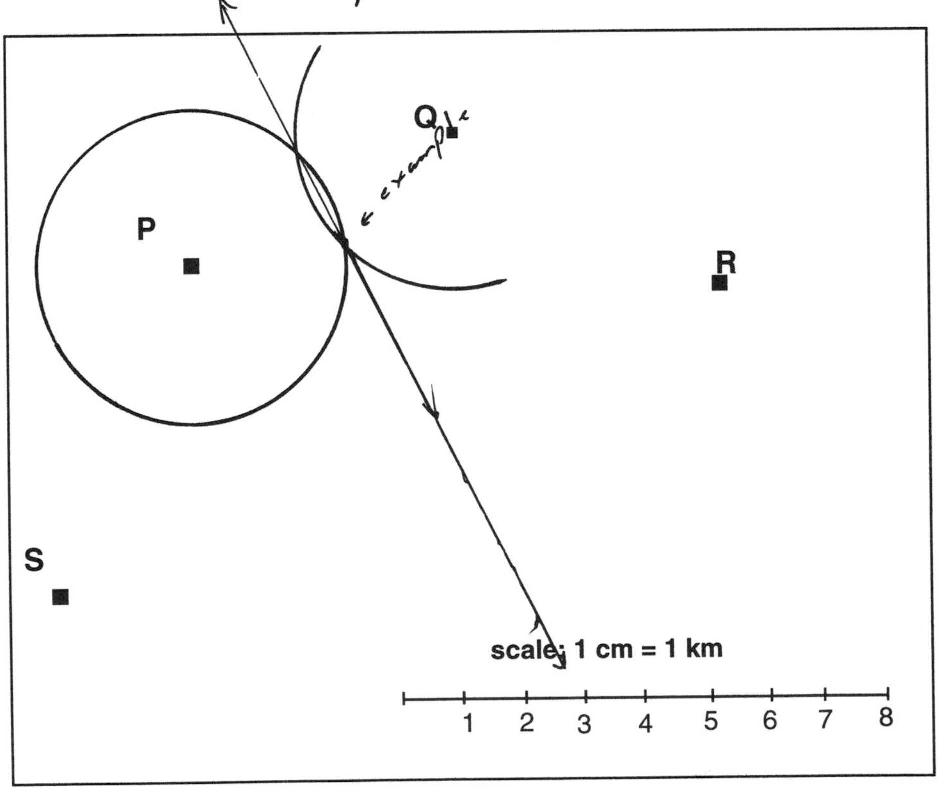

Name Angela Date

4. Now suppose lightning strikes once again at yet a different place.

a. If you know that the person at P heard the thunder 9 seconds after she saw the lightning, show on the map as many points as you can where the lightning might have struck.

b. If you learn that the person at R heard the thunder from this same lightning stroke 18 seconds after he saw the lightning, show on the map the places where the lightning might have struck.

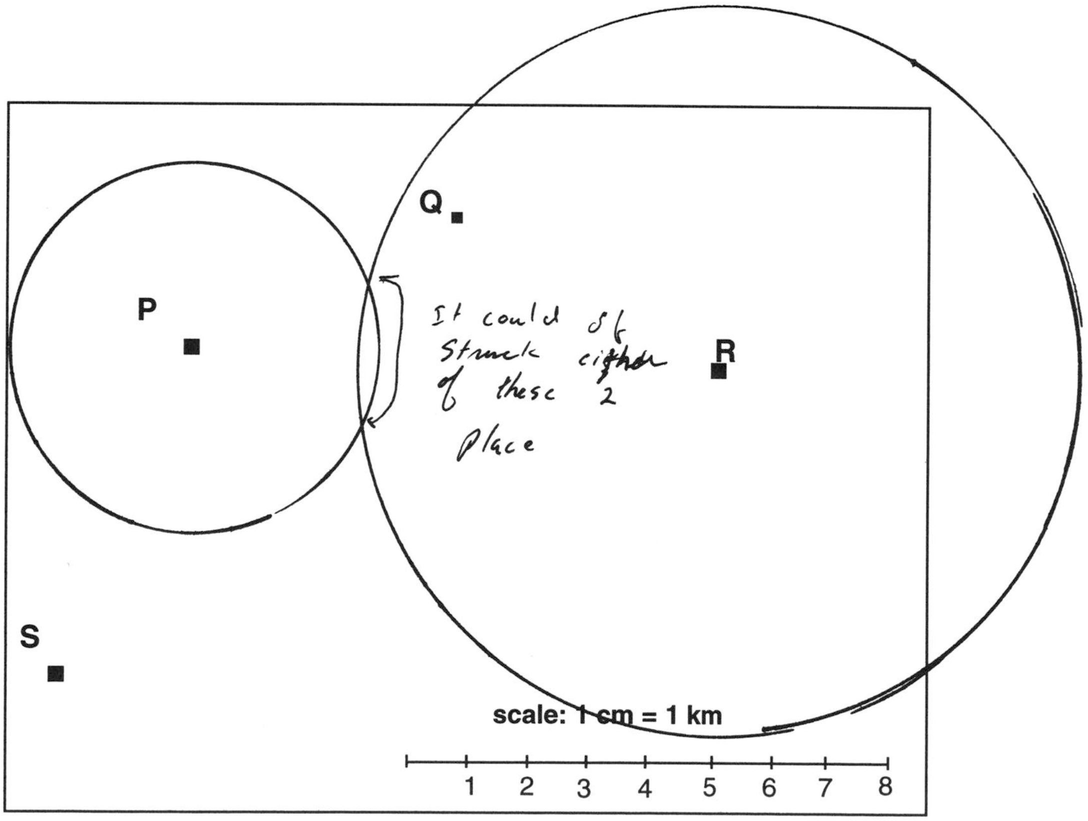

Name Anthony Date________

Lightning

The aim of this assessment is to provide the opportunity for you to:
• solve problems about real situations involving lightning and thunder;
• work from a map drawn to scale;
• use ideas from geometry to reason about distances.

In a thunderstorm, you see the lightning before you hear the thunder. This is because the light travels essentially instantaneously, whereas the sound of the thunder may take a few seconds to reach you.

One way to estimate the distance from where you are to where the lightning struck is to count the number of seconds until you hear the thunder, and then divide by three. The number you get is the approximate distance in kilometers.

1. Suppose you see a lightning flash, and count 3 seconds before you hear the thunder.

   a. How far away was the lightning?

   1 Kilometer

   b. What does the "divide by three" rule tell you about how fast the sound of thunder travels through the air? Explain.

   It means it takes three seconds for thunder to reach you if you are 1 Kilometer away

Name Anthony   Date

2. People are standing at the four points P, Q, R, and S marked in the map below. They all saw lightning strike at point L.

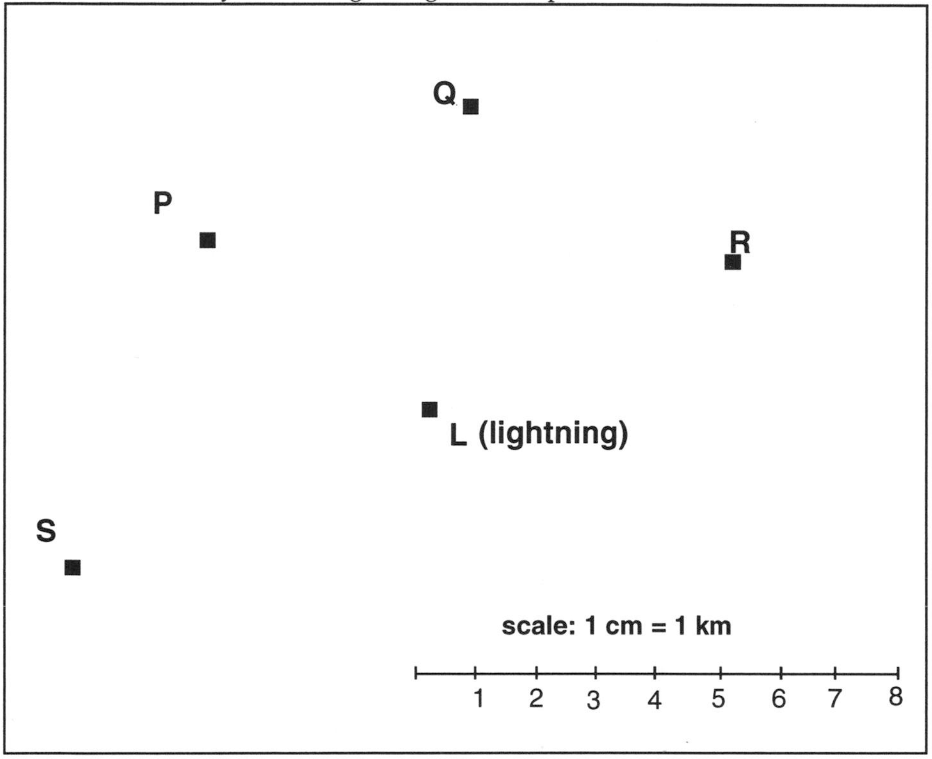

a. Who heard the thunder first? Why?

P heard it first because they were standing the closest.

b. Who heard it last? Why?

S because they were standing the farthest.

c. One of the people heard it after about 15 seconds. Who was it? Explain.

It was Q because they were 5 Kilometers away.

d. After how many seconds did the person at P hear the thunder? Show how you know.

It would be after 14 seconds because they are just under 5 Kilometers away.

Name Anthony Date

3. Now suppose lightning strikes again at a different place. The person at P and the person at Q both heard the thunder after the same amount of time.

   a. Show on the map below a place where the lightning might have struck.

   b. Are there other places where the lightning might have struck? If so, show as many of these places as you can.

   c. Can you tell which of P and R heard the thunder first? If so, say how. If not, say why not.

   No, because if you drew a line between P+R the line of lightning is not perpendicular to line P.R.

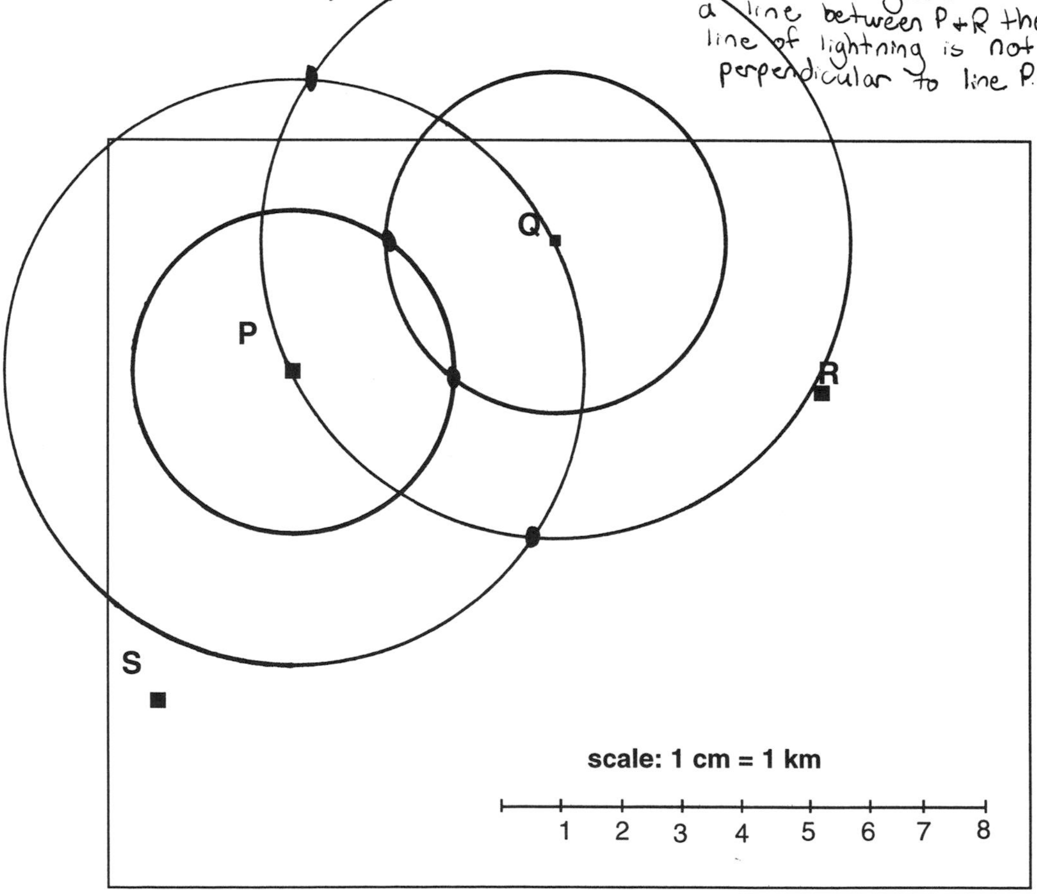

Name Anthony Date__________

4. Now suppose lightning strikes once again at yet a different place.

   a. If you know that the person at P heard the thunder 9 seconds after she saw the lightning, show on the map as many points as you can where the lightning might have struck.

   b. If you learn that the person at R heard the thunder from this same lightning stroke 18 seconds after he saw the lightning, show on the map the places where the lightning might have struck.

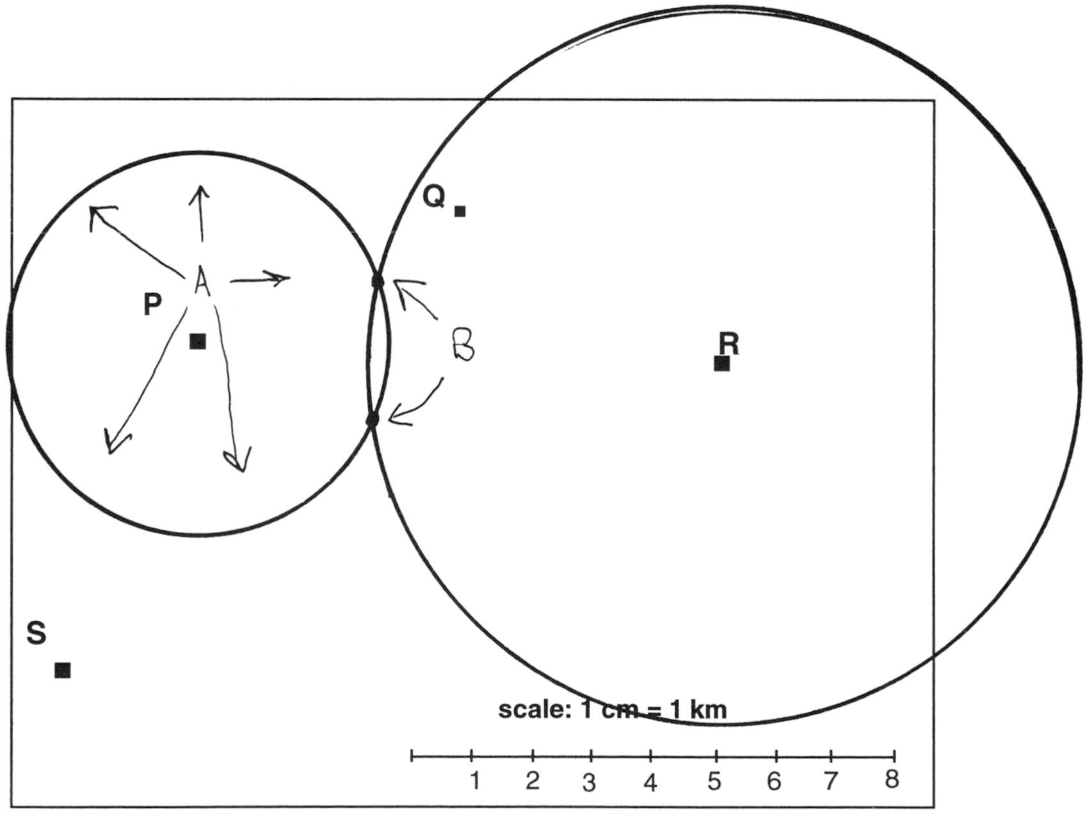

Name Ben Date

Lightning

The aim of this assessment is to provide the opportunity for you to: • solve problems about real situations involving lightning and thunder; • work from a map drawn to scale; • use ideas from geometry to reason about distances.

In a thunderstorm, you see the lightning before you hear the thunder. This is because the light travels essentially instantaneously, whereas the sound of the thunder may take a few seconds to reach you.

One way to estimate the distance from where you are to where the lightning struck is to count the number of seconds until you hear the thunder, and then divide by three. The number you get is the approximate distance in kilometers.

1. Suppose you see a lightning flash, and count 3 seconds before you hear the thunder.

   a. How far away was the lightning?

   1 Kilometer

   b. What does the "divide by three" rule tell you about how fast the sound of thunder travels through the air? Explain.

   The sound of the thunder travels a 3 seconds per hour.

Name Ben Date

2. People are standing at the four points P, Q, R, and S marked in the map below. They all saw lightning strike at point L.

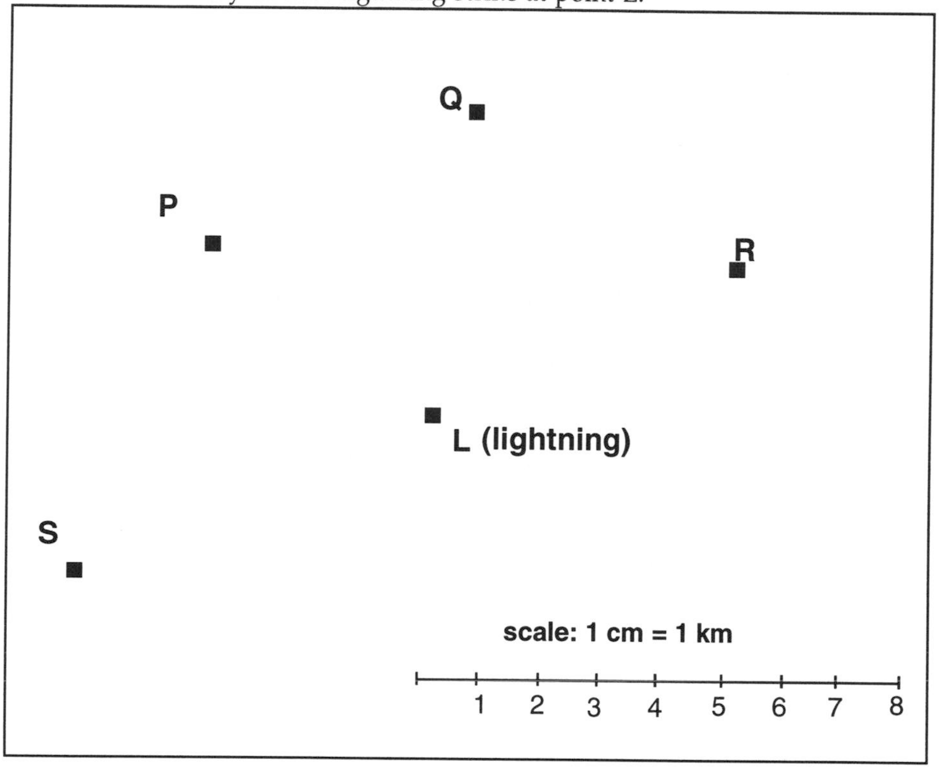

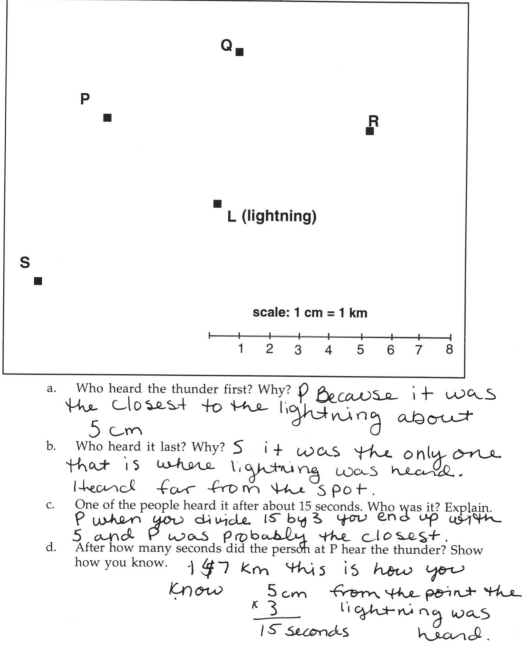

a. Who heard the thunder first? Why? P Because it was the closest to the lightning about 5 cm

b. Who heard it last? Why? S it was the only one that is where lightning was heard. Heard far from the spot.

c. One of the people heard it after about 15 seconds. Who was it? Explain. P when you divide 15 by 3 you end up with 5 and P was probably the closest.

d. After how many seconds did the person at P hear the thunder? Show how you know. 147 km this is how you know

5 cm
× 3
15 seconds

from the point the lightning was heard.

Name Ben Date

3. Now suppose lightning strikes again at a different place. The person at P and the person at Q both heard the thunder after the same amount of time.

a. Show on the map below a place where the lightning might have struck.

OK

b. Are there other places where the lightning might have struck? If so, show as many of these places as you can. Thousands. It could of struck anywhere along the line this is equal from P and Q.

c. Can you tell which of P and R heard the thunder first? If so, say how. If not, say why not. P Probably heard the lightning an extremely short time before, since my measurment shows that P is 1/10 of a kilometer closer to the area in which the lightning struck, but if anything struck above the point

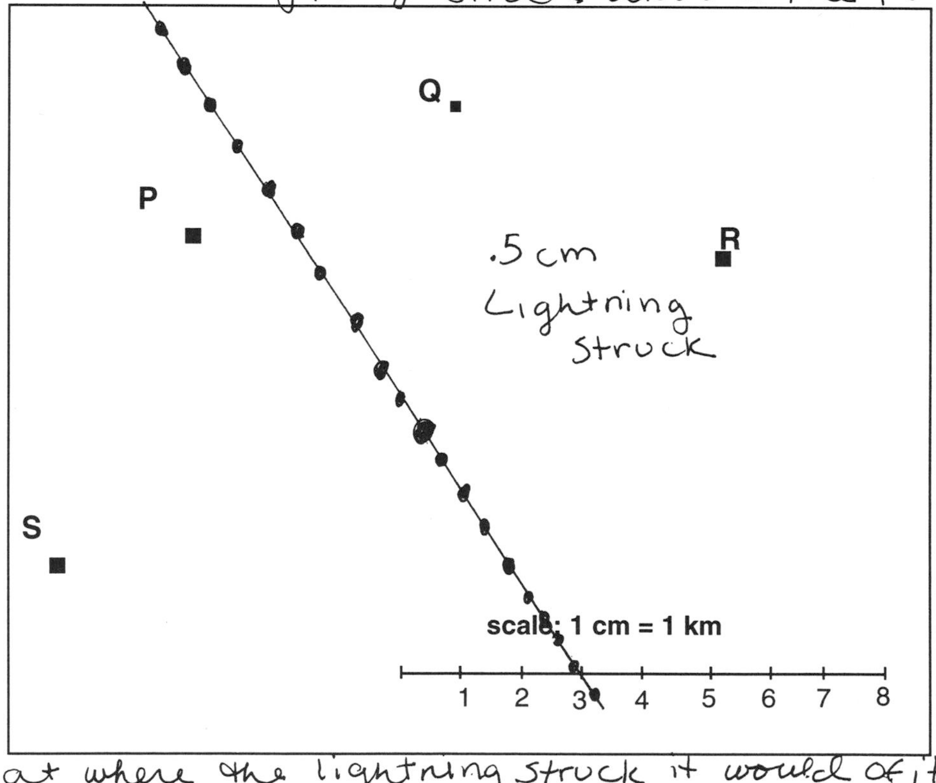

at where the lightning struck it would of it. P, but it, it hit below the point of where it is on the line it would of been heard by R. you would have a large amount of places.

Name Ben Date

4. Now suppose lightning strikes once again at yet a different place.

a. If you know that the person at P heard the thunder 9 seconds after she saw the lightning, show on the map as many points as you can where the lightning might have struck. Lightning could of struck anywhere along the circumference of the circle.

b. If you learn that the person at R heard the thunder from this same lightning stroke 18 seconds after he saw the lightning, show on the map the places where the lightning might have struck. where the two circles interesect and where they meet.

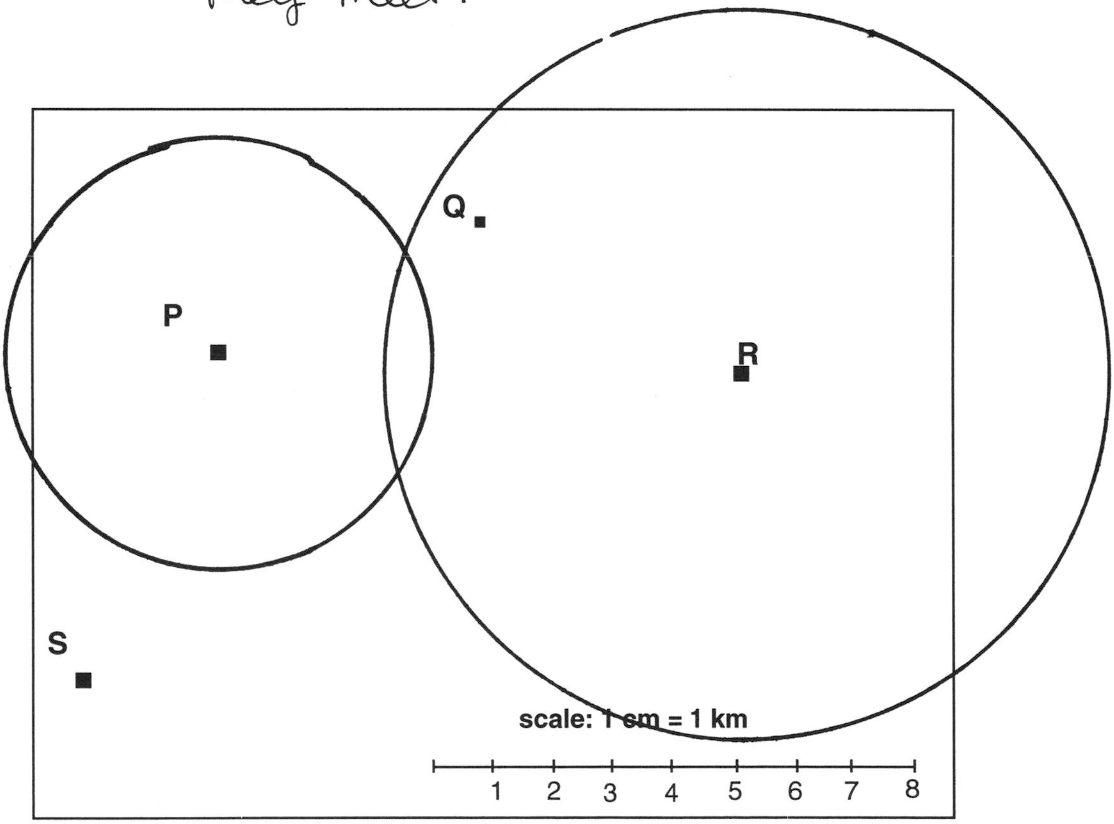

Name Johnny Date

Lightning

The aim of this assessment is to provide the opportunity for you to:
- solve problems about real situations involving lightning and thunder;
- work from a map drawn to scale;
- use ideas from geometry to reason about distances.

In a thunderstorm, you see the lightning before you hear the thunder. This is because the light travels essentially instantaneously, whereas the sound of the thunder may take a few seconds to reach you.

One way to estimate the distance from where you are to where the lightning struck is to count the number of seconds until you hear the thunder, and then divide by three. The number you get is the approximate distance in kilometers.

1. Suppose you see a lightning flash, and count 3 seconds before you hear the thunder.

   a. How far away was the lightning?

   The lightening was 1 Km away.

   b. What does the "divide by three" rule tell you about how fast the sound of thunder travels through the air? Explain.

   Light travels much faster than sound, almost exactly 1200 Km/hr faster.

Name Johnny Date____________

2. People are standing at the four points P, Q, R, and S marked in the map below. They all saw lightning strike at point L.

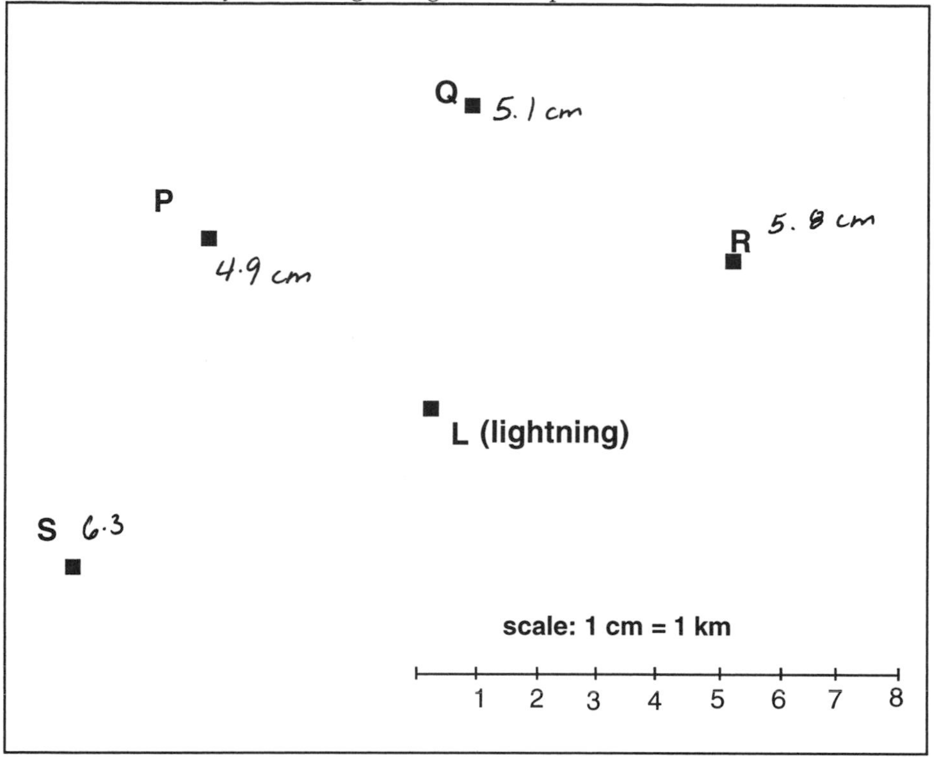

a. Who heard the thunder first? Why?

P was closest to the lightning so could have heard it first

b. Who heard it last? Why?

S was furthest away from the lighting so he would have heard it last.

c. One of the people heard it after about 15 seconds. Who was it? Explain.

3 ⟌15 = 5   5 km away Q was little more than 5 km so he would have heard it slightly more than 15 sec.

d. After how many seconds did the person at P hear the thunder? Show how you know.

4.9 × 3 = 14.7

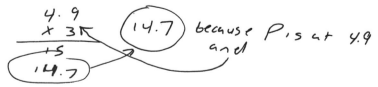

14.7 because P is at 4.9 and

Name Johnny Date

3. Now suppose lightning strikes again at a different place. The person at P and the person at Q both heard the thunder after the same amount of time.

   a. Show on the map below a place where the lightning might have struck.

   4 cm from both

   b. Are there other places where the lightning might have struck? If so, show as many of these places as you can.

   3, 5, 11

   c. Can you tell which of P and R heard the thunder first? If so, say how. If not, say why not.

   at 3 P is closer, would have heard it first
   4 P is closer, "
   5 P is closer, "
   11 R is closer, "

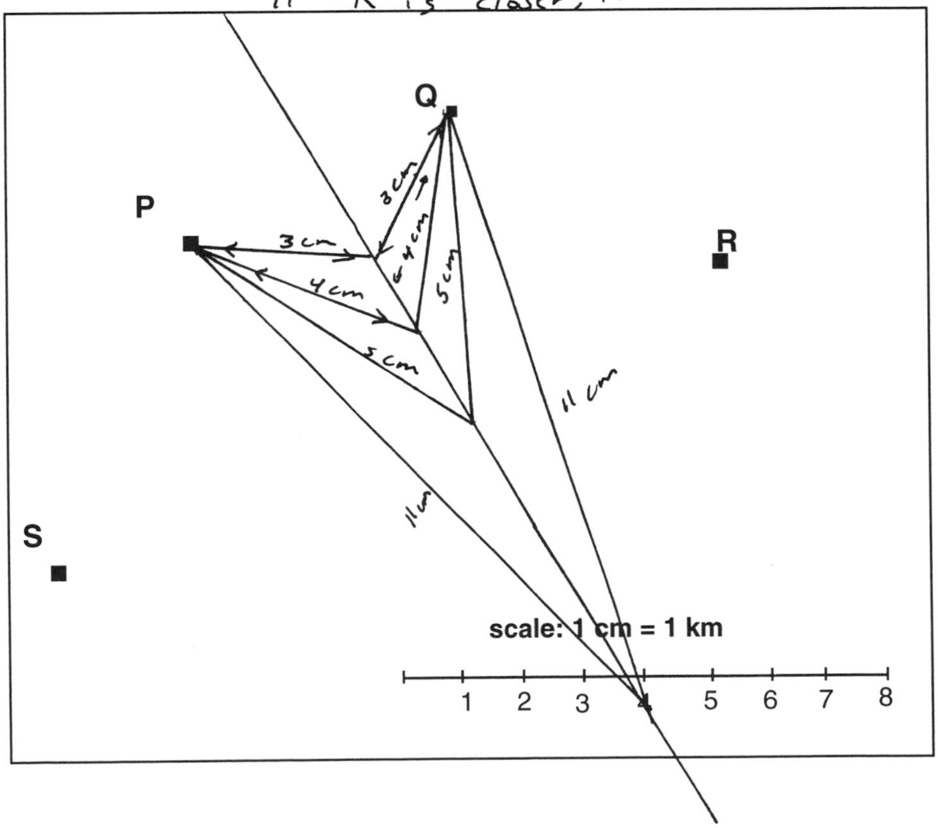

Name Johnny Date

4. Now suppose lightning strikes once again at yet a different place.

a. If you know that the person at P heard the thunder 9 seconds after she saw the lightning, show on the map as many points as you can where the lightning might have struck.

3)9 = 3   3 km away   anywhere on the circle surrounding P. the radius is 3 cm

b. If you learn that the person at R heard the thunder from this same lightning stroke 18 seconds after he saw the lightning, show on the map the places where the lightning might have struck. anywhere on the 6 inch radius circle surrounding R

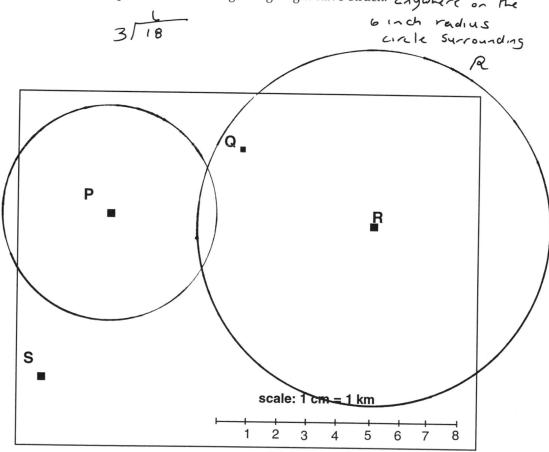

3)18 = 6

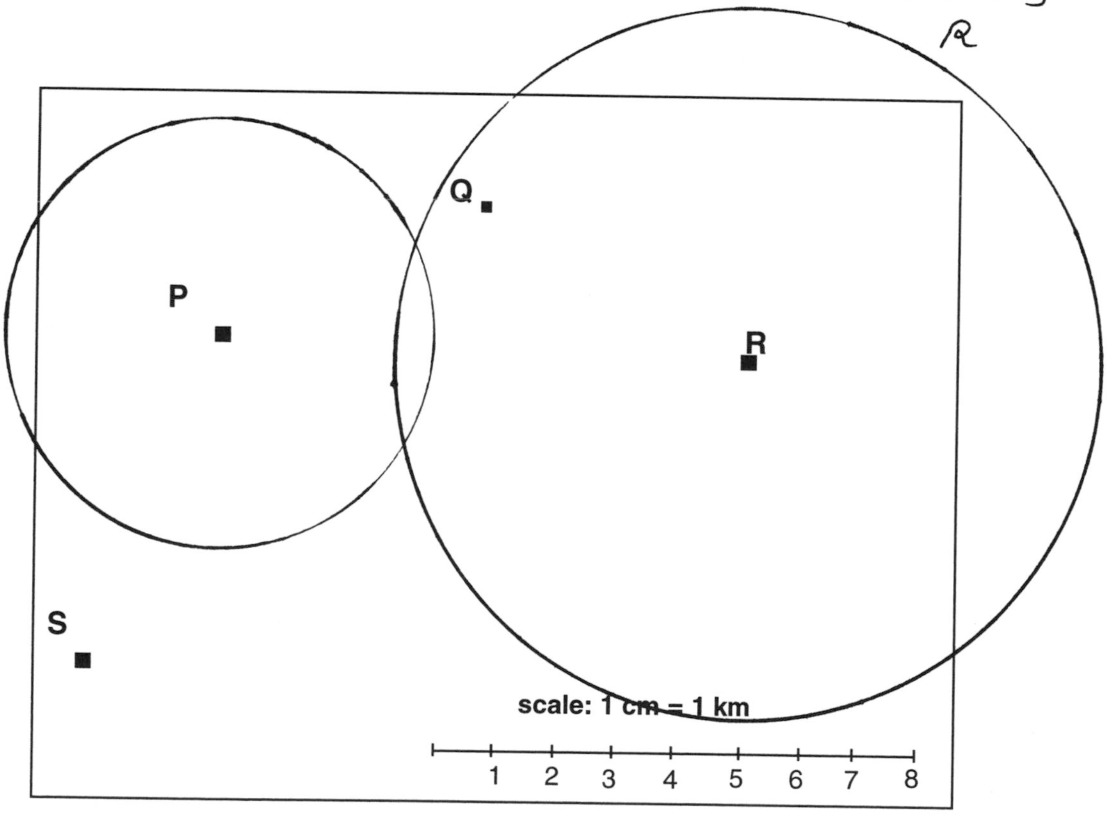

QUESTIONS FOR DISCUSSION: STUDENT WORK ON THE *LIGHTNING* TASK

- What are the ways in which students approach this task?
- To what extent do they seem to be drawing upon their work with geometric constructions?
- What can Zielinski learn about his students' progress toward the three learning goals he has for them?
- How might student work on this task shape a teachers' decisions about next instructional moves?

3

Capturing Students' Engagement With A Task

This chapter focuses on analysis of teaching and learning by examining multiple forms of documentation of students' engagement with a task. The cases are intended to provoke a discomfort with relying solely on students' written work for making claims about what they know and how they know it. The cases also provide opportunities to explore the complexity of teaching and learning in two content areas—rational numbers, and volume and surface area—where being able to use rules and formulas far too often is taken as sufficient evidence of understanding. As you read these cases, consider the following questions.

- How much do I rely on students' written work to make judgments about what they know and what they can do?
- What sorts of claims do I tend to make about students' understanding and what do I use as evidence?
- What do I learn about students' thinking when I listen to their conversations and the questions they ask?
- To what extent do I use what I learn through listening and observing to make instructional decisions?
- What do I understand about rational numbers; About volume and surface area? How does my teaching help develop students' understanding of these topics beyond rules for computing with rational numbers and formulas for calculating volume and surface area? What issues do these cases raise about teaching and learning of these ideas that I had not thought about before?
- When might I want to videotape in my own classroom and why?

CASE 6—Making Sense of Multiple Snapshots of Students' Written Work—is built around a series of vignettes of students working on a task involving fractions as parts of a whole. This case highlights one very important fact. The domain of rational numbers is a very complex set of ideas, models, representations, and applications. Developing students' deep understanding of this topic is extremely challenging. In our use of the case, we found that participants develop new insights about the nuances and subtleties of meanings and representations in this content area.

CASE 7—"Dang! This Can't Be Right:" Computation in Problem Situations—is built around a transcript of a video recording of a small group of students comparing the surface area and volume of two different juice containers. The case invites inquiry about a number of issues: meaning of measurement ideas, strategies for efficient counting, taking numbers out of context, recognizing situations that are additive and distinguishing them from ones that are multiplicative, explaining one's understanding to others.

This case is unique in that it occurs in a classroom for "learning disabled" students. This suggests a second line of inquiry about what special needs students should have opportunities to learn. It raises questions about basic skills, practice, and the use of calculators in special-education classrooms. It raises issues of how a teacher, who values writing as a way of communicating with others and developing one's own understanding, can support her students when their experiences at writing have been limited and their skills are underdeveloped.

Case 6: Making Sense of Multiple Snapshots of Students' Work

From the classroom of Karen Rohrs in collaboration with the Project Team

OVERVIEW

This case provides opportunities to

- *analyze students' written work*: examining students' written work on a fractions task using an area model—what students' responses seem to indicate about their knowledge of fractions, how they reason about parts of a whole, what counts as evidence of what they know and how they know it;
- *analyze audio and video recordings of students working on a task*: listening to and observing students as they work on a task—what can be learned of how they reason about and solve a problem that is not apparent in their written work;
- *decide instructional options based on analysis of case materials*: using analysis of students' written work and recordings of their conversations while working in small groups for the purpose of deciding where to go next in instruction;
- *explore complexity of teaching and learning rational numbers*: using different models to represent fractions, knowing what kinds of situations can be represented with different models, recognizing similar mathematical situations in new contexts; applying spatial, numerical and verbal reasoning to make sense of rational number problems;
- *evaluate potential of task for assessment*: critically examining an assessment task – what it has the potential to reveal about student understanding of multiple aspects of fractions that other kinds of tasks do not; what each question of the task contributes to a richer understanding of how students reason about fractions of a whole.

Mathematical Content: Fractions as parts of a whole.

Case Materials: Copy of Fractions of a Square task. Written work of several students on Fractions of a Square. Transcript of audio recorded conversation of one group working on the task. Video recordings and transcripts of conversations of three groups working on the task.

Additional Materials Needed: Scissors, rulers, grid paper of various sizes.

Suggested Time: Minimum of 2.5–.3 hours to investigate the case but could easily be extended beyond this time.

INTRODUCTION

This case is built around a classroom vignette of students working on a task involving fractions as parts of a whole. It provides an opportunity to work on making sense of students' written responses to the task and their conversations as they worked on the task. Our professional interpretations of student understanding vary as widely as the responses to the task by the students. However, the case materials highlight one very important fact: The domain of rational numbers is a very complex set of ideas, models, representations, and applications, and developing students' deep understanding of this topic is extremely challenging.

These materials could be used collaboratively to explore and unpack some of the subtleties and nuances of the mathematics of rational numbers that are often passed over in instruction, and the intricacies of students' efforts at making sense. Often, these understandings (partial, mis-, fragmented) persist and result in poorly constructed and incorrectly remembered rules and algorithms for computing with fractions.

In our field testing of these case materials, we found that participants begin to appreciate some aspects of the complexity of this mathematical domain that they may never have given thought to before. Some teachers have commented that they never considered when different models of fractions were appropriate, they just took it for granted—it had seemed straightfor ward.

USING THE CASE MATERIALS

Levels of Working With the Materials

Analyzing Students' Written Work. The richness of the data in this case provides the opportunity to pursue several levels of exploration. At one level, participants can have direct experience in doing analysis as they examine students' written work on a fractions task. Here they can scrutinize the information contained in students' written responses to the task, what the responses within and across the several questions suggest about students' understanding of fractions as parts of a whole, and what counts as evidence of what they know and how they know it.

Analyzing Students' Conversations. The analysis of students' written work can be complemented with an examination of conversations students had while working on the task in small groups. As participants analyze students' conversations, they can consider what these data contribute. What does this additional documentation add to understanding how students are reasoning about and trying to make sense of the mathematics in this problem? How are students applying spatial, numerical, and verbal reasoning to make sense of this task?

Deciding where to go next. From this analysis, participants can consider how this information might help a teacher decide where to go next in instruction. This may mean considering if immediate further attention is needed on some aspects of this content, or if there are some ideas that the teacher might want to revisit in subsequent units. This is likely to move the conversation to another level, where participants move outside the specifics of this particular task and consider the challenges of teaching and learning fractions. What are the various models that can be used to represent fractions? What distinguishes these models? What might be difficult in choosing and applying appropriate models in new contexts? How is teaching and learning for understanding at the middle grades influenced by students' prior experiences with fractions and decimals?

Evaluating the task. At another level, participants can evaluate the task as a tool for assessment. What does this task have the potential to reveal about student understanding of multiple aspects of fractions as parts of a whole that other kinds of tasks do not? What does each question in the task contribute to a richer picture of how students reason about fractions? Might this task be modified in light of earlier analysis of students' work on the task?

Doing deep analysis. At yet another level, participants could step back farther from the specifics of the case materials and consider a more general line of inquiry about doing analysis. Why would a teacher want to engage in deep analysis of students' written work? What can careful observation and listening as students work on tasks contribute to analysis of student learning? What might this kind of deep analysis and conversation among a group of professionals contribute to enhancing teaching and learning in mathematics classrooms?

What follows is a suggestion of how to structure the investigation of the case materials. It derives from field trials with groups of novice and experienced teachers in which we tried to engage them in the several levels of inquiry. It is deliberately staged so that participants begin by working on the task themselves, then move to analyzing samples of students' written work. As the analysis proceeds, additional data are introduced into the conversation including transcripts of an audio recording and video recordings (and transcripts) that document students working on the task. Finally, the conversation moves to a reflection on the analysis, pushing beyond the specifics of the case to consider what the analysis and the conversations have contributed to how individuals might think about their own practice.

Organizing Participants to Investigate the Case

A rather large set of materials comprises this case. We have included the written responses of one youngster, Michael J., who worked individually on the task. We have included the written responses of several students who worked in pairs or in a small group on the task: Leslie and Gil; Jeff and Chastity; Holly, Justin, Brandon, and Jonathon. Although some students worked together, each was required to turn in a paper, and we include the written work of each student.

For the students who worked in groups, we have included documentation of their conversations as they worked together on the task. For Leslie and Gil, we provide a transcript of an audio recording of their conversation. For Jeff and Chastity and for Holly, Justin, Brandon, and Jonathon, we provide a video recording and a transcript of their conversations.

The quantity and richness of the materials (the task, the written responses of 9 students and recordings of the conversations of 8 of them) make it difficult for participants to dig deeply across the entire set in less than 3 hours. To try and have all participants look at every piece of documentation in less time is likely to result in their simply "covering" the case rather than closely e xamining and analyzing the materials.

If you have less than 3 hours available, you may want to consider examining a subset of the data. We suggest that you be certain to have participants examine at least the data for Michael J., for Leslie and Gil, and for Holly, Brandon, Justin, and Jonathon. In this way, participants have the opportunity to interrogate a small but interesting set of the data, suggest interpretations of how some students reasoned about the questions, offer evidence in support of their interpretations, and consider where students' understanding is robust and where it is partial, tentative, and misguided.

Introducing The Case

This case was constructed from a set of events in the sixth-grade urban classroom of Karen Rohrs. Rohrs and her students had been working with the unit *Bits and Pieces, Part I,*[8] a unit on rational numbers, for about 2 weeks. The unit is intended to develop students' understanding of key ideas about fractions as parts of a whole, provide students with various representations of fractions, and engage them in problem-solving situations using various fraction models. In the first three investigations in this unit, students encountered three representations of rational numbers—fraction as part of a whole, fraction as a measure or quantity, and fraction as an indicated division. In the first two investigations, students were working with situations that involved a linear model. The tools they used involved fraction strips and the number line. In one investigation they used fraction strips to investigate equivalent fractions. In the third investigation, the situations involved an area model.

Rohrs was about halfway through the unit and the next investigation involved a shift from common fractions to decimal fractions. Karen decided that this would be a good place to take stock of what students were coming to understand and whether they were ready to move on to decimals. She used a task developed by the Balanced Assessment project.[9] The task, *Fractions of a Square*, provides an opportunity for students to show how they analyze and reason about rational numbers, whether and how they use numerical and spatial reasoning, and how they communicate their reasoning.

---

[8]The students in this class had been working with draft units from the Connected Mathematics Project (CMP). CMP is funded by the National Science Foundation to develop a mathematics curriculum for Grades 6 through 8. This unit is one of two focused on rational numbers for Grade 6. The published units are available from Dale Seymour, the innovative materials division of Addison Wesley Longman.

[9]Fractions of a Square was developed by Balanced Assessment for the Mathematics Curriculum (BA), a project funded by the National Science Foundation to develop high-quality performance assessment tasks. This task appears in Middle Grades Assessment Package 1, published by Dale Seymour Publications.

Most students worked in pairs but a few chose to work in larger groups, and some chose to work individually. Rohrs passed out the task, instructed students to read the directions and work on the task. She wanted to provide as little direction as possible. While students worked on the task, Rohrs documented several small-group conversations with an audio and a video recorder. Students were able to talk among themselves as they worked on the task, but each student was responsible to turn in her or his own written work.

Activity 1: Having Participants Work on the Task

We suggest you begin by having the participants work on the task themselves, either individually or in pairs. Our experience is that participants are more likely to appreciate the mathematical essence and subtleties of the task if they themselves have an opportunity to reason about it first. The following materials will need to be distributed.

- *Fractions of a Square Task*. You may want to make two copies for each participant so they have a clean copy to take back to their classrooms to try with their own students. Have a supply of tools at each table including scissors, rulers and grid paper of various sizes. Participants may choose to use some of these in working on the task.
- *Discussion Questions: Working on the Task*. Why would a teacher use a task like this? What does this task have the potential to reveal about students' understanding of fractions? What do you think students are likely to do with this task?

You may find it necessary to remind participants that you want them to *write* their responses to question #2. Our experience in using this task is that teachers are reluctant to write how they reasoned about a problem, although they are quite willing to talk with others about it. An argument we use is that teachers should experience doing some of the things they are asking their own students to do.

After participants have had sufficient time to work on and discuss the problem in small groups, these questions can be the focus of a whole-group conversation. The questions are likely to generate a rich discussion among the participants about what they think is important for middle-school students to learn and know about rational numbers and the kinds of difficulties teachers have teaching and students have learning within this domain. On occasion, we have provided a few fractions tasks from standardized tests as a concrete way to compare traditional assessment tasks with *Fractions of a Square*.

Activity 2: Examining the Written Work of Michael J.

You will need to distribute the following materials, one set to each participant.

- *Written Work of Michael J.*: Michael J. worked separately on the task.
- *Discussion Questions: Examining Students' Written Work*: The following questions can provide a focus for participants to examine the work and can elicit an engaging conversation after the close analysis of the students' written responses. What do the students seem to understand and what counts as evidence of their understanding? What do they seem to be str uggling with and what is the evidence?

Our experience is that participants tend to want to focus on students' incorrect answers. You may want to emphasize that they first consider what they think students *do* understand.

We include the work of Michael J. for two reasons. First, there appears to be evidence that he used fraction strips (a linear model) to lay on the fraction square (an area model). His work raises issues about different representations and models for working with fractions, how to know what kind of situation lends itself to a particular representation. His work led to an extended conversation among our project team members about various models commonly used to investigate problems involving fractions. We realized that many of us considered linear models and area models as fairly straightforward and had not realized that these may be complex and not easily distinguishable representations for students.

We also include Michael's work because it is the *only* documentation we have for him. Participants often raise questions and offer tentative interpretations about the students' responses that cannot be adequately answered or verified with this small amount of information. Recognizing the limitations of making judgments about student understanding and reasoning based on a single piece of data provides an easy transition to the next activity.

Activity 3: Adding to the Written Work—Listening to and Watching Students

There is a tendency for teachers to rely heavily on written work to assess what students understand about a topic. However, listening to students as they work together on a task can be a rich source of information about how they reason and make sense of a problem. By listening and observing, teachers may learn things about students' mathematical reasoning that are not apparent in their written work. Observing and listening as students work in small groups on a task gives a teacher insights into group dynamics, how students deal with one another when there are conflicts over interpretation, differences in problem solving approaches, or inconsistencies in solutions.

We include the work of three groups of students for whom we had additional documentation—in the form of audio and video recordings of their conversations as they worked together on the task. If your time is limited, we suggest that the participants consider the data for Leslie and Gil, and for Holly, Justin, Brandon, and Jonathon.

We suggest the following routine in this activity.

1. Work with materials of one group of students at a time.
2. First have participants examine closely the written work of the students in that group, using the same set of questions used to examine the work of Michael J.
3. Have them generate some questions they have for which the written work does not seem to provide an adequate answer.
4. After allowing sufficient time to carefully consider the discussion questions and other questions that arise, tell participants that the teacher documented the efforts of these groups with audio and video recordings. Then take up the additional data, one group at a time (a transcript of Leslie and Gil as they worked together, video recordings and transcripts of Jeff and Chastity and of Holly, Justin, Brandon and Jonathon).

Leslie and Gil

You will need to distribute the following materials, one set for each participant.

- *Written Work of Leslie and Gil*. After allowing some time for discussion about what students seem to understand, what counts as evidence, and what new questions arise, distribute the transcript and the Discussion Questions.
- *Transcript of Audio Recording of Leslie and Gil*.
- *Discussion Questions: Analyzing the Data for Leslie and Gil*. How does Leslie make sense of C being one-twelfth? How does Gil make sense of D being eight-sixteenths? Many students seemed to lose sight of the whole at some point in working on the task. Where does that appear to happen for Leslie and Gil and how does it seem to happen? What does this additional documentation contribute to making sense of students' written responses?

The written responses of Leslie and Gil were representative of many others in the class; they lost sight of the large square as the whole. By having a recording of their entire conversation, we see how they began the problem correctly (the large square as 1 whole unit) and then shifted to naming a portion of the square as a whole. Leslie and Gil were unique in that they were the only students who totaled their fraction pieces in question 1 as a check. However, they got a sum of 20/80, which they found by adding the numerators and adding the denominators. It is easy to pass over this because it is such a common mistake among middle-grades youngsters. However, the recording of their conversation sheds some interesting light on their efforts at making sense of this first question. Perhaps most amazing was their way of making sense of the "sum" of twenty-eightieths. From the transcript we "hear" the following.

Leslie:	Yes, but if you add eighty plus twenty that'll be a hundred. Eighty plus twenty would be a hundred.
Gil:	Uh-huh.
Leslie:	And a hundred equals a whole thing.

Jeff and Chastity

You will need to distribute the following materials, if time per mits.

- *Written Work for Jeff and Chastity* After allowing some time for discussion about what students seem to understand, what counts as evidence, and what new questions arise, distribute the transcript and the Discussion Questions, and show the video recording of this pair of students.
- *Transcript of Video Recording of Jeff and Chastity.*
- *Discussion Questions: Analyzing the Data for Jeff and Chastity*. Chastity and Jeff's conversation centers on the whole versus four pieces. How do you make sense of their dilemma? From both their written work and their conversation, what do you think Chastity and Jeff seem to understand?
- What does this additional documentation contribute to making sense of students' written responses?

From the outset, Chastity and Jeff viewed each quarter of the large square as a unit. We selected their work, in part, because they were representative of about one-third of the students in Karen's class who conceived the figure in a similar way. We have puzzled about why so many students saw the figure this way, despite the directions above the figure that the large square represented 1 whole unit. The conversation of this pair provides some insight into how they (and perhaps others) perceived the figure. We also selected their work because of the way in which Chastity made her own fraction square, particularly the quadrant she divided into "sixths."

Holly, Justin, Brandon, and Jonathon

You will need to distribute the following materials, one set to each participant.

- *Written Work of Holly, Justin, Brandon and Jonathon.* After allowing some time for discussion about what students seem to understand, what counts as evidence, and what new questions arise, distribute the transcript and the Discussion Questions, and show the video recording of this group.
- *Transcript of Holly, Justin, Brandon and Jonathon*
- *Discussion Questions: Analyzing the Data for Holly, Justin, Brandon, and Jonathon.* How do these students seem to be reasoning about F that leads them to give it two different fractional names? Which whole do you think Justin is referring to when he talks about H? How do you interpret Holly's reasoning to try and justify Brandon's answer for H?
- What does this additional documentation contribute to making sense of students' written responses?

We include the work of these four because of the richness of their conversation as they worked on the task. We puzzled over their attempts to decide whether piece F should be three-fourths or three-sixteenths. At times they seemed to be using numerical reasoning; at other points they seemed to be relying on spatial reasoning. Their conversation highlighted for us how much information about students' attempts to make sense of a problem situation is hidden by simply checking a written answer to a question on the task. We also include their work as representative of a number of students who named piece H as one-sixth. Because question 2 does not ask for a student's reasoning about piece H, we have speculated about why a significant number of students in different groups came to name H this way. Finally, their own fraction squares raised a number of questions about their understanding of key ideas about fractions that were not raised by their responses to the other questions in the task.

Activity 4: Reflecting on Analysis

Having spent considerable time investigating this case, it seems appropriate to conclude by having participants step back and consider a more general line of inquir y. You will need to distribute the following.

- *Discussion Questions: Reflecting on Analysis*. Why would a teacher want to engage in deep analysis of students' written work? What can careful observation and listening as students work on tasks contribute to analysis of student learning? What might this kind of deep analysis and conversation among a group of professionals contribute to enhancing teaching and learning in mathematics classrooms?
- What do I learn from analyzing this case that helps me think about my own instr uctional practice?

BEYOND THE CASE

This case tends to pique the curiosity of teachers and other educators about high-quality assessment tasks. In instances where we have been working with teachers over an extended period of time in a multisession professional development program, we follow up this case with an exploration of other performance-assessment tasks. We use the tasks for several purposes: to develop teachers' own subject matter knowledge; to help them learn to assess student responses to the tasks; to consider the kinds of learning opportunities students would need to have to be able successfully to engage these kinds of tasks; to help them learn more about how their own students reason about important ideas; to have them consider how the analysis of student responses ought to be link ed to an analysis of their teaching.

DELIBERATIONS WITHIN THE PROJECT

This case has been the subject of many extended conversations among the project team as we have tried to make sense of students' written work on this task and of their conversations as they worked on the task. The following captures the essence of some of our inquir y.

Making Sense of Students' Understanding

Almost Overwhelming Data. Our first line of investigation involved our own efforts to sort out what we wanted to look at. Rohrs had provided the work of two classes of students and recordings of several groups of students in those classes. There seemed to be so much to consider—in the written work and in the recorded conversations—that deciding what to focus on was challenging. At times our attention focused on the mathematical reasoning of the students. At other times our attention was drawn to the dynamics within groups as students worked together on the task. Rohrs often paid attention to individual students whose actions were particularly surprising. For example, she was amazed at Leslie's reasoning about having the right fractions because "twenty plus eighty is a hundred and you need a hundred to make a whole." Rohrs knew that Leslie had been identified as "gifted and talented" and this episode left Rohrs somewhat shaken about her own expectations simply because students had labels.

Having so much material to consider raised a very real practical question: Can teachers be expected to analyze students' written work closely and record and analyze their conversations as they work in small groups in every learning event? We felt the answer is clearly that they cannot and that was not what we were trying to promote. However, what this case demonstrated is that making claims about what students understand can be risky business and that to really get at their levels of understanding requires attending to more than just their written work. This case helped to uncover the complexities of getting a handle on what students know and how they know it, and what they are struggling with.

In our fieldtrials, teachers suggested that they might select particular points in the curriculum to do this kind of in-depth data collection. Teachers could take explicit and systematic actions to document students' work on tasks around mathematical topics that they know from their own experience are quite challenging—for them to teach and for their students to understand. Participants, familiar with the concept, have likened this to action research.

Deciding Next Instructional Moves

Connections to Teachers' Knowledge of Rational Numbers. Teachers' decisions about where to go next in instuction are shaped, in part, by their own knowledge of the content being taught. The possible courses of action available to teachers in a situation like the one presented here are constrained or enhanced in relation to their own depth of understanding about rational numbers. There is plenty of evidence to suggest that this is an area where teachers' subject matter knowledge is very weak. Their own experiences, as learners and as teachers, have done little to develop a rich conceptual understanding of the domain. They have typically learned and taught fractions and decimals as a sizeable set of rules that are to be practiced and memorized.

Issues related to developing deeper understandings of rational numbers continue to come up in our project. It seems that this is a part of the middle grades curriculum that continually causes frustration for teachers and students. In our deliberations over the materials Rohrs presented, we uncovered ways in which many of us had not appreciated some of the complexity in this domain. Using different models to represent fractions—fraction strips, fraction squares and rectangles, fraction circles, the number line—all have subtleties and nuances that some had not really thought much about. So they were taken aback when one student used his fraction strips to lay on the fraction square.

Generally in our project when we referred to learning we were talking about students' learning. However, our conversations in relation to Rohrs' case have made us aware that we need to consider what *we* understand about the topics we teach. How do we understand rational numbers? How do we reason about quantities? How do we recognize situations that are additive and distinguish them from those that are multiplicative? How do we reason proportionally? How do we build our own knowledge base about rational numbers, about how students learn rational numbers, and about how to teach rational numbers in ways that are in harmony with how students learn? What kinds of materials would support us and our students in deepening our understandings about teaching and lear ning in this domain?

Resources to Develop Understanding of Rational Numbers. There are a number of recently published resources that can support teachers who want to develop their content and pedagogical knowledge in the domain of rational numbers. One that stands out is *Providing a Foundation for Teaching Mathematics in the Middle Grades*, a collection of papers and cases edited by Judith Sowder and Bonnie Schappelle (1995). The book derives from a project in which researchers and middle-grades teachers engaged in work to study the links among teacher knowledge, teacher decisions, and student learning in number, quantity, and reasoning. The book is a rich resource of ideas that derive from research on knowledge within the domain and applications for creating learning environments and activities to carry students through the development of complex sets of ideas. It also contains three case studies of teachers who participated in the project. Although the cases each have distinctive features, a common theme is that teachers must have a deep conceptual knowledge of the mathematics they are teaching if they are to make real instructional changes that can lead to student understanding.

Another excellent resource is a recently published case book and facilitator's guide from Carne Barnett (1995) entitled *Fractions, Decimals, Ratios & Percents: Hard to Teach and Hard to Learn?* The cases are written by upper elementary and middle-grade teachers who describe their experiences teaching rational numbers. The cases invite teachers to tackle some important issues (e.g., strengths and limitations of various manipulatives and representations to teach fractions; problems that are challenging, that are worked on over several days; writing to communicate mathematical reasoning).

A third resource is *Rational Numbers: An Integration of Research*, edited by Carpenter, Fennema, and Romberg (1993). This volume presents findings from research programs that have integrated the study of problems of teaching, learning, curriculum, and assessment in this content domain. The research that is described "focuses on the attempt to understand the effects of instruction rather than on the development of prescriptions for more effective instruction" (p. 1).

There are some newly developed curriculum materials that grow out of the research on teaching and learning in this domain. These materials are shaped by the recommendations of the National Council of Teachers of Mathematics in *Curriculum and Evaluation Standards* and *Professional Standards for Teaching Mathematics*.

They are intended to engage students in problem situations, foster the use of multiple representations to explore mathematical ideas, and help students make connections—among mathematical ideas and between mathematics and real life situations. At the heart of these materials is the goal of empowering students by providing opportunities to develop a robust understanding of ideas in number and quanitity; algebra, patterns and functions; geometry, shape, and space; and probability and statistics.

However, these materials provide much more. They are written to help teachers develop their own understandings of the key mathematical ideas embedded within the investigations. Each of the projects devotes considerable attention to the domain of rational numbers. Some units focus primarily on fundamental aspects of this domain. In other units, rational numbers run through as a theme, emphasizing the connectedness of rational numbers to other ideas. For professionals who are interested in enhancing their own understanding of rational numbers as well as their students', these materials can be useful resources. We provide a list of these resources in the Appendix. The list is not intended to be exhaustive of what is available to support teachers and students in their teaching and learning within the domain of rational numbers. It does represent materials with which we are familiar and that we recommend without hesitation.

REFERENCES

Balanced Assessment for the Mathematics Curriculum. (1998). *Balanced Assessment Package, Middle Grades Package 1 and Package 2.* White Plains, NY: Cuisenaire-Dale Seymour.

Barnett, C. (1995). *Fractions, decimals, ratios, and percents: Hard to teach and hard to learn?* Portsmouth, NH: Heinemann.

Carpenter, T., Fennema, E., & Romberg, T. (1993). *Rational numbers: An integration of research*. Hillsdale, NJ: Lawrence Erlbaum Associates.

Connected Mathematics. (1998). *Connected mathematics*. Menlo Park, CA: Dale Seymour Publications.

Education Development Center, Inc. (1998). *Mathscape: Seeing and thinking mathematically*. Mountain View, CA: Creative Publications.

National Center for Mathematical Sciences Education and Freudenthal Institute. (1997). *Mathematics in context*. Chicago, IL: Encyclopedia Britanica Educational Corporation.

Sowder, J., & Schappelle, B. (Eds). (1995). *Providing a foundation for teaching mathematics in the middle grades*. Albany: State University of New York Press.

TERC. (1998). *Investigations in number, data, and space*. Menlo Park, CA: Dale Seymour Publications.

MATERIALS FOR MAKING PHOTOCOPIES AND TRANSPARENCIES

- *Fractions of a Square* Task. Prepare two copies for each participant; prepare a transparency.
- Discussion Questions: Working on the Task. Prepare one copy for each participant; prepare a transparency.
- Written Work of Michael J. Prepare one set of materials for each participant; prepare a transparency.
- Discussion Questions: Examining Students' Written Work. Prepare one copy for each participant; prepare a transparency.
- Discussion Questions: Adding to the Written Work—Listening to and Watching Students. Prepare one copy for each participant; prepare a transparency.
- Written Work and Transcripts of Leslie and Gil. Prepare one set of materials for each participant; prepare a transparency of Leslie's first page.
- Discussion Questions: Leslie and Gil. Prepare one copy for each participant; prepare a transparency.
- Written Work and Transcripts for Jeff and Chastity. Prepare one set for each participant.
- Discussion Questions: Jeff and Chastity. Prepare one copy for each participant; prepare a transparency

- Written Work and Transcripts for Holly, Justin, Brandon, and Jonathon. Prepare one set for each participant; prepare a transparency.
- Discussion Questions: Holly, Justin, Brandon, and Jonathon. Prepare one copy for each participant; prepare a transparency.
- Discussion Questions: Reflecting on Analysis. Prepare one for each participant; prepare a transparency.

Fractions of a Square

The aim of this assessment is to provide the opportunity for you to:
- analyze and reason about rational numbers
- use spatial and numerical reasoning

The large outer square represents 1 whole unit. It has been partitioned into pieces. Each piece is identified with a letter.

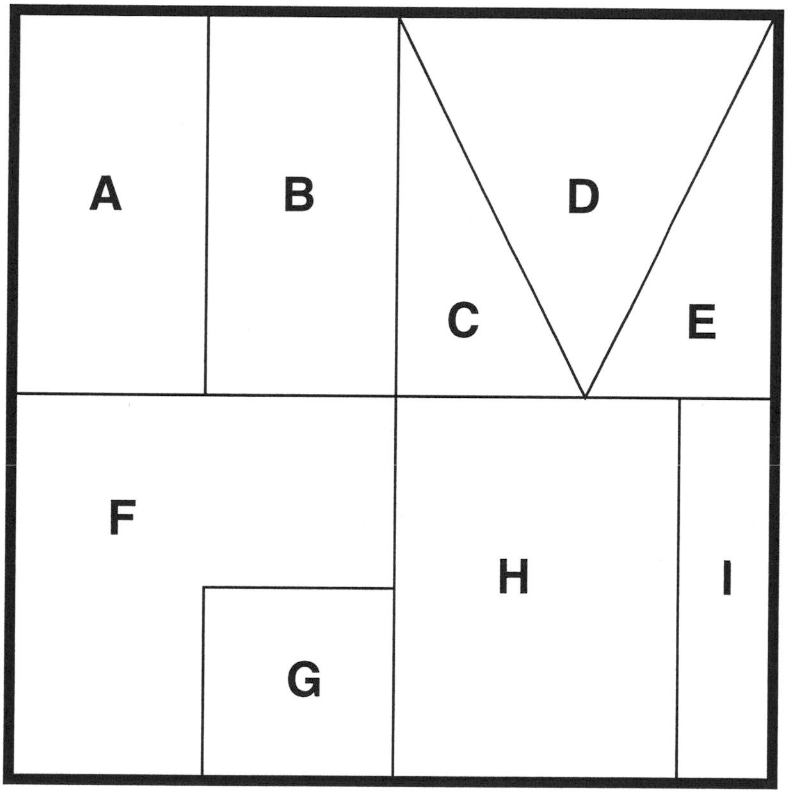

1. Decide what fraction of the whole square each piece is and write it on the shape.

2. Explain how you know the fractional name for each of the following pieces.

A

C

D

F

3. Which piece or collection of pieces from the square on the first page will give you an amount close to:

a) $\frac{1}{5}$?

b) $\frac{2}{3}$?

4.

a) Design your own fraction square using the square below. Your square must contain at least 4 differently sized fractional pieces, other than ½. At least two of your fractional pieces have to be a different size than what is in the original square (used for problems 1, 2, and 3).

b) Give the fractional names for each of your pieces.

DISCUSSION QUESTIONS: WORKING ON THE TASK

- Why would a teacher use a task like this?
- What does this task have the potential to reveal about students' understanding of fractions?
- What do you think students are likely to do with this task?

Name Michael J   Date

Fractions of a Square

The aim of this assessment is to provide the opportunity for you to:
- analyze and reason about rational numbers
- use spatial and numerical reasoning

The large outer square represents 1 whole unit. It has been partitioned into pieces. Each piece is identified with a letter.

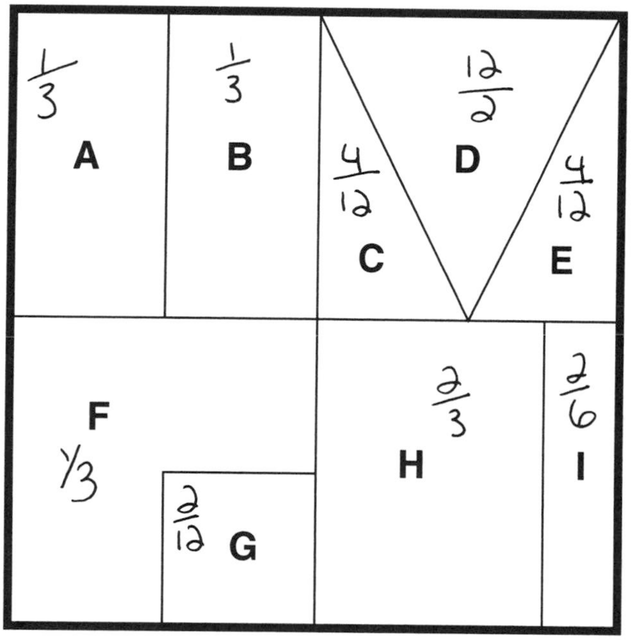

1. Decide what fraction of the whole square each piece is and write it on the shape.

Name Michael J. Date

2. Explain how you know the fractional name for each of the following pieces.

A - I took the fraction strips and I got 1/3.

C - I took the fraction strip and I got $\frac{4}{12}$.

D - I took the fraction strip and I got $\frac{12}{12}$

F - I took the fraction strip and I got anything.

3. Which piece or collection of pieces from the square on the first page will give you an amount close to:

a) $\frac{1}{5}$? It would be C and E.

b) $\frac{2}{3}$? 7 is the closest.

Name Michael J. Date .

4 a) Design your own fraction square using the square below. Your square must contain at least 4 differently sized fractional pieces, other than $\frac{1}{2}$. At least two of your fractional pieces have to be a different size than what is in the original square (used for problems 1, 2, and 3).

b) Give the fractional names for each of your pieces.

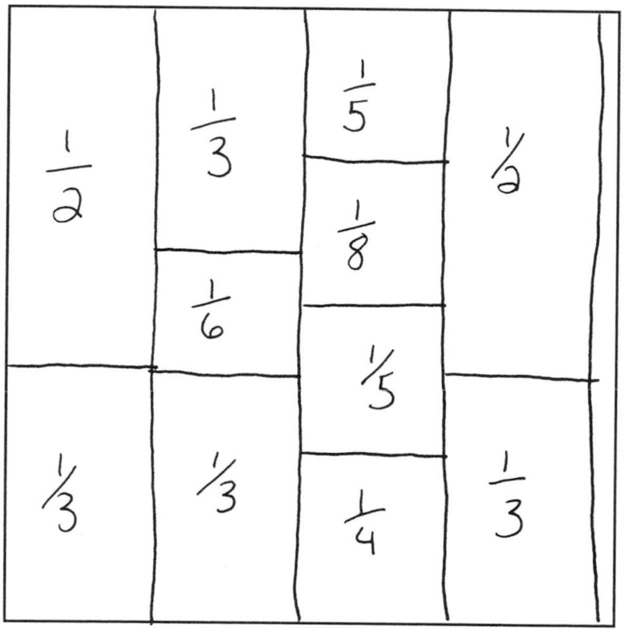

DISCUSSION QUESTIONS: EXAMINING STUDENTS' WRITTEN WORK

- What do the students seem to understand and what counts as evidence of their understanding?
- What do they seem to be struggling with and what is the evidence?

Name______________________ Date Leslie

Fractions of a Square

The aim of this assessment is to provide the opportunity for you to:
- analyze and reason about rational numbers
- use spatial and numerical reasoning

The large outer square represents 1 whole unit. It has been partitioned into pieces. Each piece is identified with a letter.

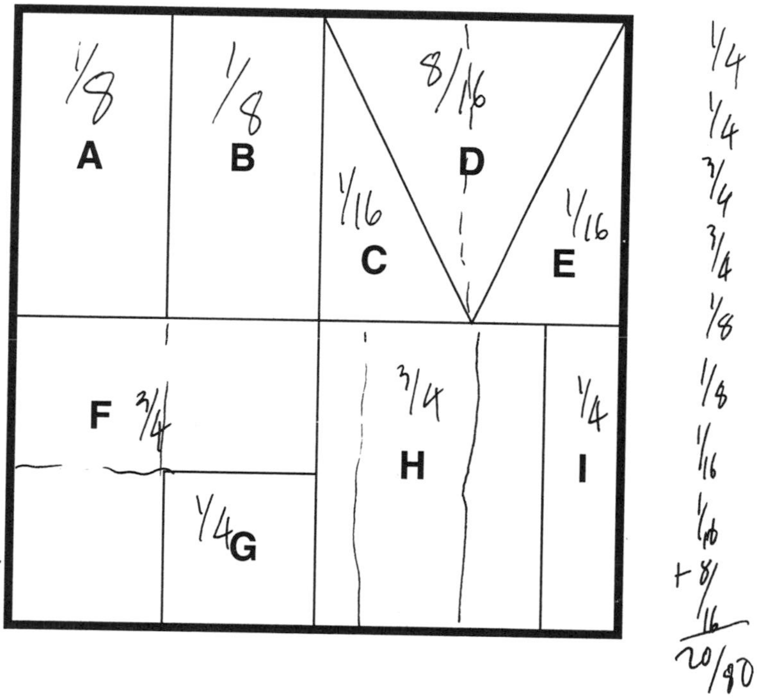

1. Decide what fraction of the whole square each piece is and write it on the shape.

Name______________________ Date______________

2. Explain how you know the fractional name for each of the following pieces.

A if you devided into 4th's and then devided each 4th in half, you would have 2, 1/8 in each square.

C If you devided into 4th's and then into 8th's and put an equalateral triangle, that would give you 1/16

D This is the same a letter C.

F if you devide the whole square into 4th's and then devide each individual square into 4th, 3 of those 4th's would be F.

3. Which piece or collection of pieces from the square on the first page will give you an amount close to:

a) $\frac{1}{5}$? G. I 1/4

b) $\frac{2}{3}$? F or H. 3/4

Name______________________________ Date____________________

4 a) Design your own fraction square using the square below. Your square must contain at least 4 differently sized fractional pieces, other than $\frac{1}{2}$. At least two of your fractional pieces have to be a different size than what is in the original square (used for problems 1, 2, and 3).

b) Give the fractional names for each of your pieces.

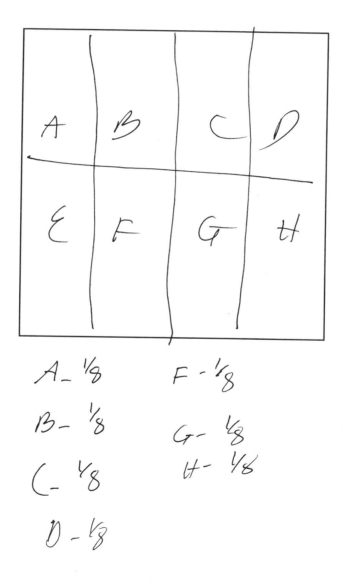

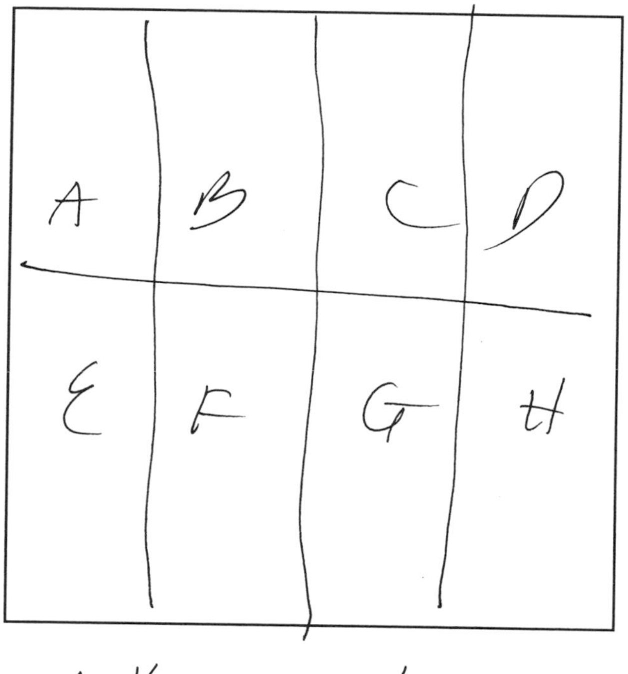

A – 1/8 F – 1/8

B – 1/8 G – 1/8

C – 1/8 H – 1/8

D – 1/8

Name Gil Date

Fractions of a Square

The aim of this assessment is to provide the opportunity for you to:
- analyze and reason about rational numbers
- use spatial and numerical reasoning

The large outer square represents 1 whole unit. It has been partitioned into pieces. Each piece is identified with a letter.

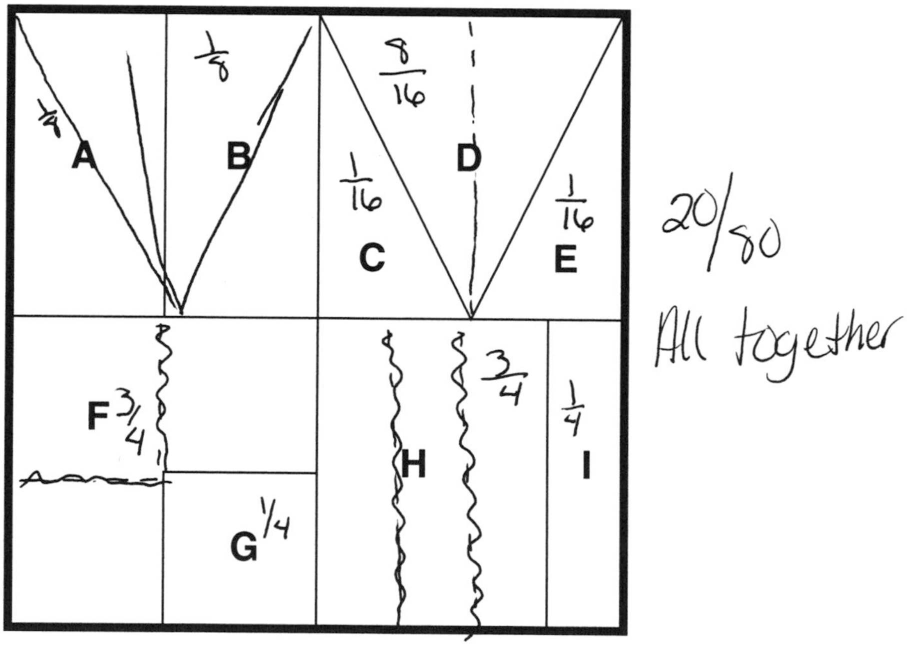

1. Decide what fraction of the whole square each piece is and write it on the shape.

Name Gil Date

2. Explain how you know the fractional name for each of the following pieces.

A If you divide the whole square into 4ths then divided them in half. 2 1/8 in each square

C If you divided the whole square into 4ths then divided those into . eights and put on equilabral, that will give you 1/16.

D this is the same as C

F If you divided it into 4ths and there each induvidual square into 4ths 3 of those fourths would be F.

3. Which piece or collection of pieces from the square on the first page will give you an amount close to:

a) $\frac{1}{5}$? G, 1/4 or I 1/4

b) $\frac{2}{3}$? What is 3/4, for H

Name G:l Date

4 a) Design your own fraction square using the square below. Your square must contain at least 4 differently sized fractional pieces, other than $\frac{1}{2}$. At least two of your fractional pieces have to be a different size than what is in the original square (used for problems 1, 2, and 3).

b) Give the fractional names for each of your pieces.

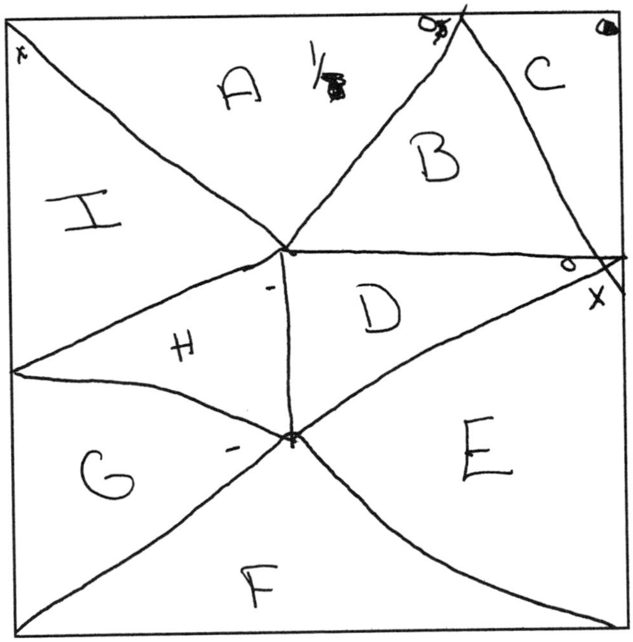

TRANSCRIPT OF AUDIO: LESLIE AND GIL

Gil: [reading the instructions to the task] The large outer square represents 1 whole unit. It has been partitioned into pieces. Each piece is identified with a letter. One. Decide what fraction of the whole square each piece is and write it on the shape.

Leslie: What would A be?

Gil: A—What do you think it would be?

Leslie: Well if it is divided into fourths then that would be two out of one of the fourths.

Gil: So eighth, one-eighth?

Leslie: Should be. Each one of those should be one-eighth.

Gil: Let A be one-eighth?

Leslie: Since A and B are the same size they should also be the same number.

Gil: Okay. For C.

Leslie: Divide it down here, down the middle of D. Each of them, they would be half of D and C would be one-eighth and [inaudible] half of one-eighth would be [pause] one-twelfth, wouldn't it?

Gil: Half of one-eighth ...

Leslie: If this is one-twelfth then ...

Gil: That's ...

Leslie: Then that's one-eighth and that would be one-twelfth.

Gil: Cause this is four right? Four-fourths?

Leslie: One of the four-fourths. Divide D down the middle, then each half would be one-eighth and that would be one twelfth.

Gil: Wait, one of four-fourths, it would be one of four fourths over here, so that's one-eighth, then one-twelfth, so it would be one-sixteenth.

Leslie: Instead of one-twelfth?

Gil: Yeah.

Leslie: Each of these would be one-sixteenth.

Gil: E and C.

Leslie: E and C would be one-sixteenth. Then D, one-sixteenth plus one-sixteenth equals ...

Gil: Two er one ...

Leslie: One thirty-second.

Gil: Wait [pause]

Leslie: Hmm. Are you still trying to figure it out?

[A pause of about 20 seconds while it appears that both are thinking about the problem.]

Gil: Well,

Leslie: One-thirty-second.

Gil: Thirty-second?

Leslie: But if … hmm.

Gil: That's one, that's one-fourth, that's one-third right there right? In this square?

Leslie: Well, if you divided that down the middle, if you divided D down the middle then, uhm, there would be, there would be four triangles … so … that would be, that's two of four.

Gil: But we're working with just D, I think, just the whole thing, and you can't divide it.

Leslie: No, I mean, you can divide it and then like if D were shaded in on both sides …

Gil: Yeah.

Leslie: Then that would be two of four … so would it be two-fourths or … two-fourths of one-sixteenth?

Gil: Two-fourths, but … wouldn't it be … eight-sixteenths? That's the same as two-fourths, but it would make it like sixteenths.

Leslie: Yah.

Gil: So it would be eight-sixteenths.

Leslie: So it would be eight-sixteenths.

Gil: Now for F … uh, o' my gosh.

Leslie: Boy, if you divided this into, if you divided F and G into fourths … like that, F would be three-fourths and G would be one-fourth out of it.

Gil: F would be three-fourths of three-fourths … three times a

Leslie: So G is automatically one-fourth, correct?

Gil: Yeah … No? Don't you wanna? You wanna add all this too.

Leslie: Hmm-hmm, yeah I know. We're going to try that, but you can always go back and erase it.

Gil: Well, you can just well twelve-sixteenths. Cause if this was in each one, like each little … no …

Leslie: This would be three-fourths. Three-fourths to get it equivalent, no you can't get it equivalent, it can't be reduced. So three-fourths.

Leslie: Okay, now H, I. If you divided them, if you divided them into thirds, fourths. If you divided H and I into fourths …

Gil: Like that. So put two lines in H.

Leslie: Yeah.

Gil: Yeah, so that would be …

Leslie: So that would be fourths.

Gil: Three-fourths.

Leslie: H is three-fourths and I is one-fourth … So then add them up … Six-fourths then eight-fourths. Eight-fourths from the bottom … which is an improper fraction …

Gil: But you can … that actually two-fourths. Cause that, no, cause that times that … two that would be …

Leslie: Eight-fourths would be four-fourths and one half …

Gil: Nooo!

Leslie: No.

Gil: It would be one of two, wouldn't it? It would be two … no it couldn't be two.

Leslie: Well there is two one-fourths and there is two three-fourths … Okay one-fourth, one-fourth, three-fourths, three-fourths, one-eighth, one-eighth, one-sixteenth, one-sixteenth, eight-sixteenths.

Gil: Then you add those.

Leslie: Uh-huh … How many does it have to be to equal a whole?

Gil: I don't know … Oh it has to be [inaudible]

Leslie: One, two … six, eight, nine, ten, eleven, twelve, … twenty. We have twenty sums of parts. Sixteen and sixteen is thirty-two plus another sixteen … forty-eight, plus another sixteen … would be…

Gil: I think we have these wrong … a couple of these…

Leslie: [unintelligible] to fix it then.

Gil: Whad you get, twenty-nine?

Leslie: I got twenty. Sixteen plus sixteen, thirty-two plus another sixteen plus sixteen is sixty-four, plus another sixteen … is, ah … sixty, no I mean eighty. That's twenty-eightieths …

Gil: Twenty-eightieths?

Leslie: Yes, but if you add eighty plus twenty that'll be a hundred. Eighty plus twenty would be a hundred.

Gil: Uh-huh.

Leslie: and a hundred equals a whole thing …

Gil: Wouldn't it be twenty-eightieths?

Leslie: Yeah, and then if you add eighty plus twenty it's a hundred.

Gil: So should I write …

Leslie: You should.

Gil: Twenty-eightieths. Twenty-eightieths all together.

DISCUSSION QUESTIONS: ANALYZING THE DATA FOR LESLIE AND GIL

- How does Leslie make sense of C being one-twelfth?
- How does Gil make sense of D being eight-sixteenths?
- Many students seemed to lose sight of the whole at some point in working on the task. Where does that appear to happen for this group and how does it seem to happen?
- How do you make sense of Leslie's comment that a "hundred equals a whole thing"?

Name Jeff Date

Fractions of a Square

The aim of this assessment is to provide the opportunity for you to:
• analyze and reason about rational numbers • use spatial and numerical reasoning

The large outer square represents 1 whole unit. It has been partitioned into pieces. Each piece is identified with a letter.

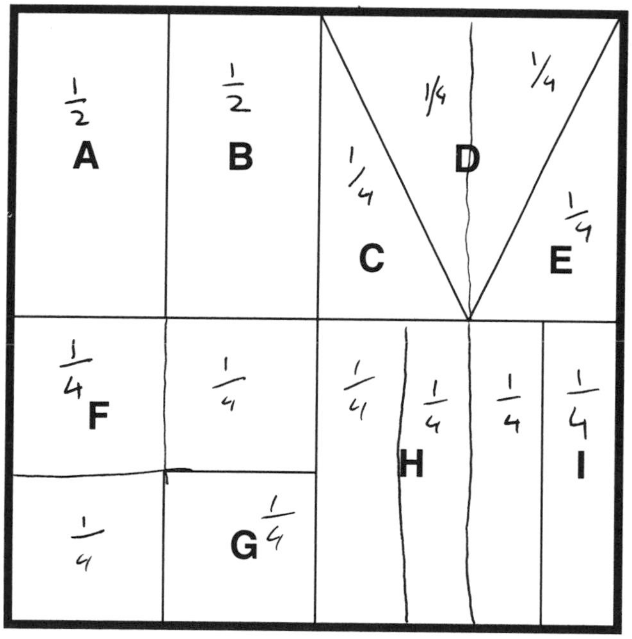

1. Decide what fraction of the whole square each piece is and write it on the shape.

Name Jeff Date

2. Explain how you know the fractional name for each of the following pieces.

A We looked at the sections and named them, Like if there 2 halves we lable them each $\frac{1}{2}$

C These were there pieces that were not equal we divide D up into two part so we could lable them all $\frac{1}{4}$

D We divide into equal parts to go with there Square

F We divided into Square to go with G.

3. Which piece or collection of pieces from the square on the first page will give you an amount close to:

a) $\frac{1}{5}$? C, D, E, F, G, H, I

b) $\frac{2}{3}$? $\frac{1}{2}$ A, B

Name Jeff Date

4 a) Design your own fraction square using the square below. Your square must contain at least 4 differently sized fractional pieces, other than $\frac{1}{2}$. At least two of your fractional pieces have to be a different size than what is in the original square (used for problems 1, 2, and 3).

b) Give the fractional names for each of your pieces.

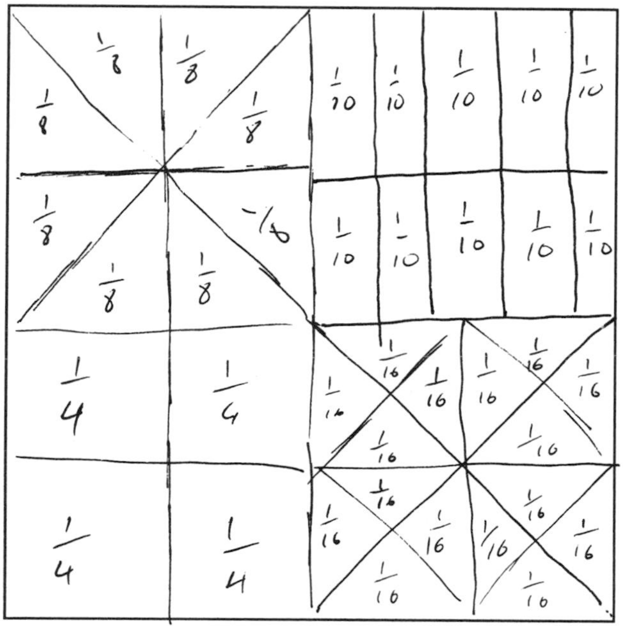

Name______________________ Date Chastity

Fractions of a Square

The aim of this assessment is to provide the opportunity for you to:
- analyze and reason about rational numbers
- use spatial and numerical reasoning

The large outer square represents 1 whole unit. It has been partitioned into pieces. Each piece is identified with a letter.

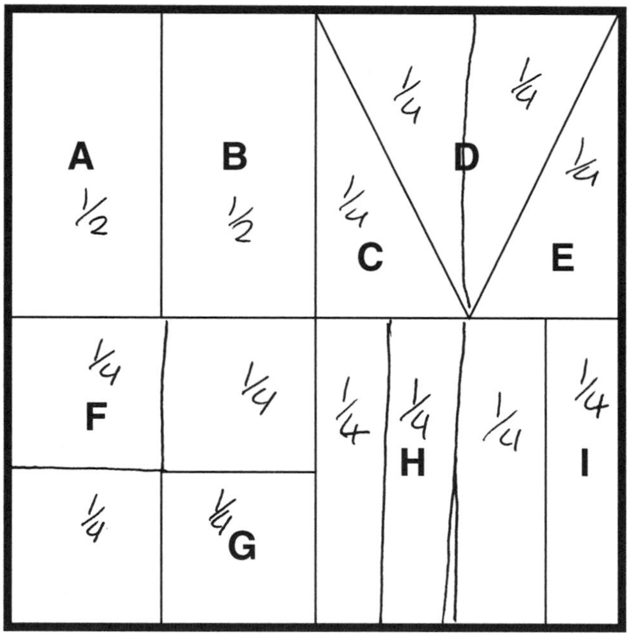

1. Decide what fraction of the whole square each piece is and write it on the shape.

Name Chastity

2. Explain how you know the fractional name for each of the following pieces.

A We looked at the sections and named them. Like if there was 2 ½'s we would label them ½ each

C There were three pieces that were not equal We divided D up into 2 part so we could label them all ¼

D We divided it into equal parts to go with there square

F We divided it into equal squares to go with G.

3. Which piece or collection of pieces from the square on the first page will give you an amount close to:

a) $\frac{1}{5}$? $\frac{1}{4}$ wich was c, d, e, f, g, h, i

b) $\frac{2}{3}$? $\frac{1}{2}$ wich was a & b

Name Chastity Date ~~Cha~~

4 a) Design your own fraction square using the square below. Your square must contain at least 4 differently sized fractional pieces, other than $\frac{1}{2}$. At least two of your fractional pieces have to be a different size than what is in the original square (used for problems 1, 2, and 3).

b) Give the fractional names for each of your pieces.

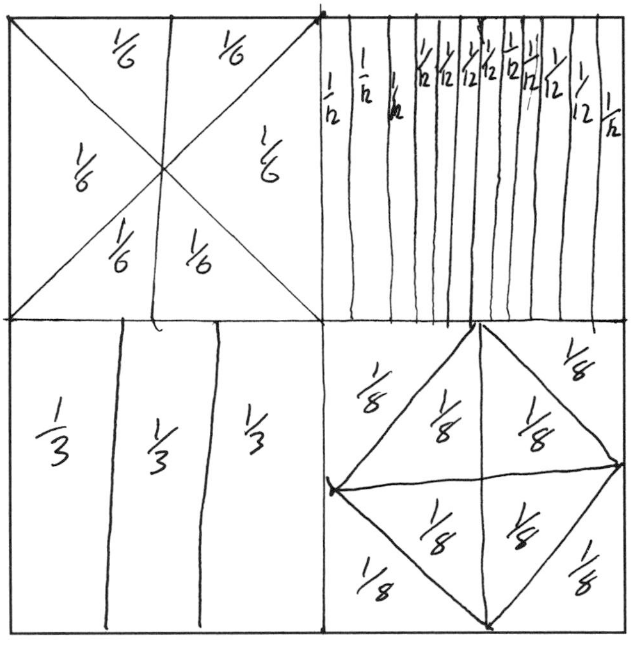

TRANSCRIPT OF VIDEO: JEFF AND CHASTITY

Jeff: Oh, look we don't know. With C, D, and E, you know, we had to put that line. We don't know if that would still be one-fourth or be two-fourth. Because there's one-fourth here [pointing to C] and one-fourth here [pointing to E] and with the line [pointing to D] it would be two-fourths and make all the pieces even. We don't know if they want to make that two-fourths cause there is two of it in D. Same down here [pointing to F] Cause you go all the way around. Don't know if this would all be three-fourths in here for F and G would only be one-fourths.

Chastity: I think it would be four-fourths because it's divided like one going down [motioning on big square] and one going across [pointing across the whole square] like four parts and those four parts are divided again. So really, you know, one, two, three, four [counting lower right square], one, two, three, four, one, two [counting upper left square], one, two, three, four ... let's go on.

Jeff: [Reading the instructions] Explain how you know the fractional name for each of the following pieces. We divided them up into equal parts.

Chastity: [Reads question to herself.]

Jeff: We divided up into even, yeah, equal parts and then we gave the names of the equal parts. If there was four pieces we called it one-fourth. So A, what did we just had to use it. C ... for C we didn't really have to divide anything. We divided D and then found that there was four pieces in that one square. And then for D, oh that was D. Then we divided

Chastity: into four parts, four squares.

Jeff: Divided that up ... And F ... Here we divided that up in four pieces that were squares ... Wait, first we looked at the, um, square, corner square. Since the big square is divided up into four pieces. We looked at the one square and it was already divided up for us.

Chastity: And it's one-half.

Jeff: Yeah, so it would be one-half [writing].

Chastity: It says Explain how you got it for A. We just counted up how many pieces it was and uh, right?

Jeff: Well, first we had to look at the big square and find out if each four—

Chastity: Oh, each of these—

Jeff: Yeah, for each section, well no, not four, we had to find each section. This would be its own section, this would be its own section, then this its own and then this its own. So, first we had to find their own sections. That's all we had to do for there.

DISCUSSION QUESTIONS: ANALYZING THE DATA FOR JEFF AND CHASTITY

- Chastity and Jeff's conversation centers on the whole versus four pieces. How do you make sense of their dilemma?
- From both their written work and their conversation, what do you think Chastity and Jeff seem to understand?

Name_______________________ Date Holly

Fractions of a Square

The aim of this assessment is to provide the opportunity for you to:
- analyze and reason about rational numbers
- use spatial and numerical reasoning

The large outer square represents 1 whole unit. It has been partitioned into pieces. Each piece is identified with a letter.

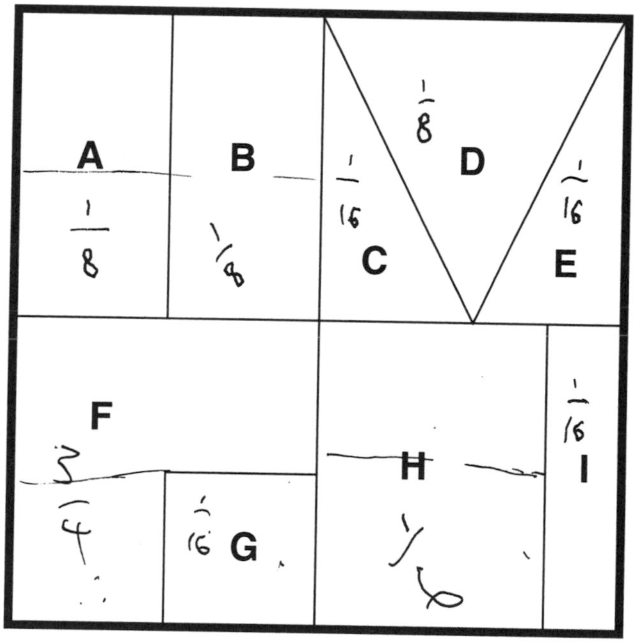

1. Decide what fraction of the whole square each piece is and write it on the shape.

Name________________________ Date________________

2. Explain how you know the fractional name for each of the following pieces.

A it's

C

D

F

3. Which piece or collection of pieces from the square on the first page will give you an amount close to:

a) $\frac{1}{5}$?

b) $\frac{2}{3}$?

Name Holly Date

4 a) Design your own fraction square using the square below. Your square must contain at least 4 differently sized fractional pieces, other than $\frac{1}{2}$. At least two of your fractional pieces have to be a different size than what is in the original square (used for problems 1, 2, and 3).

b) Give the fractional names for each of your pieces.

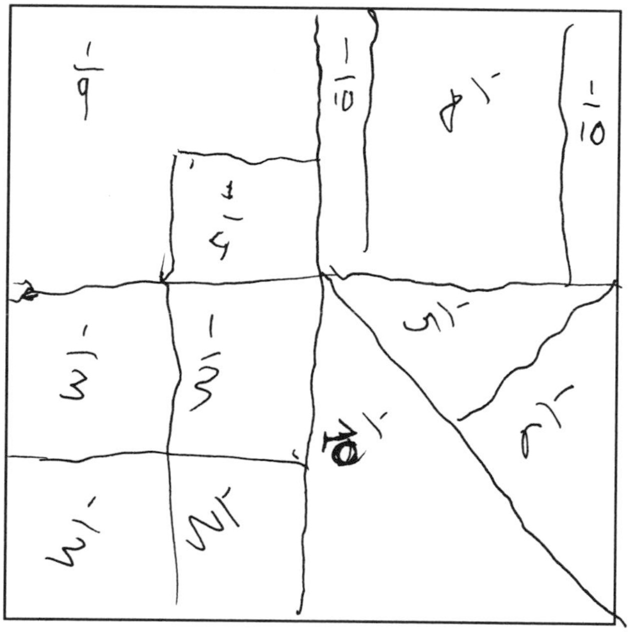

Name Jonathon Date

Fractions of a Square

The aim of this assessment is to provide the opportunity for you to:
- analyze and reason about rational numbers
- use spatial and numerical reasoning

The large outer square represents 1 whole unit. It has been partitioned into pieces. Each piece is identified with a letter.

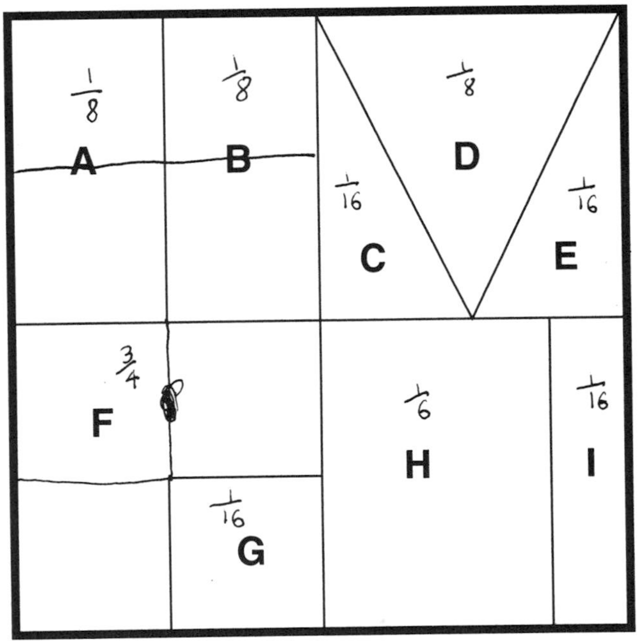

1. Decide what fraction of the whole square each piece is and write it on the shape.

Name Jonathon Date

2. Explain how you know the fractional name for each of the following pieces.

A

C

D

F

3. Which piece or collection of pieces from the square on the first page will give you an amount close to:

a) $\frac{1}{5}$?

b) $\frac{2}{3}$?

Name Jonathon Date______

4 a) Design your own fraction square using the square below. Your square must contain at least 4 differently sized fractional pieces, other than $\frac{1}{2}$. At least two of your fractional pieces have to be a different size than what is in the original square (used for problems 1, 2, and 3).

b) Give the fractional names for each of your pieces.

Name Justin Date Justin

Fractions of a Square

The aim of this assessment is to provide the opportunity for you to:
- analyze and reason about rational numbers
- use spatial and numerical reasoning

The large outer square represents 1 whole unit. It has been partitioned into pieces. Each piece is identified with a letter.

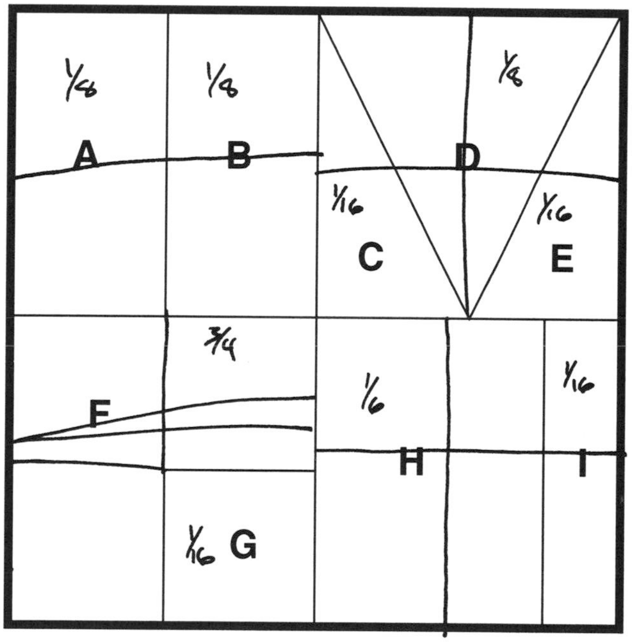

1. Decide what fraction of the whole square each piece is and write it on the shape.

Name Justin Date

2. Explain how you know the fractional name for each of the following pieces.

A Because it is split in half

C If you put the two triangle together it would be a whole but it isn't so it is 1/16

D It is a whole triangle so it is 1/8

F It is most of the square except for a little square on the bottom so it is 3/4

3. Which piece or collection of pieces from the square on the first page will give you an amount close to:

a) $\frac{1}{5}$? H is closest

b) $\frac{2}{3}$? F is closest.

Name Justin Date

4 a) Design your own fraction square using the square below. Your square must contain at least 4 differently sized fractional pieces, other than $\frac{1}{2}$. At least two of your fractional pieces have to be a different size than what is in the original square (used for problems 1, 2, and 3).

b) Give the fractional names for each of your pieces.

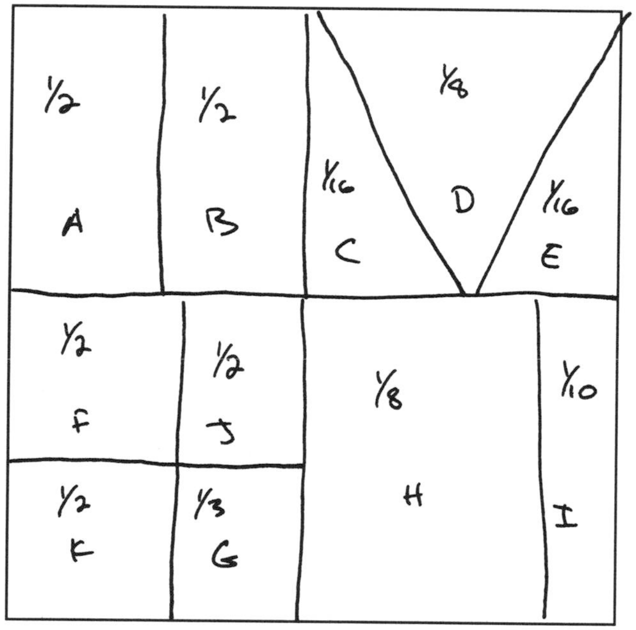

Name Brandon Date

Fractions of a Square

The aim of this assessment is to provide the opportunity for you to:
- analyze and reason about rational numbers
- use spatial and numerical reasoning

The large outer square represents 1 whole unit. It has been partitioned into pieces. Each piece is identified with a letter.

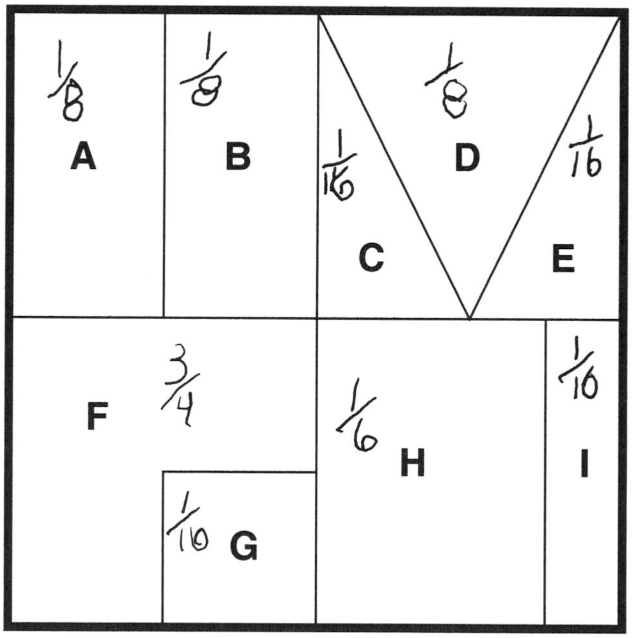

1. Decide what fraction of the whole square each piece is and write it on the shape.

Name Brandon Date

2. Explain how you know the fractional name for each of the following pieces.

A I checked to see how many would fit

C If you put the two triangle together it would be a whole but it was't so it is $\frac{1}{16}$

D It is a whole triangle so it is $\frac{1}{8}$

F It is most of the square so it is $\frac{3}{4}$.

3. Which piece or collection of pieces from the square on the first page will give you an amount close to:

a) $\frac{1}{5}$? h is closest

b) $\frac{2}{3}$? F is closest

Name Brandon Date

4 a) Design your own fraction square using the square below. Your square must contain at least 4 differently sized fractional pieces, other than $\frac{1}{2}$. At least two of your fractional pieces have to be a different size than what is in the original square (used for problems 1, 2, and 3).

b) Give the fractional names for each of your pieces.

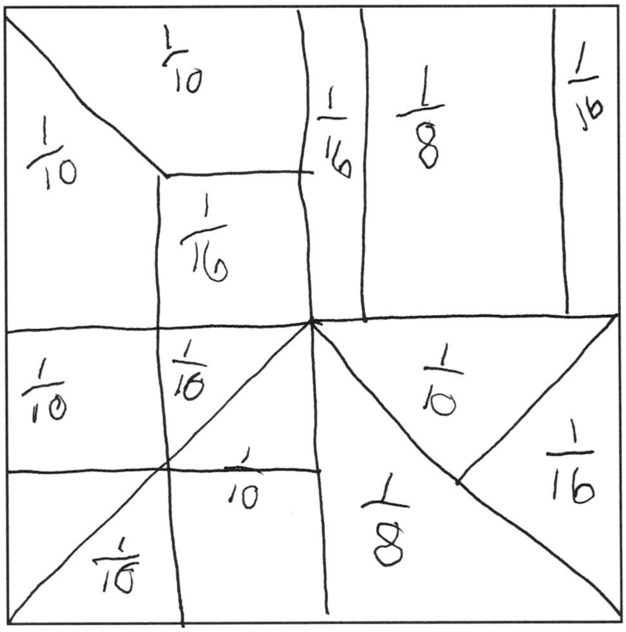

TRANSCRIPT OF VIDEO: HOLLY, JUSTIN, BRANDON, AND JONATHON

Brandon: What do you think about A?

Justin: I think it would be about one-eighth. Because there would be half and half would be about fourth each so if you split them up, add them together would be eighth.

Brandon: So it would be one-eighth.

Brandon: B is equal to A so that would be one-eighth, too.

Justin: Now C, I would say about.

Brandon: I got one-sixteenth.

Jon: That's what I got.

Justin: But how would it be one-sixteenth?

Brandon: Take one of these [referring to C], I don't know, take one of these. Flip it over and there, there would be half in the box. Another one put it there and there would be four to a box.

Jon: That's good.

Brandon: Four, four, four and four [pointing to each of the four quarters of the big square].

Holly: So for D if we put C and E together there would be D. So it would be one-eighth.

Jon: I had problems with F.

Holly: D would be one-eighth ... F? Me too!

Brandon: What D would be? Flip these over and stick them in the slots they would be exactly equal to D.

Jon: Yep.

Holly: It would be one-eighth, cause—

Justin: So I would say about one-eighth—

Holly: [with Justin] Cause one-sixteenth, Yep

Brandon: Should we go on to F?

Holly: Yeah, he had trouble. Okay, if we divided this one like this and like this, that's three equal parts. So it would be, wouldn't it be—

Brandon: Three-fourths.

Holly: Three-fourths?

Justin: But, see, but G, that little box in there would be one-sixteenth. See. But if you broke that, you probably have to break that down into three.

Brandon: Then again instead of three-fourths this piece could be three-sixteenths. A one-sixteenth, a one-sixteenth and one-sixteenth.

Justin: Yeah, ...

Holly: And this is a sixteenth, right? One of them is a sixteenth [pointing to G]. And these wouldn't be three-fourths cause four and four is eight cause is twelve.

Justin: But see you can break them down, too.

Holly: Three of them is twelve.

Justin: So it would be three-fourths.

Brandon: Yeah, but if we divided them like this it would be one, two, three, four, and four to a box with these lines weren't here.

Jon: Yeah.

Brandon: There would be four parts to a box.

Jon: Yeah.

Holly: To each box?

Brandon: Yeah, so wouldn't that be a sixteenth? Three-sixteenths?

Holly: Yeah, three-sixteenths.

Justin: ... See but you could also write sixteenths down into each box.

Holly: Oh, yeah, and four goes into sixteen four times and those four little boxes.

Brandon: But how do we get four out of one.

Holly: Four out of one?
[pause]

Holly: Because one, two, three, four, four boxes.

Justin: See look there's four boxes and we only need to use three boxes.

Holly: [with Justin] three boxes. So wouldn't it be ...

Justin: And you could use three-fourths

Holly: And four goes into six, four goes into sixteen.

Brandon: Yeah, but if it's three boxes, four don't go into three.

Holly: Yeah, I know.
[pause]

Holly: Sixteen, cause three goes into sixteen.

Brandon: No, maybe it's three-fourths.

Holly: That's what I think. Do you think it's three-fourths?

Justin: Yeah.

Jon: I think it's really three-fourths.

Holly: Me, too.

Jon: Let's put it down.

Justin: Now what about H? Cause that's big, that's like a big one out of a whole.

Brandon: I think it would be, um, one-sixth.

Justin: But how, cause look, if you, you took all that—

Brandon: I is one-sixteenth.

Holly: If we divided it in half. What would that be Brandon?

Justin: If we took, if we took—

Holly: —half of six. So it would be one-third. Look if we divided it in half like this it would be one-third and one-third and that's one-sixth all together.

Jon: Yeah, but look we got that little I over there.

Holly: I know, we have it.

DISCUSSION QUESTIONS: ANALYZING THE DATA FOR HOLLY, JUSTIN, BRANDON, AND JONATHON

- How do these students seem to be reasoning about F that leads them to give it two different fractional names?
- Which whole do you think Justin is referring to when he talks about H?
- How do you interpret Holly's reasoning to try and justify Brandon's answer for H?

DISCUSSION QUESTIONS: REFLECTING ON ANALYSIS

- Why would a teacher want to engage in deep analysis of students' written work?
- What can careful observation and listening as students work on tasks contribute to analysis of student learning?
- What might this kind of deep analysis and conversation among a group of professionals contribute to enhancing teaching and learning in mathematics classrooms?
- What do I learn from analyzing this case that helps me think about my own instructional practice?

Case 7: "Dang! This Can't Be Right": Computation in Problem Situations

From the classroom of Patricia Wagner in collaboration with Sandra Wilcox

OVERVIEW

This case provides opportunities to

- *examine a teacher's account of a small group of students as they worked on a task to find and compare the surface area and volume of two closed containers*: making sense of what students do as they work on a task—what tools they use, what they do when they are unsure about how to procede, what they seem to be struggling with, how they know if they are right;
- *consider the challenges to teacher and students in linking conceptual and procedural knowledge*: helping students link computational skill and conceptual understanding of measurement—where the linkage breaks down and what seems to account for it, how the students know that something is amiss, what they do to reconcile their different ways of carrying out procedures;
- *examine the interaction of individual students as they work on a task in small groups*: what role each person is taking on, to what extent they are working together, building on each other's ideas, helping each other understand the situation and ways of attacking the problem;
- *explore issues of equity in mathematics classrooms*: what does it means to have a commitment to develop the mathematical power of *all* students and to act on that commitment? What does it mean to say that students are "learning disabled" in mathematics; what kinds of learning opportunities in mathematics should be available to "learning disabled" students?

Mathematical Content: Volume and surface area.

Case Materials: Teacher narrative of a class activity with transcription of a video recording of a small group as they worked on the task. Students' written work on the task.

Additional Materials Needed: Juice cans (11.5 fl. oz. size) and juice boxes (12 fl. oz size), enough for each group of 3 to 4 participants; centimeter grid paper; centimeter cubes; rulers, scissors, and calculators.

Suggested Time: Minimum of 2 hours to investigate the case.

INTRODUCTION

This case is built around the teacher's narrative of a small group of her middle school students working on a problem to find and compare the surface area and volume of two different juice containers—a juice box and a juice can. The narrative includes some of the actual conversations the students had while working on the task. The dialogue was transcribed from a video recording of the group as they used several strategies to find the measures of the containers, struggled about what calculations to do, and reasoned about and decided when they had solved the problem. The transcript is accompanied by drawings to represent the actual activity of the students as they wrapped grid paper around the containers and stacked centimeter cubes on and next to the containers.

USING THE CASE MATERIALS

The several paragraphs in the next section provide the context for the materials that make up this case. We typically describe some curricular detail of the events that led up to this assessment activity and what the teacher did in getting herself and her students ready for the assessment. We do not reveal at the outset that this is a special education classroom for "learning disabled" students. Our experiences in working with teachers in a variety of settings is that some well-meaning professionals may exhibit a tendency to hold low expectations for students with special needs. We think that teachers are more likely to give this classroom event more serious consideration if they do not have the "special education" filter through which they view the case materials. We suggest adding this additional piece of data later as a final component in the case investigation.

Introducing the Case: Setting the Context

The students in Patricia Wagner's seventh and eighth grade classroom had been working for several weeks on a set of investigations and problems to develop their understanding of volume and surface area of rectangular boxes and cylinders. This unit followed earlier work with investigations of perimeter and area of polygons and irregular figures. In this latest unit, students had engaged in the following kinds of activities:

- filling rectangular boxes and cylinders with unit cubes, counting and estimating the number of cubes necessary to fill an object;
- wrapping rectangular boxes and cylinders with centimeter grid paper, calculating the number of squares required to cover an object;
- developing strategies for finding volume and surface area (e.g., estimating, counting, filling, stacking, subdividing, generalizing to formulas).

As a mid-unit assessment intended to take stock of how students were making sense of the two measurement ideas, Wagner created a task in which students were to compare the surface area and volume of two different juice containers. Because the students had done most of the investigations in the unit in small groups, Wagner decided to have them work on the assessment task in small groups of 2 or 3 students. She provided each group with a 12 fl. oz. rectangular box of Bok u juice and an 11.5 fl. oz. can of V-8 juice.

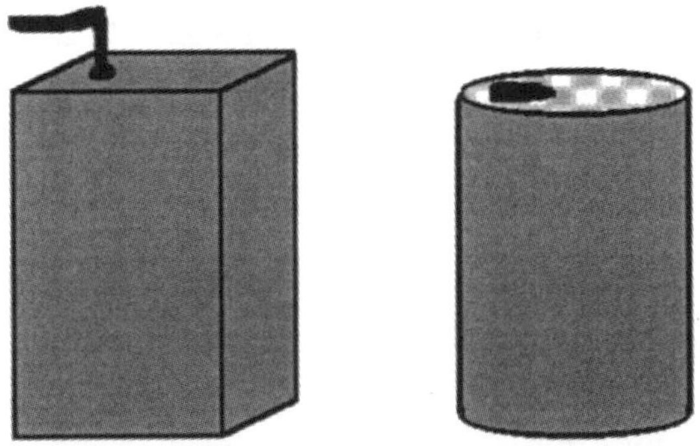

Each group was to find the surface area and the volume of the containers and to answer two questions: [a] Which juice container holds the most and how do you know? [b] Which juice container would be the cheapest to wrap and how do you know?

On the following day, Wagner planned to ask each group to explain in writing their methods for determining volume and surface area of a rectangular container and of a cylinder. These explanations would be written on large paper and hung in the classroom. As the event unfolded, she asked only for an explanation of how to find the surface area of a cylinder.

Doing the Task First. Wagner worked on the task herself prior to giving it to her students. Her own approach initially was to measure the containers and then apply the appropriate formulas. But she doubted that her students had fully made sense of the formulas they were beginning to generalize from patterns they discovered in their investigations. They continued to rely on other strategies. She decided to approach the task as she thought her students would. She thought that would alert her to difficulties they might encounter. As she worked further on the task, she realized that her students' answers might show considerable variation depending on what materials they selected and what strategies they used for counting and estimating. In previous activities, students had been encouraged to make their own estimation decisions—how to take into account gaps that were left when filling a container with centimeter cubes; how to count the partial squares on grid paper that resulted from covering a container.

Worried about the possible range of solutions, Wagner considered setting up some guidelines about counting partial squares and cubes before she launched her students on the task. On further consideration, she decided not to provide any further guidance. Instead, she saw the task as a good opportunity for her to learn more about students' strategies, their own sense making of the problem, how they accounted for partial squares and cubes, and the extent to which they considered the "closeness" of their answers to the actual measures.

Launching the Task. Wagner launched the task by first having a brief whole class discussion about the work that they had been doing in the unit on surface area and volume. Several students volunteered strategies they had been using: wrapping an object with grid paper to find the surface area; filling an object with cubes to find the volume. Wagner introduced the task and told students that materials—unit cubes, grid paper, rulers, calculators, scissors, and tape—were available for their use. She said that each group was to decide what tools they needed and to get them from the materials table. Students were encouraged to rely on each other if they had questions and to call her only as a last resort.

Documenting Students' Engagement with the Task. Wagner decided to document students' work on the task in two ways. In addition to collecting students' written work on the task, she planned to observe the small groups and to video record the efforts of one group—Natasha, Randy, and Kevin. After the class, Wagner viewed the video of Natasha's group and wrote a narrative description, with some dialogue of the actual conversation.

Activity 1: Having Participants Work on the Task

After using the information just cited to set the context of the case in a way appropriate for your particular setting, have participants themselves first work on the task. To do this you will need to provide the following.

- *The Juice Task*. Each participant will need a copy of the task that the students worked on.
- *11.5 fl. oz. juice cans and 12 fl. oz juice boxes*. One box and one can for each group of 3 to 4 participants is sufficient.
- *Centimeter grid paper*.
- *Centimeter cubes*.
- *Rulers, scissors, and calculators*.

Tell participants you have provided a variety of materials for their use and they should decide what tools they need. Some are likely to use formulas they remember. Those who rely on formulas may struggle with the cylinder, unsure about the formulas for circumference and area of a circle and when to use which one. Others may make use of cubes and grid paper. Some may not be sure what to do because they cannot remember the appropriate formulas and do not seem to have any other way to approach the problem.

After participants have had sufficient time to work on the task, begin a discussion by asking them to share the strategies they used and what they think their own students might do with this task. This is likely to surface a number of issues about various strategies. For example:

Should middle-grades students be allowed, even encouraged, to use materials such as grid paper and cubes in solving a measurement problem?

Should middle-grades students be expected to know and apply formulas for volume and surface area?

What does being able to use formulas tell a teacher about what students understand conceptually about these measures?

What do I do when I can't remember a formula?

Treat the issues raised as questions the group will return to as they investigate the case. With some important issues now a part of the conversation, it is appropriate to move on to the case materials.

Activity 2: Reading and Discussing the Classroom Vignette

You will need to distribute the following materials, one set for each participant.

- *A Classroom Vignette: Natasha, Randy, and Kevin Work on Solving the Problem*. The vignette was written by Wagner and she is the narrator. There is a transcription of students' actual conversation on the video recording.
- *Questions for Discussion: Natasha, Randy, and Kevin Work on Solving the Problem*. The following questions can help frame the reading and subsequent discussion of the vignette. What strategies do these youngsters use to work with the task? What do they seem to know about surface area and volume and what is the evidence? How would you characterize what they are struggling with and what is the evidence? What answers do you think they wrote on their paper for volume and surface area of the two containers?

We have found that it works best if the facilitator reads the vignette aloud to the participants as they follow along on the handout. After you have read the narrative of the event, invite participants to take up *Questions for Discussion: Natasha, Randy, and Kevin Work on Solving the Problem* in small groups.

When you feel participants have had sufficient time to consider the questions in their small groups, bring participants together. You can begin by having them make a list on a large piece of paper of what they think students understand, at what level and what they take as evidence of that understanding. Then have them make a list of what they think students are struggling with and what they take as evidence. Our experience is that participants offer quite a range of interpretations of understanding and difficulties. Some are quite upset that these grade 7 and 8 students do not seem to know or at least are not inclined to apply formulas to solve the problem. This would be an opportune time to return to the question posed earlier: What does being able to use formulas tell a teacher about what students understand conceptually about these measures? What do I do when I can't remember a formula?

Activity 3: Examining Students' Written Work

Although Wagner had a video recording of Natasha's group only, she did have the written work of all five groups that had worked on the task. At this point you will need to distribute the following, one set for each participant.

- *Students' Written Work on the Juice Task*. We have included copies of the written work of each of the groups.
- *Questions for Discussion: Students' Written Work on the Task*. These questions invite participants to consider what analysis of students' written work on the task might reveal about their reasoning in this problem. How do you think students got their numbers for the surface area and volume measurements? What might account for the wide range of answers? What do you make of the responses to the two comparison questions? What would you like to know that you cannot tell from the written work?

The day following this vignette, Wagner had each group write the strategies they used to find surface area of a cylinder on large pieces of paper that were hung in the classroom. Have participants examine students' written explanation of their strategies and consider a second set of questions. You will need to distribute the following materials, one set to each participant.

- *Students' Written Explanations of Their Strategies to Find Surface Area of the Cylinder*. Our data set contains the written explanations of three of the groups, one of which was Natasha's group.
- *Questions for Discussion: Students' Written Explanations of Strategies*. The following questions will help frame the discussion, but others are likely to emerge in the course of the conversation. What do you make of these written explanations? Given your analysis of the materials and your conjectures about what you think students understand and what they are struggling with, how would you use this information to decide where to go next in instruction?

Activity 4: Helping All Students Develop Mathematical Power

It is likely that participants will already have made inquiries about the nature of this classroom, sensing that there may be something special about it based on students' ways of interacting with the task and writing about their strategies. This would be an appropriate time to add further data about this classroom.

Wagner teaches in an urban middle school. She teaches mathematics and language arts to classes of 7th- and 8th-grade students of color identified as "learning disabled." We put the words in quotes because we are increasingly unsure about what it means to say that students are learning disabled in mathematics. This part of the case investigation is intended to raise issues that arise in working toward a goal of helping *all* students develop mathematical power.

At this point you will need to distribute the following.

- *Questions for Discussion: Helping All Students Develop Mathematical Power*. The questions are intended to consider explicitly important issues embedded in this case. Some of these questions and others may have already come up in your discussion. What issues does this assessment event raise about what "learning disabled" children should be learning in their mathematics classes? What do you think special needs youngsters should be spending their time learning and what arguments would you make to support your belief? What issues about basic skills, practice, and the use of the calculator are raised by this classroom event? What kinds of experiences might help students reason about different kinds of situations and whether a particular situation lends itself to addition or to multiplication? How can a teacher, who values writing as a way of communicating with others and developing one's own understanding, support her students when their experiences at writing have been limited and their skills are underdeveloped? What larger issues of equity in mathematics education does this case raise?

DELIBERATIONS WITHIN THE PROJECT

Wagner brought this case to a project meeting because she was deeply puzzled. Some of her questions emerged from watching the video of Natasha's group. Why did the students seem confused about what computational procedures to use? Why were some in the group so willing to accept the directions of others, particularly when they sometimes sensed the directions were wrong? And in what ways did their working together get them on the wrong track?

Some of her questions emerged from looking over the written work of all the groups. Why was there such a range of answers given for the measures of surface area and volume? Why did some groups seem not to draw on the answers they got for volume and surface area to respond to the two comparison questions?

Examining Students' Answers

Our examination of students' answers for volume and surface area of the juice box revealed some numbers that were reasonably close to what Wagner had hoped they would find and others that were quite far off.

Natasha's group had used cubes to measure the height of the juice box—which they found to be 13—and to make a rectangle approximately the size of the bottom of the box—which they found to be 6 cubes by 4 cubes. Using these numbers, they correctly calculated the volume as 312. Three other groups calculated the volume of the box as 390, a number consistent with measuring the height with 13 cubes and making a rectangle 6 cubes by 5 cubes to match the bottom of the box.

We were puzzled as to how the groups arrived at their answers for surface area. The numbers they gave were inconsistent with the numbers of cubes they had used to calculate the volume. Wagner had observed that all groups had wrapped their boxes with grid paper rectangles to determine the surface area. Although Wagner was not able to tell for sure from the video, we thought it might be that the rectangles that Natasha cut from the grid paper to cover each of the sides of the box gave her some partial squares and that in counting the number of whole squares she needed to do some estimation.

Our own work at finding the volume and surface area of the can of juice gave results of approximately 420 cu. cm. and 320 sq. cm., respectively. Natasha's group had an answer for the volume that was consistent with Kevin's and Randy's reasoning that it would take 32 cubes to make one layer of the juice can and there would be 12 layers to fill it up. However, when they calculated the surface area, they used some numbers different from what they had used for the volume. Natasha had cut a rectangle to wrap the can that they counted as 13 squares wide and 21 squares long. Randy then counted 29 cubes to cover the top of the can. These numbers should have given them a surface area of 331. We were unable to reconcile the answer of 370 that they had written on their paper.

Some answers that students gave were reasonable and probably dependent on how closely they tried to estimate the number of cubes covering the top of the can and the number of squares in the rectangle covering the side of the can. For example, Monique's group gave 372 for the volume of the can. We had a hunch that the students estimated that 31 cubes would cover the top of the can and that it was 12 cubes high. Twelve layers with 31 cubes in each layer would yield a total of 372 cubes to fill the can. This group calculated the surface area at 326. We had a hunch that they cut a 12 x 22 rectangle to cover the side of the can and disregarded the amount of overlap. Rasheed's group gave 336 as the volume of the can, a figure consistent with estimating that 28 cubes would cover the top of the can. We were unable to make sense of the answer of 240 from Tameka's group.

The responses to the two questions that asked students to compare the surface area and volume of the two containers held some surprises. Two groups answered the comparison questions in ways that were inconsistent with the measures they had found for surface area and volume. Natasha's group said the juice box held the most juice "because it looks like it" even though their answer for the volume of the can was calculated at 384 and the volume of the box was calculated at 312. Tameka's group said the can held the most juice even though they had calculated the volume of the can at 240 and the volume of the box at 390. Their explanation was that "it take [sic] the most surface and volume area." It appeared that some students were not drawing on their work at calculating the measures to answer these questions.

Making Sense of What Students Understand

Meaning of Measurement Ideas. Wagner's observations of the groups as they worked led her to feel confident that students understood the meaning of surface area as the number of square units it takes to cover an object, and the meaning of volume as the number of cubes it takes to fill an object. Without prompting, they used grid paper to cover an object to find the surface area and they stacked cubes to find the volume.

Strategies for Efficient Counting. There was some evidence of a tendency to use more efficient strategies for finding the total number of squares or cubes besides counting every individual object. In several instances, students calculated the number of squares in a rectangular array by counting the number of squares in one row and then multiplying by the number of rows. Similarly, in calculating volume, students counted the number of cubes in one layer and then multiplied by the number of layers.

Taking Numbers Out of Context. At the same time, students exhibited some uncertainty about what to do when faced with "naked numbers," numbers taken out of context. For example, the students in Natasha's group on more than one occasion were uncertain about what to do with some numbers they got for counts of squares and cubes. Natasha stacked cubes against the side of the juice box and she made a rectangle about the same size as the bottom of the box. She gave Randy three numbers—6, 4, and 13 (the height of the box and the length and width of the rectangle matching the bottom of the box)—but then neither of them seemed to know what to do with the numbers. In calculating the surface area of the cylinder, Randy knew that the number of squares covering the top and bottom needed to be included but he told his group to *multiply* the number of squares covering the side of the can by the sum of the number of squares covering the top and the bottom. It was only when they got an answer that Natasha knew was much too big that they decided to add the numbers instead.

Knowing What Kinds of Situations are Additive or Multiplicative. The students in this class often could not recall multiplication facts. Wagner refused to let that stand in the way of their having opportunities to engage in rich mathematical investigations. A multiplication chart was prominently displayed on the bulletin board and calculators were always available for computation. It seemed to us the matter of concern was the difficulty students had in deciding whether a situation was additive or multiplicative. Once students had some numbers, they sometimes seemed to abandon making a connection to what they had done physically with the squares or cubes and just randomly applied some operation.

Students had been instructed to write an explanation of the process their group had used to find the measures. A close examination of student explanations revealed that two groups did not mention a mathematical operation. One group described wrapping a cylinder with grid paper and counting one layer of squares all the way around and then counting the height. But they did not tell what to do with those number counts. Natasha's group wrote that you "do something with the numbers." A third group wrote that "we multiply the side, top, and middle."

The students seemed to have an intuitive, but only partial understanding of these measurement concepts. That is, they understood at a conceptual level that these measurements involved wrapping and filling. It appeared that their estimates of some of the relevant dimensions—number of squares to wrap a container, number of cubes to fill one layer of the container—were reasonable. But at a procedural level there was still some uncertainty about what to do with the numbers they got from their counts and estimates. The video revealed that Natasha's group hesitated on more than one occasion when faced with numbers with which they needed to do something. The answers of the other groups also suggested that being able to decide on the correct computational procedure was not well in hand.

Explaining to an Audience. Students explanations of how they found the surface area of the can were rather meager. We considered possible interpretations of students' limited description of the strategies they used. We did not know how students interpreted the request for them to explain what they had done to solve the problem. How much did they think they needed to tell their teacher and how much could they assume their teacher knew (and so they did not feel obliged to provide great detail)? One thing we have learned from several of our cases is that students are more likely to give detailed explanations if an audience is specified. For example, Wagner might have asked them to write to a classmate who was absent about how they found the volume and surface area of each container.

Using Knowledge in Flexible Ways. In previous investigations in this unit, students had not been asked to make comparisons of surface area and volume of different shaped objects. This was also the first time that students had been asked to find the volume of a closed container. In all other activities, they had been able actually to stack cubes to "fill" the container. In this particular activity, Wagner was pushing at the boundaries of their knowledge, asking them to use the ideas they had been developing in an unfamiliar situation. However, when deciding which object held more juice or which would be cheaper to cover, students relied on more intuitive notions—"It looks bigger." They did not connect the work they had done to find the surface area and volume of each container as data that would help them answer the questions.

Students had opportunities in earlier units to do some comparisons. From those experiences, Wagner learned that this was a difficult idea for her students and that she needed to provide many occasions where they were asked to make comparisons. This event further reinforced for her the notion that students need many examples and models of making mathematical comparisons that draw on student-generated data rather than intuitive, naive, gross comparisons.

Thinking About Where to Go Next in Instruction

We considered a number of options available to Wagner about where she might go next based on the foregoing analysis.

- Revisit the written strategies of the several groups for a whole-class conversation about whether what they had written would effectively communicate the strategies they had actually used. The task might be reframed in the following way.

  > Suppose that one of your classmates had been ill and not able to work on the problems. Would your explanation have helped the classmate understand exactly how you found the answer for the surface area and volume of each object? How could you revise your explanation so that someone else would know exactly what you had done and could follow your directions?

- Focus the group on the difficulty that most students had about deciding what to do with the numbers they got when they counted squares and cubes. This would provide an occasion to consider what kinds of situations are additive and which kinds are multiplicative. It would be an occasion to help students connect operational–computational procedures to their conceptual understanding of surface area and volume.
- Return to Natasha's formulation that to find the volume of a rectangular box, you multiply length times width times height. It was not clear whether Natasha recalled this formula from some previous experiences or if she deduced it from observing patterns and it was not clear what sense she made of it. But it was a strategy that could be put before the entire group for their consideration. Does this strategy make sense and, if so, why? Will it always work? Is it a reasonable way to find the volume of a box? This seemed like an opportunity to see if the students could generalize from the particular circumstance of this problem and previous examples to create a formula for finding the volume of a rectangular box.
- Revisit the answers they got for surface area and volume and consider which ones were reasonable and how the answers might help them decide which container held the most and which container would cost the least to cover.

Acting to Ensure Equity in Mathematics Classrooms

Some might question whether Wagner is spending her time wisely with children who are "learning disabled." Often she must justify her decisions about the kinds of learning experiences she provides for her students. She encounters some who think that what these youngsters need is a good dose of "basics," and "drill and practice" with whole numbers, fractions, and decimals. She has been accused of not acting in students' best interests when she spends time on geometry, probability, or statistics. Wagner has come to realize that many of these well-intentioned adults hold minimal expectations for her students—as learners and as future adult citizens, workers, and consumers.

Wagner has steadfastly refused to return to a minimum competency, basic skills curriculum—"drill and kill," to use her words. Her work over the past 5 years with curriculum materials that engage her students in mathematical investigations and problem solving has revealed abilities of her students that a drill-and-skill-based curriculum always obscured. She has seen excitement, enthusiasm, and self-confidence replace the boredom, resistance, and self-doubt that characterized her students in the past.

Yet she still worries. Will her students be prepared to deal with the mathematical experiences they are likely to encounter in their high-school mathematics classrooms? What is the nature of their disabilities and how and to what extent does it affect their mathematical reasoning and sense-making? Is she adapting the curriculum materials she selects so as to meet the specific needs of these youngsters? What knowledge is "basic" and what role can and should practice play in her classroom? She knows there are no quick, easy answers to her questions, only partial and tentative ones. But she is committed to providing the kinds of learning opportunities that she thinks will develop deeper and richer mathematical understandings, and she acts on that commitment.

MATERIALS FOR MAKING PHOTOCOPIES AND TRANSPARENCIES

- The Juice Task. One copy for each participant; one transparency.
- A Classroom Vignette: Natasha, Randy, and Kevin Work on Solving the Problem. One copy for each participant.
- Questions for Discussion: Natasha, Randy, and Kevin Work on Solving the Problem. One copy for each participant; one transparency.
- Students' Written Work on the Task. One set for each participant.
- Questions for Discussion: Students' Written Work on the Task. One copy for each participant; one transparency.
- Students' Written Explanations of their Strategies to Find Surface Area of a Cylinder. One set for each participant; one transparency.
- Questions for Discussion: Students' Written Explanations of Strategies. One copy for each participant.
- Questions for Discussion: Helping All Students Develop Mathematical Power. One copy for each participant; one transparency.

The Juice Task

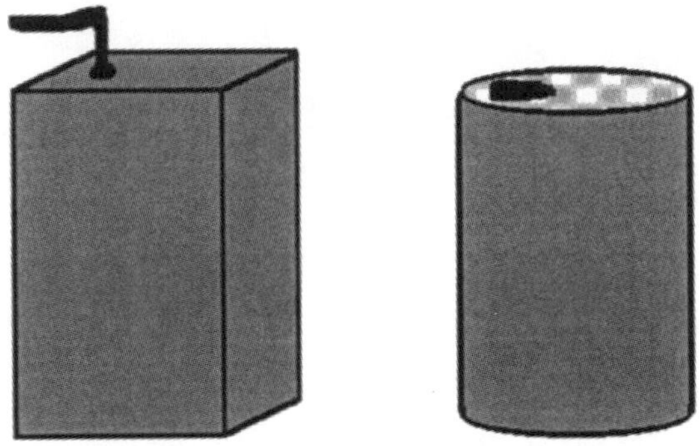

1. Find the volume and surface area of a cylindrical and a rectangular juice container.
2. Which juice container holds the most? How do you know?
3. Which juice container would be the cheapest to wrap? How do you know?

A CLASSROOM VIGNETTE:

Natasha, Randy, and Kevin Work on Solving the Problem

The following is Wagner's account of Natasha's group as they worked on the task. Her primary source was the video recording she made as they work ed in their group.

Natasha, Randy, and Kevin appeared to begin confidently by dividing up the work. They got centimeter cubes, grid paper, a calculator, and tape from the materials table. Natasha began stacking cubes against the side of the juice box. She also made a rectangle of cubes the same size as the bottom of the juice box.

She counted the number of cubes high in the stack but then hesitated.

Randy: What's the height?
Natasha: Thirteen.
Randy: How do we get the surface area for that one [pointing to the juice box]?
Natasha: I got six, four, and thirteen.

The numbers Natasha gave were the number of cubes she counted in the length (6) and width (4) of the rectangle that was like the bottom of the juice box, and the number of cubes she counted in the height (13) of the stack. But then none of the three students in the group seemed to know what to do with these three numbers.

Natasha then took some grid paper and cut out rectangles to cover the top, bottom, and each side of the box. While Natasha worked with the box, Kevin worked with the can. He put a layer of cubes on the top of the can and he stack ed cubes up against the side of the can.

Kevin: There's thirty-two cubes on top and it's 12 cubes high.
Randy: You got to divide the numbers.

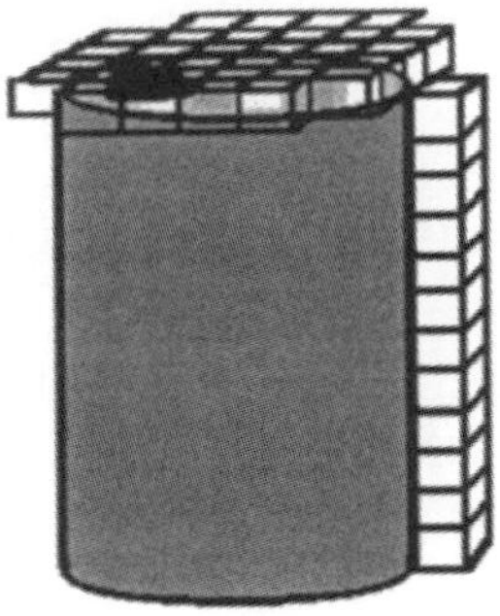

Both Kevin and Natasha stopped what they were doing and seemed puzzled by Randy's order to divide. All three began to look around at other groups in the room to see what they were doing.

Within moments, Kevin returned to his can, saying he was going to find the volume.

Kevin: There's 32 on top.

Randy: I count 12 high. [pause] It takes twelve layers to fill the whole thing, I think. [pause] So now what?

Kevin began doing some pencil-and-paper calculations, multiplying 12 times 32 (although his computation contained an error). I moved toward the group and suggested to Randy that he look at what Kevin was doing. Randy said he agreed with what Kevin was doing and when I asked why that made sense, he responded.

Randy: It takes 12 layers to fill it up and there's 32 on one layer.

I suggested that Randy check Kevin's work which he did with a calculator and they corrected the computational error.

Randy then moved to find the volume of the juice box that Natasha was covering with grid-paper rectangles, counting the cubes she had earlier stack ed next to the box.

Randy: We found the volume of the can. We got to find the volume of the box. [Counting the number of cubes in the bottom layer] It's 24. [Counting the number of cubes high of the stack] That's 13.

Natasha: [She seemed to be doing some figuring] 37.

Randy: That should be the answer 'cause that's how many cubes fit in the box.

Natasha had a puzzled look on her face. Randy did not challenge her answer of 37 but none of the students wrote down the number on their paper. Natasha then took the box from Randy and began to count squares on the grid paper rectangles.

Natasha: There's 78 on the front.

Randy: You're figuring the surface area 'cause you're counting the outside.

Together, Natasha and Randy calculated the surface area of the box. They counted squares on each grid-paper rectangle she had made. Then they appeared to add that count as many times as a rectangle was needed to cover the box. But they continued to be puzzled over the volume.

I could see they were having difficulty with the volume of the box so I went to the group and asked them what volume meant. Each student responded that it was the amount needed to fill the box. I asked if they recalled finding the volume of other objects, pointing out some earlier examples. Natasha responded with a formula.

Natasha: Length times width times height would give us the volume.

With that, the three quickly computed the volume with a calculator.

Randy decided that they still needed to find the surface area of the can. Kevin cut some grid paper to wrap around the can and then began to count the squares on the grid paper. As he counted, he marked each individual square. Natasha told him that another way to find the total number of squares was to count the number of squares in one row around and count the number of squares in the height of the can and then to multiply those two numbers.

Randy: Thirteen rows with twenty-one.
Kevin: I times it and got 273.
Randy: We have 13 rows with 21 squares.
Natasha: What do we do? Times?
Kevin: Yea, that's what I did.
Randy: I guess, 13 times 21.
Natasha: Two hundred seventy-three [after computing with the calculator].
Randy: Wait! We got to do the top. [Counting cubes on the top] Twenty-nine and the bottom makes fifty-eight.
Kevin: We had 273.
Randy: Times 58.

Natasha picked up on Randy's last comment and multiplied 273 times 58 on the calculator. She looked at the answer on the calculator display and shouted:

Natasha: Dang! We're supposed to plus, it's too many!

Natasha seemed startled by the size of the number and was even unable to read it correctly from the calculator. She showed the number to Randy and Kevin. They all agreed this was too much and that they should add. Natasha added two numbers on the calculator and they recorded their answer.

QUESTIONS FOR DISCUSSION: NATASHA, RANDY, AND KEVIN WORK ON SOLVING THE PROBLEM

- What strategies do these youngsters use to work with the task?
- What do they seem to know about surface area and volume and what is the evidence?
- How would you characterize what they are struggling with and what is the evidence?

Name: Natasha's group

Test

Directions: Find the volume and surface area of a cylindrical and a rectangular juice container.

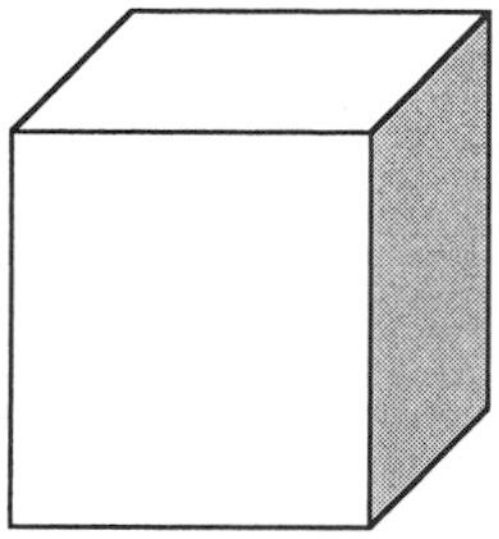

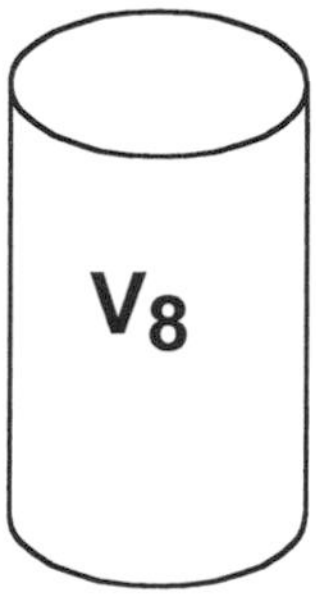

1. Volume = 312

Surface Area = 292

2. Volume = 384

Surface Area = 370

Which juice container holds the most? BOKU
How do you know? Because it looks like it.

Which juice container would be the cheapest to wrap? Can Juice
How do you know? Volumn and surarea is more than box.

Name: Monique's group

Test

Directions: Find the volume and surface area of a cylindrical and a rectangular juice container.

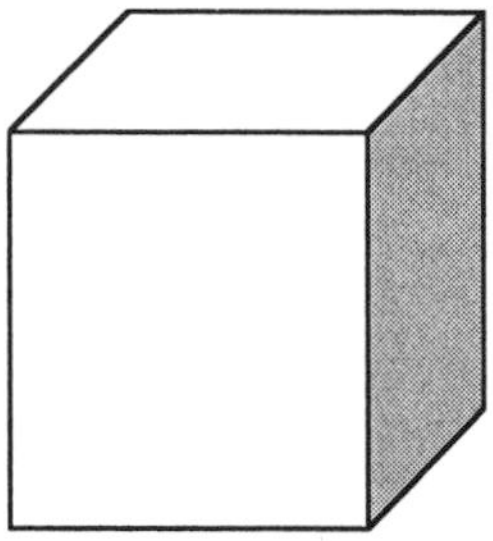

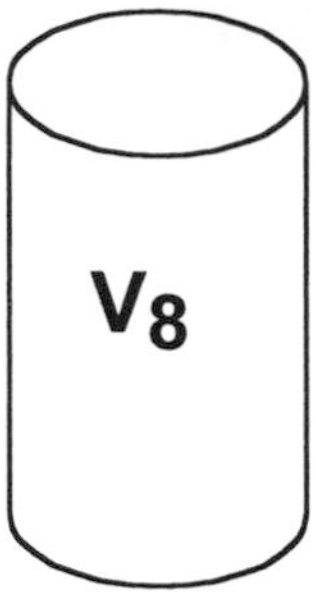

1. Volume = 390

Surface Area = 322

2. Volume = 372

Surface Area = 326

Which juice container holds the most? Boku

How do you know? Because it's more room inside the Boku

Which juice container would be the cheapest to wrap? Boku

How do you know? Because it's less wrapping than the V8

Name: Rasheed's group

Test

Directions: Find the volume and surface area of a cylindrical and a rectangular juice container.

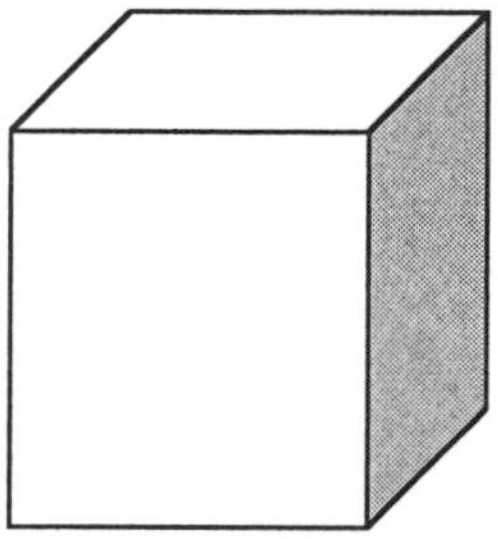

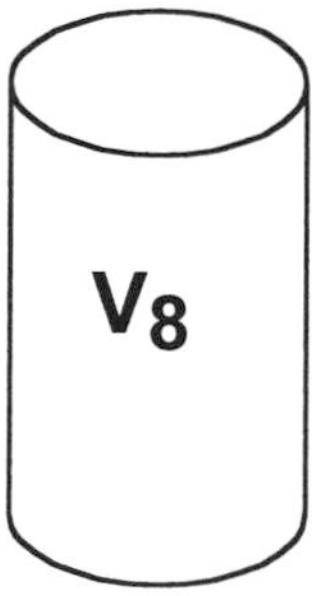

1. Volume = 288

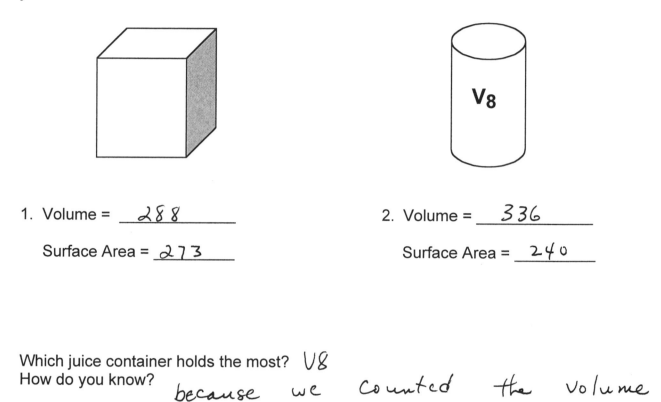

   Surface Area = 273

2. Volume = 336

   Surface Area = 240

Which juice container holds the most? V8
How do you know? because we counted the volume

Which juice container would be the cheapest to wrap?
How do you know? because V8 surface is least

because we counted the surface area

Name: Antonio's Group

Test

Directions: Find the volume and surface area of a cylindrical and a rectangular juice container.

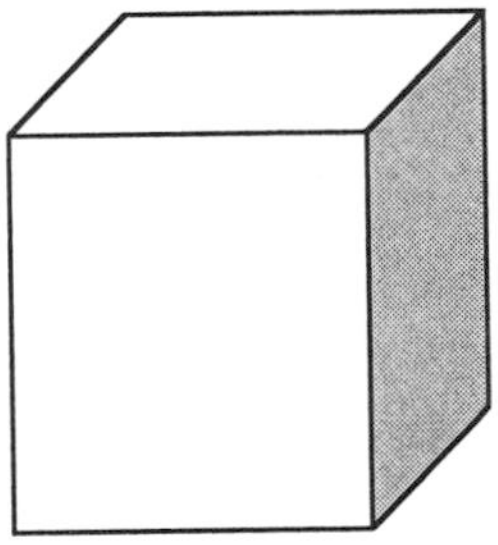

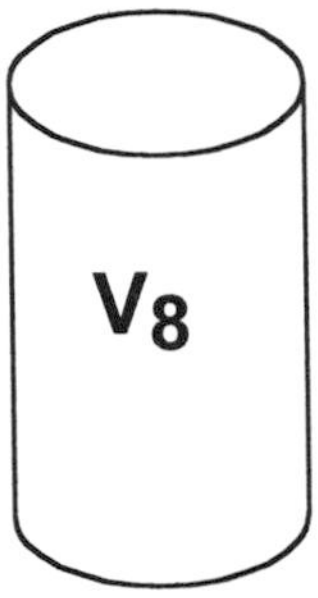

1. Volume = 390

   Surface Area = 269

2. Volume = 288

   Surface Area = 322

Which juice container holds the most? box
How do you know? Be cause of the volume

Which juice container would be the cheapest to wrap? box
How do you know? Be cause of the susface area

Name: Samekas group

Test

Directions: Find the volume and surface area of a cylindrical and a rectangular juice container.

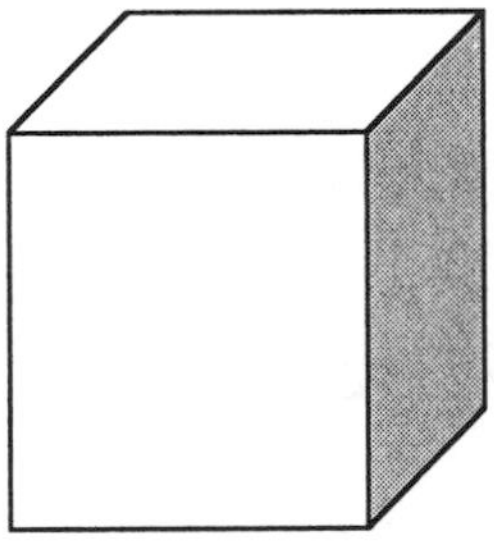

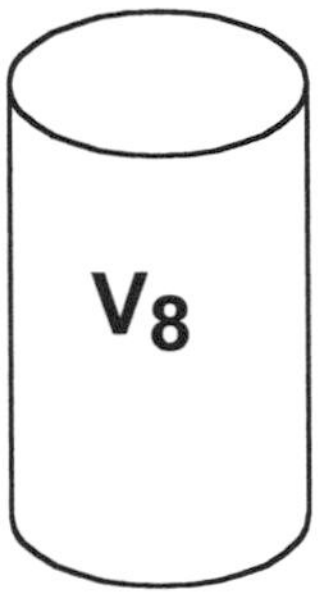

1. Volume = 390

   Surface Area = 320

2. Volume = 240

   Surface Area = 296

Which juice container holds the most? V8

How do you know? because it take the lost surface and volume area

Which juice container would be the cheapest to wrap? Boku

How do you know? because we wrap the Boku box

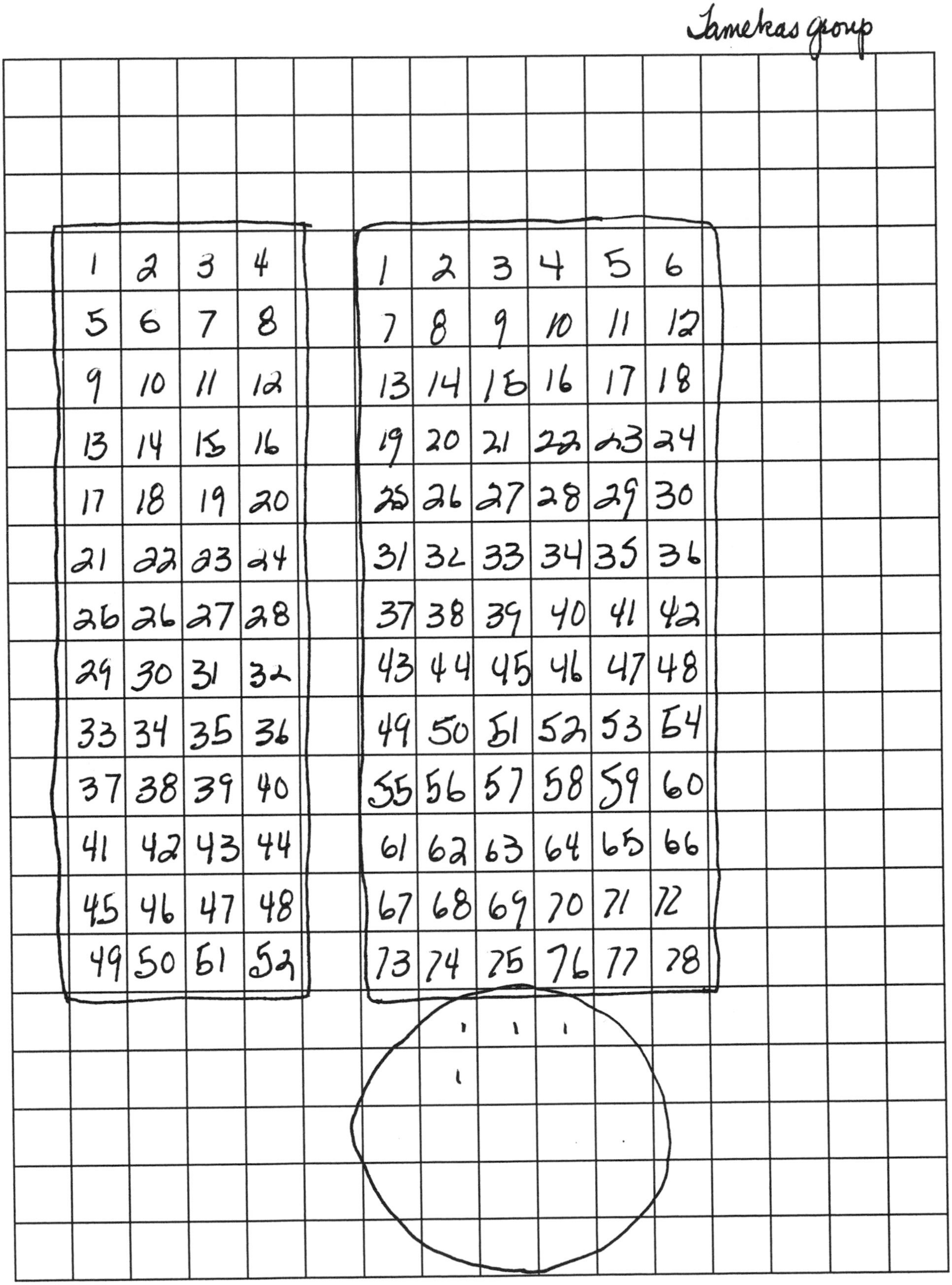
Tamekas group

QUESTIONS FOR DISCUSSION: STUDENTS' WRITTEN WORK ON THE TASK

- How do you think students got their numbers for the surface area and volume measurements and what might account for the wide range of answers?
- What do you make of the responses to the two comparison questions?
- What would you like to know that you can't tell from the written work?

STUDENTS' WRITTEN EXPLANATIONS OF THEIR STRATEGIES TO FIND SURFACE AREA OF THE CYLINDER

One group wrote:

We wrap the can up with grid paper, and grid went all the way around the cylinder. We counted one layer going around the can. Then we counted the height that's how we got surface area.

A second group wrote:

We draw a circle of the cylinder to find the surface area and we multiply the side, top and middle.

Natasha's group wrote:

Rap the outside of the cylinder count a row of cubes count how high it is do something with the numbers and you will have to count the top and bottom.

QUESTIONS FOR DISCUSSION: STUDENTS' WRITTEN EXPLANATIONS OF STRATEGIES

- What do you make of these written explanations?
- Given your analysis of the materials and your conjectures about what you think students understand and what they are struggling with, how would you use this information to decide where to go next in instruction?

QUESTIONS FOR DISCUSSION: HELPING ALL STUDENTS DEVELOP MATHEMATICAL POWER

- What issues does this assessment event raise about what "learning disabled" students should be learning in their mathematics classes?
- What do you think special needs youngsters should be spending their time learning and what arguments would you make to support your belief?
- What issues about basic skills, practice, and the use of the calculator are raised by this classroom event?
- What kinds of experiences might help students reason about different kinds of situations and whether a particular situation lends itself to addition or to multiplication?
- How can a teacher, who values writing as a way of communicating with others and developing one's own understanding, support her students when their experiences at writing have been limited and their skills are underdeveloped?
- What larger issues of equity in mathematics education does this case raise?